Microsoft® Exchange In Business

RUSSELL BORLAND

Microsoft® Press

PUBLISHED BY
Microsoft Press
A Division of Microsoft Corporation
One Microsoft Way
Redmond, Washington 98052-6399

Library of Congress Cataloging-in-Publication Data
Borland, Russell, 1946–
Microsoft Exchange in business / Russell Borland.
p. cm.
Includes index.
ISBN 1-57231-218-1
1. Business enterprises--Communication systems. 2. Information networks. I. Title.
HD30.335.B67 1996
650'.0285'53--dc20 95-44648
CIP

Printed and bound in the United States of America.

1 2 3 4 5 6 7 8 9 QMQM 1 0 9 8 7 6

Distributed to the book trade in Canada by Macmillan of Canada, a division of Canada Publishing Corporation.

A CIP catalogue record for this book is available from the British Library.

Microsoft Press books are available through booksellers and distributors worldwide. For further information about international editions, contact your local Microsoft Corporation office. Or contact Microsoft Press International directly at fax (206) 936-7329.

Acquisitions Editor: Casey Doyle
Manuscript Editor: John Pierce
Project Editors: Wallis Bolz, John Pierce, Editorial Services of New England
Technical Editor: Kurt Meyer

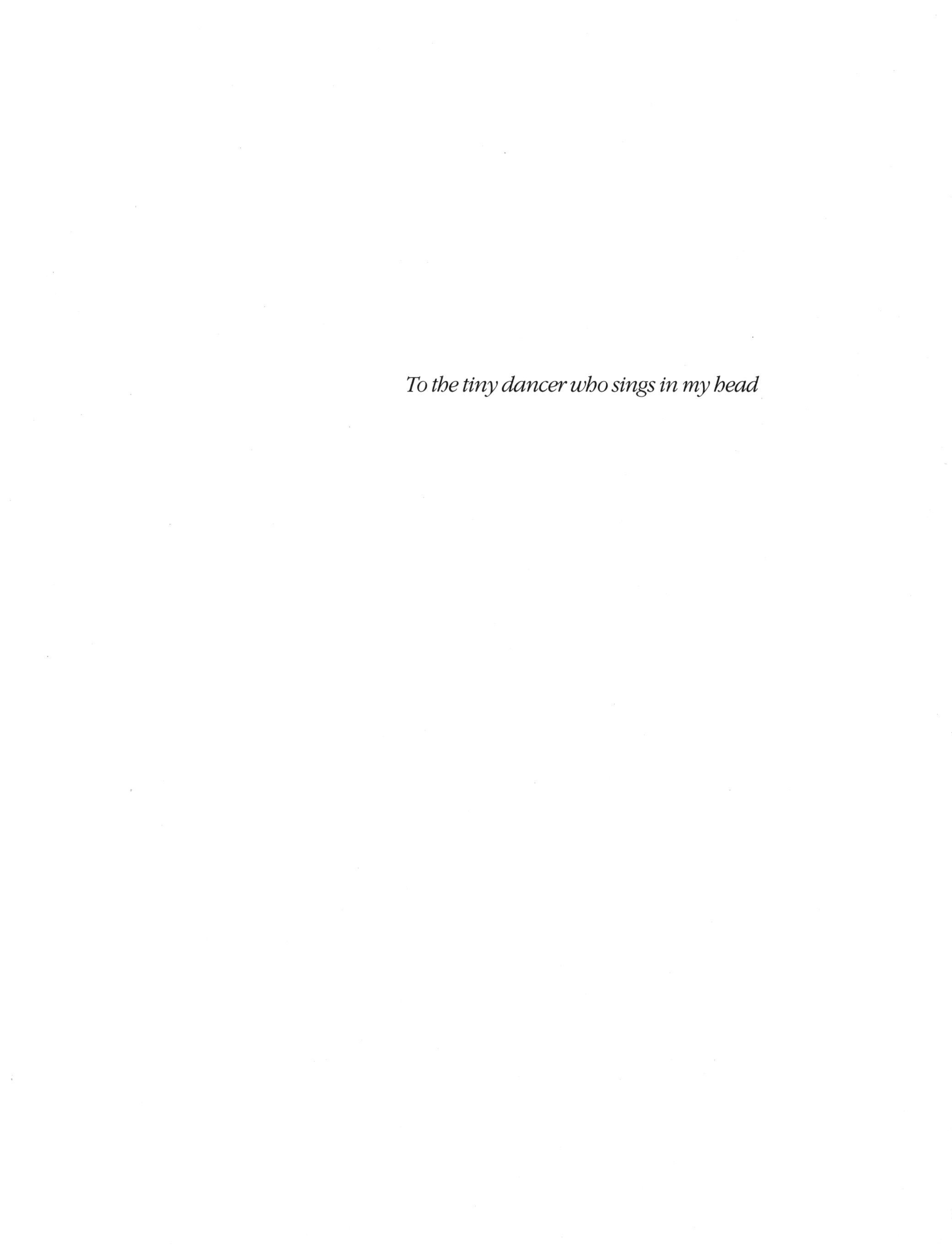

To the tiny dancer who sings in my head

Acknowledgments

A quiet word of thanks to the quiet man, John Pierce, who very ably shepherded this book through the major part of the project and extracted from a sometimes very mangled manuscript a book. Even though our senses of humor don't always match, John managed much better than I to keep our working relationship amiable. And to John's deputy, Wallis Bolz, who shepherded the final stages of this project, thanks for her energy and irony—both welcome qualities when it's time to count the chips.

A quiet word of thanks to the other quiet man, Kurt Meyer, who struggled better than I against the chaotic, evil forces of error and inaccuracy. Kurt slew this two-headed dragon with cool aplomb and disentangled the artwork from the twin evils of stray bits and moiré shades to render the pictures in this book in splendid, living gray scale.

A quiet word of thanks to Bonnie Jo Collins, Michelle Neil, and the staff of Editorial Services of New England for skillful proofreading and indexing and for rendering the text and art printable. Their very visible contributions to the production of this book were made totally out of my sight and hearing. Perhaps one day I'll ride my Harley into their lobby, and we'll get very well acquainted?

It's only fair to acknowledge that I first heard the term bozo bit from the working title of Jim McCarthy's book, *Dynamics of Software Development* (Microsoft Press, 1995). Jim is in no way responsible for my misuse and distortion of his elegant turn of phrase, "Don't flip the bozo bit."

And to all the members of the acquisitions, production, manufacturing, marketing, sales, and distribution groups at Microsoft Press, thank you for getting this book into the hands of the people for whom it is intended.

Lazaruss Acres, 1996

Contents

Introduction

"Share!" your parents exhorted. Share with your siblings, share with your friends, share with your classmates. In most modern companies and organizations, sharing information is a key strategy for success. Most modern organizations operate through teamwork—whether in a strongly collaborative manner (several team members together perform a single task) or in a looser manner (each team member is a specialist for one part of the overall task). Yet team members cannot work as productively as possible without knowing what other team members and other teams in the organization are doing. Information about engineering, marketing, sales, production, manufacturing, shipping, financial results, and human resources that is shared across traditional divisions of the organization leads to more efficient and proficient action by everyone. All the more so in an organization whose "product" is information.

Traditionally, information was parceled to people by word of mouth, memos, reports, phone calls, and, more recently, electronic mail. When taken together, these lines of communication *can* get information to those who need it. But too often the information isn't available right when it's needed. Sometimes people don't even know the information exists. Now Microsoft Exchange can change all that.

Exchange is an information sharing system. Besides using electronic mail for sending messages from one person to another or to a group, team members can use Exchange to share memos, reports, and many other kinds of information. Furthermore, teams can use Exchange to arrange meetings, to set and monitor schedules and tasks, and to select and sort out specific information from the welter of information that surrounds and infuses a single project as well as the operation of the entire organization.

What's All This About Information Exchange?

As Microsoft never tires of telling us, from the beginning the company had a vision of a computer on every desk and in every home. The key to this vision is the availability of useful computer programs. Initially, many of the computer programs that Microsoft and others developed were for individuals' work on personal computers. But developing a program that replaced one method of work (for example, handwriting) with another (such as word processing) has limited value if you can't share the information the program produces with someone else, or if others can't reuse the information whenever possible. And low-level, private use of a personal computer is rarely as efficient, pleasant, or effective as something like handwriting.

The real value of computers comes from connections between them—connections by which each computer user can share his or her individual work with a group, and vice versa. With connections, the office in your home isn't an isolated computer room; it becomes a doorway to the library, the workplace, the market, friends, associates, and relatives. With connections, the personal computer in an office isn't just a tool for one person's work; it becomes a gateway through which information passes among computer users and their business community.

Microsoft Exchange provides the means for you to connect with a larger computing community—to exchange messages, to exchange comments on issues, to organize and share your work, to collect information and view it in a formal way. Exchange lets you push information into the hands of others and pull in information from public collections. Exchange lets you organize and view all this information in a variety of selective ways.

What You've Got in This Book

As the thematic artwork in this book suggests, Exchange has many parts that are connected the way subway stations are. The lines of connection make it possible to perform many business and personal messaging, scheduling, and information sharing tasks. The trick is to build a mental map of the line you need to take through the various parts of Exchange.

This book concentrates on helping you set up and work through a variety of tasks for which Exchange is suited. Rather than walk you through various features of each part of Exchange, I'll describe how to set up Exchange for the ways you really work. As you follow each scenario that's described in the book, you'll find directions for actions to take.

Because this book teaches Exchange by using scenarios rather than by describing features, you're likely to find some overlap as you read through the parts of this book. I really wasn't trying to make the book as fat as possible, rather I wanted to give you all you need, for the most part, within each scenario, so that you don't always have to chase through all of the book's parts looking for this or that procedure. That said, however, I do provide you with a healthy number of cross-references so that you don't have to read everything twice and can also find the information you need easily.

You'll start with the personal side of Exchange, and then you'll gradually work toward more expanded uses—discussion forums (also known as bulletin boards), project information, and information-at-work (customer information). At the end of this book, you'll find chapters about extending Exchange—directions for using Exchange from remote locations and details about adjusting Exchange options. This book also contains information about moving your Microsoft Mail 3.x messages to Exchange, a list of my favorite tips for using Exchange, and a quick reference guide to the commands and toolbar buttons for each part of Exchange with cross-references to applicable discussions in this book.

Before you leap into learning about the virtues of working with Exchange, however, you might find the guided tour that starts next illuminating.

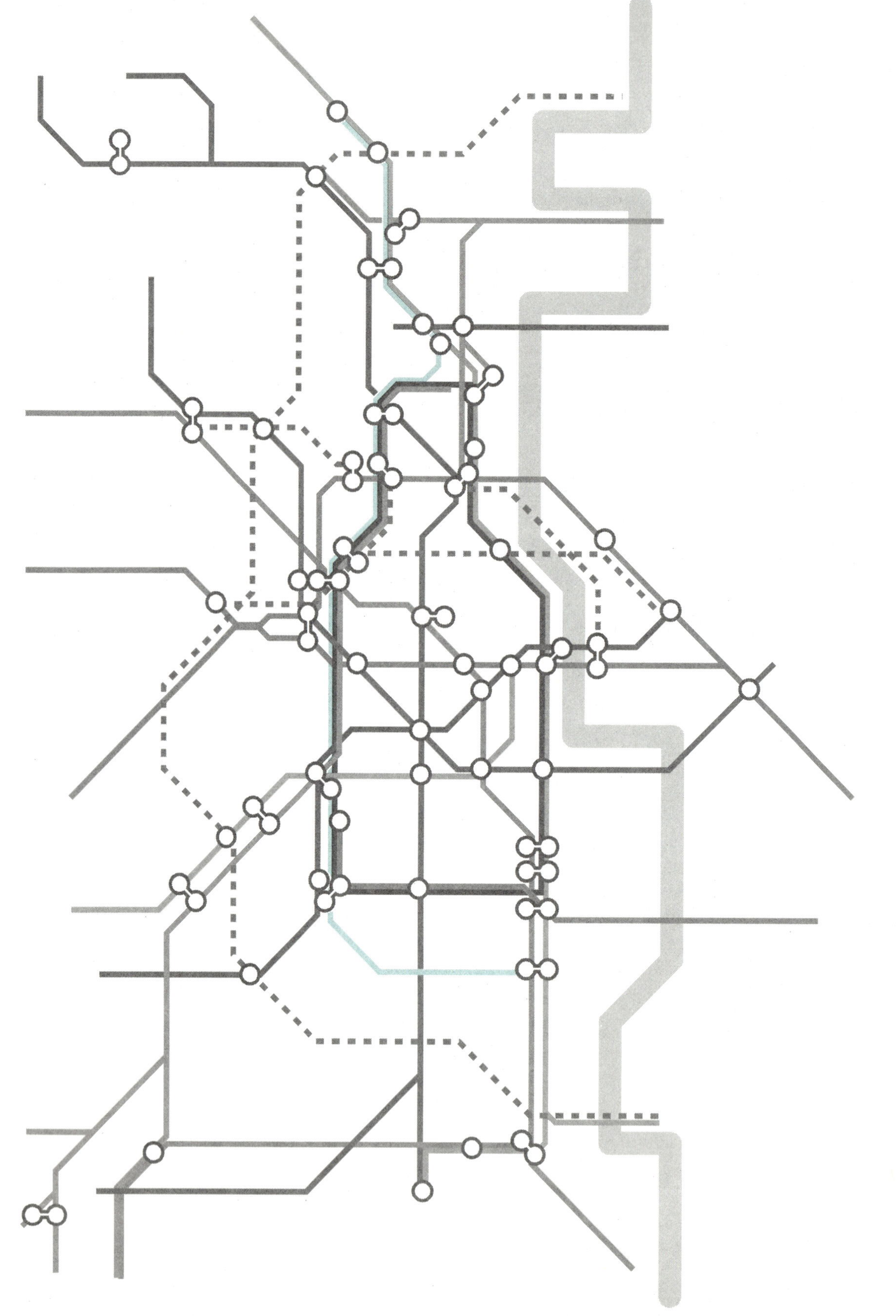

Guided Tour of Exchange

«Aller Anfang ist schwer.» "The first step is the hardest." So goes the German proverb. The assumption behind a graphical computer system, such as Microsoft Windows or the Apple Macintosh, is that by putting pictures, icons, windows, and other graphical elements on the screen for you, beginnings won't be quite so *schwer*. All the same, getting started and getting familiar with the pictures, icons, windows, and other graphical elements in an application is an important but not always entirely easy first step.

Scenes from This Tour

In this guided tour, you'll be introduced to Microsoft Exchange and its related parts so that you have a complete view of all that Exchange has to offer. You'll learn how to start Exchange and its related parts, what they're made of, and how to log off the Exchange system.

Getting Started

So you think you want to join the electronic mail revolution, eh? Or are you one of those who already uses electronic mail, but now you want the latest? Well, to get there, whether you're just starting on the trip or you're retracing a trip you've taken before (but this time on a brand-spanking-new system), you've got to climb aboard; that is, you've got to start Exchange.

That's where you'll start this guided tour—at the start-up sequence. Then you can explore and observe the scenic beauties along the way.

Starting Microsoft Exchange

Starting Exchange is really complicated—you have to double-click a mouse button. What do you double-click on? An icon. Which icon? That depends. Depends on what? It depends on which computer system you're using—Windows 95, Windows 3.1, Windows 3.11, Windows NT, or the Macintosh.

- **For Windows 95**—Double-click on the Inbox icon on the desktop.

- **For Windows 3.1 or 3.11, Windows NT, and the Macintosh**—Open the Microsoft Exchange window (program group), and then double-click on the Microsoft Exchange icon.

Logging On

Before you can see Exchange or do anything in it, Exchange needs to know who you are. How you identify yourself depends on various factors. Here are the most common scenarios:

- **For Windows 95**—If you are logged on to your organization's computer network, Exchange knows who you are and doesn't ask for your logon name and password. Exchange will start connecting you to your Exchange server, usually. (See the sidebar, "The Lines Are Down! What Now?" on page 5, for a different situation.) Your Exchange server is a computer that stores messages you send and receive.

  If you're not logged on to a network, you'll see a message that tells you that you must first log on. Choose to do this now. Then, when you're logged on, Exchange will start connecting you to your Exchange server.

- **For Window 3.1 or 3.11 and Windows NT**—You'll see a logon dialog box, like this one:

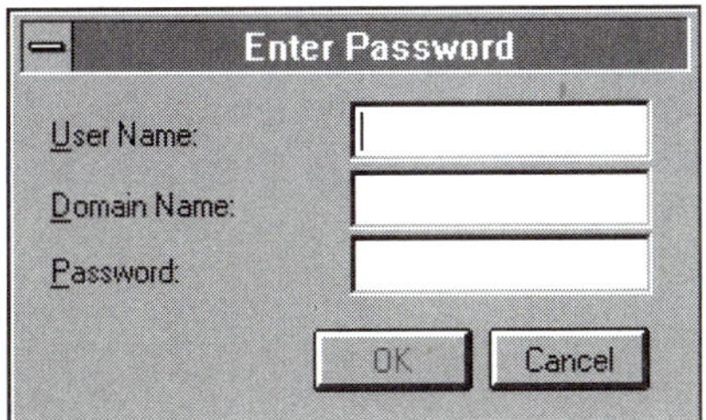

Type your logon name (if it's not already in the dialog box), your domain name, and then your password. Click on OK to start up Exchange.

To help set up the options that you'll use in Exchange, Exchange uses what's known as a *profile*. You'll learn how to set up and manage profiles in Chapter 4, "Developing Your Profile." The first time you start Exchange, you will probably have only one profile set up. If you happen to have more than one profile set up and have turned on the option to be prompted for which profile to use, Exchange displays the Choose Profile dialog box, which looks like the one at the top of the next page.

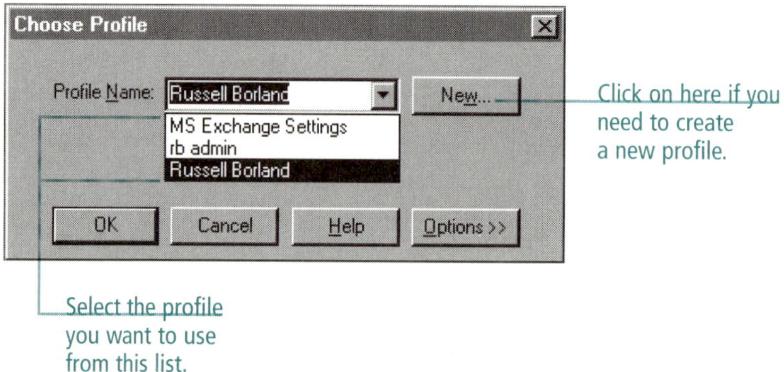
Choose Profile
Profile Name:
Russell Borland
New...
MS Exchange Settings
rb admin
Russell Borland
OK
Cancel
Help
Options >>
Click on here if you need to create a new profile.
Select the profile you want to use from this list.

Select the profile you want to use, and then click on OK.

If Exchange is set up for use away from your network connection, Exchange next displays a dialog box like the following, which asks if you want to connect to the network or work offline:

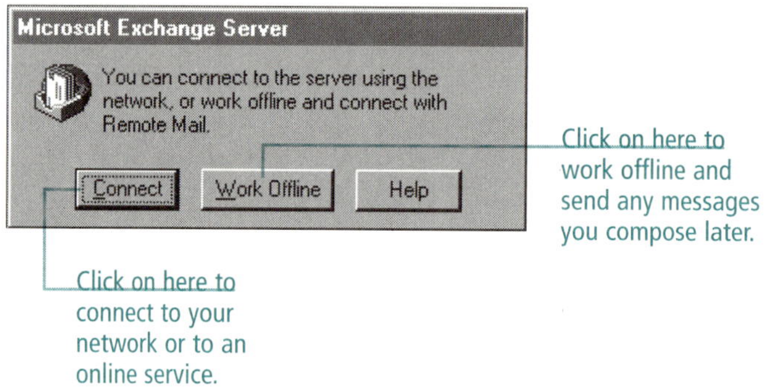
Microsoft Exchange Server
You can connect to the server using the network, or work offline and connect with Remote Mail.
Connect
Work Offline
Help
Click on here to work offline and send any messages you compose later.
Click on here to connect to your network or to an online service.

- If the network is available and you want to connect to your Exchange server to send and receive messages, click on the Connect button.
- If you regularly connect to an online service (such as MSN, the Microsoft online network; CompuServe; America Online; or AT&T) and you want to connect to it to send and receive messages, click on the Connect button.

- If you want to work offline (because the network is down, because you don't have a direct connection to it, or because you want to compose messages or perform other tasks before you connect), click on the Work Offline button. When you work offline, you can compose messages for sending later, and you can review any messages that you have stored on your computer (rather than on the Exchange server). Later you can connect to the network or other online service to send your messages and to receive any messages that are waiting for you.

Now that you've logged on, whaddaya see? That's what you'll read about next.

The Lines Are Down! What Now?

Networks and servers are wonderfully bizarre at times. They love to go down (that is, stop working) just to give some beleaguered system administrator something to do—namely, restart the network or server.

If you try to start Exchange when the server or the network isn't working, you'll see a dialog box like this:

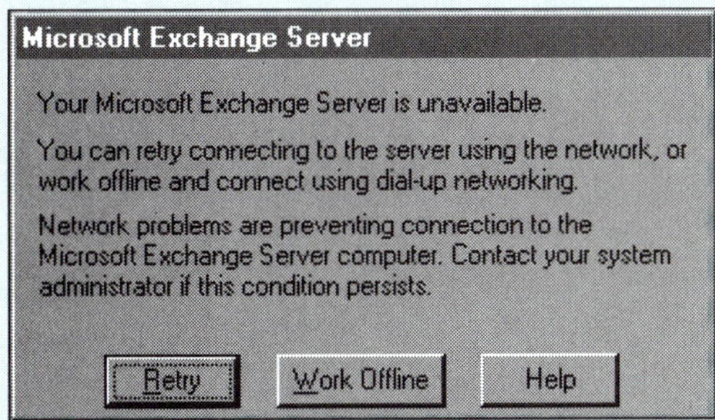

In this case, select one of the choices in the dialog box, and then click on OK.

- Select Retry to try again.
- Select Work Offline if you're working away from a network connection and will be using phone lines to connect later.

Whaddaya See?

The first thing you see is the Exchange window, which looks like this:

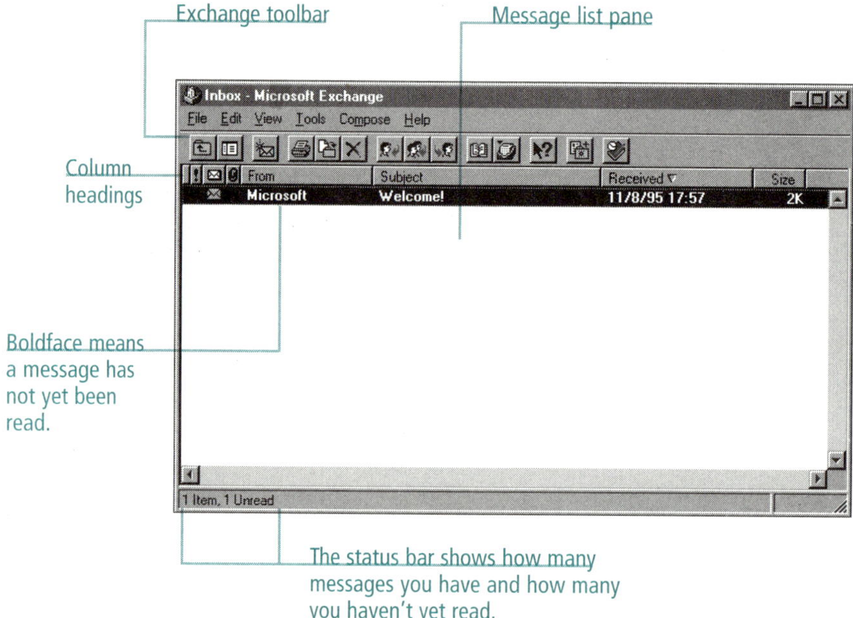

When you start Exchange, Exchange always displays the contents of the Inbox folder, which is where you receive messages. This way you can read your new messages first thing. (You'll learn more about folders in the next section.) Your Inbox should have at least a Welcome! message in it and might have other messages as well (or instead). New messages appear in boldface. Messages you've already read appear in normal typeface (not boldface). Each message line contains an envelope icon (which means it's a message), the name of the person who sent you the message, the subject line of the message, and the date and time of the message. To learn about reading a message, see "Whaddaya Want? Reading a Message," on page 39.

In the previous illustration, you don't see folders, just the message list pane. But you can make the folder pane visible.

If you don't see folders along the left side of the window, click on the Show/Hide Folder List button on the Exchange toolbar. The Show/Hide Folder List button looks like this:

Inbox - Microsoft Exchan
File Edit View Tools Comp
Show/Hide Folder List
Microsoft
Click on this button to show folders and the message list. Click on it again to show only the message list.

When the folder pane is visible along with the message list pane, you see the folders that hold messages and postings, like this:

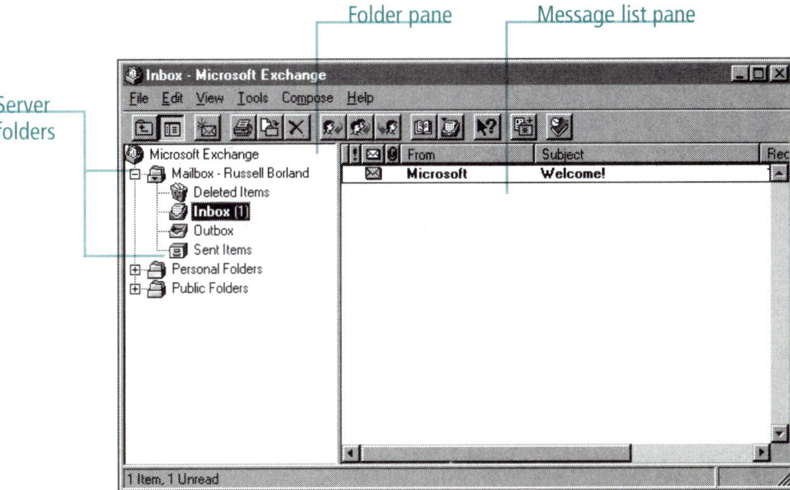

On the right you see the contents of the current folder.

Folders

A folder can hold messages, postings (notes), forms, and documents (files). When you're connected to the Exchange server, you see two or three sets of folders. You always see server folders and public folders, and if your computer is set up to take on the road—as a laptop often is—you might also see personal folders.

Folders can either be online folders—folders that are available only when you're connected to your Exchange server or to an online service—or offline folders—folders that are available both when you're connected to your Exchange server and when you're not connected. Personal folders are always offline folders. When you set up a folder as an online and offline folder, Exchange changes the folder's icon. (This doesn't happen with the four main server folders and their duplicates in Personal Folders, which I'll discuss in a minute.) Here's what the icons look like:

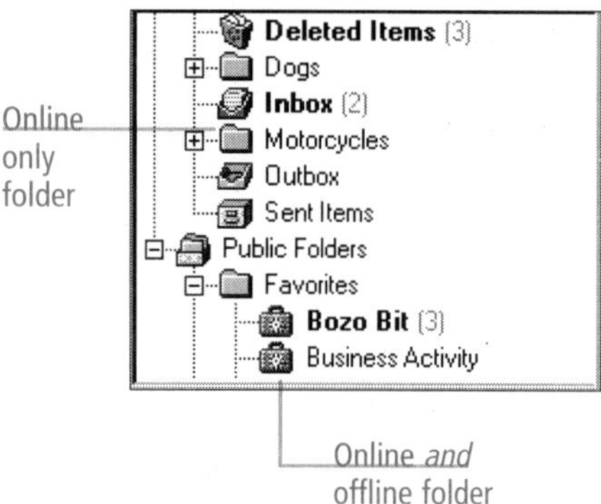

The following sections give you more information about the various types of folders.

Server Folders

At the top of the folder pane, you see an icon labeled Microsoft Exchange, under which appears an icon labeled Mailbox, followed by your name. The Microsoft Exchange icon represents your server. The server folder contains four standard folders: Deleted Items, Inbox, Sent Items, and Outbox. These four folders are always available both online and offline.

Deleted Items contains messages you have deleted. You can retrieve messages from the Deleted Items folder, but after the Deleted Items folder is emptied, the messages are gone forever.

Inbox contains new messages that you haven't read, plus any messages you've read and haven't deleted or moved to another folder.

Sent Items contains copies of messages you've sent. You can use this folder as a record of the messages you've generated in case you need to refer to them again or in case you need to resend a message.

Outbox temporarily holds messages you've sent but which the Exchange server has not yet pulled from your computer to the server. When you're connected, messages stay in your Outbox folder only a short time. If you're working offline, the Outbox folder holds your sent messages until you're connected again. Then the Outbox folder sends your messages to the Exchange server.

You can add any additional folders you want to the server folders.

Public Folders

The Exchange server contains some variety of public folders. These are folders that most people can use. Public folders contain messages that everyone who can open the folder can read. A public folder can also contain postings—notes that ask questions, provide answers, or state opinions and facts—as well as documents. Public folders are intended to present and record public discussion of a specific topic. Depending on the generosity of your Exchange administrator and the capacity of your Exchange server, there could be hundreds of public folders or possibly only a few.

Some public folders might have limited access. Some folders might be available only to particular people. For example, there could be a project folder to which only the project team members have access.

For more information about public folders, see "Neighborhood Gossip—Bulletin Boards and Public Folders," on page 13.

Personal Folders

Below your Mailbox folder you might see an icon labeled Personal Folders. This folder contains duplicates of your four main server folders (Deleted Items, Inbox, Outbox, and Sent Items). These duplicates work the same as the main server folders when you're working offline. They also work as backup folders in which you can keep duplicates of the messages in your server folders. Exchange stores your personal folders on your computer's hard disk.

You can also create new folders inside either your server folders or your personal folders. These additional folders are where you'll usually keep messages that you want to have around for a while but don't want to leave lying around in your main folders. By creating new folders, you can sort messages into groups for easier access when you want to read them again.

Other Exchange Window Parts

Let's look again at the Exchange window. In particular, let's look more closely at the parts that appear and what you can do with them. To orient yourself, refer to the illustration at the top of the next page.

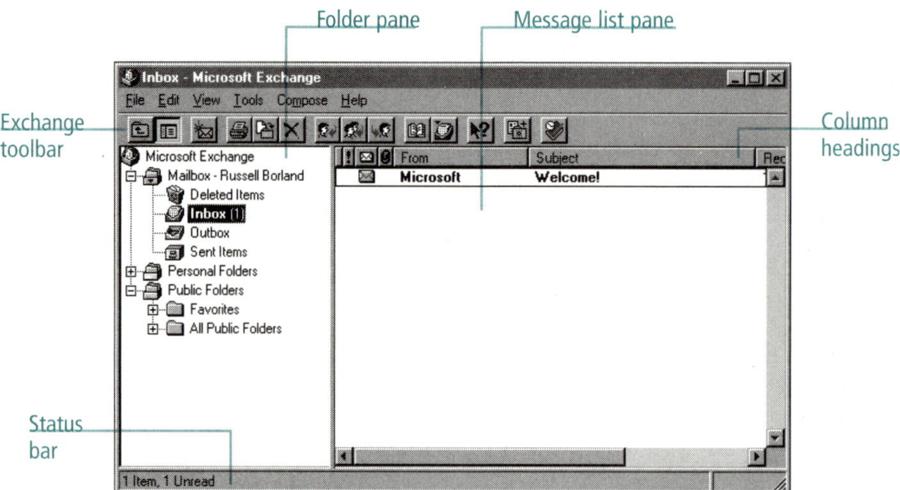

As you might expect, most parts of the Exchange window are fairly self-explanatory. Still, it will be helpful for you to zoom in on the toolbars and to look at them in more detail. Also, I'll give you a first look at a message window and its toolbars.

Exchange Toolbars

Like all good applications that run under a graphical operating system, Exchange windows have toolbars. The main Exchange window has a toolbar that contains buttons for working with messages. Here is what the buttons on the Exchange toolbar do.

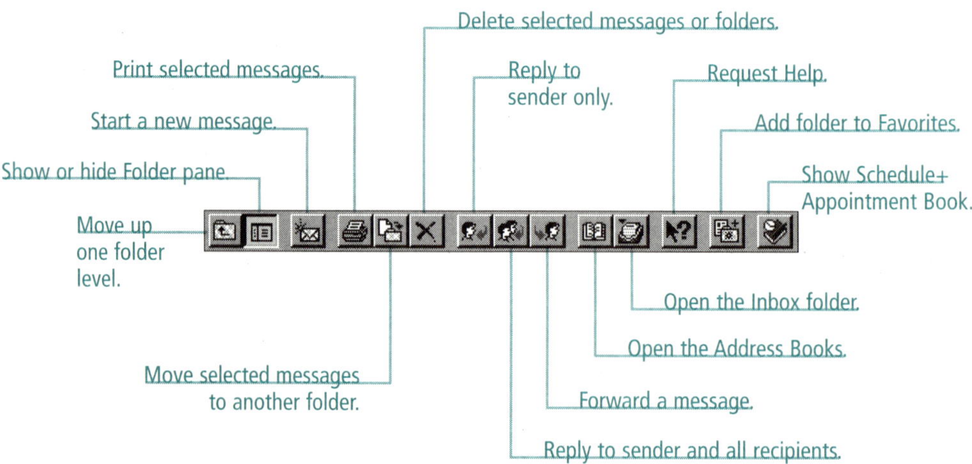

To open a message, simply double-click on its message line. When you open a message in Exchange, you'll see a window such as the next one. (For more about reading—and sending—messages, see Chapter 1, "Electronic Mail.")

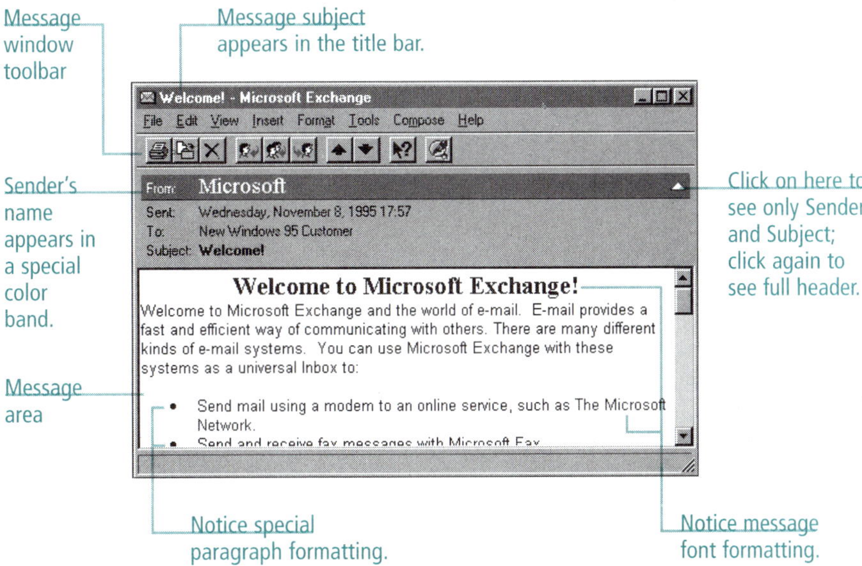

As you can see, a message window contains a variation of the Exchange toolbar. If your toolbar looks different, it could be because the person who set up your Exchange client turned on an option that lets you create messages using a Microsoft Word window. (See "Creating a Project Message Template," on page 256, for information about how to turn off this option.) Here is what the buttons on the Message window toolbar do.

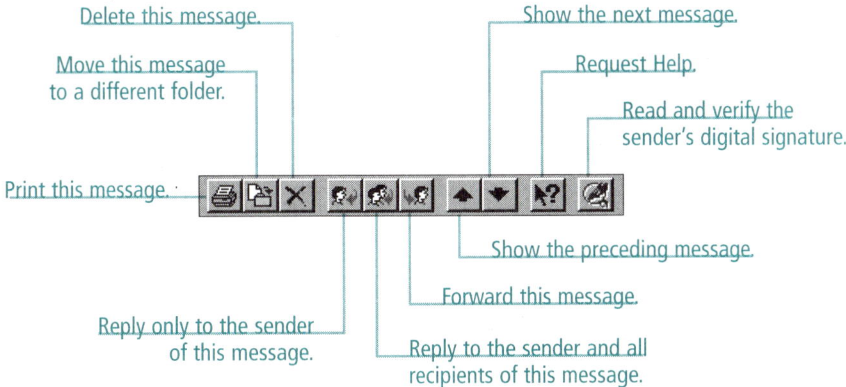

Delete this message.
Move this message to a different folder.
Print this message.
Show the next message.
Request Help.
Read and verify the sender's digital signature.
Show the preceding message.
Forward this message.
Reply only to the sender of this message.
Reply to the sender and all recipients of this message.

To compose a new message, simply click on the New Message button on the Exchange toolbar. When you compose a new message, you'll see a window like the following:

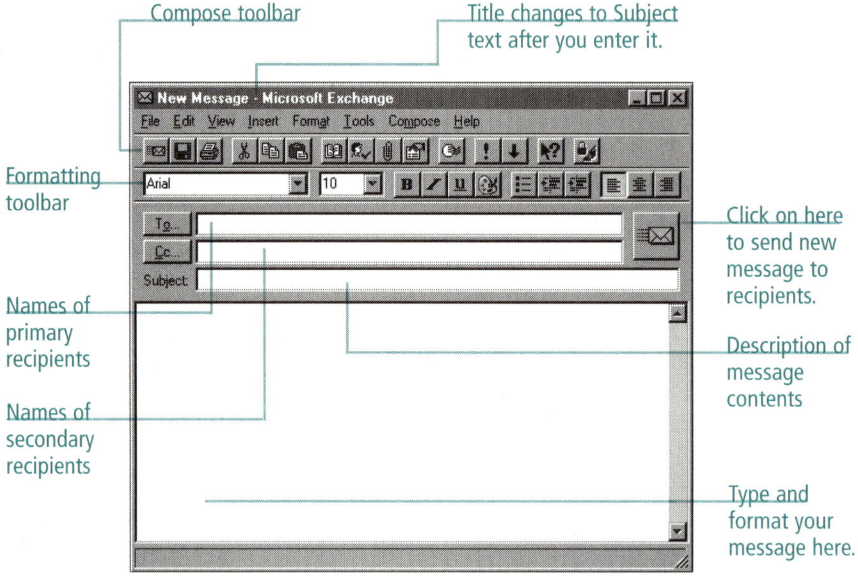

As you can see, a compose message window contains a variation of the Exchange toolbar. Here is what the buttons on the Compose toolbar do.

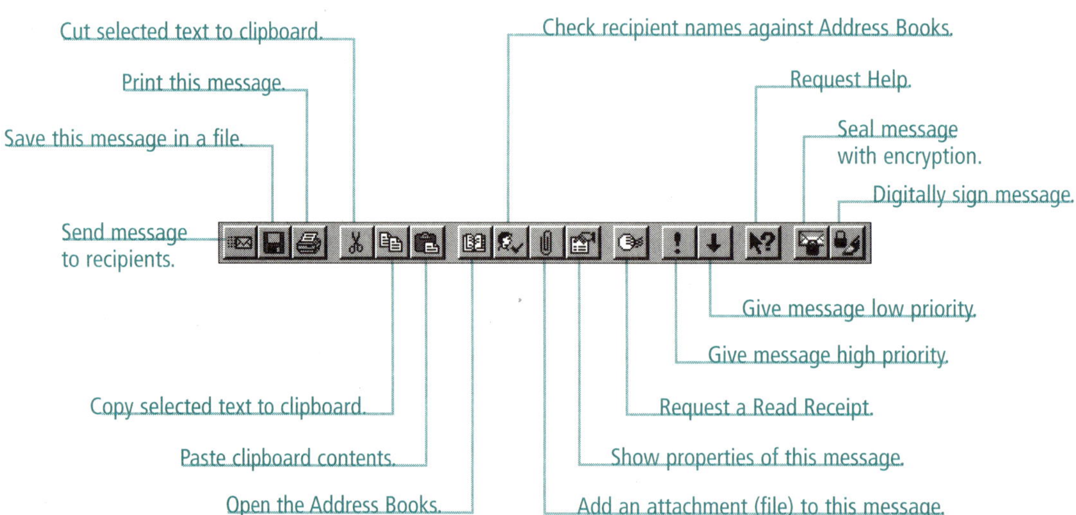

Note The buttons for encrypting a message and for adding a digital signature are enabled only if you have been set up for advanced security features by your Exchange adminsistrator.

A compose message window also contains a Formatting toolbar, which you use to change the font and paragraph formatting of message text. Here is what the fields and buttons on the Formatting toolbar do.

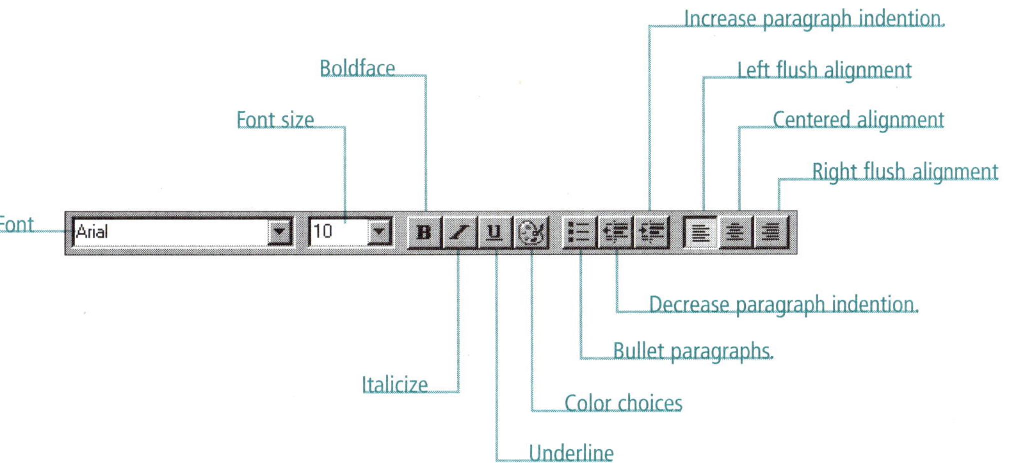

Neighborhood Gossip—Bulletin Boards and Public Folders

Part of the power of Exchange comes from how you can use it to disseminate public and private information. Exchange can provide public folders to which you and others using Exchange can send messages, post notes, and share documents. A public folder can provide a forum for a discussion and for gossip that many people can view at once, at their leisure, without having to deal with a flood of messages interrupting their work and filling their inboxes. You can learn about using a public folder for a discussion forum in Part 2.

Public folders can be made very private. It's possible to limit access to a public folder to a very few people, even to only one person. The power to limit access makes a public folder a useful receptacle for project information or for customer information, as you'll find in Part 3 and Part 4.

Within the Public Folders folder, you'll see two subfolders: Favorites and All Public Folders. The number and nature of public folders in the All Public Folders folder depend on the capacity of your Exchange server and on the graciousness of your Exchange administrator. The public folders that you see will be unique to your organization. But to give you an idea of the kinds of public folders that you might see, here is an illustration. (You'll see the folders in this illustration used later in this book.)

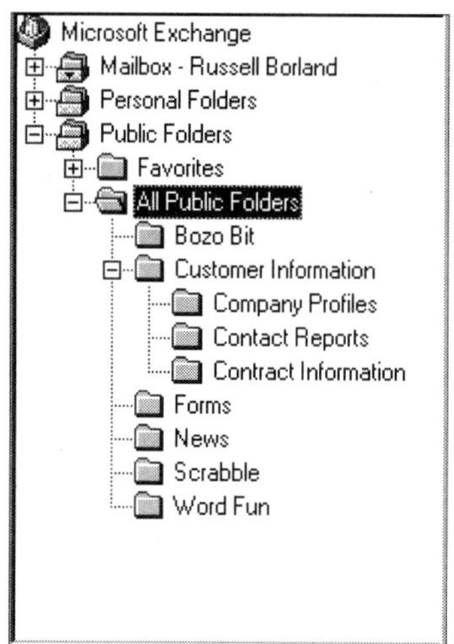

To view the contents of a public folder, click on the folder icon. When you do, the message list pane shows you a list of the subfolders (if there are any), as well as the messages, postings, and documents in the folder.

If a folder in the folder pane has a plus sign next to it, that means the folder contains subfolders. To see the list of subfolders in the folder pane, click on the plus sign to expand the list of subfolders.

The number and arrangement of public folders can be extensive and almost perversely complex. As a special bonus, you can set up quick access to any public folder. To do this, you add a public folder to the Favorites folder. This way, when you want to look in a particular public folder, you click on its icon in the Favorites folder to jump immediately to the public folder's contents. Here is an illustration of my Favorites folder:

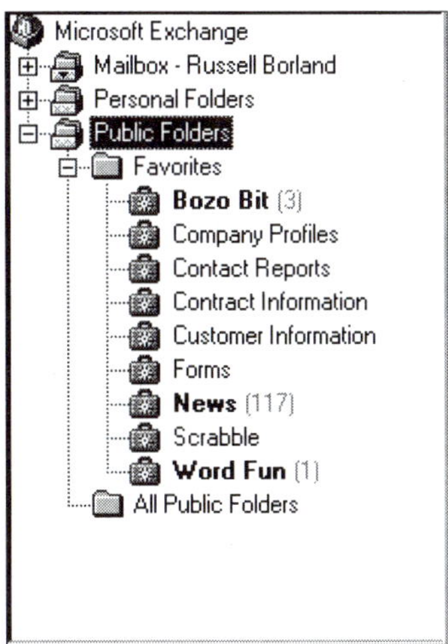

As noted earlier, you can also mark a folder in the Favorites folder as an offline folder so that you can see the public folder's contents when you're working away from your network connection. You'll learn more about offline folders in Chapter 15, "Having a Remote Idea of Exchange."

From Now to Eternity— The Appointment Book

An intimate partner of Exchange is Microsoft Schedule+ 7.0. You start this Exchange partner by clicking on the Show Schedule button on the Exchange toolbar. You can also start it separately if you want, either from the Windows 95 Start button or from the Exchange window or program group.

When you start Schedule+, you see the Daily appointment page for today, as shown at the top of the next page.

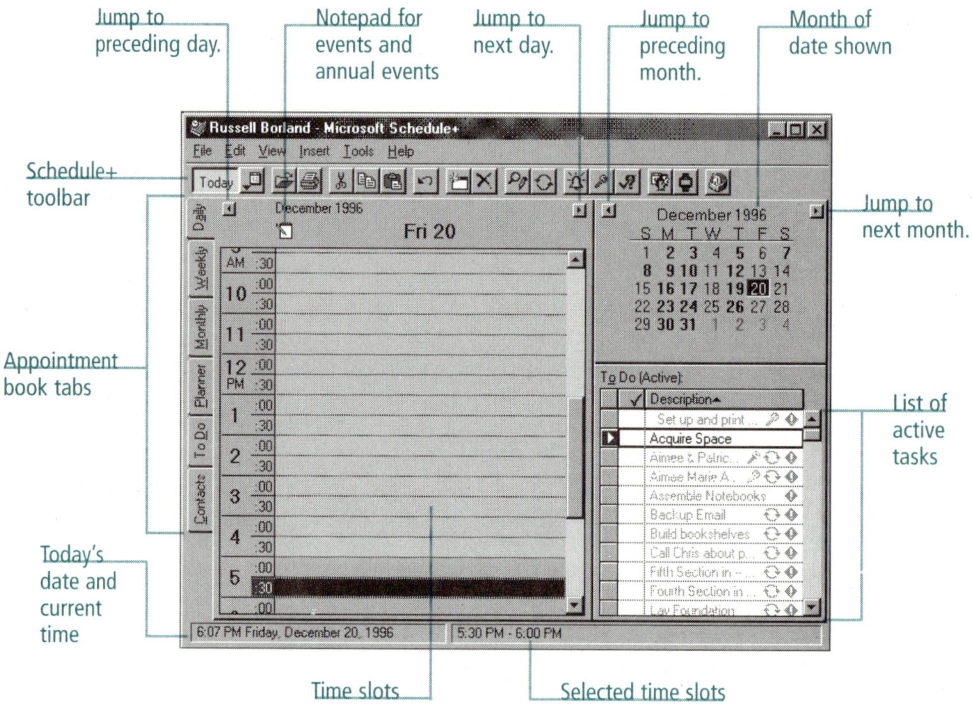

If you have tasks set up, you also see a Daily Reminder window, which appears over the top of your appointment book, as shown here:

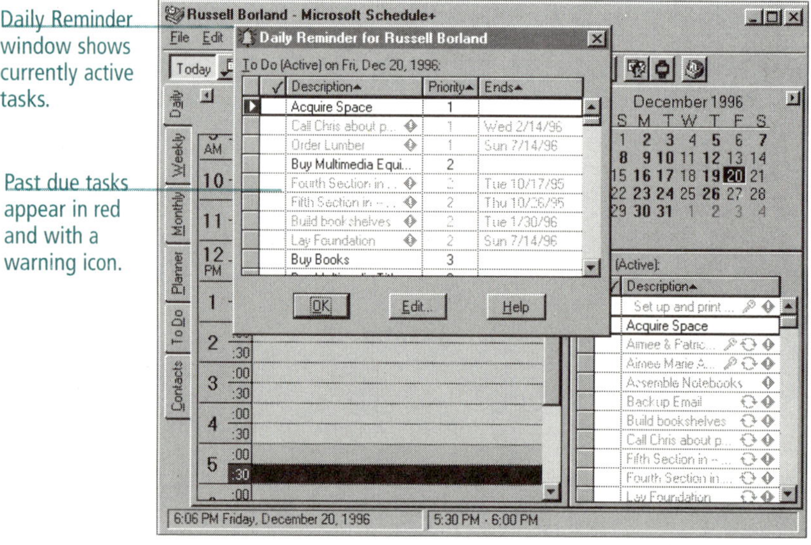

You can work on your task list directly in this window, or you can click on OK and work on your task list later. In your Schedule+ appointment book you can keep track of your appointments, contacts, and tasks. To learn the basics of using Schedule+, refer to Chapter 2, "Personal Scheduling."

Schedule+ Tabs

Clicking on the tabs along the left side of the Schedule+ appointment book displays various pages of information. Here's an illustration of what clicking on the tabs displays. To see the displays for yourself, click on the tabs.

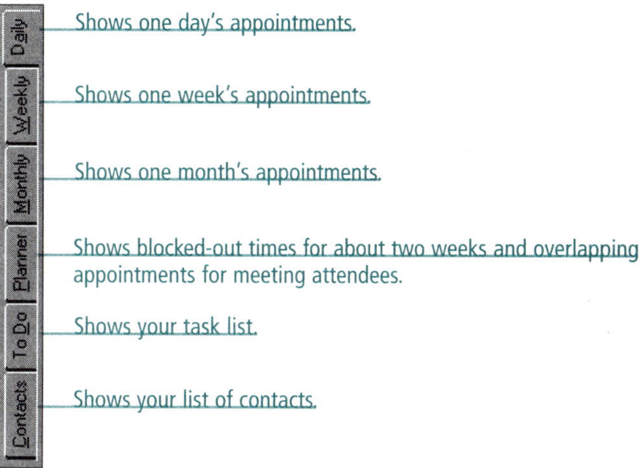

Schedule+ gives you a way to change the number and the order of tabs in your appointment book. (For information about changing the tab setup, see Chapter 2.) If you or the person who installed Exchange for you changes the tab setup, your appointment book might look a little different from the tab setup shown here.

Schedule+ Toolbar

The Schedule+ toolbar contains buttons for most of the record keeping actions you'll perform. Here's some detail about the toolbar buttons and what they do.

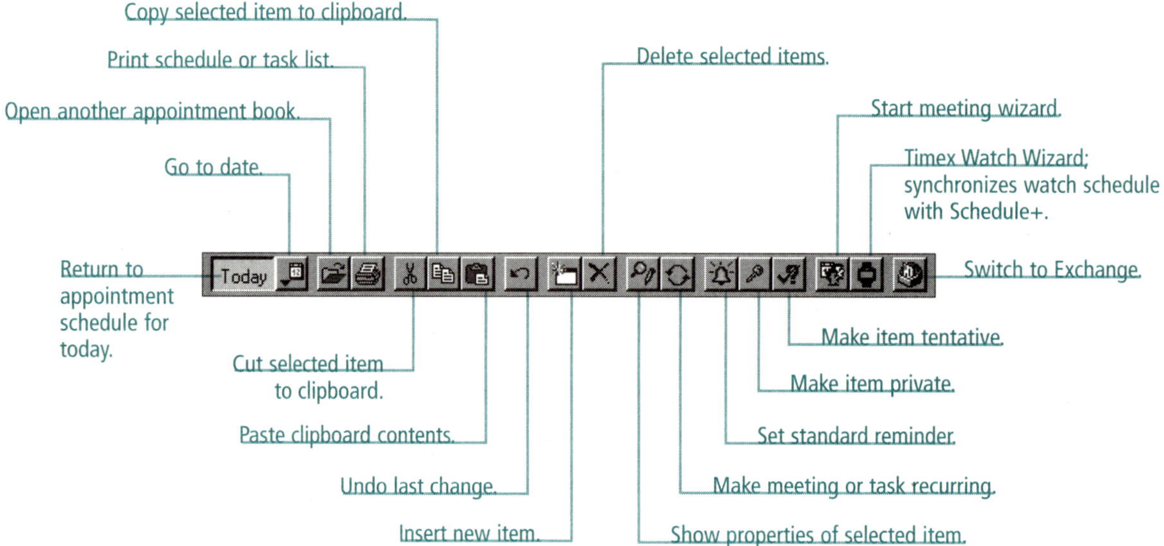

Different Actions of Some Schedule+ Toolbar Buttons

Some of the buttons on the Schedule+ toolbar perform a similar but different action depending on which tab is visible in the appointment book. I've noted these differences in the following table. The Appointment Tabs column includes the Daily, Weekly, Monthly, and Yearly tabs. The To Do Tabs column includes the To Do and Seven Habits tabs.

Button	Appointment Tabs	Contacts Tab	To Do Tabs
Insert New	Insert a new appointment.	Insert a new contact.	Insert a new task.
Delete	Delete an appointment.	Delete a contact.	Delete a task.
Edit	Edit an appointment.	Edit a contact.	Edit a task.
Recurring	Insert a recurring appointment or convert a one-time appointment to a recurring one.	(Not applicable—there's no such thing as a recurring contact.)	Insert a recurring task or convert a task to a recurring one.

(continued)

continued

Button	Appointment Tabs	Contacts Tab	To Do Tabs
Reminder	Set a reminder for an appointment.	(Not applicable—you don't need a reminder for a contact, do you? If so, set it up as a task.)	Set a reminder to do a task.
Private	Mark an appointment as private.	Mark a contact as private.	Mark a task as private.
Tentative	Mark an appointment as tentative.	(Not applicable—there's no such thing as a tentative contact.)	(Not applicable—there's no such thing as a tentative task.)

According to Form

Exchange uses forms for just about everything you do with it. Exchange uses a form for composing and reading messages and for composing postings and replies to postings. For much of what you do in Exchange, you'll find standard forms. But in addition, the Exchange package includes Microsoft Exchange Forms Designer.

In your organization, someone (probably someone designated by your Exchange administrator) might act as an electronic forms designer. This forms designer will create standard forms for use by all members of your organization to report information and to order goods and services. These forms are called *organization forms*. Using them is a simple matter of selecting the form you need, filling it out, and sending it to the appropriate person or persons through Exchange. You select the form you need with the Compose New Form command, which displays the New Form dialog box, shown at the top of the next page. Or, if you're working in a folder that already has forms in it, you'll see forms for that folder listed at the bottom of the Compose menu. In this case you simply choose the name of the form you need from the Compose menu.

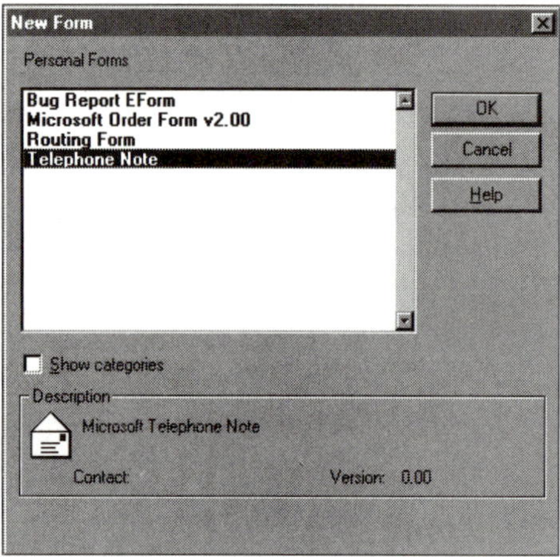

With the Exchange Forms Designer, you can create forms of your own for sending messages and for posting notes to folders. You can also create forms for reading messages or postings. The Forms Designer gives you the ability to tailor the collection and presentation of information in a way that suits your circumstances and needs.

Here is an illustration of a special form you'll learn to create in Part 3.

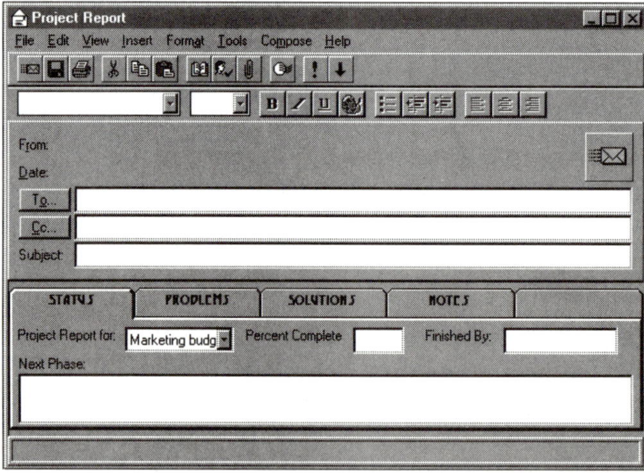

Note The Exchange Forms Designer must be installed separately from Exchange. This means that your Exchange administrator must give you access to the Exchange Forms Designer before you can create your own forms. When you have access to the Exchange Forms Designer, you'll be able to create forms for your own use. You'll be able to create *organization* forms if you're the designated forms designer for your organization.

Whenever you create or read a message or posting that uses a special form, Exchange installs the form on your computer and then opens it. For this reason, when you open a message or posting that uses a special form, you'll see a message while Exchange installs the form. This installation makes it possible for you and others to read messages and postings that use any Exchange form, even if it's a private form rather than an enterprise form.

Getting Off and Out—Quitting Exchange

You've got a couple of ways to quit Exchange. You can exit or you can exit and log off.

Exit

When you quit Exchange or Schedule+ by simply exiting, you quit only that one program. The other program continues to run. You can quit Exchange or Schedule+ in all the usual Windows ways. Here's the list:

- Choose the File Exit command.
- Choose the Close command from the Control menu or press Alt+F4.
- For Windows 95, Windows 3.1 or 3.11, or Windows NT, double-click on the Control menu icon.
- For Windows 95 and the Macintosh, click on the Close button on the title bar.
- For Windows 95, right-click on the title bar, and then choose Close from the shortcut menu.

Exit and Log Off

When you quit Exchange or Schedule+ by exiting and logging off, you quit both programs at the same time. The only way to exit and log off is to choose the File Exit And Log Off command.

MICROSOFT EXCHANGE IN BUSINESS

PART 1

"Charity begins at home," goes the adage. Before information can be available to a group, someone has to create the information—or at least put it in an electronic form so that the information can be shared. In this part, you'll learn how to send and receive e-mail messages as a private citizen of the network. You'll also learn how to use Schedule+ for your appointments and assignments. You'll learn how to organize, find, and view information in public folders, and you'll learn how to develop individual profiles that personalize your various sessions with Microsoft Exchange.

Personal Information

CHAPTER
1

Electronic Mail

You have sumthin' to say and you wanna say it. Someone else has sumthin' to say, and you wanna hear it. You know something someone else needs to know; someone else knows something you need to know. You want to swap lies (as well as facts). Well, to swap tales with other people, you send them a mail message or they send you one—you start a "conversation" through Microsoft Exchange.

The scene is set. Now you need to know how to swap facts, lies, tales, and hearsay with others. That's the story of this chapter.

Scenes from This Chapter

The process of electronic mail is like a swap meet. You send up a message on a hard disk somewhere (on a computer known as a server) so that the person whom you want to see the message (and only that person) can pull it down and read it. It's the same for everyone who sends a message—send up and read, send up and read. The messages you pull down (receive), someone else sent up to you. (You can also send up messages for yourself.)

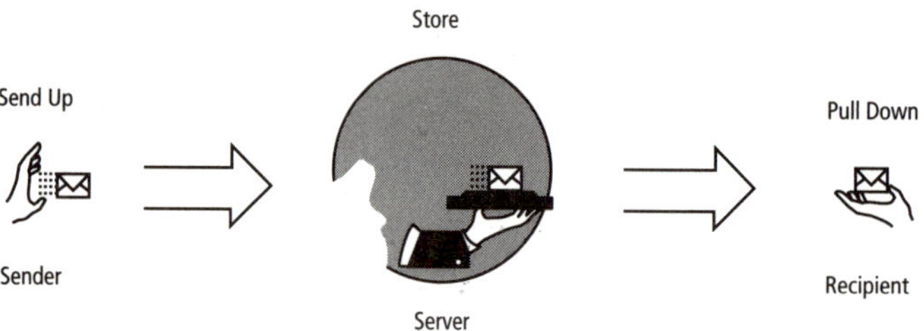

There are three important parts to electronic mail: composing the message you want to send, sending the message to the right place, and reading the messages others send to you.

Your message can include words and numbers (text), pictures, charts and graphs, audio, and video; in fact, it can include any type of information that you can create in a Windows-based application. (See "Adding Text from a File," on page 31, and "Text Plus Other Stuff," on page 33.) You can add special effects and decorations to the text—boldface, italic, underlining, color, bullets, and paragraph indention. (See "Text Decorations," on page 29, for information.)

After you compose and decorate (format) a message, you're ready to address the message so that you can send it to the right place for those you want to see it. Important to addressing a message is your address book. To find the right person, you need to use the right address book at the right time, plus make your address book as useful as possible. (See "Mucking About in Address Books," on page 55.) After you address the message, you push it along, whether by sending, forwarding, or replying.

And, of course, when someone else stuffs a message in your mailbox, you want to read it (maybe), and then deal with it in some way or other. Because a message can contain any object created by any Windows-based application, some parts of a message might appear as icons. You'll want to know how to make an icon open up and reveal its contents. You

might also have more than one place to store mail messages—in various Exchange folders and in files outside Exchange. (See "Gathering Messages from the Beyond," on page 41, and "Moving Messages," on page 46.)

Getting the Word Out: Sending a Message

Let's see. I need to send a message to my team about new information I have for them. I want to send a message to Sirch about having lunch together. I should also send my comments on the new bylaws to the officers of my professional group.

Only the first of these messages is strictly business related, but all of them are probably tinged with some elements of business life.

Just the Text

The fastest and easiest way to send a message is simply to type the text and send the message. In this basic case, your message looks tidy but unspectacular, yet it also requires of you the least effort.

To send a simple message, do the following:

1. Click on the New Message button (the envelope with one sparkling corner) on the Exchange toolbar.

2. In the New Message window, click on the To button to display the Address Book dialog box, shown on the next page.
3. Type *Sirch* (or the beginning of the name of the person you want to send the message to). Exchange jumps to the spot in the list that matches the name you've started to type. Select the correct name from the list.

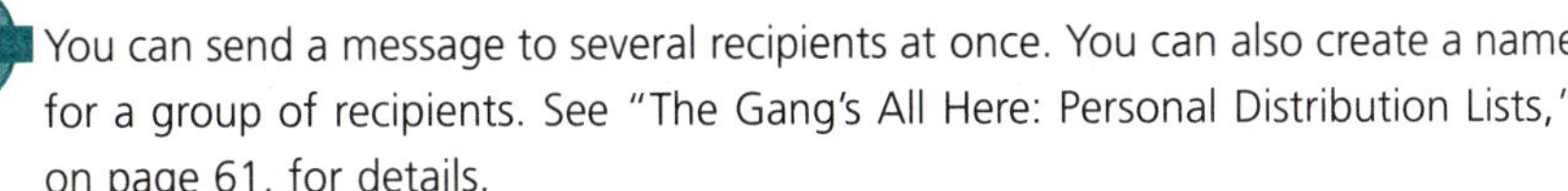

TIP You can send a message to several recipients at once. You can also create a name for a group of recipients. See "The Gang's All Here: Personal Distribution Lists," on page 61, for details.

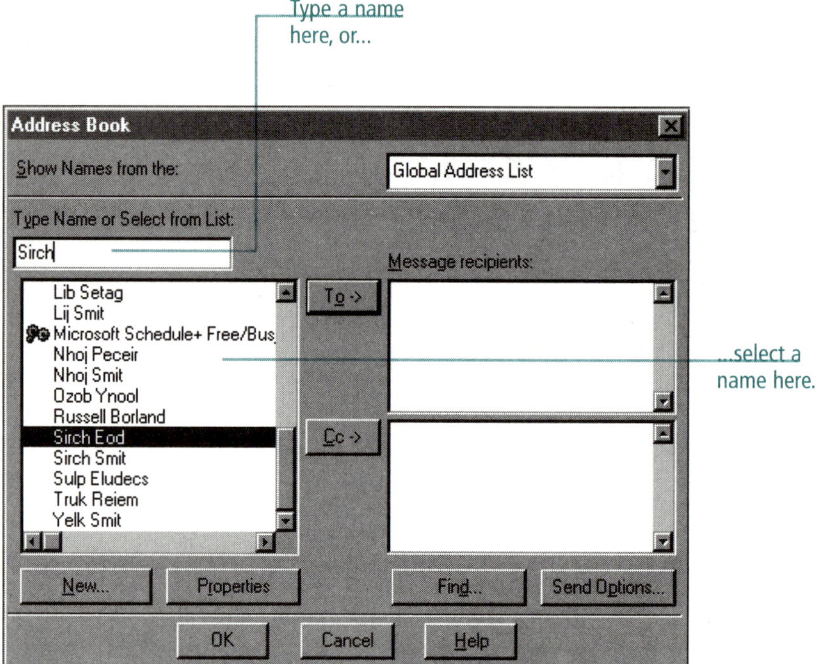

4. Click on the To button, and then click on OK.
5. Click in the Subject box and type a brief description of the subject of your message, such as *Doing Lunch.*
6. Press the Tab key to move to the message text area, and then type your message, such as:

    Sirch,

    Can we do lunch today? I want to talk with you about upcoming projects and find out how house-hunting is going. I want to hear ALL your war stories.

    Russell
7. When your message is ready to send, click on the Send button (the flying envelope) beside the To and Cc boxes in the message window header.

Text Decorations

A message like the one to Sirch is quick and easy, but you might want to decorate the message's text a little, just to make e-mail life more lively. Exchange provides several wonderful ways to enhance the appearance of your mail messages. Here's the list of basic text decorations you can use:

- Boldface, italic, and underlining
- Color
- Various fonts and sizes
- Bullets
- Paragraph indention
- Paragraph alignment

To apply decorations to the text in a message, you use the buttons and boxes on the New Message Formatting toolbar, shown here:

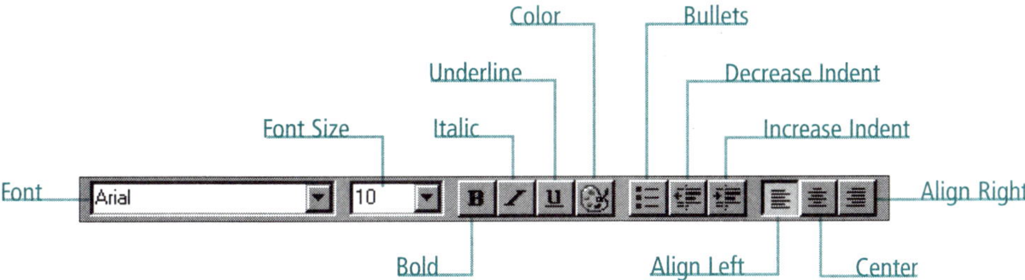

While you probably won't use all of these decorations at the same time, or even in the same message, the following example gives you a sense of what's possible.

A Text Decoration Sampler

You just espied a bunch of news about your new project. You want to share it with your team. To do so, you compose a new message addressed to *Bozo Bit*, which is a personal distribution list you created. (See "The Gang's All Here: Personal Distribution Lists," on page 61, for details.) Your message will look like the illustration on the next page. Follow the labels to apply the text decorations. Remember, for text effects (boldface, italics, underlining, and color), you first have to select the text. For paragraph effects (bullets, indention, and alignment), position the insertion point anywhere in the paragraph.

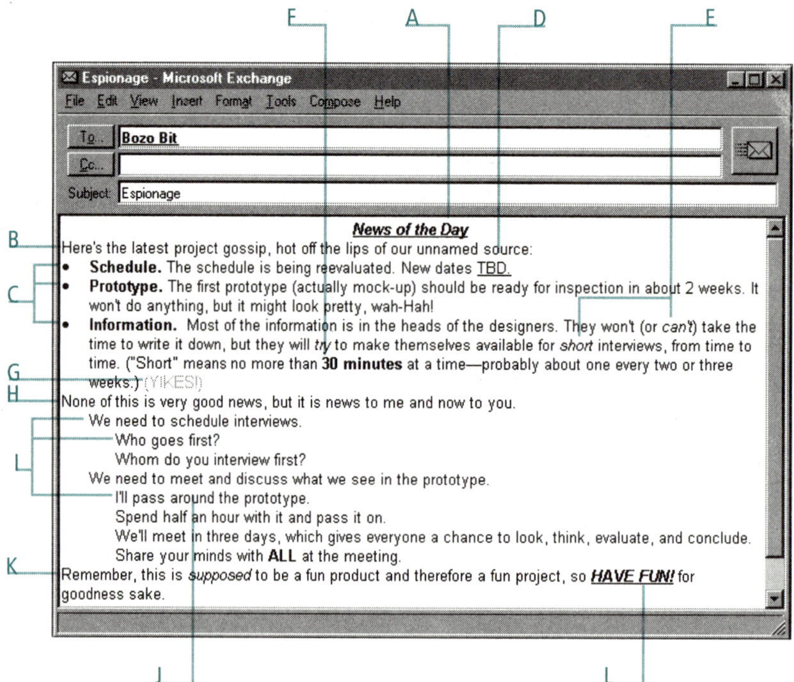

A. Click on the Center, Bold, Italic, and Underline buttons. Type *News of the Day*, and then click on the Bold, Italic, and Underline buttons again to turn off these formats.

B. Press Enter to start a new paragraph, click on the Left Align button, and then type the text.

C. Click on the Bullets and Bold buttons, type the text, and then click on the Bold button again to turn off boldface.

D. Click on the Underline button, type *TBD*, and then click on the Underline button again to turn off underlining.

E. Click on the Italic button, type the text, and then click on the Italic button again to turn off italics.

F. Click on the Bold button, type the text, and then click on the Bold button again to turn off boldface.

G. Click on the Color button, select Fuchsia, type *(YIKES!)*, and then click on the Color button again and select Auto to turn off color.

H. Click on the Bullets button to turn off bullets.

I. Click on the Increase Indent button once.

J. Click on the Decrease Indent button once.

K. Click on the Decrease Indent button twice.

L. Click on the Bold, Italic, and Underline buttons, type *HAVE FUN!*, and then click on these buttons again to turn off these formats.

Menu Commands and Key Combinations for Formatting

Besides clicking on the buttons on the toolbar, you can add and remove text decorations with menu commands and key combinations.

Menu commands. The Format menu contains two commands: Font and Paragraph. The Font dialog box contains selections for fonts, font sizes, boldface, italic, underlining, and color. The Paragraph dialog box contains selections for paragraph bullets, indention, and alignment.

Key combinations. To add (or start using) a text decoration from the keyboard, press the key combination. To remove the decoration (or stop using it), press the key combination again. The following table shows the text decorations and their corresponding key combinations.

Text Decoration	Key Combination
Boldface	Ctrl+B
Italic	Ctrl+I
Underline	Ctrl+U
Stop all text decorations	Ctrl+spacebar
Stop all paragraph formatting	Ctrl+Q

Adding Text from a File

If you have a text file stored on disk, you can insert the text file as part of your message. You can attach files to any message you send, whether it is a new message, a forwarded message, or a reply. (See

"Passing the Buck: Forwarding a Message," on page 44, and "Take That! Replying to a Message," on page 42.

To attach a file to a message, follow these steps:

1. Click on the Insert File button on the message window toolbar. If the Insert File button isn't visible, choose the View Toolbar command to display the toolbar.

2. Select the disk and folder that contain the file you want to attach to the message.

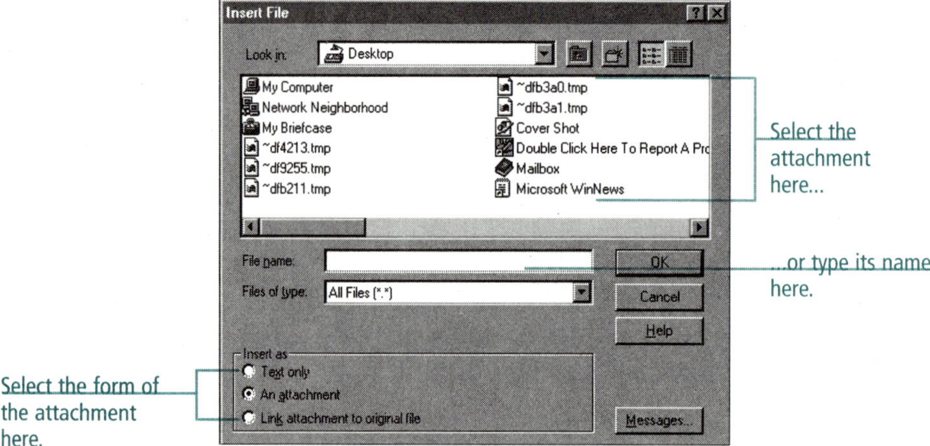

3. Select the file you want to attach. (You can select only one file at a time. To insert another file, repeat this procedure.)
4. Select the form you want the file to have in your message:
   - Text Only inserts the file as plain text with no formatting.
   - An Attachment inserts the file as an icon, which the recipient opens and reads with the program you used to create the file.

- Link Attachment To Original File links the attachment and its original file. This makes the message move through Exchange faster because the message is much smaller. To do this, the file must be in a shared folder—a folder that the recipients can connect to in order to read the attached file—on a hard disk.

5. Click on OK.

Text Plus Other Stuff

Exchange provides a way to add "other stuff" (stuff other than text) to your message. What you can add besides existing files depends on which Windows-based applications you have available on your computer. If, for example, you have Microsoft Office Professional installed, you can add the following:

- Microsoft Paint pictures and Microsoft Object Packager objects
- Microsoft Word for Windows documents, charts from Microsoft Graph, math and scientific equations from Microsoft Equation Editor, and text effects from Microsoft WordArt
- Microsoft Excel spreadsheets and charts
- Microsoft PowerPoint pictures, presentations, and slides
- Microsoft Access database files

If you and your recipients have sound cards installed, you can add sound objects. If you have Microsoft Video for Windows installed, you can add video clips.

Note For you technoid readers, "other stuff" is called "attachments"—usually files created by other Windows-based applications. For really technoid readers, "other stuff" can also be any OLE object. Phewh!

You can attach "other stuff" to any message you send, whether it is a new message, a forwarded message, or a reply. (See "Passing the Buck: Forwarding a Message," on page 44, and "Take That! Replying to a Message," on page 42.)

To insert a new piece of "other stuff," do the following:

1. Choose the Insert Object command, and then select Create New.

2. From the Object Type list, shown next, select the type of object you want to add to your message, and then click on OK.

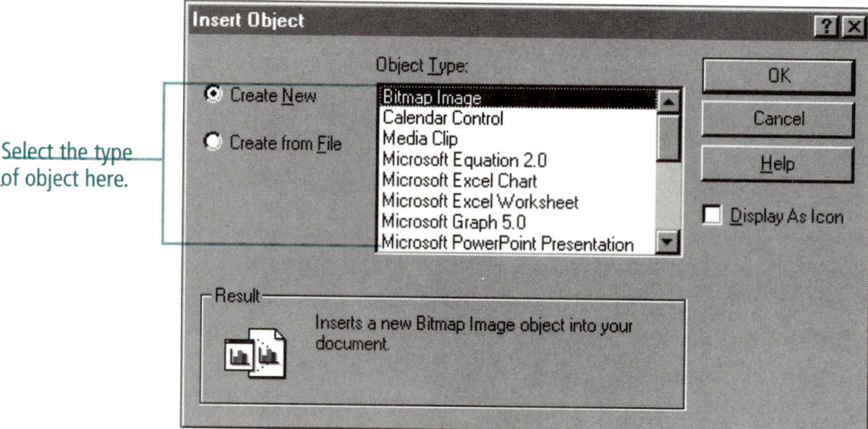

3. In the window that appears, create the object as you usually do in the application associated with the object. Here is an example of a Bitmap Image object window.

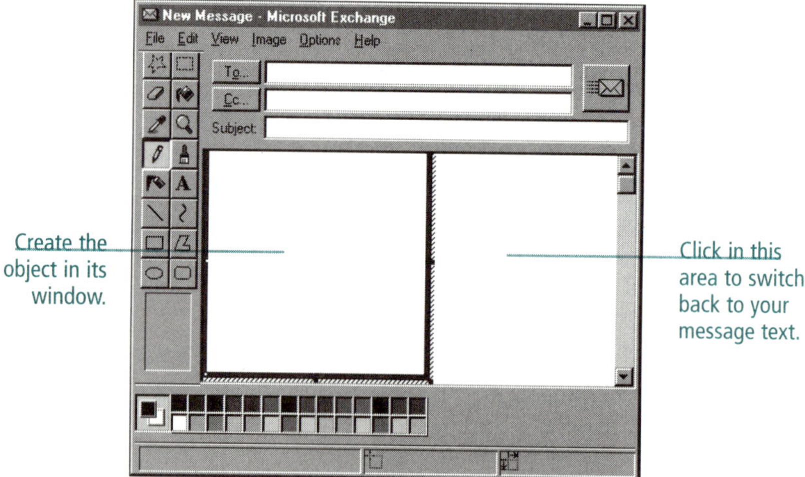

4. When you're finished creating the object, click in the message area outside the object window.

To insert an existing piece of "other stuff" from a file, follow these steps:

1. Choose the Insert Object command, and then select Create From File.
2. Click on the Browse button to find the file.
3. Select the disk and folder that contain the file, select the file, and then click on the Open button.
4. If you want to link the inserted file to the original file (rather than send the entire file through the mail system), turn on the Link box.
5. To display the file as an icon that must be double-clicked to show its contents, turn on the Display As Icon box. If you want the recipient to see the file contents without having to double-click an icon, leave the Display As Icon box turned off.
6. When you're all set, click on OK.

Anytime you're sending a very large or very long file in your message, it's better to send it as an icon. An icon takes up less space in the message window, and usually it's easier for people reading the message to view a large file in the window of the application you used to create the file. Also, Exchange has a 2 MB limit on message size. If you're sending a very large file, it's better to link it, which reduces message size considerably. Remember that a linked file must reside on a disk and in a folder to which the recipient has read access.

Attaching Messages

Usually, to send a copy of a message to someone—even lots of someones—you just forward the message. That's fine if you want to send only *one* message. But suppose you want to forward several related messages? For that you need to attach messages to your new message. You can attach messages to any message you send, whether it is a new message, a forwarded message, or a reply. (See "Passing the Buck: Forwarding a Message," on page 44, and "Take That! Replying to a Message," on page 42.

To attach an existing message to a new message, take these steps:

1. Click on the Insert File button on the message window toolbar.
2. Click on the Messages button. (The name of the button then changes to Files so that you can switch back to the list of files.)

3. In the Insert Message dialog box, select the mail folder that contains the message you want to attach.

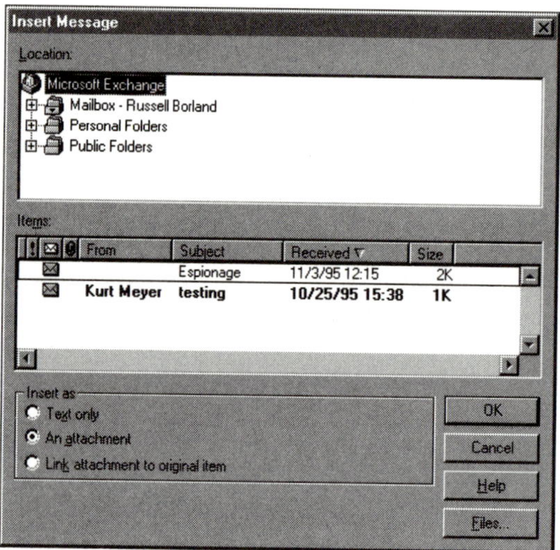

TIP You can select the Insert Message command to jump straight to the Insert Message dialog box.

4. Select the message you want to attach. To select more than one message, hold down the Ctrl key as you click the additional messages. If the messages are listed consecutively, click on the first message, hold down the Shift key, and then click on the last message; Exchange selects all the messages from the first one you selected to the last.
5. Select the form you want the existing message to have in your new message:
   - Text Only inserts the message as plain text with no formatting.
   - An Attachment inserts the message as an envelope icon with the Subject line as its label. The recipient double-clicks the icon to open and read the message. The recipient can also save each attached message as a separate message in an Exchange folder. See "Saving Message Attachments," on page 52.

- Link Attachment To Original Item links the attachment and its original item. This makes the message move through Exchange faster because the message is much smaller. The message must be in a folder that the recipients can connect to in order to read the attached item.

6. Click on OK.

Stamping Your Signature

Have you ever received a message with a bunch of standard closing lines at the end of it? Say, in addition to the sender's name, there's an e-mail address, a postal address, and some pithy saying? Have you ever added such lines at the end of your messages? Would you like to? Exchange gives you AutoSignature for just this case.

AutoSignature automatically adds whatever closing you want to your new messages. AutoSignature can also add a closing to replies and forwarded messages; you decide. And, you can use AutoSignature to store text you don't want to have to type. Instead, you type it once, store it, and then you can insert an AutoSignature selection anytime, anywhere in a message.

To use AutoSignature, you first set up a selection, and then you designate the selection as the closing you want on your messages.

To set up an AutoSignature, do this:

1. Choose the Tools AutoSignature command.

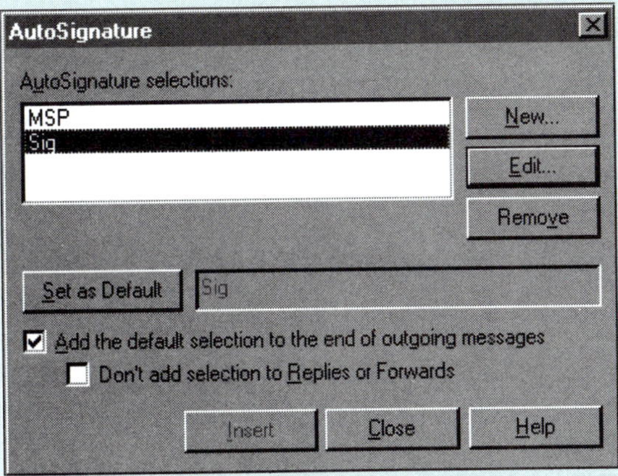

2. Click on the New button.

(continued)

Stamping Your Signature *(continued)*

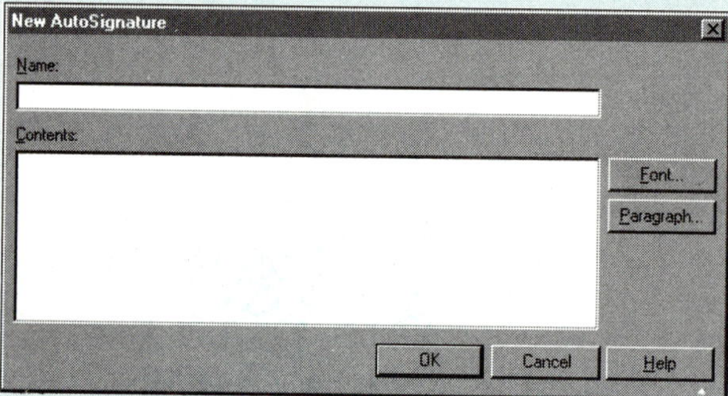

3. In the Name box, type a name for this AutoSignature selection.
4. In the Contents box, type the words and lines you want to use as an AutoSignature.
5. If you want this AutoSignature to have special formatting, click on the Font button to decorate the words in the Contents box. Click on the Paragraph button to format the paragraphs in the Contents box.
6. When the AutoSignature is set up as you want it, click on OK to return to the AutoSignature dialog box.
7. If you want a particular AutoSignature added to every new message, select its name in the AutoSignature Selections box, click on the Set As Default button, and then click to place a check in the Add The Default Selection To The End Of Outgoing Messages check box.
8. If you don't want to add the default AutoSignature to replies and forwards, click to place a check in the Don't Add Selection To Replies Or Forwards check box.
9. When your AutoSignature is set up, click on the Close button.

The next time you send a message, Exchange adds your default AutoSignature selection at the end of the message. For replies and forwards, Exchange adds the AutoSignature *above* the copy of the message you are responding to or forwarding.

(continued)

Stamping Your Signature *(continued)*

If you want to insert a passage of text (or your default AutoSignature) as an AutoSignature selection elsewhere in a message, first set up an AutoSignature selection using step 1 through step 9 above, and then follow these steps:

1. Position the insertion point in the message text where you want to insert the AutoSignature.
2. Choose the Tools AutoSignature command.
3. Select the AutoSignature selection you want to insert, and then click on the Insert button.

Whaddaya Want? Reading a Message

Whether you're "Hooked on Phonics" or you learned to read the old-fashioned way—"See Dick. See Jane. See Dick and Jane."—you'll probably want to apply your reading skills to at least some of the messages you receive. (One side effect of having electronic mail is that people tend to read *every* message for a while. Then they become more selective. It's a lot like people new to television—they watch everything in the beginning, can't turn it off, and have no powers of discrimination for a while. Eventually people become more discerning about how much television they watch and what they watch—whether you like their taste or not!)

To learn how to automatically dispatch incoming messages to the dustbin or to other places in Exchange or your file system, see "Inbox Assistant" on page 410.

A mail message can contain text that you read in the message window as well as attachments (other stuff) that you have to open (as you would open an envelope around a paper letter).

To read mail message text, do the following:

1. Double-click on the message line.
2. If parts of a long message fall below the bottom of the window, scroll through the message window to read them.

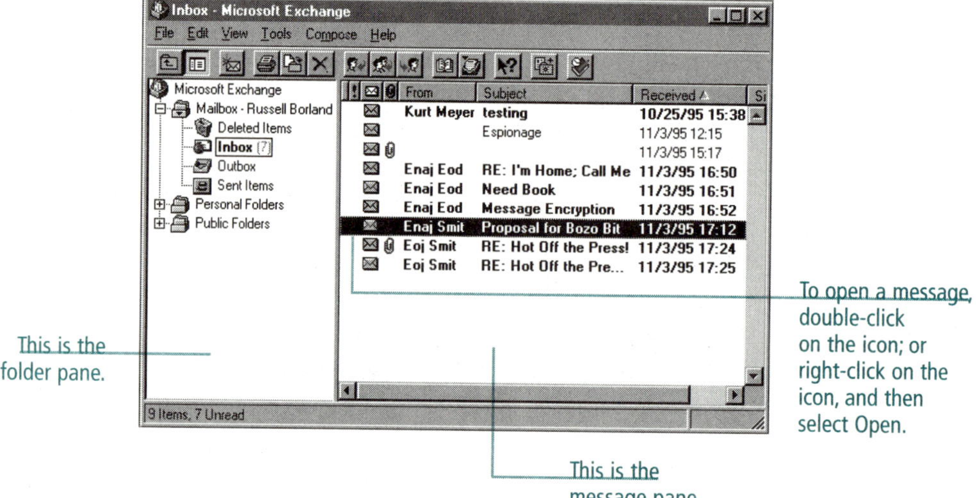

Seeing Other Stuff

The "other stuff" in a mail message can be any type of information in any form that's created with a Windows-based application. For example, a message could contain a video clip of your family picnic, complete with Uncle Slim dancing the limbo in his Hawaiian shirt and Jamaican straw hat. Usually, "other stuff" appears in the message as an icon.

To see the "other stuff" inside an icon in a mail message, do this:

1. Double-click on the icon in the mail message.

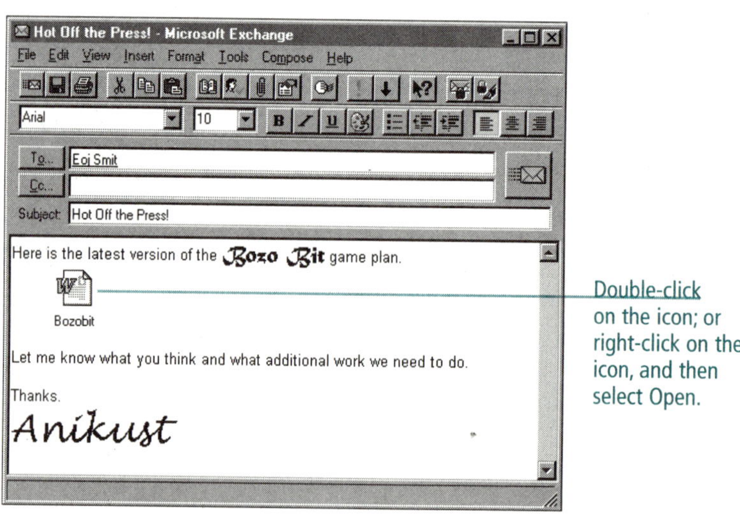

2. View the "other stuff" as you would usually view information in the application used to create this "other stuff."
3. When you're finished looking at the "other stuff," close the file. (You can also close the application if you wish.)
4. Return to Exchange. (If you close the application that displays the "other stuff," you return to Exchange automatically.)

Gathering Messages from the Beyond

Think about receiving e-mail in terms of physical mail—letters, magazines, and packages. You can receive them at your abode, you can receive them at a box at a U.S. post office, you can receive them at a package center that has private post boxes, or you can receive them at a commercial carrier's offices. Each of these locations is a different place to receive items. So it is with other services in Exchange.

If you are signed up for other electronic mail services, you can use Exchange to read the messages you receive through these services. For example, you could have an account on MSN, The Microsoft Network online service, or on CompuServe, America Online, or AT&T.

Most of your messages will probably come to you through Exchange. Every so often, Exchange checks for new messages for you. But unless you keep a connection to these other services open all the time, Exchange won't automatically check for new messages. So you have to tell it to deliver your messages.

To request message delivery, do this:

1. Choose Tools Deliver Now Using, and then select the service from which you want to get your new messages.

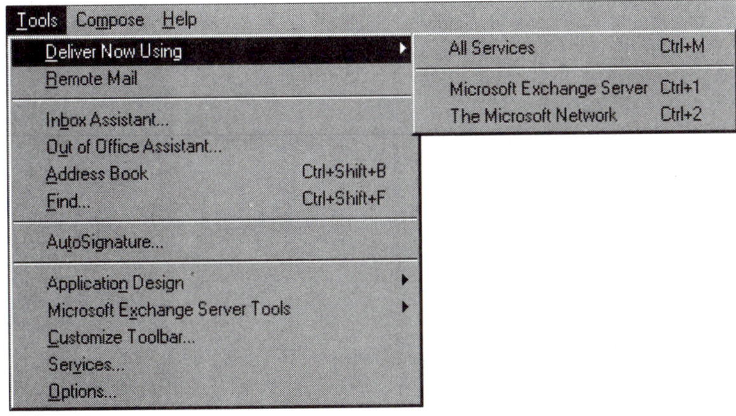

2. If the message service is one that you have to sign on to, Exchange starts that service's log-on routine.
3. After you log on (if necessary), Exchange collects your messages, and they appear in the Exchange Inbox.

   Now you can read your messages from the other service just as you read any other messages you receive through Exchange.

To get all your messages from all your mail services at once, choose Tools Deliver Now, and then select All Services.

Take That! Replying to a Message

Oftentimes a message provokes you to respond. So what do you do? Send back a reply. You can direct your response to only the person who sent the message, or you can respond to everyone who received the message.

To reply to a message, do the following:

1. Select the message line in the message list or open the message.
2. To reply to one person, click on the Reply To Sender button on the Exchange toolbar. To reply to the entire audience, click on the Reply To All button on the Exchange toolbar.

3. Type your response anywhere in the message area. (Exchange automatically positions the insertion point at the top of the message area, above the original message.) You can type your response at the top, at the bottom, or anywhere within the original message. You can format the text and add any "other stuff" just as you can for a new message.

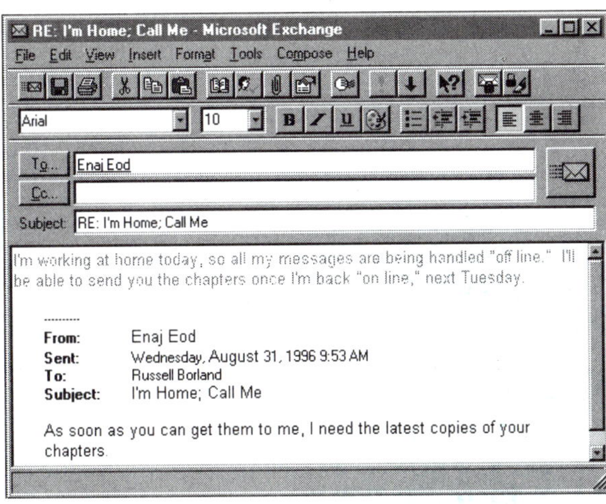

5. Delete any parts of the original message that you don't want or need to send back.
6. Click on the Send button on the message window header.

You'll notice that Exchange indents the original message when you reply either to the sender or to all those who received the message. Also, Exchange includes the entire original message. You can set up Exchange to not indent the original message or to exclude the original message when you reply. In addition, you can choose the font effects you want for your reply. To set these options, choose the Tools Options command and select the Read tab. Turn the check boxes on or off as appropriate, or click on the Font button to change the font or color of the text you type in your reply.

TIP Too often, people simply add their comments to the message that came in and then reply to all. After half a dozen replies to everyone, the message gets quite long. Most of this extra baggage isn't really necessary. Throw away the excess baggage. Keep the message short and crisp for the sake of your hard disk and for the sake of the Exchange system's performance.

Passing the Buck: Forwarding a Message

Now someone has sent you a really important message—as Rocky says to Bullwinkle, "And now for something *really* important." You think that other people might want or need the information in the message, even though they weren't originally recipients. In this case, you can forward the message to other interested parties.

To forward a message, follow these steps:

1. Select the message line in the message list or open the message.
2. Click on the Forward button on the Exchange toolbar.

3. Fill in the To box with the names of the recipients you want to receive the message. Remember, you can use group names, too. (See "The Gang's All Here: Personal Distribution Lists," on page 61, for information about Personal Groups.)
4. If you want to add your own two-cents worth as a preface to the message, type your response anywhere in the message area. You can use any text decorations or add any "other stuff" just as you can for a new message.

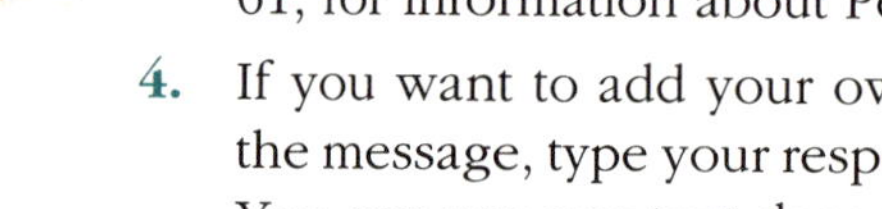

5. Delete any parts of the original message that you don't want or need to send on.
6. Click on the Send button on the message window header.

You can set up Exchange to automatically forward messages of interest. To do so, see "Inbox Assistant," on page 410.

Keeping Things Tidy: Dealing with Messages

You'll see. You're going to get lots of messages that you won't need to keep after you get them. You'll also receive some messages you'll treasure and want to keep forever. Once in a while, you'll discard a message and then want it back. If you practice a little self-discipline (yeah, right!), you might be lucky enough to retrieve a discarded message from the dustbin before it's gone for good. And now and then, you'll receive a message with "other stuff" in it. You'll want to save the "other stuff" but not necessarily the message itself (though you can do that, too).

The next sections describe all these various ways of dealing with messages.

Deleting Messages

Clutter, clutter, clutter! What a mess! You'll find that you receive many messages that you don't need and don't want to keep. Just like postal deliveries that you don't want to keep and quickly dump in the recycling bin (or the trash, if you don't live next to a clear-cut, as I do), you can dump mail messages in the Deleted Items folder.

To delete a message, do this:

1. Select the message line in the message list or open the message.
2. Click on the Delete button on the Exchange toolbar.

As an alternative, you can click on the Delete button on the message toolbar, or you can move the message to the Deleted Items folder. (To move the message, see "Moving Messages," on page 46.)

Retrieving Messages

How many times have you thrown something away only to want to retrieve it later? This is especially true on a computer, where the discarded item isn't physically lying around waiting for you to take it back. Exchange gives you some grace when you delete messages. After you delete a message, you can retrieve it from the Deleted Items folder by moving the message to another folder. You must retrieve the message *before* you purge (empty) the Deleted Items folder. After that, the message is gone for good. Your only recourse then is to have someone send you a copy of the message, if possible (and it ain't always so). For the steps you take to move a message from the Deleted Items folder to another folder (as the means to retrieve the message), see "Moving Messages," next.

Note Exchange is set up to automatically purge your Deleted Items folder when you quit. To prevent this, choose the Tools Options command, click the Empty The Deleted Items' Folder Upon Exiting check box to turn it off, and then click on OK. From now on, you'll have to empty the Deleted Items folder yourself. See "Purging Messages and Folders," on page 55.

Moving Messages

Even if you delete the messages you don't want to keep and don't need, your Inbox folder can become overloaded with messages that you *do* want to keep. Having lots of messages in your Inbox makes it difficult to find the messages that are important to you. They don't have much organization, and scrolling up and down a long list of messages is tiresome.

Before you move a message to another folder to store it, you might want to delete parts of the message that you don't want or need to keep. This keeps your Exchange files smaller. You can also add your own notes and comments to a message before you store it. To edit a message, you open it and then change the message as you would change any reply, forwarded message, or new message.

Exchange offers a clever way to organize your messages and keep your Inbox folder tidy. To do so, you move messages to other folders in Exchange or in your file system (*file system* means anywhere on a disk on your computer).

To move a message to another folder, follow these steps:

1. Select the message line in the message list or open the message.
2. Click on the Move Item button on the Exchange toolbar.

3. From the list in the Move dialog box, select the folder you want to move the message to. If the folder is a subfolder, click on the plus sign next to the folder that contains the subfolder, and then select the subfolder.

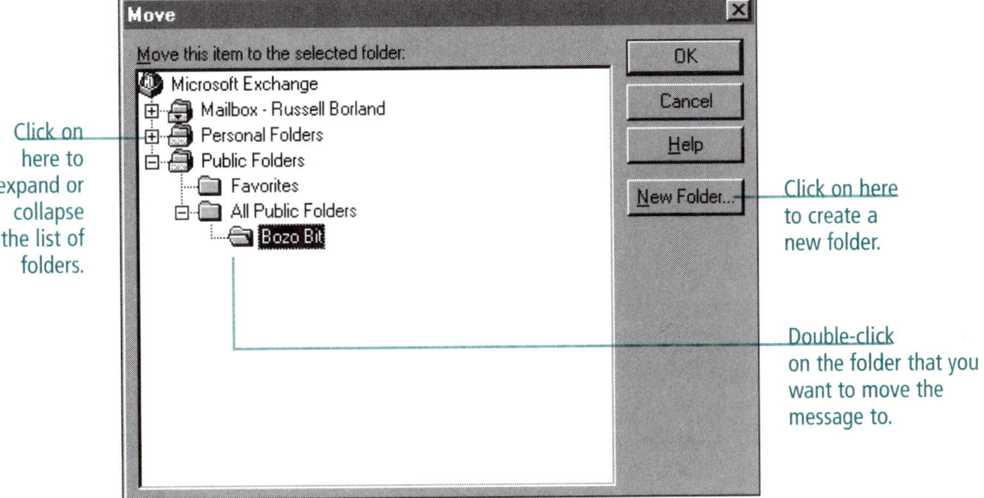
Move
Move this item to the selected folder:
Microsoft Exchange
Mailbox - Russell Borland
Personal Folders
Public Folders
Favorites
All Public Folders
Bozo Bit
OK
Cancel
Help
New Folder...
Click on here to expand or collapse the list of folders.
Click on here to create a new folder.
Double-click on the folder that you want to move the message to.

4. If the folder you want to use doesn't exist yet, select the folder in which you want to add a new subfolder, click on the New Folder button, type a name for the new folder, and then click on OK.
5. Double-click on the folder where you want the message to go.

As an alternative, you can drag the message line from the message list to the folder where you want the message to go.

You can move multiple messages at the same time by selecting all the messages you want to move before you click on the Move Item button or before you drag the messages to the new folder.

But what's that you say? You don't have any folders except Inbox, Sent Mail, Outbox, and Deleted Items? Well, you can create all the folders you want or need. See "Creating New Folders," next.

You can also delete folders you no longer need. See "Deleting Unwanted Folders," on page 49.

The Exchange Folder System

Exchange has two main folders—Mailbox and Public Folders. You can also have Personal Folders, which you must set up separately.

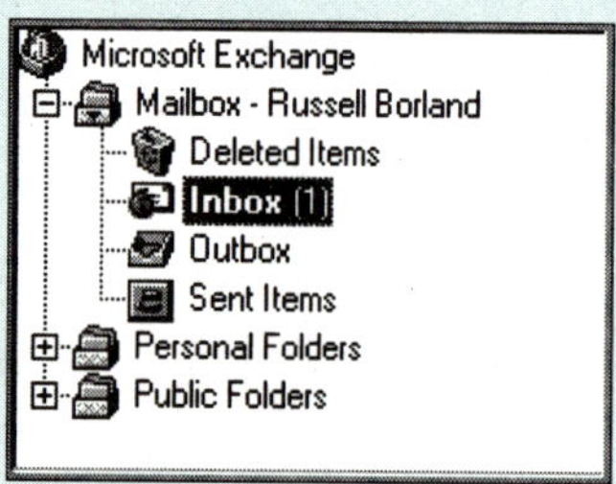

The Mailbox and Personal Folders folders contain the same subfolders: Deleted Items, Inbox, Outbox, and Sent Items. (Exchange lists them in alphabetic order rather than in some more logical order of use or usefulness.)

The difference is this: Microsoft Exchange folders are stored on your Exchange server; Personal Folders are stored on your computer's hard disk. To let you work on your messages offline, your Mailbox folders are set up for use both online and offline. You can also move messages to your Personal Folders Inbox while you're still online, but this isn't necessary.

Public Folders themselves are also stored on an Exchange server. To work with public folder contents offline, you must set up Public Folder Favorites, and then set up the favorites for work offline. For details, see Chapter 15, "Having a Remote Idea of Exchange."

Creating New Folders

Creating a new folder is a pretty simple task. You can create a folder inside any folder or subfolder in your Microsoft Exchange and Personal Folders folder.

To create a new folder, take these steps:

1. Select the folder that you want the subfolder to live in.
2. Choose the File New Folder command.

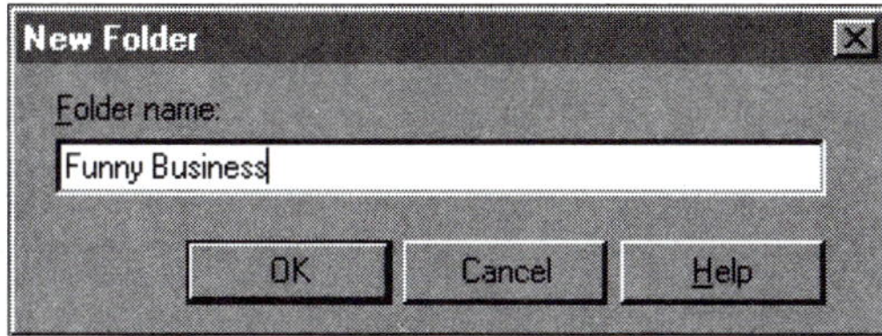

3. Type a name for the folder.
4. Click on OK.

Deleting Unwanted Folders

Some days are just like that—you wake up one morning and realize that you've got a folder that you no longer need. And if you don't need it, you certainly don't want it, do you? So here's what you do to rid yourself (well, okay, rid your mail system) of those unwanted folders.

To delete a folder, follow these steps:

1. Select the folder you want to delete. You can select the folder either in the folder pane or in the message list pane. The folder can be any folder at any level.

> **Caution** Exchange gives you no warning that deleting the folder also deletes all the messages and subfolders in the folder. Be sure that you really want to delete the folder. If you want to keep any subfolders or messages that live in a folder that you want to delete, move them before you delete the folder. See "Moving Messages," on page 46, and "Moving Folders," next. Then go back and delete the folder you no longer need.

2. Click on the Delete button on the Exchange toolbar.

When you delete a folder, Exchange moves the folder and its contents to the Deleted Items folder. From there you can retrieve the folders and their contents if necessary before you delete them from the Deleted Items folder. To retrieve a folder, move it to some other folder.

To completely delete messages and folders from Exchange, you must delete them from the Deleted Items folder. (See "Purging Messages and Folders," on page 55.)

Copying Folders

What's that you say? You want to *copy* a message so that you have it in two folders at the same time? No problem. Here's how you do it. Hold down the Shift key and drag the message line to the new folder. Or, choose the File Copy command, and, in the Copy dialog box, double-click on the folder to which you want to copy the message.

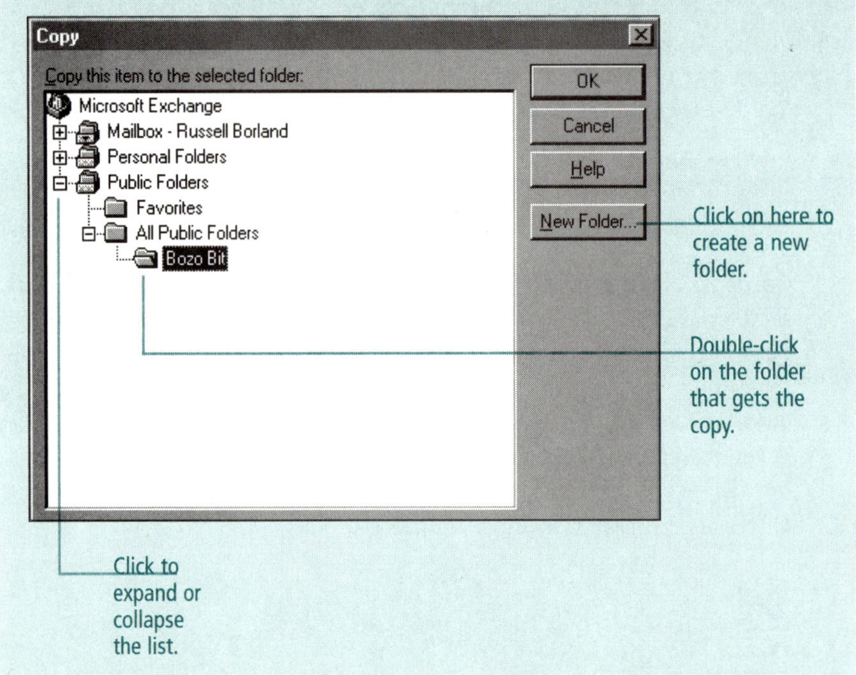

Moving Folders

Sometimes you just don't get it right the first time (or the second or third time, either). You've got a folder stuck somewhere in your mail system and you want to stick it somewhere else. What to do, what to do? Here's what you do. Move that folder!

To move a folder into another folder, follow these steps:

1. Select the folder.

2. Drag the folder to the folder in which you want to store the moved folder.

You can drag a folder to the Microsoft Exchange folder, to the Personal Folders folder, or to any other folder within these two folders, where it becomes a subfolder.

Note Unless you have permission from the system administrator, Exchange won't let you move a folder to the Public Folders folder.

Saving Messages in Files

Sometimes a message is so important or useful that you'll want to save it in a file that you can open in another application.

To save a message in a file, do this:

1. Select the message from the message list or open the message. You can save several messages in the same file by selecting all these messages at the same time.
2. Choose the File Save As command.

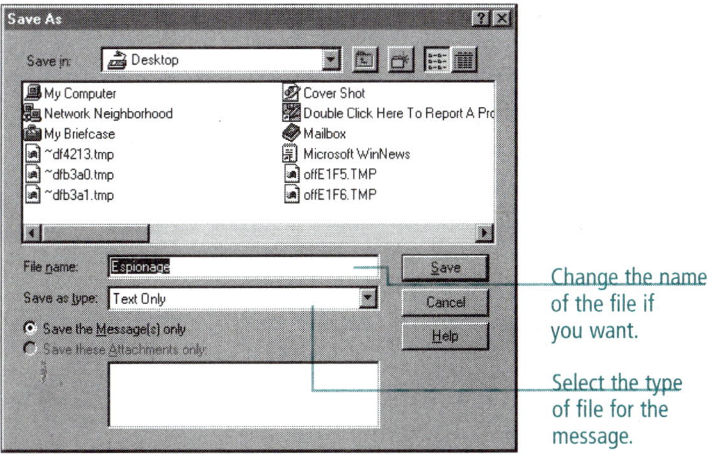

Change the name of the file if you want.

Select the type of file for the message.

3. Exchange creates a name for the file by using the subject line of the first message you selected to save. If you want, you can type a different name, select a different disk, or select a different folder.

4. In the Save As Type box, select the format for the type of file you want to save. The following types are available:

Text Only	Saves the text of the message but none of the formatting and none of the "other stuff."
Rich Text Format	Saves the text, formatting, and "other stuff" in the message for use in another application.
Message Format	Saves the message as a message, including information about the sender, recipients, and the subject. You can import the file into Exchange later.

5. To save only the message text, click on the Save button. To save attachments too, see "Saving Message Attachments," next.

Saving Message Attachments

So your good buddy Eromej sends you a message like this:

Hey, Ozob!

Look at this way cool picture I found. You'll want to hold on to it, I bet!

Argyle.bmp

You open the attachment (as directed in "Seeing Other Stuff," on page 40) and decide that Eromej is right; you *do* want to save this picture.

Note The following steps work only for attachments that are files. You'll know an attachment is a file because the filename appears below the file icon. If you don't see a filename, the "other stuff" is an OLE object. To save "other stuff" that's not an attached file, use the steps listed in "Saving 'Other Stuff' from a Message," on page 54.

To save a message attachment, do the following:

1. Open the message.
2. Choose the File Save As command.
3. Turn on the Save These Attachments Only option.

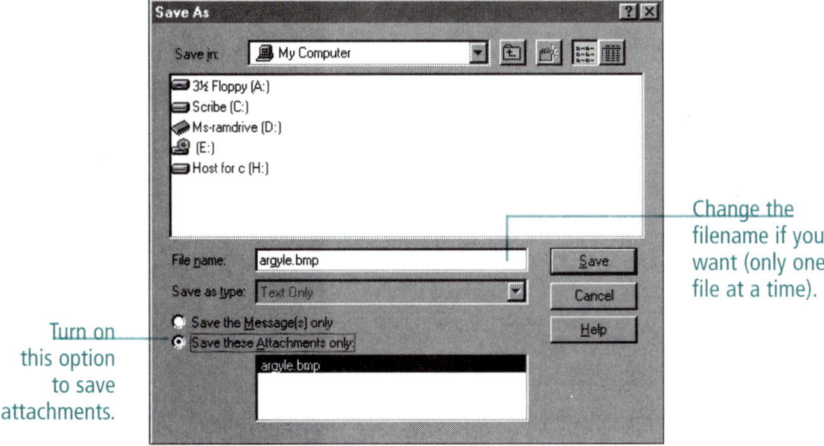

Change the filename if you want (only one file at a time).

Turn on this option to save attachments.

Exchange shows the name of the attached file in the Save These Attachments Only box.

4. If you want, you can type a different name, select a different disk, or select a different folder for the new file. To change the name, select the attachment name in the Save These Attachments Only list, and then type the new name in the File Name box.

Note If you want to change the name of an attachment, you must select and save only one attachment at a time. To save any other attachments, you must repeat these steps.

5. Click on the Save button.

You can save any number of attachments (if a message includes more than one) or all of them. To save some (but not all) of the attachments, select the names of the attachments you want to save in the Save These Attachments Only list, and then click on the Save button. To save all the attachments at once, select all the attachment names, and then click on the Save button. Exchange saves each attachment in a separate file.

Note If you choose to save all the attachments at once, you can select the disk and folder for the attachment files, but you cannot change the filenames.

Saving "Other Stuff" from a Message

Some kind souls like to insert pictures and other kinds of stuff directly in a mail message without creating a file for the stuff. Saving these kinds of "other stuff" is a little different, but it's not really very difficult.

To save "other stuff" from a message, do the following:

1. Double-click on the item you want to save.
2. The Exchange window changes to show the menu bar and toolbar of the application that the message sender used to create the item. Select the sections of the item that you want to save, and then press Ctrl+C to copy your selection to the Clipboard.
3. Start the appropriate application, and then press Ctrl+V to paste the selection into a new document in the other application.
4. Save the document with the item you inserted.
5. Close the other application.
6. Switch back to your Exchange message, and then click anywhere outside the item to bring back the Exchange menu bar and toolbar.

Saving Orphaned Items

Some types of "other stuff" might be created with an application that does not save its work in files, for example, Microsoft Draw, Microsoft Graph, Microsoft Equation Editor, and Microsoft WordArt. This "other stuff" is called an orphaned item. In these cases, you have to use a more indirect method to save the "other stuff" in a file.

To save an orphaned item in a file, do the following:

1. Select the item in the mail message.
2. Press Ctrl+C or choose the Edit Copy command to copy the item to the Clipboard.
3. Start an application that accepts the item, such as Microsoft Word, Microsoft Excel, or possibly Microsoft Paint.
4. Press Ctrl+V or choose the Edit Paste command to paste the item from the Clipboard.
5. Save the document as you normally save a document in the application.

Purging Messages and Folders

Well, like all good citizens of the e-mail community, you've been putting your litter (unwanted messages and folders) in the Deleted Items folder—that is, you've been deleting messages and folders right and left to keep your folders tidy. Now your Deleted Items folder is stuffed. (Well, there's not really any danger of overflowing the Deleted Items folder; it's just a turn of phrase.) So now you want to purge your Deleted Items folder and just get rid of all those discarded messages and folders once and for all.

Remember that Exchange automatically empties the Deleted Items folder in your Mailbox folder when you quit. If you have turned off this option, and you either want to empty the folder while you're still working or you want to empty the Deleted Items folder in your Personal Folders folder, follow these steps:

1. Open the Deleted Items folder and select the messages and folders you want to delete.
2. Click on the Delete button on the Exchange toolbar, or choose the File Delete command, or press Ctrl+D.
3. When Exchange asks if you want to permanently delete the selected items, click on the Yes button.

Unlike deleting messages and folders from other folders (which sends the message or folder to the Deleted Items folder), deleting messages and folders from the Deleted Items folder wipes out the messages and folders forever.

Mucking About in Address Books

Think of your Personal Address Book as your "little black book." In your address books, you keep the name and "address"—an e-mail identification, a fax number, or any other electronic identification—of each of your correspondents.

You can add new names, change names, and remove names as much as you want, but an electronic address book is much easier to keep straight than a paper address book. No ugly erasures, no running out of space. And your Personal Address Book—as well as all the other address books you can use—help you find names many different ways.

Opening an Address Book

Who'd have ever thought that adults would need directions for opening an address book? Zseesh! How hard can it be? It's not hard, once you know where to go and what to do.

To open an address book, simply click on the Address Book button on the Exchange toolbar. Exchange displays the names that are in your default address book.

Switching Address Books

Most Exchange users will have more than one address book. First and foremost, you'll have your Personal Address Book, in which you'll keep the names and addresses of the people you send e-mail to most often. Second, you'll probably have some kinds of organizational address books—one for the entire organization, one for your department (your network domain), possibly some for other departments (other network domains), and perhaps an offline address book. You will also have a separate address book for each online service you use to send and receive e-mail. For example, if you use MSN, you'll have a separate address book for your MSN e-mail account.

Note What's a network domain? It's all the people who share the same Exchange server, which is a computer that serves as your post office.

Because names and addresses might not be repeated across address books, you'll sometimes need to switch between address books to find the person you want to contact with e-mail.

To switch address books, do the following:

1. Click on the Address Book button on the Exchange toolbar.
2. Click the Shows Names From The box, and select the address book you want to open.

   The names in the address book appear in the big box.

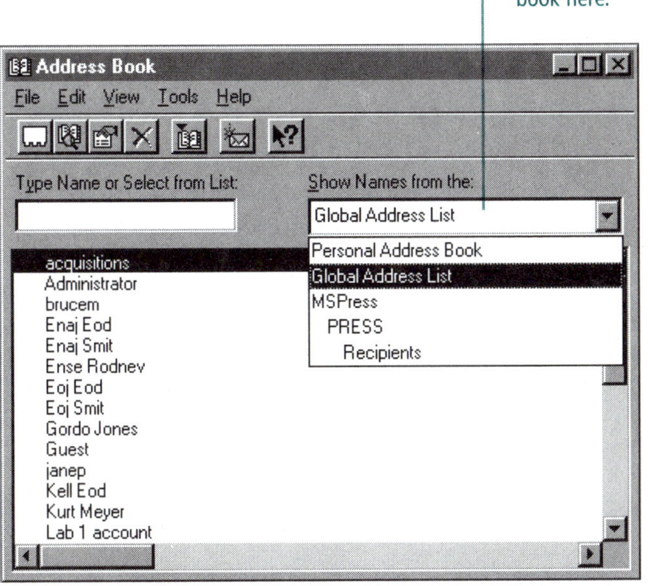

Finding People

Even if you have only one or two address books, the number of names an address book can hold makes finding a certain person time-consuming and possibly even tiresome. You need a way to locate a name quickly and efficiently so that you can get on with creating and sending the message and then on to other tasks. Exchange provides a Finder tool for locating that certain someone easily and quickly.

To find a name in your address books, take these steps:

1. Click on the Address Book button on the Exchange toolbar.
2. In the Shows Names From The box, select the address book you want to look in.
3. Type the beginning of the name in the Type Name Or Select From List box. Exchange jumps to the spot in the list that matches the name you've started to type. You can, of course, simply scroll the list of names in the big box to find the name you're looking for.

Finding Someone by Other Means

Typing part of a person's name in the Type Name Or Select From List box uses only one piece of information about a person. Perhaps you don't know the name or can't remember it accurately, but you do know something else about the person—perhaps an e-mail name (such as reVisionary) or the company name.

The Find button allows you to find a person's name by using other pieces of information. To do so, follow these steps:

1. Click on the Find button.

2. Type the information you do know, such as the first part of the name, in the Display Name box, and then click on OK.

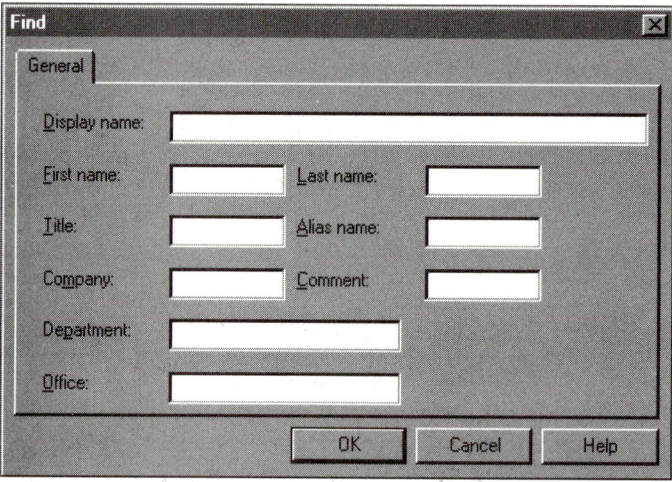

Exchange returns to the Address Book dialog box, and the list shows only those names that match the information you typed in the Find dialog box. Now it's easier to find the name you're looking for.

Notice also that the Shows Names From The box shows "Search Results." To return to a full address book list, select the address book name in the Show Names From The box.

Adding Someone

When you first start using Exchange, your address books will contain a standard list of names of people within your organization or of members of an online service. Because many people around the country and around the world now use e-mail regularly, you'll make "pen pals" as well as professional contacts with whom you'll want to exchange messages. You can, of course, simply type their e-mail address in each message you send, but e-mail addresses are singularly weird. It's really hard to remember them. Consider, for example, a CompuServe address. It's nine numbers with a comma in the middle. And you have no way of knowing who the heck resides behind some random number. On most other online services, people can select their own "handle"—their visible name, which seldom looks anything like their legal name. For example, my MSN "name" is reVisionary.

To avoid confusion, to reduce memorization, and to make sure you use the correct e-mail address every time, add the name and address to your Personal Address Book.

Note You can add new names only to your Personal Address Book. Only Exchange administrators can add names to organizational address books.

To add a name and address to an address book, do the following:

1. Click on the Address Book button on the Exchange toolbar.
2. Click on the New Entry button on the Address Book toolbar.

3. In the New Entry dialog box, select the type of address you want to add in the Select The Entry Type box, and then click on OK.

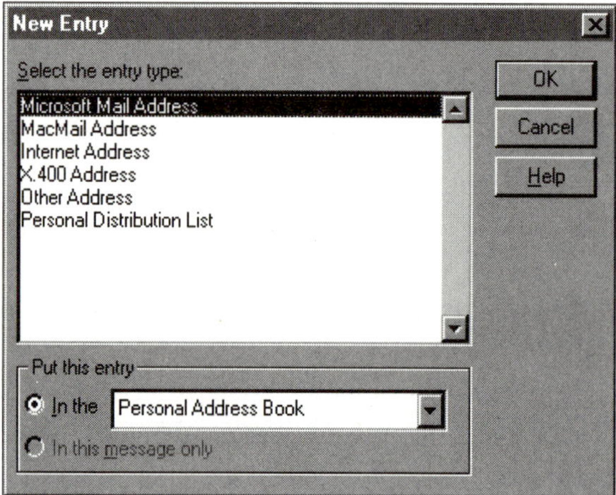

4. In the Properties dialog box that appears (the title bar shows the type of address you're adding), type the name you want to see in the address book in the Display Name box. You *must* fill in this box to create a new entry.

5. In the E-mail Address box, type the e-mail address. (This is the techy-looking address, something like *russb@microsoft.com* or *reVisionary@msn.com*.) You *must* fill in this box to create a new e-mail entry. (For fax-only recipients, see Chapter 4, "Developing Your Profile.")

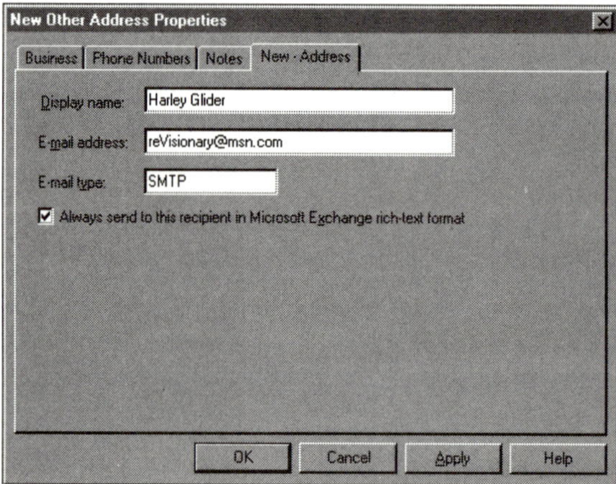

6. In the E-mail Type box, type the designation for your organization's e-mail system. Check with your Exchange administrator for the designation you should use. You *must* fill in this box to create a new entry.
7. If this recipient uses Exchange, be sure to turn on the Always Send To This Recipient In Microsoft Rich-Text Format box.
8. Fill in the boxes on the other tabs with as much information as you want. For example, the Business tab gives you boxes for addresses and a phone number. The Phone Numbers tab gives you boxes for various phone numbers.

   Exchange requires you to fill out only the boxes on the New Address tab. You can leave the other tabs blank for now and fill them in anytime later. You do that with the Properties button on the Address Book toolbar.

   The Properties button displays the same dialog box that you see after you click on OK in the New Entry dialog box.

You can use the information on the Business tab to fill in mailing labels in Microsoft Word for Windows 95.

9. When you finish filling out the tabs (at least as much as you want to for now), click on OK.

The Gang's All Here: Personal Distribution Lists

Do you know a bunch of people to whom you want to send e-mail regularly? To do so, you have to remember everybody's name every time. And, you have to type or select all those names every time. Too slow. Too prone to errors. Too boring!

Instead, you can create personal groups. A personal group is a name that you give to a bunch of e-mail correspondents. You add their names to a personal group, and then, when you want to send e-mail to the group, you just select or type the group name. Exchange takes care of sending your message to all those lucky people.

Exchange gives you the tools you need to create personal groups, to edit a personal group (to add and delete names), to delete personal groups, and to give a personal group a new name.

Creating a Personal Distribution List

Once you've decided to set up a personal group, the steps are pretty easy. You simply name the group, open the address book or books with the names you need, and select the names.

To create a new personal distribution list:

1. Click on the Address Book button on the Exchange toolbar.
2. Click on the New Entry button on the Address Book toolbar.
3. In the New Entry dialog box, select Personal Distribution List in the Select The Entry Type box, and then click on OK.

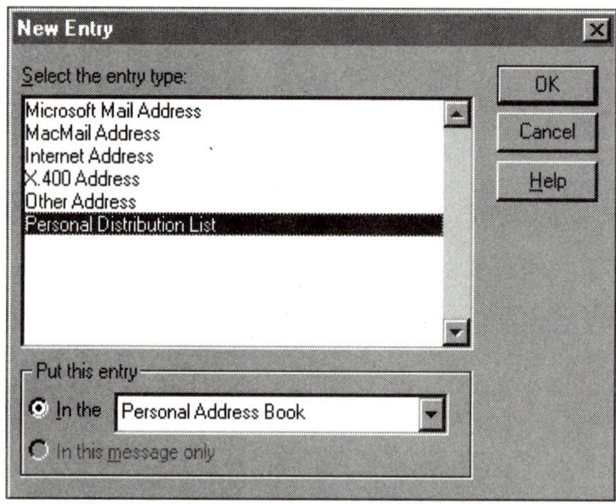

4. In the Name box, type a name for your personal group.

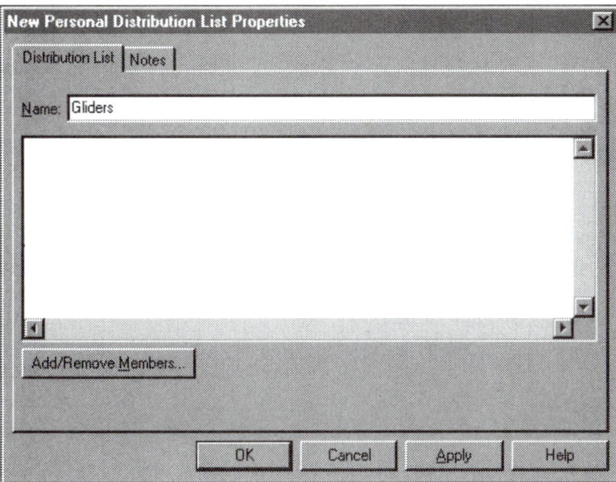

5. Click on the Add/Remove Members button.
6. In the Edit Members Of dialog box, select the address book with the names you want to add to this personal group. You can switch to different address books at any time to add names from several address books.

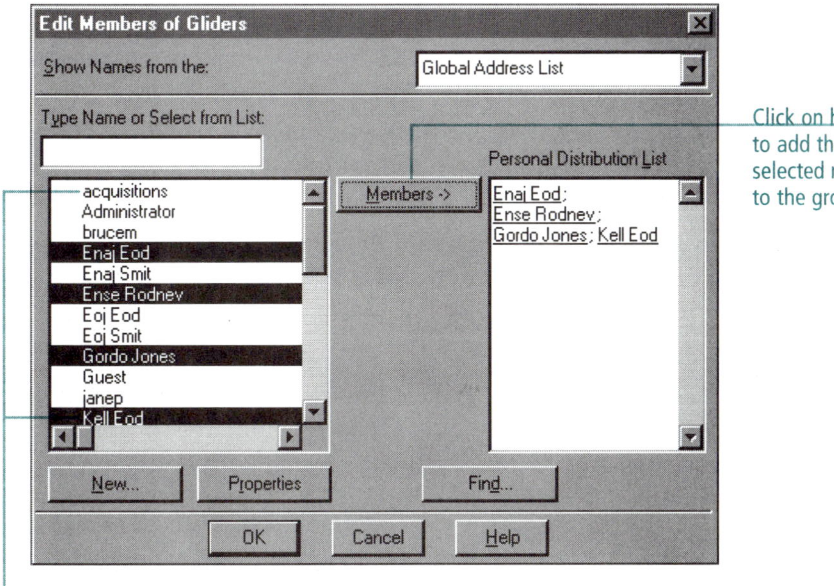

Note The title of the Edit Members Of dialog box shows the name of the Personal Distribution List. For example, if the new name is Gliders, the title bar shows Edit Members Of Gliders.

7. Select the names you want to add.

   To add several names listed one right after the other, select the first name you want to add, hold down the Shift key, and then click on the last name you want to add. Exchange selects all the names from the first to the last you clicked on.

   To add more than one name to the selected names, hold down the Ctrl key and click on the names. These names don't have to be listed consecutively.

   To find a particular name in a large address book, click on the Find button, type the first part of the name in the Display Name box (or appropriate information in one of the other boxes), and then click on OK. Exchange returns to the Edit Members Of dialog box, and the list shows only those names that match the information you typed in the Find dialog box. Now it's easier to find the name you're looking for.

8. Click on the Members button. The names now also appear in the Personal Distribution List box.

   You can add new names to your Personal Address Book as you're creating your personal group. To do so, click on the New button. Follow the steps for "Adding Someone," on page 59. You can also change the information for a person. To do so, select the name, and then click on the Properties button.

9. When you're finished adding members to your personal distribution list, click on OK.

   In the New Personal Distribution List Properties dialog box, you can click on the Notes tab and enter any information that you want about this personal group. This information can be handy if someone asks you what this group is about. You can copy this information into a reply and save yourself some time and effort by not having to remember and type a description of this personal group.

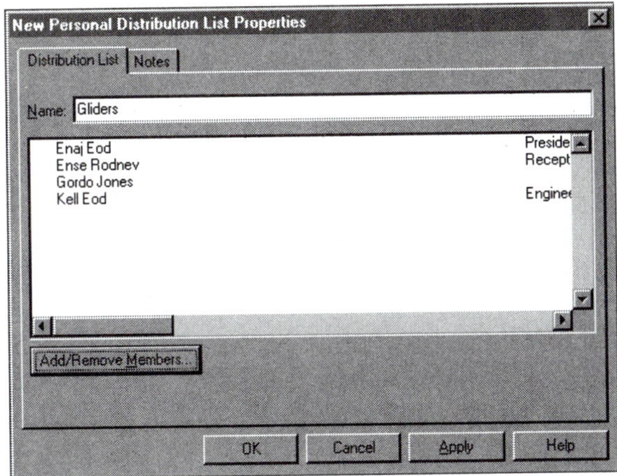

10. When the properties for this new personal distribution list are all set, click on OK. The new personal distribution list now appears in the address book with a "group" icon next to the name, as shown here:

Editing a Personal Distribution List

People come and people go. From time to time, a personal distribution list changes. New people want to be in your club; others want out. (And there are always a few you just want to throw out!) For your personal distribution list to be fully useful all the time, you need to add and remove names as the need arises.

To add a name to an existing personal distribution list, do this:

1. Click on the Address Book button on the Exchange toolbar, and then select your Personal Address Book.
2. Select the personal distribution list you want to change.
3. Click on the Properties button on the Address Book toolbar.
4. Click on the Add/Remove Members button.
5. In the Show Names From The box, select the address book that contains the name you want to add, select the name from the Type Name Or Select From List box, and then click on the Members button.

6. Click on OK.

To remove a name from a personal distribution list, follow the first four steps above, select the name from the Personal Distribution List box, and then press the Delete key. When you're finished, click on OK.

Note When you delete a name from the Personal Distribution List box, be sure to delete the extra semicolon and space that separates the deleted name from the names surrounding it in the list.

Deleting a Personal Distribution List

Sometimes groups disband—not even the Beatles lasted forever, though one fears that the Rolling Stones might. When you no longer want or need a personal distribution list, you can remove it from your Personal Address Book.

To delete a personal distribution list, follow these steps:

1. Click on the Address Book button on the Exchange toolbar, and then select your Personal Address Book.
2. Select the name of the personal distribution list you're removing, and then click on the Delete button on the Address Book toolbar.
3. When Exchange asks if you want to permanently remove the selected users from the address book, click on Yes.
4. Click on the Close button on the Address Book title bar.

Note The individual names of the group members remain in your Personal Address Book. If you want to remove them as well, select the names, and then click on the Delete button on the Exchange toolbar.

Changing a Personal Distribution List Name

Maybe a group changes its colors; maybe a group changes its mind; maybe you just want to use a different distribution list name for whatever reason. Exchange provides a way to change the name of a personal distribution list without too much trouble.

To change a personal distribution list name, do the following:

1. Click on the Address Book button on the Exchange toolbar, and then select your Personal Address Book.
2. Select the group name you want to change.
3. Click on the Properties button on the Address Book toolbar.

Sharing a Personal Distribution List with Others

After you create a personal distribution list name, you'll want others in the group to use it. But it's sometimes a pain in the neck to get an Exchange administrator to set up a public distribution list, especially if it's a "private" or social group rather than a business group, so here's how to send your personal distribution list name and its members to others.

1. Click on the Address Book button on the Exchange toolbar, and then select your Personal Address Book.
2. Select the personal distribution list name and click on the Properties button on the Address Book toolbar.
3. Click on the Add/Remove Members button.
4. Select all the names in the Personal Distribution List box.
5. Copy the names to the Clipboard by pressing Ctrl+C.
6. Close all the dialog boxes and the address book.
7. Compose a message to the people to whom you want to send the group names.
8. Paste the names from the Clipboard into the message area by pressing Ctrl+V.
9. Send the message.

When the recipients receive the message with the names, they can use it to create a personal distribution list, as follows:

1. Select all the names in the message and copy the names to the Clipboard.
2. Create a new personal group.
3. Click on the Add/Remove Members button.
4. Paste the names from the Clipboard into the Personal Distribution List box.
5. Close all the dialog boxes and the address book.

The recipients will then have a personal distribution list just like your original list.

4. Type the new name of the personal distribution list in the Name box, and then click on OK.

CHAPTER
2

Personal Scheduling

Keeping track of your daily appointments, tasks, and activities is important for doing your job and running your life. You want to be reminded in advance when it's time for a meeting or an appointment you don't want to miss. You want to keep track of all the little chores you have to do from day to day and of your personal contacts and anniversaries. You can use Microsoft Schedule+, a component of Microsoft Exchange, to keep a calendar and record of your daily schedule. That's what this chapter is about: working smarter with your personal time.

Scenes from This Chapter

Viewing the Calendar

Any view you want, you got it. Any view you need, you can have it.

At the click of a mouse button, you can see your calendar in one of three views—daily, weekly, and monthly. To switch to a different view, click on the tab for that view along the left edge of the Appointment book.

What's Going on Today? Daily View

Click on the Daily view tab to see a single day's appointment times in half-hour bands. (You can, of course, change the time span of the bands, and you can set appointments that start and stop at times different from what the bands show. I'll explain how in "Setting the Time Scale," on page 104, and "Fine-Tuning an Appointment," on page 76.)

Here's a typical Daily view with a few appointments and notes.

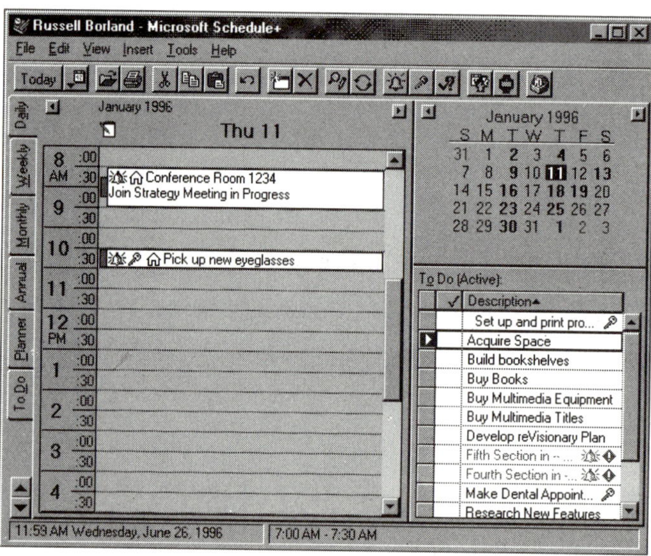

You'll note that the bands for times before 8:00 A.M. and after 5:00 P.M. are darker than the bands for times from 8:00 A.M. to 5:00 P.M. The lighter bands show your business hours; the darker bands show your off-work times. You can set the start and end of your business hours to fit your daily routine. See "Setting the Time Scale," on page 104, for details.

The Week in Review: Weekly View

See the week at a glance. Just click on the Weekly tab, and Schedule+ shows your appointments for the week.

Here's a typical five-day (work) week in Weekly view.

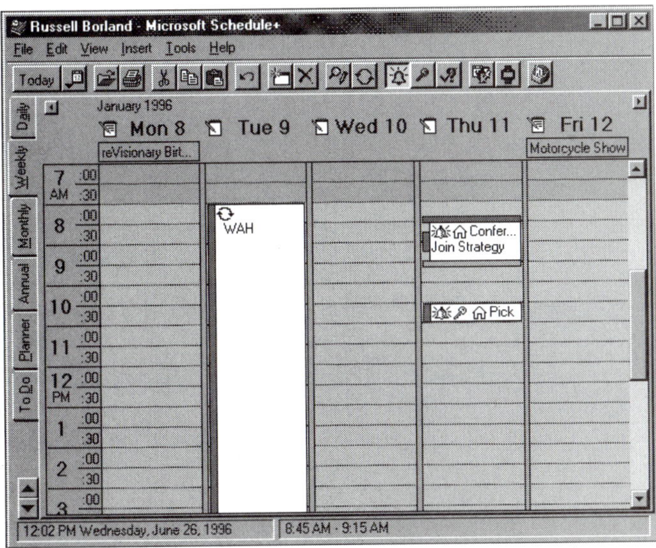

Of course, you can set the week to six or seven days, or four, three, or two days. You can't, however, like the Beatles, set the Weekly calendar to "eight days a week." See the sidebar "How Many Days Do You Want?" next, for details.

How Many Days Do You Want?

When you choose View Number Of Days, a submenu with the numbers 1 through 7 on it drops down. Select the number of days you want to see from this list of numbers. Schedule+ then displays that number of days. The View Number Of Days command is available only in Daily view and in Weekly view. Schedule+ dims the command in Monthly view.

To hone in on a particular appointment, double-click on the appointment. Schedule+ displays the Appointment dialog box, which shows details for the appointment.

Glancing Ahead or Behind: Month View

For hyper-planners who like to see the month ahead, click on the Monthly tab. You can see all the days of the month and the first word or two of each appointment for an entire month.

Here's a typical month view.

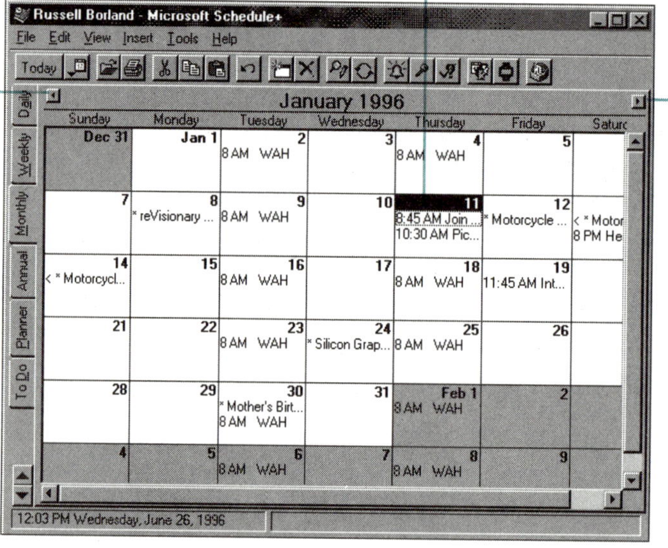
Double-click on an appointment to see details; or right-click on an appointment, and then select Edit Item from the shortcut menu.
Click on here to see the preceding month.
Click on here to see the next month.
Russell Borland - Microsoft Schedule+
January 1996
12:03 PM Wednesday, June 26, 1996

You'll note that you can see all the days in one month, plus a few days from the preceding and following months. You can't set Month view to start in the middle of a month.

To see the details for an appointment on a particular day, double-click on that appointment. Schedule+ displays the Appointment dialog box.

To view the next month, click on the right arrow button at the top of the calendar. To view the previous month, click on the left arrow button at the top of the calendar.

To jump to a month that's several months away, use the Edit Go To command. See "Finding a Date," next, for details.

Finding a Date

Sometimes single people have difficulty finding a date. In Schedule+, however, this isn't a problem. You can jump to any date you want to find—even if you don't know the precise date—because besides looking for a specific date, you can also look for a date that includes a particular appointment.

To jump to a particular date, take these steps:

1. Choose the Edit Go To command.

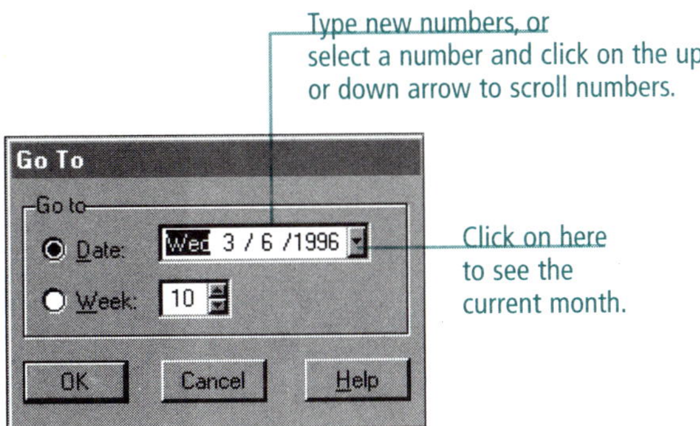
Type new numbers, or
select a number and click on the up
or down arrow to scroll numbers.
Go To
Go to
Date:
Wed 3 / 6 /1996
Week:
10
OK
Cancel
Help
Click on here
to see the
current month.

2. In the Date box, select or enter the month number, date number, and year number, and then click on OK.

What Happened Before 1900? And What Will Happen After 2999?

Well, one suspects that you don't have many appointments, tasks, or events listed in your Schedule+ calendar before 1900. And you're probably not really sure where you'll be after 2999, but it's probably safe to say you won't be using Schedule+ version 7.0!

So what's important about these two years? In the Year slot of the Go To dialog box, if you type numbers less than 1900, Schedule+ changes it to 1900. If you type a number greater than 2999, Schedule+ lops off the first three digits or changes it to 1900 if the last digit is zero. You cannot view a date before 1/1/1900 or after 12/31/2999.

To jump to a particular week in the current year only, do this:

1. Choose the Edit Go To command.
2. Click on the Week button, select or type the week number, and then click on OK.

Note You cannot use the Edit Go To command to jump to a particular week in a year other than the current year—even if the calendar shows a different year.

To jump to a particular day of the week in a month or year:

1. Choose the Edit Go To command.
2. Select or type the month and year numbers. Press the first letter of the day of the week you want to find. Each time you press the letter, Schedule+ advances the date to the next such day of the week. For Tuesday and Thursday, which both start with *t*, you must press the letter twice to advance a whole week. When the correct date is displayed, click on OK.

To find the date of a particular appointment, do the following:

1. Choose the Edit Find command.

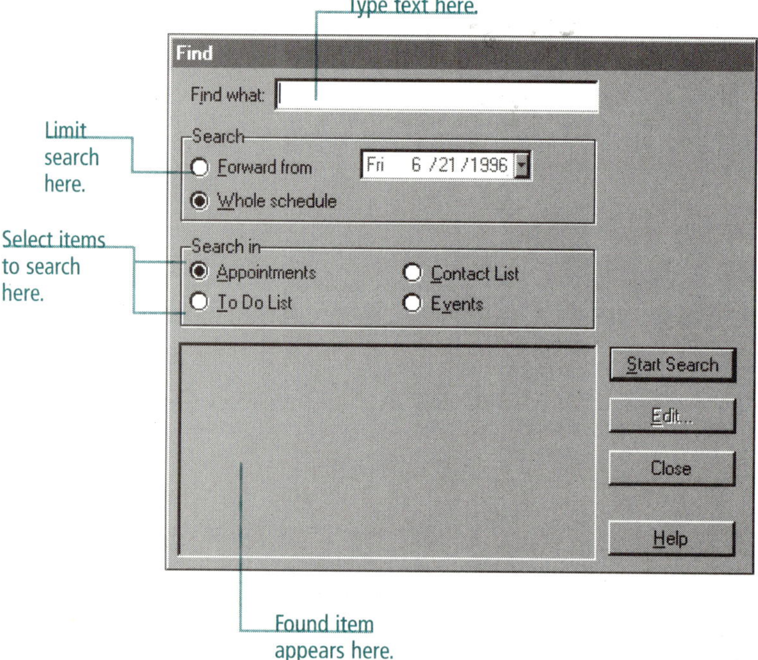

2. In the Find What box, enter some text that's part of the description, location, or notes for the appointment you want to find. (See "Fine-Tuning an Appointment," on page 76.)

3. Under Search, select the option to search the entire schedule or the option to search from a particular date forward. Select the Whole Schedule option when you want to find all the appointments you have had and will have for a particular purpose. Select the Forward From option when you want to find appointments after a particular date.

   You can also use the Edit Find command to find tasks (To Do List), particular people (Contact List), or particular Events. To find something in one of these other lists, select the list you want in the Search In area.

4. Click on the Start Search button.

   If Schedule+ finds a matching appointment, task, person, or event, you see it listed at the bottom of the Find dialog box, and the Start Search button changes to the Find Next button. To look for another appointment, click on the Find Next button.

   If you want to make changes to the item or items Schedule+ finds, click on the Edit button. Schedule+ displays the dialog box for that item. (The dialog box you see depends on what you searched for.) Make your changes in the dialog box, and then click on OK to return to the Find dialog box.

5. When you're done searching, click on the Close button.

Scheduling an Appointment

Information doesn't do you any good if it's only in your head. Write it down! That is, put your appointments in Schedule+. Not only do you have a record, but you also can set a reminder to alert you when it's time to go to or prepare for your appointment.

Schedule+ is especially helpful for setting up a series of appointments. For example, suppose you play soccer every Thursday at 7:00 P.M. And suppose that you have a weekly staff meeting every Monday at 10:00 A.M. You can set up recurring appointments for cases like these.

For both one-time and recurring appointments, you can designate the appointment as private or public. For example, your soccer matches are private, as are your weekly golf lessons at 4:00 P.M. on Tuesdays, your doctor, dentist, and eye appointments, and your car repair. Your staff meetings and other business meetings are public. You'll learn more about public and private appointments a little later in this chapter.

Just a One-Time Appointment

Most of us fill our days and nights with one-time appointments. Even a series of appointments with the dentist won't always be on the same day and time each week but will come up on different days and at different times.

To set up a one-time appointment, take these steps:

1. Switch to the date of the appointment. (Use the Edit Go To command, or click to select the date from the monthly calendar.)
2. If necessary, switch to Daily or Weekly view.
3. In the time scale, select from the start time to the end time. (Press down the left mouse button on the start time, drag to the end time, and then release the mouse button.)
4. Type a description for the appointment.

Fine-Tuning an Appointment

Sometimes you'll want to set an appointment that begins at a time other than on the hour or half-hour. For example, your soccer game might start at 8:15 P.M. In this case, you need to enter the appointment using the Appointment dialog box.

To do so, follow these steps:

1. Select the nearest start time, and then click on the Insert New Appointment button.

2. In the Appointment dialog box, change the start time to match the actual appointment time and then set the end time. To change the start time, select the hour or minute and either scroll to the time you want or type the number. For truly odd minutes, such as 18, you'll have to type the number.
3. Type a description of the appointment in the Description box.
4. If you want to, type the location of the appointment in the Where box.
5. Set the Reminder, if you want one, and set the Private and Tentative boxes if they apply.
6. Select the Notes tab and add a note if you want.
7. Click on OK.

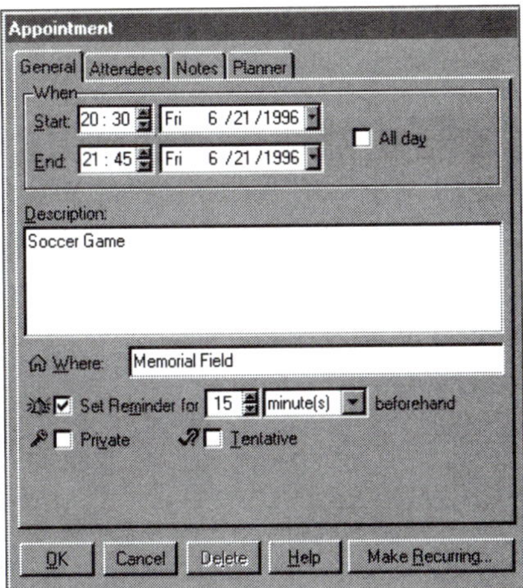

After you set an appointment that starts at a time not shown on the time bands, you can see the precise time for the appointment. To see the odd appointment times:

1. Select the appointment, and then position the mouse pointer on the top, left, or bottom border of the appointment. In the top and left borders, the mouse pointer becomes a four-headed arrow. In the bottom border, the mouse pointer becomes a two-headed arrow.
2. Hold down the left mouse button. The start and end times of your appointment appear in a small box next to the mouse pointer.

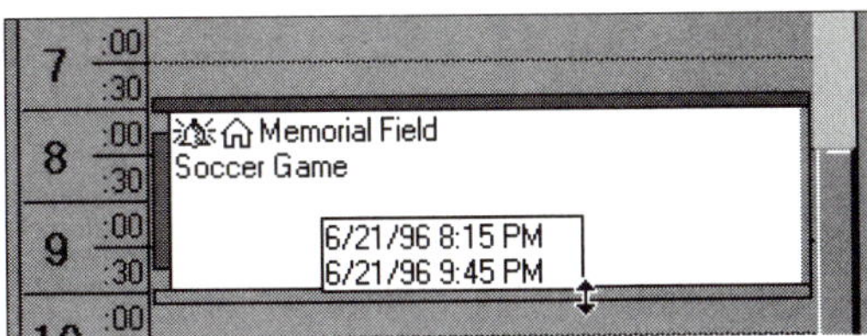

3. Release the mouse button to hide the odd appointment times.

Note You can use these steps for any appointment. This is handy if you have difficulty detecting the exact start and end times of an appointment from the time bands.

Public and Private Appointments

When you set up a new appointment, Schedule+ makes it a "public" appointment. A public appointment is one that you don't mind others seeing when they read your schedule (only by permission, of course). By keeping an appointment public, you let others know the importance of the appointment. (You'll learn more about seeing others' appointment books in Chapter 10, "Scheduling Project Meetings.")

You'll probably want to keep most of the meetings that relate to your job public. But you'll have other meetings and appointments that you'll want to mark "private." Because Schedule+ makes a meeting or appointment public when you set it up, you must purposely set an appointment to private for it to not be a public appointment.

You designate an appointment as private when others don't need to see the nature of the appointment. Most of us are uneasy about showing doctor, dentist, eye, legal, and court appointments to others. Of course, you might inform your supervisor about such appointments, but you don't necessarily want everyone who can read your appointment book to see the nature of these private appointments, especially appointments "after hours."

When an appointment is private, others can see that you are busy during the time of the appointment, but they can't see what you'll be doing. To make an appointment private, click on the Private button on the Schedule+ toolbar. (You can also turn on the Private check box in the Appointment dialog box.)

To switch a private appointment back to public, click on the Private button on the Schedule+ toolbar again.

Remind Me Again What I'm *Supposed* to Be Doing: Setting Reminders

One of the great advantages of keeping your appointments in Schedule+ is reminders. With reminders, Schedule+ can ding you when it's time for the appointment. You can set a reminder for several hours, days, weeks, or months ahead of an appointment to remind you to prepare for it.

Whenever you set up a new appointment, Schedule+ automatically sets a reminder for 15 minutes before the appointment time. To turn off a reminder for an upcoming appointment, select the appointment and then click on the Reminder button on the Schedule+ toolbar. To turn a standard reminder back on, click on the Reminder button again.

Note As you can see, all appointments with reminders show a bell icon beside the appointment description.

You can change the time of the reminder for each appointment. Here's how:

1. Select the appointment, and then click on the Edit button on the Schedule+ toolbar.

2. In the Set Reminder For area of the Appointment dialog box, select the unit of time and enter the number of units. For example, to set a reminder two weeks prior to the appointment, select Week(s) and enter *2*.
3. Click on OK.

You can also set up Schedule+ to use a different standard reminder time. For details, see "Standard Reminder Time," on page 108.

Changing an Appointment

Nothing holds as strongly as an appointment—until someone changes it, that is. Sometimes you have to move an appointment to a different time or day or both. Sometimes an appointment has to be longer than originally set, and sometimes, if you're very, very lucky, an appointment can be shortened.

Moving an Appointment

When you need to move an appointment, you've got two choices. You can use the Edit Move Appt command, or, as long as the appointment's original and new times are both visible, you can drag the appointment to move it.

To move an appointment by dragging it, follow these steps:

1. Select the appointment, and then position the mouse pointer in the top or left border of the appointment. The mouse pointer becomes a four-headed arrow.
2. Drag the appointment to the new time.

   If the time is earlier or later than the bands of time shown on the screen, drag the appointment into the border of the time bands. Schedule+ scrolls the time bands.

The scrolling point is very narrow—about 1 pixel tall. You might have to move the arrow back and forth across the top or bottom border to scroll the time bands.

If the appointment needs to be rescheduled for a new date, click on the Weekly tab. Select the appointment, position the mouse pointer in the top or left border so that it becomes a four-headed arrow, and then drag the appointment horizontally to the new date and time.

Remember, you can show as many as seven days in Weekly view. Use the View Number Of Days command to select the number of days to see in Weekly view.

If the appointment is next week or next month or anytime beyond the current week, you must use the Move Appt command. To do so, take these steps:

If right-clicking is unavailable, select the appointment, and then choose Move Appt from the Edit menu.

1. Right-click on the appointment, and then select Move Appt from the shortcut menu.
2. In the Move Appointment dialog box, set the new time and new date, and then click on OK.

Tailoring an Appointment: Longer or Shorter

Say you've set up your meeting and then someone suggests additional topics to discuss. You agree, but now the meeting must be longer. Or,

what happens if you decide to forgo discussing some items on the meeting agenda, and now the appointment can be shorter?

Here's what you do:

1. Select the appointment, and then position the mouse pointer on the bottom border of the appointment. The mouse pointer becomes a two-headed arrow.
2. Drag the bottom border up to shorten the appointment or down to lengthen the appointment.

I'll Be in a Meeting All Day

Some meetings are like that—they take up your entire day. Schedule+ makes it simple to set an all-day appointment. Just follow these steps:

1. Switch to the date of the meeting.
2. Click on the Insert New Appointment button.
3. Select the All Day check box.

   "All day" means from midnight to midnight. If the meeting really lasts only from 9 to 5, set the start and end times to the actual start and end times.
4. Type a description of the meeting, note its location, set other items in the dialog box as you want, and then click on OK.

Let's Set Aside Every Tuesday at 2 O'Clock: Recurring Appointments

When you are part of an event that happens repeatedly at the same time, you can save yourself a lot of effort by setting a recurring appointment. You have several choices for the recurring time period—daily, weekly, monthly, and others.

To create a recurring appointment, do the following:

1. Select the date and time of the first appointment, and then click on the Recurring button.

2. Type a name for the appointment in the Description box and the location of the appointment in the Where box, as seen next.

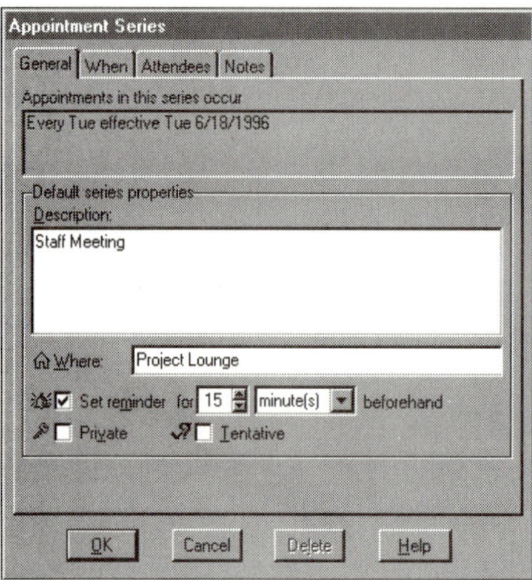

3. If you want a reminder, set the advance notice time. If you don't want a reminder, turn off the Reminder check box.
4. If you want to make this series of appointments private, click to place a check in the Private check box.
5. Click on the When tab, and then select the interval for the appointment. The interval can be Daily, Weekly, Monthly, or Yearly. The table on the next page describes the various intervals you can select.

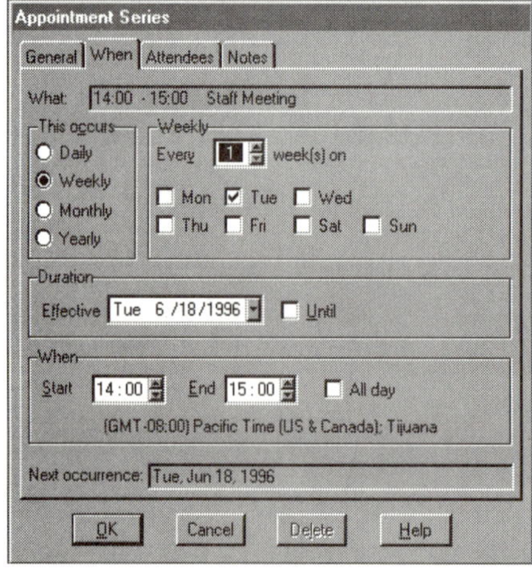

Intervals	Choices
Daily	Select the number of days between occurrences. You can select from 1 to 999 days (about 2¾ years).
Weekly	Select the number of weeks between occurrences. You can select from 1 to 99 weeks (just under 2 years). Also select the days of the week for the appointment. You can select from 1 to 7 days. To turn off a day, click it again.
Monthly	For a specific day, select the Day option, then select the day of the month and the number of months between appointments, from 1 to 99 months. Or, select the The option, and then select an occurrence of a day in a month. Your choices are First, Second, Third, Fourth, and Last. Also select the day, which can be a specific day of the week or a type of day (such as a weekday or a weekend day), and the number of months between appointments, from 1 to 99 months.
Yearly	For a specific date, select the On option, and then select the month and date. Or, select the The option, and then select an occurrence of a day in a month. Your choices are First, Second, Third, Fourth, and Last. Also select the day and the month.

6. If the series of appointments ends at a specific date, click to place a check in the Until box. A box for the end date appears. Set the end date. If the appointments, such as a series of weekly staff meetings, will go on indefinitely (or at least you hope so . . . you *do* hope to remain employed, don't you?), leave the Until box turned off.
7. If you want to jot down some notes about this series of appointments, click on the Notes tab, and then type your notes.

Note The only way to see notes you type for an appointment is to edit the item. To do so, right-click on the appointment, select Edit Item from the shortcut menu, and then click on the Notes tab.

8. Click on OK.

Jump to the various dates and times to see an appointment set for the duration of the appointment series.

Scheduling a Task

Don't you make a list of things to do? I bet you do. (I've got a nickel that says you do.) It's a scrap of paper or an organizer or a Filofax, right? Well, you might be one of those lighted-up people who use an electronic organizer. You might even use version 1.0 of Schedule+. Version 7.0 of Schedule+ provides the same basic to do list as version 1.0, but there are some added tools, too.

By setting up your tasks in Schedule+, you have a record of what you have to do. You can set reminders to warn you that a task is coming due. When you're done with the task, you can mark it completed, and Schedule+ crosses out the task but leaves it in your To Do list as a record of your accomplishment. Not only does keeping your list of things to do in Schedule+ help you remember them all, but it also lets you see at a glance how many pots you have simmering on the stove. In addition, you can see which pots require the most attention—and the most immediate attention. In addition, each day you start Schedule+, it shows you your current task list and even marks past-due tasks in red so you can see how far behind you've fallen (or not).

If you have a task that recurs (that is, comes due over and over again on a particular day, week, month, or year), you can set up a recurring task. For example, you can set up a task for your weekly status report in Schedule+. You can also divide your tasks under project headings to organize them better.

Schedule+ can also make and keep track of meetings and tasks for a project group. More about the topic of group scheduling appears in Chapter 10, "Scheduling Project Meetings," and Chapter 11, "Setting Up and Tracking Project Tasks."

Just the One-Time Task

Suppose your supervisor comes to your office and asks you to prepare a proposal for a new service. The due date for the proposal is three weeks away. So, let's set up the task in Schedule+.

1. Select the To Do tab along the left edge of the Schedule+ window.
2. If you have projects set up, select the project to which you want to add a new task. (You can learn about setting up projects in the To Do List in Chapter 11, "Setting Up and Tracking Project Tasks.")

3. Click on the Insert New Task button on the Schedule+ toolbar.

4. In the Task dialog box, fill in the Description box.

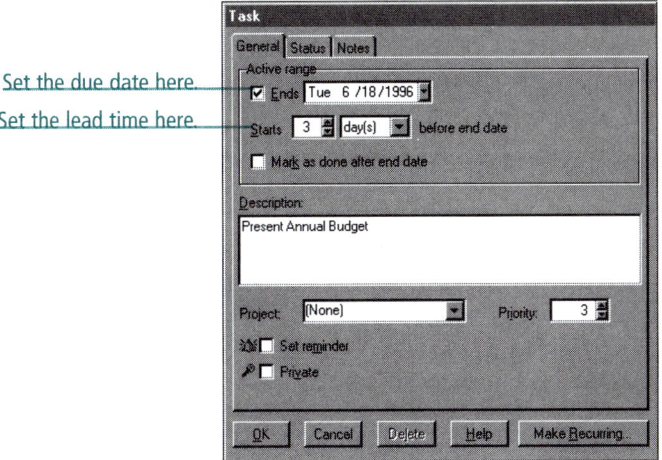

Schedule+ always assigns priority 3 to new tasks. To learn more about priority settings, see "Who's on First? Ranking Tasks (Priority)," next.

5. If the task has a due date, click to place a check in the Ends check box, and then set the end date.
6. If you need to start the project before the end date (that is, if the project will take more than one day), set the advance time in the Starts box. For example, for this little three-week project that your supervisor gave you, you'd enter *3* in the Starts box and select Week(s).
7. If you want a reminder, click to place a check in the Set Reminder check box. Three more boxes suddenly appear. Use the first two to set the units of time and the number of units for

the reminder. In the third box, select either Start Date or End Date—Schedule+ sets the reminder ahead of whichever of these two choices you select.

8. If you want to mark a task as private, click to place a check in the Private check box. Schedule+ displays the key icon beside the name of a private task.
9. Click on OK to add the new task to the selected project.

Who's on First? Ranking Tasks (Priority)

Schedule+ is set up to assign priority 3 to new tasks. If a task is more important to you than the standard priority 3, you can boost the priority by selecting a lower number (1 or 2). If a task is less important, drop the priority by selecting a higher number or a letter (4–9, A–Z).

TIP You can always use letters instead of numbers for priority rankings. Some time management schemes use the letters A, B, C, and D for ranking. If you prefer the letter system, you can change the standard task priority to one of these letters. See "Changing the Standard Task and Project Settings," on page 110, for details.

You have two places in which you can change task priority—the Task dialog box and the To Do List. Typically, you'll use the Task dialog box to change the priority as you set up a new task; you'll use the To Do List to change the priority of a task that's already on the To Do List.

To change task priority in the Task dialog box, take these steps:

1. Display the Task dialog box. You do this either by clicking on the New Task button (for a new task) or by selecting a task and clicking on the Edit button (for an existing task).
2. Type or select the new priority. You can use the numbers 1–9 or the letters A–Z.
3. Click on OK.

To change task priority in the To Do List, take these steps:

1. Click on the Priority number for the task you want to change. Schedule+ displays up and down arrows.

2. Type or select the new priority. You can use the numbers 1–9 or the letters A–Z.
3. Press Enter or click elsewhere in the Schedule+ window.

Changing a Task

Ever had a task that went the way it was planned from the beginning? Me neither. Sometimes you have to revise the schedule for a task, or you have to change the task—and then it needs a new description. You might also want to increase or decrease a task's priority. In Schedule+, you can also keep track of your progress with a task by setting the percentage completed. Even if you're such a good planner that you never have to change a task in other ways, you might want from time to time to change the percentage completed for the task—just to let others know how well you're getting on.

To change a task in Schedule+, do the following:

1. Select the To Do tab to display the task list.
2. Right-click on the task you want to change, and select Edit Item from the shortcut menu.
3. On the General tab of the Task dialog box, change the dates, duration, description, priority, project, reminder, and privacy settings.
4. On the Status tab, change the percentage complete, the actual effort, the estimated effort, the date completed, the contact, the billing information, the mileage, and the role (the part you or the person who is to perform the task plays—just type a new role if it's not already in the list).
5. On the Notes tab, add, change, or delete any notes you want to record for this task.
6. If this task becomes a recurring task, click on the Make Recurring button and fill out the information as you would for a recurring task. For details, see "Changing a Recurring Task," on page 89.
7. When you're finished making changes, click on OK.

If right-clicking is unavailable, choose the Edit Edit Item command.

You're Going to Do It Over and Over Until You Get It Right: Recurring Tasks

Once a week I back up my e-mail. Every 60 days I change my password. Once a month I give my dog a heartworm pill. These tasks and others that you perform on a regular schedule are recurring tasks. Schedule+ gives you a means to keep a list of recurring tasks, along with reminders to do them.

To set up a recurring task, do the following:

1. Select the To Do tab.
2. Select the project for the new recurring task.
3. Right-click on the project name and select Recurring Task from the shortcut menu.

If right-clicking is unavailable, click on the Recurring button on the To Do toolbar.

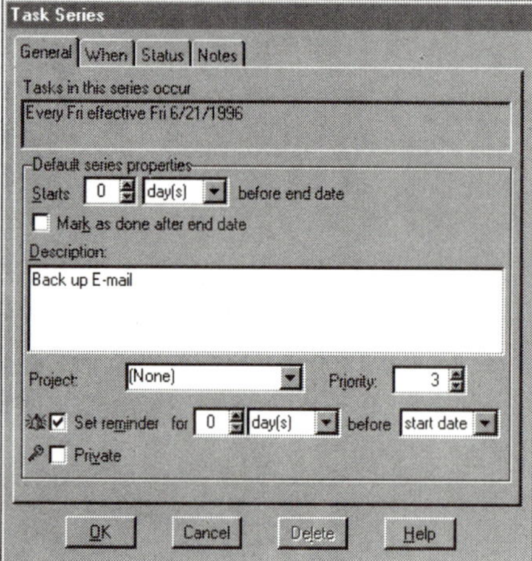

4. Type a description of the recurring task, such as *Back up E-mail.*
5. Because you want to perform this task on the day it's due, leave both the Starts box and the Reminder box set to zero days before the start date.
6. If this is a private task, select the Private check box.
7. Click on the When tab, select settings for how often you perform the task, which days you perform it, the Effective date, and the end date (if it ever ends).

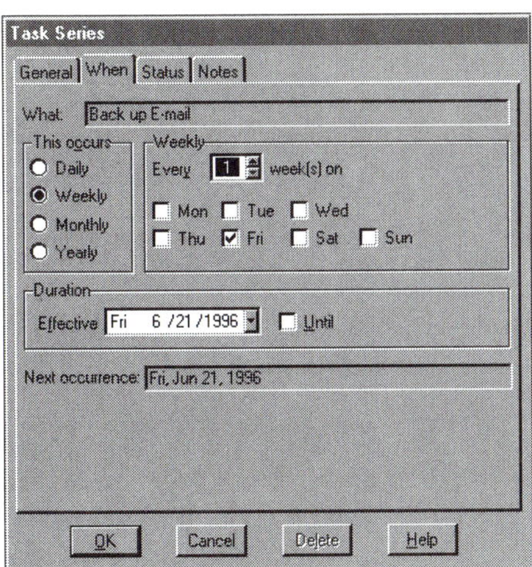

For details about selecting an interval, see the table on page 83.

8. If you want to add some notes to yourself about this task, click on the Notes tab, and then type your notes.
9. Click on OK. You see your task in the To Do List with a circle icon (for a recurring task), a bell (for a reminder), and a key icon (if it is a private task).

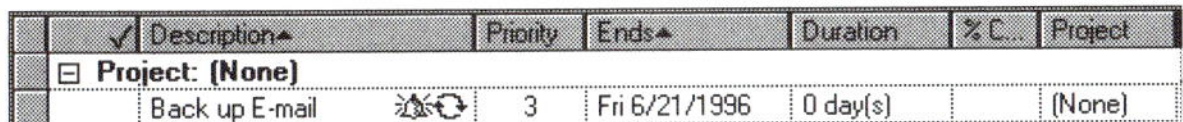

Changing a Recurring Task

Recurring tasks might receive less abuse from the variations in your life and work, but sometimes you still need to change some aspect of a recurring task. You might, for example, decide to back up your e-mail file on Mondays instead of Fridays. You also might need to change the estimated effort for each task so that the actual effort and the estimated effort are more in sync.

To change a recurring task, do this:

1. Choose the Edit Edit Recurring command, and then select Tasks from the submenu.
2. Select the recurring task you want to change, and then click on the Edit button.

3. Make the changes you need to make (using the steps in "You're Going to Do It Over and Over Until You Get It Right: Recurring Tasks," on page 88), and then click on OK.
4. If you need to change another recurring task, repeat step 2 and step 3.
5. When you're finished changing recurring tasks, click on the Close button.

In the Recurring Tasks dialog box, you can also add new recurring tasks and delete recurring tasks that you no longer perform. To add a recurring task, click on the New button, and then follow the steps in "You're Going to Do It Over and Over Until You Get It Right: Recurring Tasks," on page 88. To delete a recurring task, select it, and then click on the Delete button.

Marking Tasks Done

When you've finished with a task, you'll want to mark it completed. Doing so keeps Schedule+ from reminding you repeatedly that the task is overdue, when it no longer is.

You have three ways to mark a task completed:

- **Automatically.** Click on the To Do tab, either insert a new task or select a task, and then click on the Edit button on the Schedule+ toolbar. Click on the General tab, turn on the Mark As Done After End Date check box, and then click on OK. Schedule+ marks the task done when the due date passes.
- **Check Mark.** Click in the ✓ column for the task in the Daily Reminder window, on the To Do tab, or in the task list on the Daily tab.
- **Set the % Complete column on the To Do tab to 100%.** Click on the To Do tab, click in the % Complete box for the task, type or scroll to 100, and then press Enter.

When a task is marked completed, Schedule+ draws a line through the task, but keeps it in your To Do list for historical records. Completed tasks disappear from the To Do (Active) panes on the Daily tab, the Weekly Schedule tab, the Monthly Schedule tab, and the Daily Reminder window.

Special Events

Every now and then, something special happens on a particular day, and you want to make a note of it. Maybe it's a trade fair you want to see, or a special exhibition at a museum or gallery. There's no appointment to keep and no task to perform; it's just a special event. The event probably goes on for several hours or all day or for several days, and you can drop in anytime.

In your Schedule+ appointment book, you can add notes about special events. Here's how to do it.

1. Go to the date on which the special event occurs or begins.
2. Click on the Notepad icon at the left of the date above the time bands. (You can also choose the Insert Event command and skip step 3.)

Click on here to see the shortcut menu.

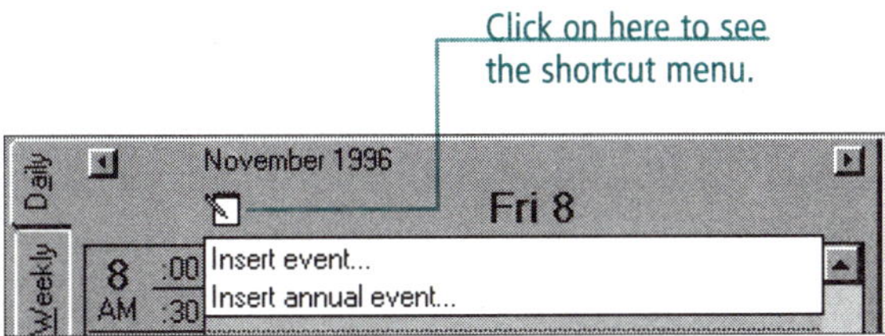

3. Select Insert Event from the Notepad shortcut menu.

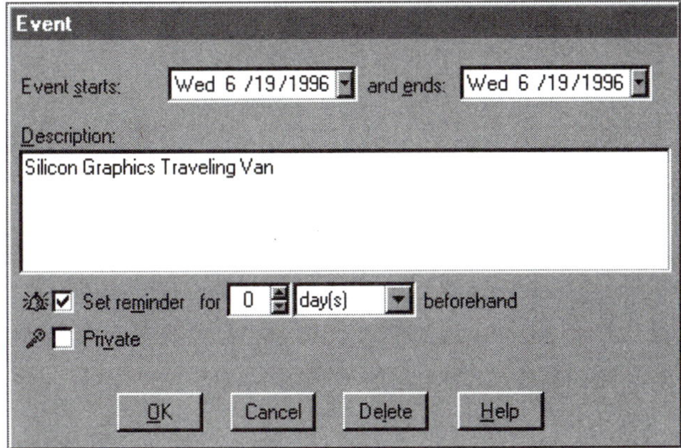

4. Type a description of the event.

5. If the event lasts more than one day, set the end date. (If you didn't jump to the start date of the event in step 1, you can change the start date in the Event dialog box.)
6. In most cases, you'll want a reminder. (If you don't, click on the Set Reminder check box to turn it off.) It is unlikely, however, that you'll want the standard 15-minute advance notice. You might want a day or two of advance notice or zero days' advance notice, which gives you a reminder on the first day of the event.
7. If this is a private event, click to place a check in the Private check box.
8. Click on OK. Schedule+ lists the event below the Notepad icon and date, just above the time bands.

An event note in place

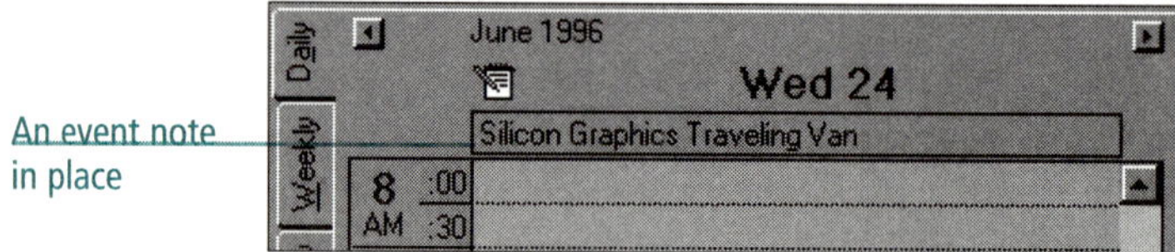

Note If you post additional events, Schedule+ increases the size of the list by two lines, which shrinks the number of time bands that you can see. If you insert more than two events or annual events, Schedule+ adds a down arrow to the events box. Click anywhere in the events box to see the entire list. Click anywhere outside the events box to collapse the list.

Anniversaries and Other Annual Events

Quick! When's your anniversary? When's your mother's birthday? When's your boss's birthday? Or your mother-in-law's? You get the picture. You want to note the birthdays, anniversaries, and other annual events in your life, in your work, and in the lives of those you know and love. So, use Schedule+ to keep track of annual events.

To add an annual event to your appointment book, do this:

1. Click on the Notepad icon above the time bands.
2. Select Insert Annual Event from the shortcut menu.

You can choose the Annual Event command from the Insert menu instead of performing step 1 and step 2.

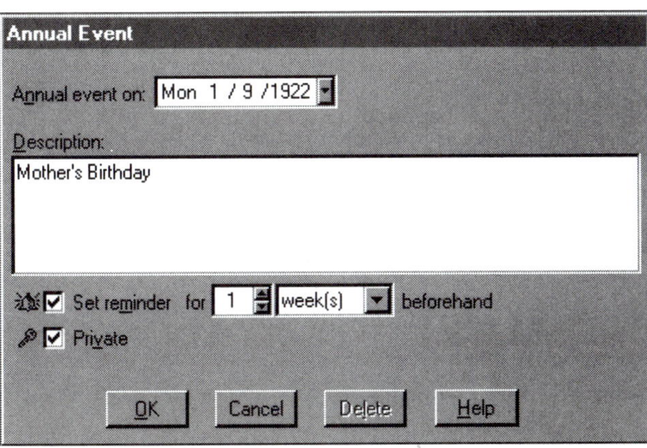

3. Select the date of the annual event in the Annual Event On box.

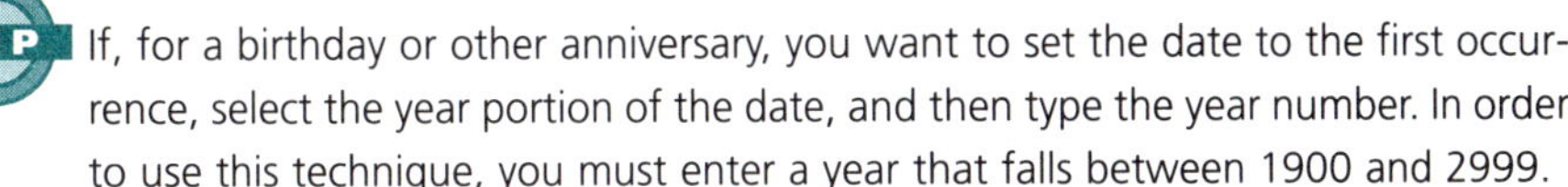

TIP If, for a birthday or other anniversary, you want to set the date to the first occurrence, select the year portion of the date, and then type the year number. In order to use this technique, you must enter a year that falls between 1900 and 2999.

4. Type a description of the annual event in the Description box.
5. If you want a reminder, set the amount of time before the annual event that you want to see a reminder.
6. If this is a private annual event, select the Private check box.
7. Click on OK. Schedule+ lists the annual event, along with one-time events, in the events list between the date and the time bands. There is no difference between the appearance of special events and annual events.

Changing an Event or Annual Event

Sometimes events are postponed or rescheduled. Some annual events occur on a schedule that Schedule+ can't quite cope with. For example, one annual event I track usually occurs the first weekend (Saturday and Sunday) of October. Fine, that's easy for Schedule+. But every once in a while, about every 11 years, October 1 lands on Sunday, and the event starts on Saturday, September 30. In another case I know of, an annual event was scheduled for the third weekend in July for 15 years. Then the organizers decided to move the event to the fourth weekend in July. In cases like these, I have to adjust my annual event schedule.

To edit an event or an annual event:

1. Jump to the date of the event or annual event.
2. Click on the event list. Schedule+ displays a list of events for the day on the shortcut menu.
3. Click on the event you want to change.
4. Make the changes in the Event or Annual Event dialog box, and then click on OK.

You can display a list of all the events or of all the annual events in your calendar and then edit any or all of the listed events or annual events. For details, see "Massaging the Entire List of Events or Annual Events," at the bottom of this page.

Canceling an Event or Annual Event

Well, there's just nothing you can do. They've gone and canceled the special event you've been waiting for. And, now that your divorce is final, you don't really want to keep track of your wedding anniversary. Or, because you've taken a new job, your hire date at your previous employer is no longer very interesting to you, is it?

So you want to erase the event or annual event from your appointment book. To do so, follow these steps:

1. Jump to the date of the event or annual event.
2. Click on the event list between the date and the time bands.
3. Select the event or the annual event from the shortcut menu.
4. In the Event or Annual Event dialog box, click on the Delete button.

Massaging the Entire List of Events or Annual Events

If you have more than one event or annual event to edit or delete, you can choose to see the entire list of events or the entire list of annual events at once. You can then select each event or annual event you want to massage, work it over, and then select another event or annual event. While you're doing this, you can even add new events or annual events. You can do this until your list of events or annual events is current.

To work on several events at once, take these steps:

1. Choose the Edit Edit List Of command, and then select Events from the submenu.

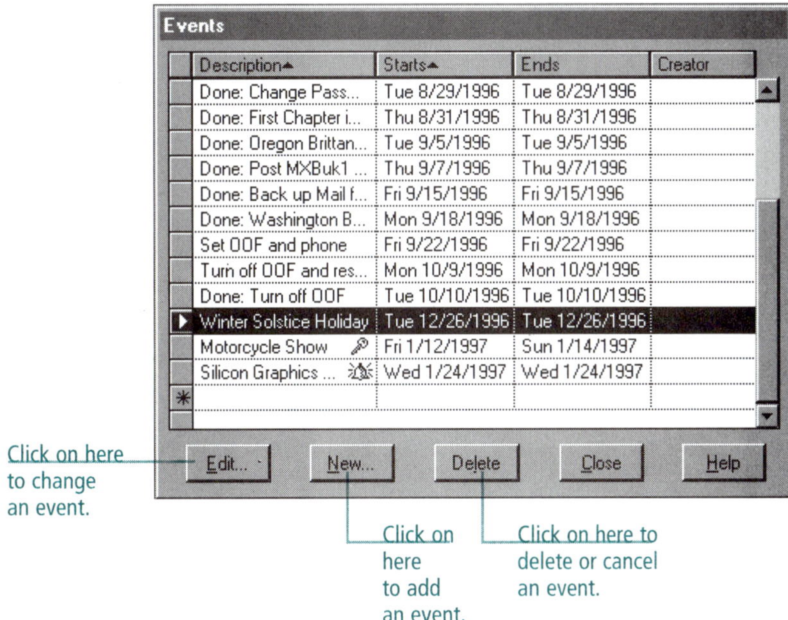

2. In the Events dialog box, do one of the following:
   - To change an event, select it, and then click on the Edit button.
   - To add a new event, click on the New button.
   - To cancel an event, select it, and then click on the Delete button.
3. Click on the Close button when you're done editing, adding, or canceling events.

To work on several annual events at once, do the following:

1. Choose the Edit Edit List Of command, and then select Annual Events from the submenu.

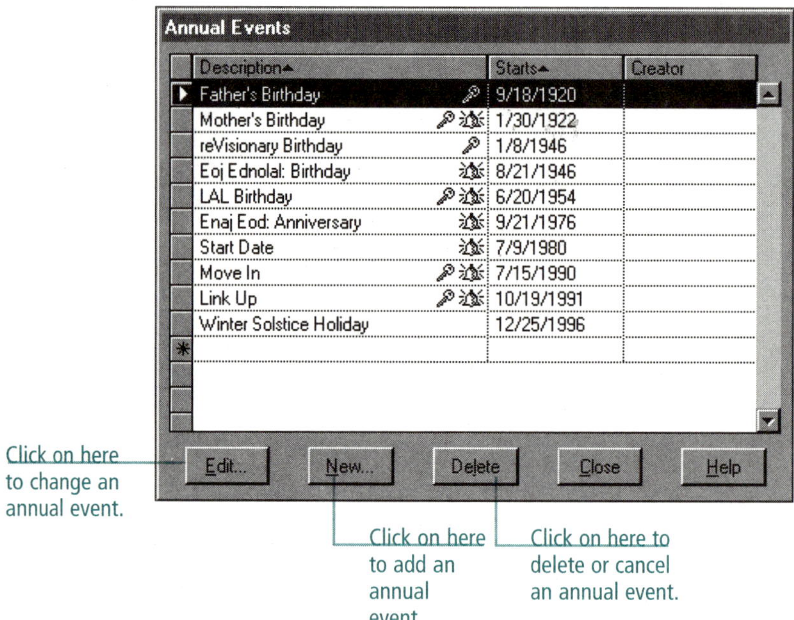

2. In the Annual Events dialog box, do one of the following:
   - To change an annual event, select it, and then click on the Edit button.
   - To add a new annual event, click on the New button.
   - To cancel an annual event, select it, and then click on the Delete button.
3. Click on the Close button when you're done editing, adding, or canceling annual events.

Keeping Your Little Black Book

In Hollywood in particular, and in Los Angeles in general, people believe that the Filofax is their most valuable possession. (Well, at least that's what movies and television shows lead us to believe.) Most people who have to deal with other people keep some kind of list of names, addresses, phone numbers, and fax numbers. In some cases, this is a rotary file; in other cases, it's a box, a pouch of business cards, or an address book (the infamous "little black book"); and in still other cases, it's a calendar or personal secretary or an electronic personal information device.

Schedule+ can keep a list of your contacts, along with all the information you want to keep about each one (or at least all the information you *have* about each one). You see your contact list by selecting the Contacts tab in your Schedule+ appointment book.

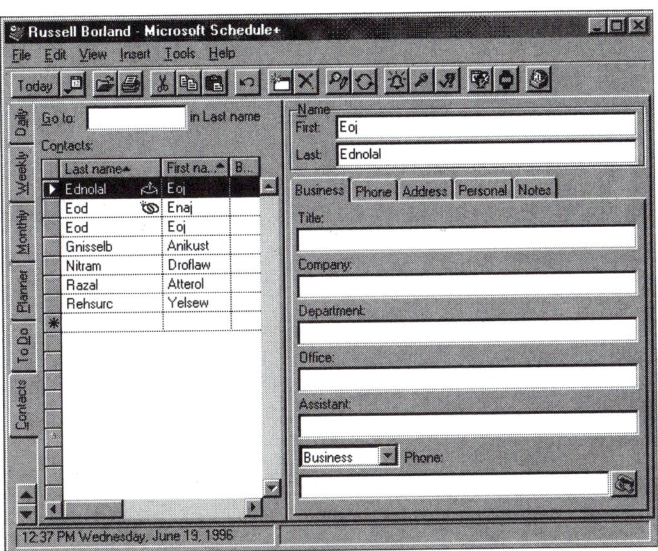

Names and Addresses and Phones and Faxes

The first task in compiling a useful list of contacts is to set up entries for the people with whom you work and socialize regularly. You can (and probably will want to) add information for all your friends and family members, too.

To add a new contact to your contact list, follow these steps:

1. Click on the Insert New Contact button on the Schedule+ toolbar.

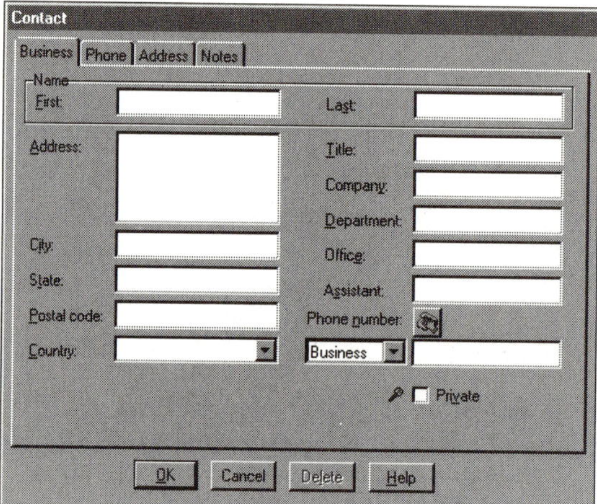

2. Fill in the boxes on the Business tab.
3. Click on the Phone tab, and then fill in the numbers for the contact's voice telephones and faxes, the contact's assistant, and his or her pager—or at least all the numbers you have.

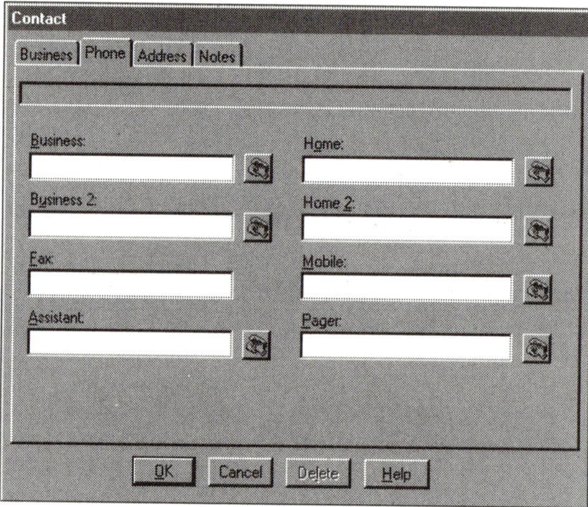

4. Click on the Address tab, and then fill in the boxes for home information. If you know (and care about) your contact's spouse's name, you can add that. You can also add the contact's birthday and anniversary.

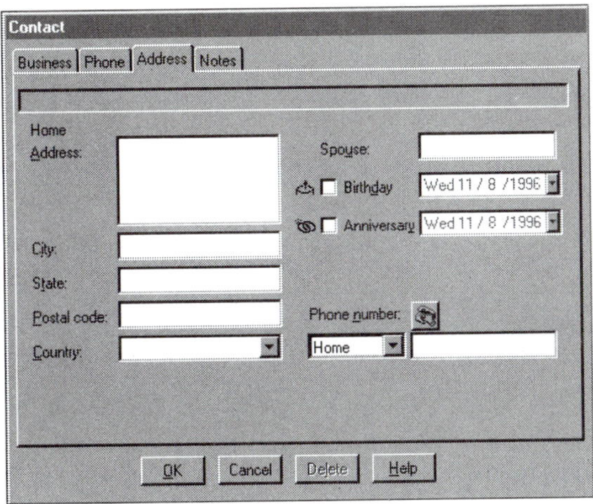

5. If you want to add notes about this contact—what business or other relationship you have with the contact, for example—click on the Notes tab and fill in the boxes.
6. Click on OK to add this contact to your contact list. If you list the birthday for the contact, you see a candle icon beside the last name. If you list the anniversary for the contact, you see two overlapping rings beside the last name.

To change information about a contact, do the following:

1. Select the name of the contact. The tabs for the contact appear on the right side of the Schedule+ window.
2. Select the tabs that display the information you want to change, and then change the information.

To remove a contact, follow these steps:

1. Select the name of the contact.
2. Click on the Delete button on the Schedule+ toolbar.
3. Schedule+ warns you that any tasks associated with this contact will be deleted. If that's okay, click on Yes. If you want to keep the tasks, click on No. If you decide not to delete the contact's name, click on Cancel.

For information about associating tasks with a contact, see Chapter 11, "Setting Up and Tracking Project Tasks."

Dialing from Your Contact List

As you compile your contact list, notice that the Dial Phone button appears beside each telephone number on each tab that has a telephone number.

If you have a telephone, fax, or data modem hooked up to your computer, and the device is set up for your operating system, you can click on the Dial Phone button to dial any of the phone numbers listed for a contact.

Taking It All with You: Printing Your Schedule

You're on the go. You want a constant visible reminder of your schedule or tasks. And you want a printed list of your contacts to stuff in your briefcase and carry with you. Anytime you want a paper copy of the information you've stored in Schedule+, you can print it.

Not only can you print the information, but you can also print it in a variety of formats. Do you have one of those small pocket calendars? You can print your schedule to fit into it. Do you have a large binder for your calendar, notes, contacts, and tasks? You can print your Schedule+ information to fit that, too.

To print your Schedule+ information, take these steps:

1. Choose the File Print command.

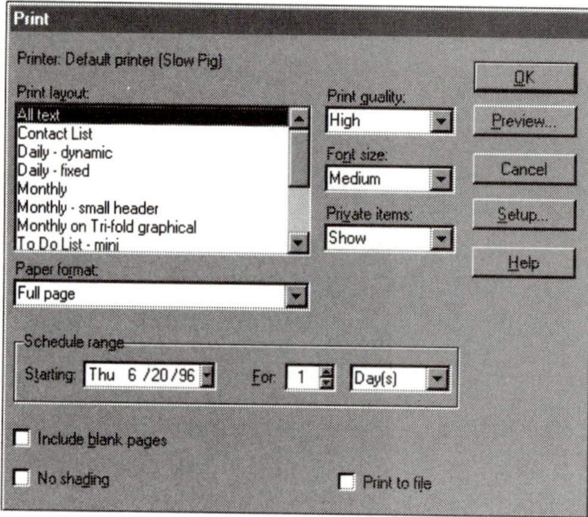

2. From the Print Layout list, select what you want to print. Refer to the following table for descriptions of the choices.

Print Layout	Description
All Text	Print events and appointments as a text-only list. For each date, Schedule+ prints events first and then appointments. For multiple months, Schedule+ prints each week on a separate page.
Contact List	Prints the first and last names of your contacts.
Daily—Dynamic	Prints appointments, events, and tasks from the daily schedule.
Daily—Fixed	Prints appointments, events, and tasks from the daily schedule, with a space for noting other appointments.
Monthly	Prints the monthly schedule. Calendars of the preceding and following months appear at the top.
Monthly—Small Header	Prints the monthly schedule without calendars of the preceding and following months.
Monthly On Tri-Fold Graphical	Prints information for a tri-fold sheet: the daily schedule on the left fold, a yearly calendar—that starts two months earlier than the month you specify—on the middle fold, and events and your active tasks on the right fold.
To Do List—Mini	Prints your active tasks with the priority, description, and due date (if any) in a vertical list.
To Do List—Normal	Prints your active tasks with the priority, description, start date (if any), due date (if any) in a vertical list, and a calendar for the month of the starting date of the schedule range. (See step 4 on page 102.)
To Do List—Text	Prints your active tasks with only the description and a calendar of days for the month of the starting date of the schedule range. (See step 4 on page 102.)
Weekly—5 Day	Prints appointments for five days.
Weekly—7 Day	Prints appointments for seven days.
Weekly—7 Day With Calendar	Prints appointments for seven days and a calendar for the month of the starting date of the schedule range. (See step 4 on page 102).

3. In the Paper Format box, select the size and shape of the paper you want the information printed on. The list includes the most popular sizes for appointment books, plus Full Size, which is standard letter paper (8½"x11" in the U.S.).
4. Set the range of time you want to print. In the Starting box, select the starting date for the items you want to print. In the For boxes, select the time units (Days, Weeks, or Months) and the number of time units (from 1 to 99).
5. At the bottom of the dialog box, turn on the Include Blank Pages check box to print days on which you have no appointments or events. Leave this check box turned off to omit blank pages.
6. To print faster and with more legibility, turn on the No Shading check box. Some Print Layout choices use shading for parts of the page when this box is turned off.
7. In the Print Quality box, select the quality of printing. You'll see more detail with a higher setting, but the information prints more slowly. If you lower the setting, you'll see less detail but print faster.
8. In the Font Size box, select the font size you want to use. Your choices are Small, Medium, and Large. For small paper formats, you'll probably want the Small font size. Large size is for those of us who need reading glasses to see normal print.
9. In the Private Items dropdown list, select how you want Private items treated. You have three options:
    - **Show.** Prints appointments, projects, tasks, and contacts that you have marked as Private.
    - **Hide.** Omits appointments, projects, tasks, and contacts that you have marked as Private.
    - **Hide Text.** Prints appointments, projects, tasks, and contacts that you have marked as Private with (Private) in place of the description.
10. To print the information to a file rather than to paper, turn on the Print To File check box.
11. If you need to adjust your printer settings, click on the Setup button, make your adjustments to the printer setup, and then click on OK.

12. As a last-minute check before you start printing, click on the Preview button.

    Schedule+ shows you a page as it will be printed. In Preview mode, you can:

    - Click on the Zoom In button to look at the page more closely
    - Click on the Zoom Out button to see the whole page again
    - Click on the Next Page button to view the next page of the printout (if there is one)
    - Click on the First Page button to jump back to the first page of the printout
    - Click on the Close button to return to the Print dialog box

13. Click on the Close button in the Print Preview window. Make any changes you want to the way Schedule+ will print the information, and check the Preview again if necessary.

14. When you're ready to print, click on OK.

    If you turned on the Print To File check box in step 10, you'll see the Print dialog box shown in the next illustration. Select the disk and folder where you want to store the file, type a name for the file, and then click on the Save button.

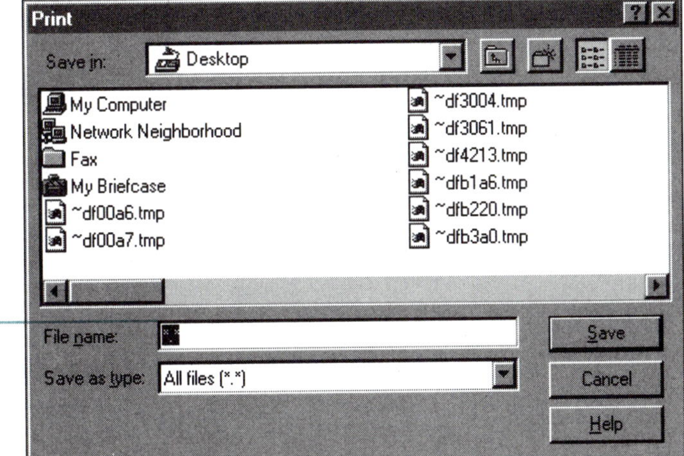

Type a complete filename with filename extension, if you want one.

Making Schedule+ Your Own: Adjusting Options

Do you work an unusual schedule—say 10:00 A.M. to 7:00 P.M.? Do you dislike the colors in Schedule+? Are half-hour time bands too restrictive? Too narrow? Do you want your standard reminder time set to 10 minutes before an event rather than 15 minutes?

These are the kinds of changes you can make to Schedule+ to make your appointment book work better for you and look more attractive. (Just *try* to make some of these changes to a paper schedule keeper!)

You can also change the standard settings for tasks—standard priority, reminders, duration, and estimated effort—and you can customize your Schedule+ appointment book in other ways. All of these standard settings appear on tabs in the Tools Options dialog box.

In addition, you can change the tabs that appear along the left side of the appointment book—delete some, add some, change their order, and even change the name that appears on the tab itself. For these moves, you use the Tab Gallery, described in "How Many Tabs Do You Really Need? How Many Do You Want?" on page 115.

Setting the Time Scale

You can decide whether you want to use a U.S. calendar week (a week starts on Sunday) or a European calendar week (a week starts on Monday). You can block out the hours you don't work. You can decide how much time each time band in the appointment book represents. You can also set the standard reminder time. These are some of the important options relating to time that you can set in Schedule+.

Where the Week Begins

Does your week start on Sunday or Monday? Calendars in the United States usually show Sunday as the first day of the week, but is that the way you really work? Isn't Monday the beginning of your week and Saturday and Sunday your weekend? (Well, I've been led to believe that many people have Saturdays, and even Sundays, off regularly.) You can have Schedule+ start the week on any day of the week. To change the first day of the week from Sunday to some other day, do the following:

1. Choose the Tools Options command, and then click on the General tab.

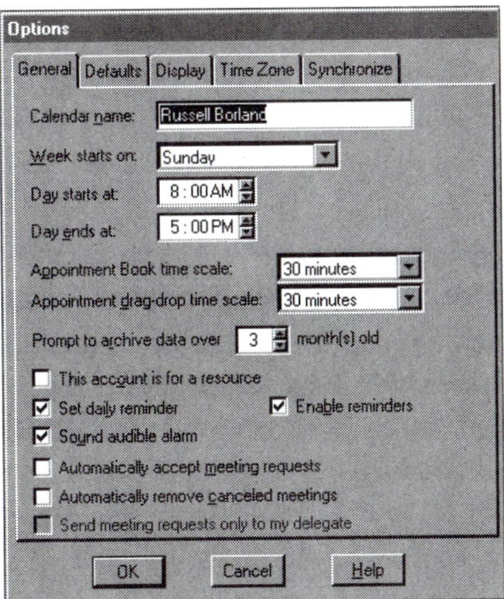

2. In the Week Starts On box, select the day of the week on which your week starts, and then click on OK.

You'll see the effects of selecting a different day to start the week when you view the calendar or jump from week to week:

- When you switch to Monthly view, the first day of the week is the leftmost column. In Weekly view, if you set the number of days to 7 and then scroll at least once to a different week, the Weekly view displays the first day of the week in the leftmost column. For other Number Of Days settings, Schedule+ scrolls by the number of days set, except for 5 days, which always scrolls to Monday as the starting day. Also, in Daily and Weekly views, the month calendar in the upper left corner of the appointment book shows the first day of the week as the leftmost column.
- When you use the Edit Go To command to jump to a specific week, Schedule+ lands on the first day of the week you set. For example, if you set the first day of the week to Monday and then jump to Week 3 in 1996, Schedule+ lands on January 15, 1996.

Work Hours

Schedule+ takes a very conventional view of the work day—8:00 A.M. to 5:00 P.M. Do you work this schedule? I don't. I work 10:00 A.M. to 7:00 P.M. Well, maybe I work more or less than this, but I don't want anyone scheduling a meeting for me before 10:00 A.M., at least not if I can help it. So I set the work hours in Schedule+ to match these nominal hours of work. (It doesn't always do much good—it seems I'm forever being dragged into meetings at 9:00 A.M. anyway! Ach, well.)

To change the work hours, do this:

1. Choose the Tools Options command.
2. On the General tab, change the start time in the Day Starts At box, then change the quitting time in the Day Ends At box, and then click on OK.

You'll notice that in Daily and Weekly views, the time bands before your new start time and the time bands after your new quitting time are darker. In my case, the time bands before 10:00 A.M. and after 7:00 P.M. are darker.

Note You can't set your work day for the graveyard shift—for example, from 8:00 P.M. to 5:00 A.M.—because Schedule+ requires that the start time fall before the quitting time.

Changing the Bands of Time

Ever since Victorian times, the half hour has been a standard unit of meeting time. In numerous Victorian novels, people come to visit and "spend a pleasant half hour." How often do you have a half-hour meeting? Have you *ever* been in a meeting that lasts less than one hour? Don't most of your meetings and other appointments start on the hour—some hour or other? Maybe you want your appointment book to show one-hour time bands, or perhaps you prefer to break up your time into quarter hours? Whatever you need, you got it. Well, sort of.

To change the bands of time, do the following:

1. Choose the Tools Options command.
2. In the Appointment Book Time Scale box on the General tab, select the interval of time you want for each time band.

   Your choices are 5 Minutes, 6 Minutes, 10 Minutes, 15 Minutes, 30 Minutes, and 60 Minutes.

3. Click on OK.

When you look at the Daily and Weekly views of your appointments, you'll see the new time scale reflected in the labeling of the time bands, as shown here for an appointment book with 60-minute time bands.

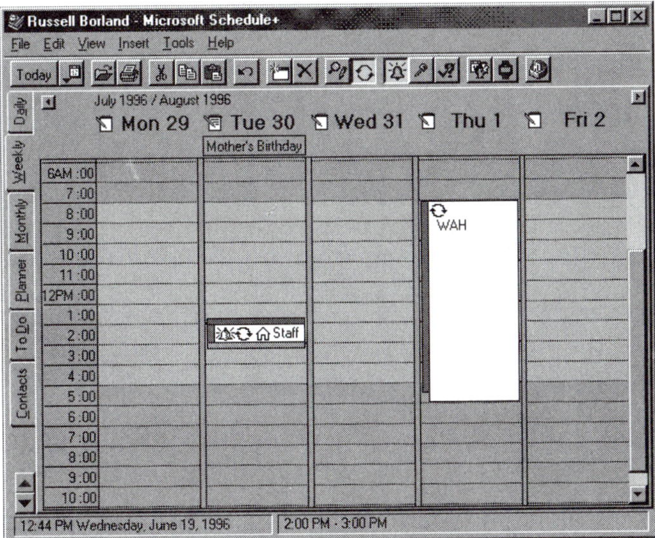

Dragging the Bands of Time

If you regularly drag appointments that change to a new time slot, you might want to adjust the scale for dragging appointments. Schedule+ is set up with a 30-minute scale for dragging appointments around. But you might want to be able to drag appointments in smaller time units, whether or not you change the size of the time bands.

To change the drag-and-drop time scale, do this:

1. Choose the Tools Options command.
2. In the Appointment Drag-Drop Time Scale box on the General tab, select the time scale you want to be able to drag to.

   Your choices depend on the time bands. For 30-minute time bands, the choices are 10 Minutes, 15 Minutes, and 30 Minutes.
3. Click on OK.

The effect of this change is apparent when you drag an appointment to a new time. (To change an appointment time by dragging, select it, position the mouse pointer on the top or left border of the appointment, and then drag up or down.) Watch the times in the pop-up box change as you drag.

Also, if you lengthen or shorten an appointment by dragging, you see the amount of time change by the drag amount you set. (To add or take away time from an appointment by dragging, select the appointment, position the mouse pointer on the bottom border of the appointment, and then drag down to lengthen the appointment or drag up to shorten the appointment.)

Standard Reminder Time

All the reminders for appointments, whether one-time or recurring, are set up with a standard 15-minute early warning. You can, of course, change the amount of reminder time for individual appointments, and I'm sure you'll do this fairly often. If your meeting is across the hall (or in your office), 15 minutes might be more than you want or need. If your appointment is across town, you might need half an hour just to get to the meeting place; 15 minutes isn't enough time in this case.

In fact, you might find that there are very few times when you want 15 minutes' notice. You might find 10 minutes or 5 minutes better. Or you might want 20 or 30 minutes to prepare and collect your thoughts and papers before going to the meeting.

TIP When Schedule+ notifies you with a reminder, you can tell Schedule+ to repeat the reminder in a few minutes or days or whenever in the Reminder dialog box. In this way, you can make the reminder like a repeating alarm clock—the first notice alerts you to the approaching meeting so that you can start your preparation; the second notice alerts you that it's time to go off to the meeting.

If you want to change the standard amount of time that Schedule+ uses for each new appointment, do this:

1. Choose the Tools Options command, and then select the Defaults tab.

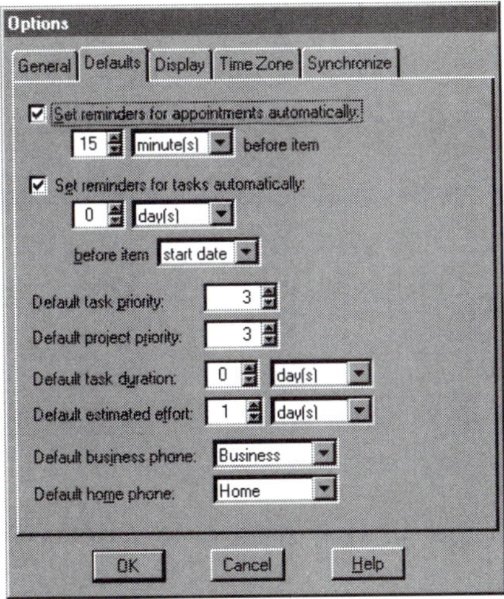

2. Under the Set Reminders For Appointments Automatically check box, type or select the number of time units for the reminder.
3. Select the unit of time in the Before Item box, and then click on OK.

Your appointment book will now show the two time zone slots side by side. In the blank box above the time zone setting, you can type a time zone label, such as GMT or PST, to identify the zone of each time scale.

If you don't want Schedule+ to set reminders automatically, click on the Set Reminders For Appointments Automatically check box to turn it off. Turning off this check box "freezes" the standard reminder time at its current setting. This is important to remember because when you decide to add a reminder to an appointment, Schedule+ will use the setting for automatic reminders. If you want advance warning at a time period other than 15 minutes, set the standard reminder time before you turn off automatic reminders.

What Zone You In, Man?

Do you travel a lot, Bunky? Does your boss send you hither and yon and back again, criss-crossing time zones like cross streets in your neighborhood? Do you need to keep track of the time zone you're in, as well as the time zone back home? What if you want to schedule a meeting with the folks back home, but you're still two time zones away. How do you do that? Set a secondary time zone, that's how.

To set a secondary time zone, do this:

1. Choose the Tools Options command.
2. Click on the Time Zone tab.

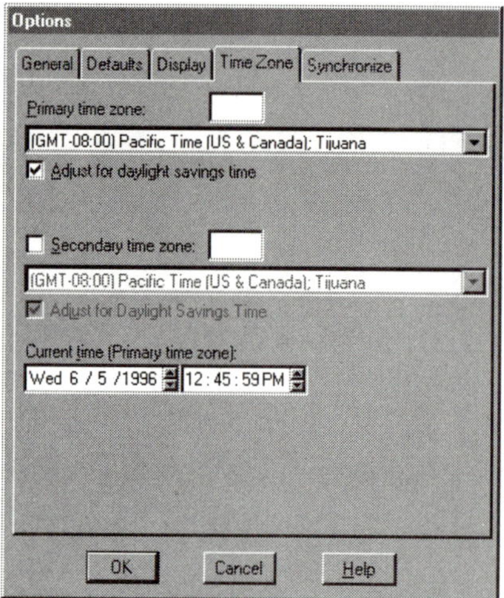

3. In the Secondary Time Zone box, select the time zone you're in (or the one you'll be working in when you're away from home base), and click on OK.

Changing the Standard Task and Project Settings

Whenever you set up a new task or a new project, Schedule+ provides some standard settings for reminders, for task priority, for project priority, for task duration, and for the estimated effort for a task. For some people, perhaps many, these settings will be unimportant. For others, their importance lies in project tracking—keeping an account of the time and effort required to complete a task and estimating effort as part of advanced planning. Also, reminders and priority help you decide when to work on a task or project and how much time and effort to give to it at any one time.

The standard settings come from some kind of logic; what logic isn't important at this point. You might find that you're forever fiddling with the settings when you set up a new task or project. If that's the case, it might well be time to adjust the standard settings to better match your work habits and the types of tasks and projects you work on.

Task Reminders

The standard reminder for all tasks, whether one-time or recurring, is zero days early warning—that is, you're reminded on the day your work is supposed to be finished. You can change the amount of reminder time for individual tasks, and you may need to do this fairly often. Unless a task has to be performed at a specific time and needs little or no advance preparation, zero days isn't much of a reminder to do something.

In most cases, you'll probably find that one or more days or weeks or months of advance notice fits most of the tasks you do.

TIP When Schedule+ notifies you with a reminder, you can tell Schedule+ in the Reminder dialog box that pops up, to repeat the reminder later. In this way, you can use the reminder service to help you keep track of your progress. The first notice alerts you to start the task, the second notice alerts you to a pending milestone, and the final notice alerts you that you're behind schedule—er, I mean that your project is due.

If you want to change the standard amount of time that Schedule+ uses as a reminder for each new task, do this:

1. Choose the Tools Options command, and then select the Defaults tab.
2. Under the Set Reminders For Tasks Automatically box, type or select the number of time units.
3. Select the unit of time.
4. Select the Start Date option or the End Date option in the Before Item box. A reminder before your start date warns you that it's time to start working on a project. A reminder before your end date warns you that you're about to miss a deadline.
5. Click on OK.

Task and Project Priority

Schedule+ starts all new tasks and projects at priority level 3. To my way of thinking, if a task or project is important enough to put on my to do list, it should be at least a priority level 2, if not level 1. Also, some time-management systems use the letters A, B, C, and D for ranking tasks and projects. If either of these scenarios fits your work style, you need to change the standard task and project priority levels.

For setting the priority of tasks and projects, Schedule+ provides the numbers 1–9 and the letters A–Z. Schedule+ ranks tasks and projects in that order. If you prefer to use the letters A, B, C, and D to indicate priority levels, tasks and projects at level A will still rank above those at level B, and so on.

To change the default task priority level for new tasks, do this:

1. Choose the Tools Options command, and then select the Defaults tab.
2. In the Default Task Priority box, type or select the priority level you want for new tasks.
3. Click on OK.

To change the project priority level for new tasks, do this:

1. Choose the Tools Options command, and then select the Defaults tab.
2. In the Default Project Priority box, type or select the priority level you want for new projects.
3. Click on OK.

Task Duration

How long does it take you to complete a task? Less than a day? More? In Schedule+, all tasks have an initial projected duration of exactly zero days. Huh? Well, you know: less than one day. (Zero is still less than one in most mathematical systems.)

If setting the task duration is an important part of your time and money budgeting, you might want to set a different standard duration for new tasks rather than always having to adjust the duration from zero.

To change the standard duration for new tasks, do the following:

1. Choose the Tools Options command, and then select the Defaults tab.
2. In the Default Task Duration box, type or select the number of time units for task duration.
3. In the box to the right of the number of units, select the unit of time. Your choices are Days, Weeks, and Months.
4. Click on OK.

Task Estimated Effort

Even though the standard duration for new tasks is zero days, the standard estimated effort for new tasks is one day. (This is *really* new math, folks; 0 = 1!) If the majority of your tasks require more than one day's effort, you might want to change the standard estimated effort for new tasks.

To do so, follow these steps:

1. Choose the Tools Options command, and then select the Defaults tab.
2. In the Default Estimated Effort box, type or select the number of time units for estimated effort.
3. In the box to the right of the number of units, select the unit of time. Your choices are Minutes, Hours, Days, Weeks, and Months.
4. Click on OK.

Decorating Your Calendar

Unless you are using a particularly vivid color scheme for your windows or you are using one of the Desktop Themes in Windows 95, your appointment book probably has a pretty bland appearance—gray and yellow. It's very businesslike, yes, but also kind of boring. Do you want a little more visual stimulation as you plot your time and track your tasks? Then decorate the parts of your appointment book.

To change the appearance of your appointment book, follow these steps:

1. Choose the Tools Options command, and then select the Display tab. The Options dialog box appears, as shown on the next page.

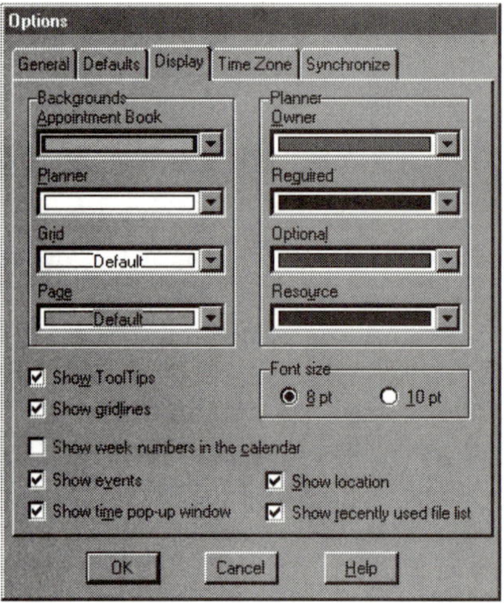

2. Use the options on the Display tab to change the appointment book's appearance and the informaton it displays. The following table describes the options you can choose.

Backgrounds	Select colors for the Appointment Book, Planner, Grid (To Do list and Contacts list), and the Page (all the other areas of the appointment book).
Planner	Select colors for the owner of the appointment book (you, unless you keep an appointment book for someone else), for required appointments, for optional appointments, and for resources (rooms, A/V equipment, and so on).
Font Size	Choose whether you want to see the descriptions of appointments and tasks and the information for contacts in 8-point or 10-point type.
Show ToolTips	Select this option if you want to see a label for each button on the toolbar and other buttons in the appointment book. To forgo ToolTips, turn off this box.
Show Gridlines	Select this option if you want gridlines in the To Do list and the Contacts list. To see the contents of these two tabs without gridlines, turn off this box.
Show Week Numbers in the Calendar	Select this option if you want to see week numbers. The week numbers take up extra space on the appointment tabs, and this

	reduces the amount of space available to show appointment, task descriptions, and other information.
Show Events	Select this option if you want events listed above the time bands.
Show Time Pop-up Window	Select this option if you want to see the little box that pops up when you hold down the left mouse button on an appointment.
Show Location	Select this option if you want Schedule+ to display the location of an appointment (the text in the Where box in the Appointment dialog box) for each appointment. To hide this information, turn off the Show Location box.
Show Recently Used File List	Select this option if you keep someone else's appointment book; otherwise turn off the option. This list, which appears at the bottom of the File menu, lists the last four appointment books you opened. If you don't keep an appointment book for someone else, or if you don't set up separate appointment books for particular projects, you don't need this list. If you do keep someone else's appointment book or set up separate appointment books for each of their projects, leave this box turned on.

3. When you've finished decorating your appointment book, click on OK.

How Many Tabs Do You Really Need? How Many Do You Want?

Along the left side of the Schedule+ window, you see tabs for the various sections of your appointment book—Daily, Weekly, Monthly, Planner, To Do, and Contacts are the tabs that Schedule+ originally sets up for you. Schedule+ provides options for displaying several more tabs. You can select additional tabs, replace tabs, remove tabs, rename tabs, and change their order. Your Schedule+ appointment book can contain the information you need most often.

All the work you do takes place in the Tab Gallery. To display the Tab Gallery, choose the View Tab Gallery command. You'll see the dialog box shown on the next page.

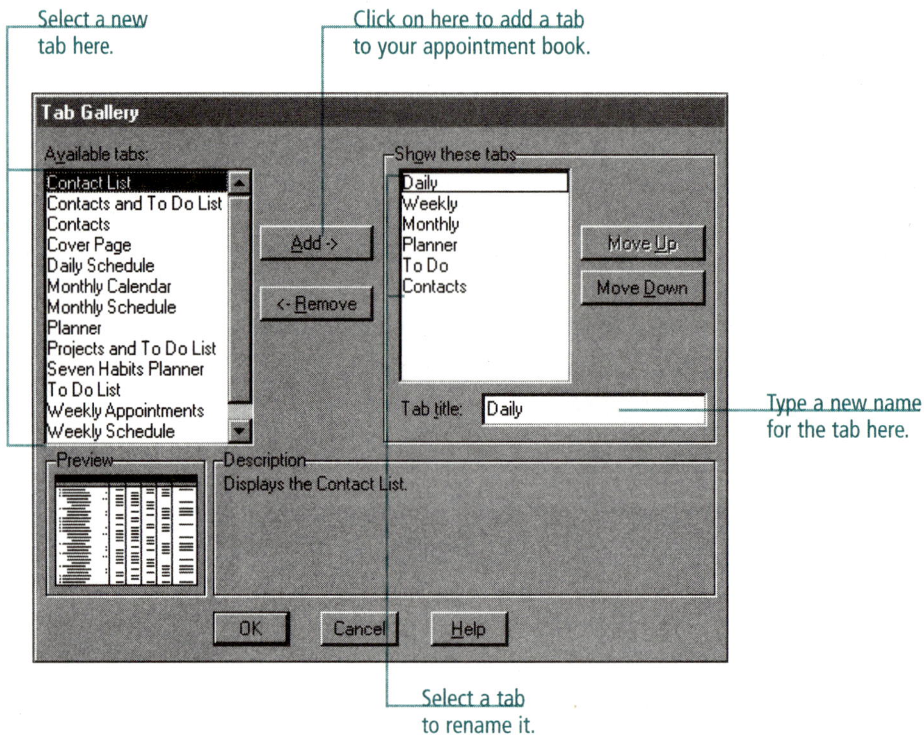

Adding Tabs

The following table lists the tabs that you can add to those that are originally set up for you.

Contact List	Displays the Contact List in a list format instead of using tabs and fields as on the Contacts tab.
Contacts And To Do List	Displays the Contact List and related tasks.
Cover Page	Displays a cover-page drawing.
Monthly Schedule	Displays a month of appointments and the To Do List.
Projects And To Do List	Displays the Project List and related tasks.
Seven Habits Planner	Displays daily appointments for as many as seven days, as well as the To Do List grouped by Seven Habits roles. (For more information about the Seven Habits roles, choose the Seven Habits Help Topics command from the Help menu.)
Weekly Schedule	Displays daily appointments for as many as seven days, as well as the To Do List.

Yearly Calendar	Displays up to 12 calendar months, which you can scroll to view dates in the past or future. Days on which an appointment occurs appear in bold.

To add a tab divider to your appointment book, do the following:

1. Right-click on a tab, and then choose Tab Gallery from the shortcut menu.
2. From the Available Tabs list, select the tab you want to add to your appointment book. A description appears in the Description box and a picture of the tab page appears in the Preview box.
3. Click on the Add button. If you want to add more tabs, repeat steps 2 and 3.
4. When you're done with the Tab Gallery, click on OK.

If right-clicking is unavailable, choose Tab Gallery from the View menu.

Example: Adding a Cover Page to Your Appointment Book

Would you like to have a handy cover page you could whip over your calendar and To Do list whenever someone walks up behind you? Would you like to be able to cover your appointment book while you are away from your desk? One of the tab dividers in Schedule+ is called Cover Page.

To add a cover page to your appointment book, do this:

1. Choose the View Tab Gallery command.
2. From the Available Tabs list, select Cover Page.
3. Click on the Add button, and then click on OK.

The first tab in your appointment book now looks like this:

If you add tabs without removing any, you might have more tabs than you can fit in the height of the Schedule+ window. When that happens, Schedule+ adds up and down arrows at the bottom of the tab dividers. Click on the down arrow to see the tabs hidden below the bottom of the window. Click on the up arrow to see tabs hidden above the window.

Adjusting the Order of Tabs

You can adjust the order of the tabs to suit yourself, whether or not you add any new tabs.

To adjust the order of tabs, take these steps:

1. Right-click on the tab you want to move, and then choose Reorder Tabs from the shortcut menu. Schedule+ selects that tab's name in the Show These Tabs list of the Tab Gallery. (If right-clicking is unavailable, choose the View Tab Gallery command, and then, in the Show These Tabs list, select the name of the tab you want to move.)
2. Click on the Move Up or Move Down button to move the tab. If you want to move other tabs, repeat steps 2 and 3.
3. When you're finished with the Tab Gallery, click on OK.

Removing, Replacing, and Renaming Tabs

If you see a tab you don't need, you can remove it. You can also replace a tab with another that's more useful. And if you find that a tab's name isn't to your liking, you can rename it.

To remove a tab divider from your appointment book, do this:

1. Right-click on the tab you want to remove, and then choose Remove Tab from the shortcut menu. (If right-clicking is unavailable, choose the View Tab Gallery command, and then select the name of the tab you want to remove. Click on the Remove button, and then click on OK.)
2. When Schedule+ asks if you want to remove the current tab, click on the Yes button.

To replace a tab with a different tab, do the following:

1. Right-click on a tab, and then choose Tab Gallery from the shortcut menu. (If right-clicking is unavailable, choose the View Tab Gallery command.)

2. Remove the tab you want to replace (see the previous procedure).
3. Add the new tab you want as the replacement. (See "Adding Tabs," on page 116.)
4. Adjust the order of the tabs to suit you. (See "Adjusting the Order of Tabs," on the opposite page.)
5. When you're done with the Tab Gallery, click on OK.

To change the name on a tab, take these steps:

1. Right-click on the tab you want to rename, and then choose Rename Tab from the shortcut menu. Schedule+ selects the tab's current name in the Tab Title box. (If right-clicking is unavailable, choose the View Tab Gallery command, and then, in the Show These Tabs list, select the name of the tab you want to rename.)
2. In the Tab Title box, type the new name for the tab.
3. When you're done with the Tab Gallery, click on OK.

For additional ways to customize your views of tasks and contacts, see "Worlds of Views: Columnbining, Grouping, Sorting, and Filtering Tasks," on page 295.

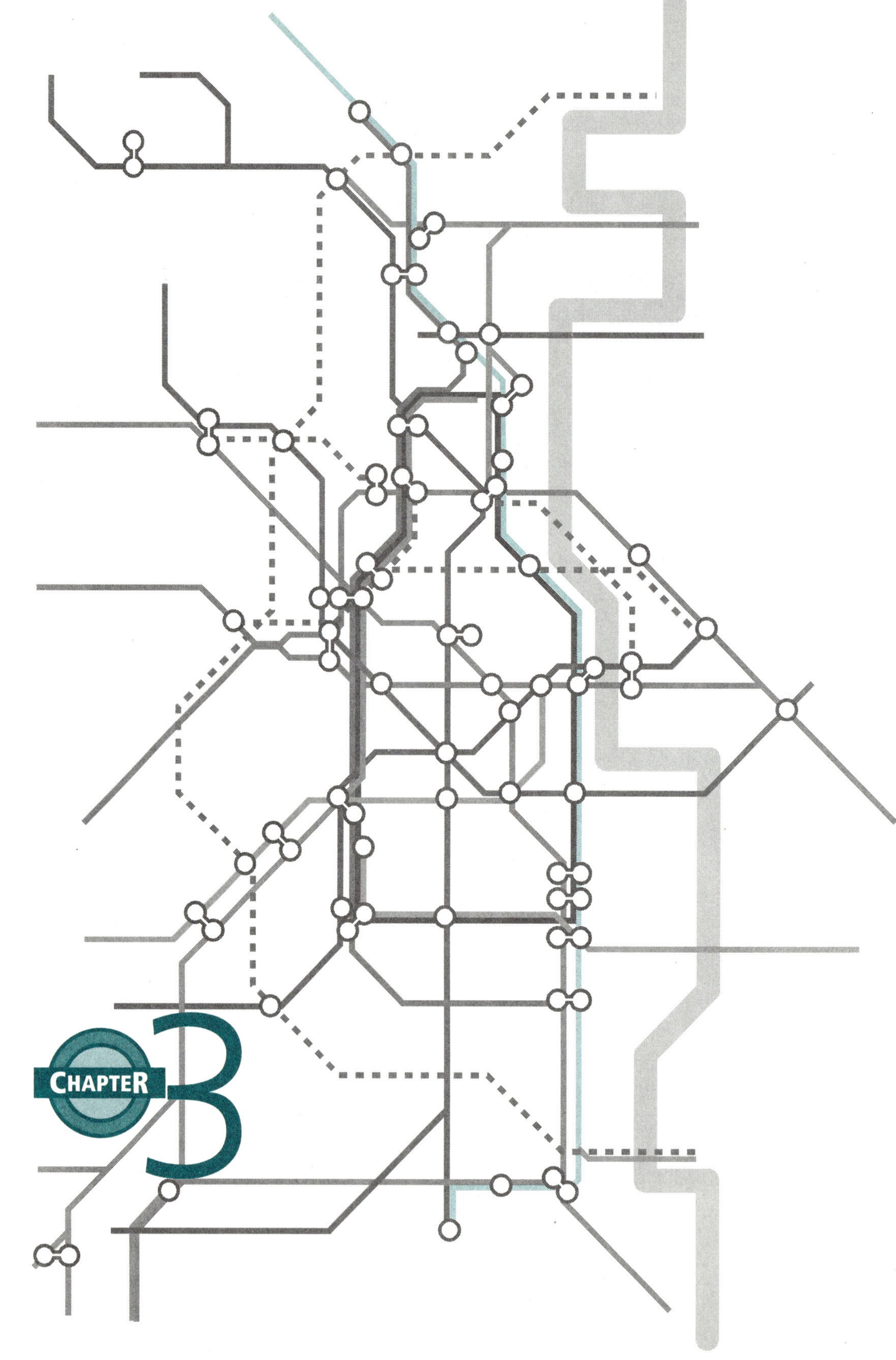
CHAPTER
3

Public Information Options

One of the many advantages of Microsoft Exchange over a plain e-mail program is the availability of public folders. Public folders provide an easy way to distribute and collect information you need. Through the Public Folders folder in Exchange, you can open and view all the public folders available on your Exchange system. In this chapter, you'll learn how to view a list of public folders and how to quickly open specific public folders.

Scenes from This Chapter

A public folder is a storage place on the Exchange server. A public folder is "public" because almost everyone who uses the Exchange server can read the items in a public folder. A public folder differs from your personal folders and your Exchange folders in that no one can get into your private folders but you.

A public folder can contain messages, postings, and files. Your Exchange administrator can also set up public folders to receive messages sent to distribution lists. For example, if you have an organizational distribution list named "Motorcycle" for employees who ride motorcycles, Exchange can add all the messages sent to "Motorcycle" to the related public folder.

A public folder can also contain subfolders, which in turn can contain messages, postings, files, or additional subfolders. In fact, in most cases, your Exchange administrator will create many levels of subfolders in order to keep information about various aspects of any given topic grouped together. To quickly jump to a specific public folder, you can set up a shortcut to a folder that you want to see regularly. This way, you can quickly find the folder you want or need to see, rather than have to rummage through acres and acres of public folders.

Note This chapter gives you a quick introduction to public folders for personal uses. A more lengthy discussion of public folders as the basis of discussion forums appears in Part 2, "Discussion Forum." Using public folders to help manage projects is described in Chapter 8, "Setting Up a Project Folder."

What's the News? Opening Public Folders

Public folders live inside the folder labeled "Public Folders" in the folder pane of the Exchange window. To view the list of public folders, click on the plus sign next to the Public Folders folder in the folder pane.

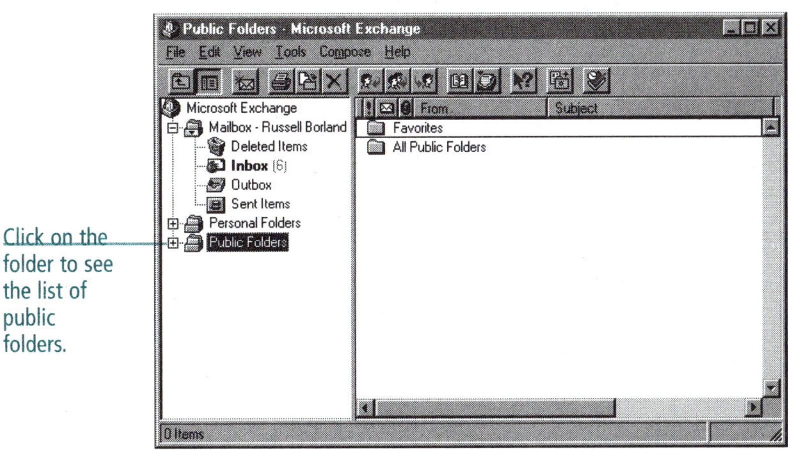

Click on the folder to see the list of public folders.

The first level of public folders appears, showing just two folders: Favorites and All Public Folders. You'll notice that these two folders also appear in the Message List pane.

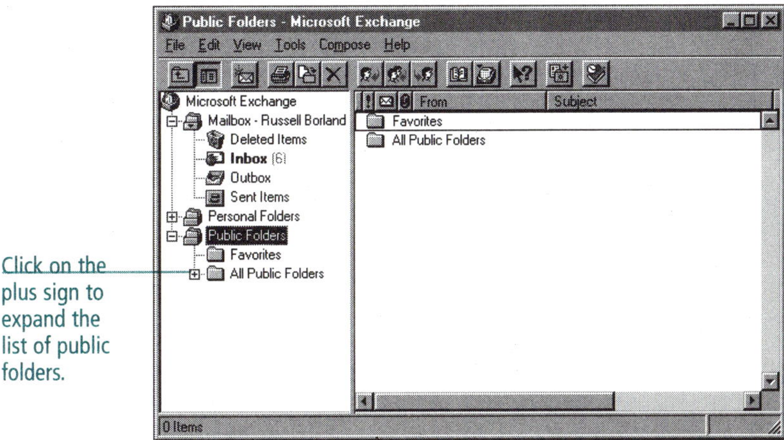

Click on the plus sign to expand the list of public folders.

To see the list of public folders, click on the plus sign next to the All Public Folders folder in the folder pane.

Each of the folders can contain items (messages, postings, and files) for a specific discussion topic or area. Each public folder can also contain subfolders. You'll know a folder has subfolders if you see a plus sign next to it in the folder pane. To see the subfolders, click on the plus sign. Click on additional plus signs to open the entire collection of folders. Each folder and subfolder at any level can contain both items and additional subfolders.

To read an item, follow these steps:

1. Open a folder. The list of messages, postings, and files appears in the message list, just as a mail message appears in the message lists for your e-mail folders (Inbox, Sent Mail, Deleted Items, and other folders you create and add messages to).

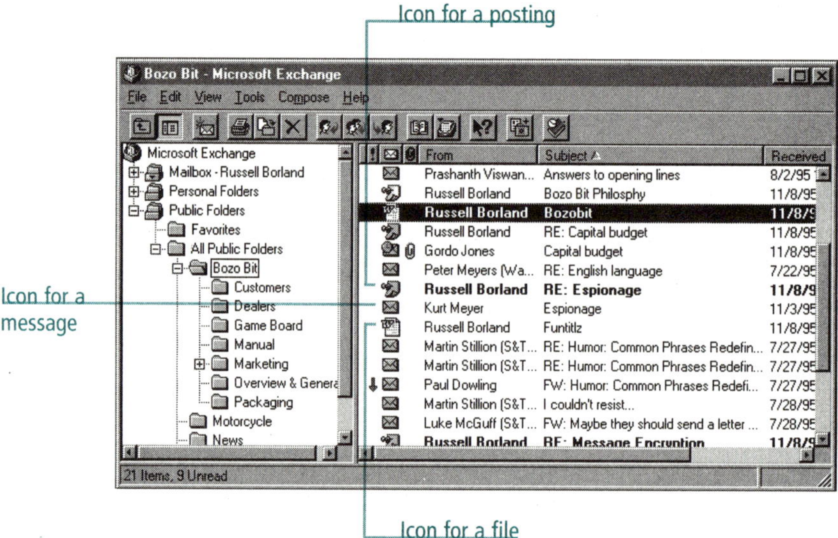

2. Double-click on the item's line in the message list.

From this point on, you treat items in public folders the same way you treat a mail message, except that you probably can't delete the items or move them—unless you have administrative privileges, are the owner of the folder, or you put the message, posting, or file in the public folder yourself. You can, however, copy an item to other folders in your Mailbox and Personal Folders folders or save an item as a file on one of your drives.

To move to the next item, click on the Next button on the message window toolbar. To see the previous item, click on the Previous button. (This works the same as with reading e-mail messages.)

Adding Information to a Public Folder

When you want to add new information to a public folder, you can either post a notice for a new topic or respond to a previous posting.

To post a new notice in a public folder, follow these steps:

1. Choose the Compose New Post In This Folder command.

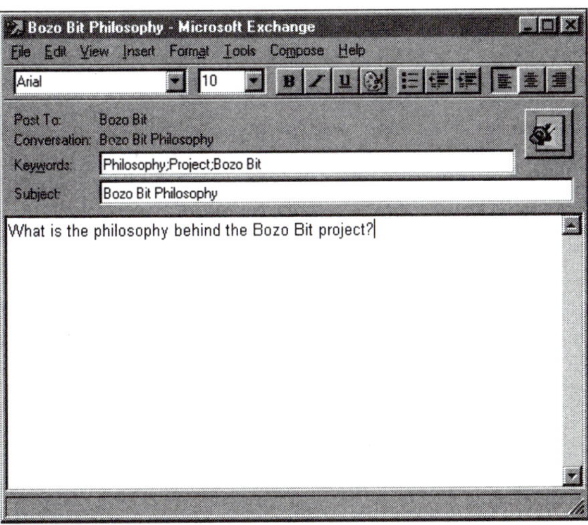

2. Type a description of the posting on the Subject line, and then type your note.
3. Click on the Post button.

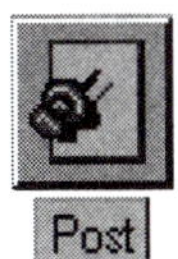

To respond to a posting, take these steps:

1. Select the item to which you want to reply.
2. Choose the Compose Post Reply In This Folder command.

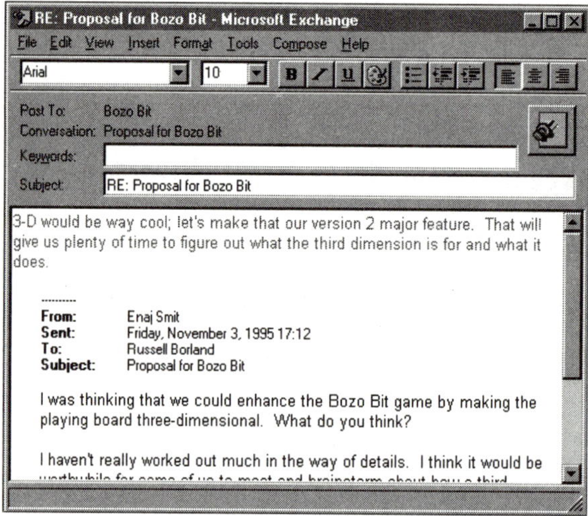

3. Press the Tab key and type your reply.
4. Click on the Post button.

Note If you select a posting or a file, the Compose Reply All command is not available. If you select a message, the Compose Reply All command is available. For all three types of items—a file, a posting, and a message—you can post a reply note, send a reply message to the poster or sender, or forward the message or posting.

For information about putting messages and files into a public folder, see "Adding Materials to the Project Folder," on page 206.

Public Folder Favoritism

Many Exchange systems have a large number of public folders and cover a broad and diverse array of topics. Finding the folder you want might take considerable time. When at last you locate a public folder that you want to consult often, it's time to set up a quick way to jump to it so that you don't have to go through all that searching again.

To set up a public folder as a favorite, take these steps:

1. Select the public folder you want as a favorite.
2. Choose the File Add To Favorites command.

A new folder appears in the Favorites folder inside Public Folders, displaying an asterisk on the folder cover to indicate it's a shortcut to a favorite public folder rather than the folder itself. Here's an illustration of a few public folder favorites.

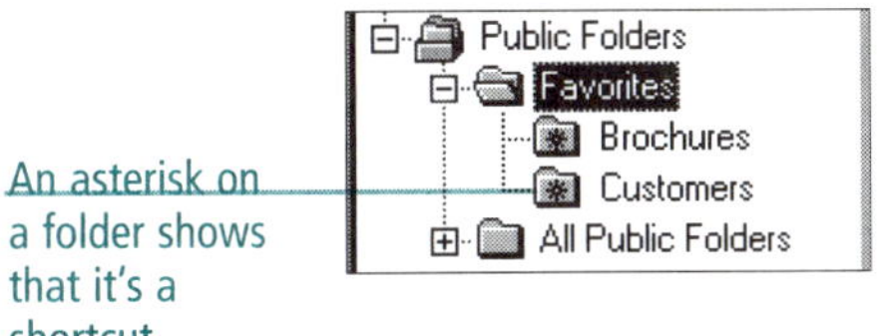

An asterisk on a folder shows that it's a shortcut.

Cutting Off Your Favorites

Have you ever gotten tired of a magazine you subscribe to? Or just found the magazine no longer fits your interests or needs? I should think so. At that point, you simply let your subscription to the magazine lapse.

With public folders, it's a little different. Your subscription runs forever—or at least until the folder becomes defunct. So, if you want to cancel a public folder favorite, you have to act; you must "send a cancellation notice."

To cancel a favorite folder, follow these steps:

1. Select the public folder favorite.
2. Choose the File Remove From Favorites command.

You're now totally free of that pesky subscription.

CHAPTER
4

Developing Your Profile

Microsoft Exchange keeps track of who you are and what you like. Whenever you log on, Exchange sets itself up to accommodate you—the way you work and the way you want Exchange to work.

Scenes from This Chapter

Each Exchange session is governed by the personal profile you select when you start Exchange. For example, you can set up one profile to use with Exchange when you're at your office, connected to a network. You can set up other profiles for when you take your computer home with you or take it on your travels, business or otherwise.

Here's another example: Say your boss puts you in charge of fielding questions about a special project, product, or service. Rather than have all messages you receive clutter your personal mailbox, you can have the Exchange administrator give you a separate Exchange account to handle only those messages. To read and send messages for this separate account, you set up a separate profile.

Where's the Profiler?

This chapter shows you how to set up, change, remove, and use profiles in Exchange for Windows 95. Most of the steps for working with profiles are the same for versions of Exchange that run under Windows 3.1 and 3.11, Windows NT, and Macintosh. For all of these operating systems, you run the Exchange Profile Wizard. What is not the same for these various operating systems is how you start the Profile Wizard.

- In Exchange for Windows 95, you double-click the Mail And Fax icon in the Control Panel to start the Profile Wizard.

Mail and Fax

- In Exchange for Windows 3.1, for Windows for Workgroups 3.11, and for Windows NT, you double-click the MS Exchange Services icon in the Microsoft Exchange program group to start the Profile Wizard.

(continued)

Where's the Profiler? *(continued)*

- In Exchange for the Macintosh, double-click the Exchange Profiles icon in the Microsoft Exchange folder.

Who Are You? Creating a Profile

When you (or some techno-guru) set up Exchange, you got a profile for Exchange. If you always use Exchange in one place and time, this single profile is very convenient; you don't need any other profiles. But suppose Exchange is set up for your office, where you connect to the Exchange server through your organization's network. Now you go on the road with your laptop, and you want to connect to your Exchange server to read mail messages, to consult public folders, and to schedule appointments and tasks. Your original profile can be set up for the home-and-away games, but you'll face a slower startup for Exchange because you'll see several dialog boxes on the way in.

For a more convenient and well-tailored startup of Exchange, you can set up a new profile for this situation. To do that, you start the Profile Wizard and create a new profile, which you'll use when you're away from your office. (And you'll edit the original profile for use when you're back in the office, right?)

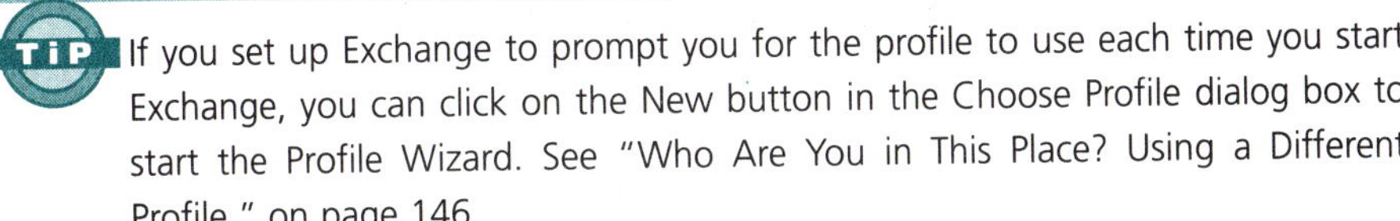

TIP If you set up Exchange to prompt you for the profile to use each time you start Exchange, you can click on the New button in the Choose Profile dialog box to start the Profile Wizard. See "Who Are You in This Place? Using a Different Profile," on page 146.

To create a new profile, follow these steps:

1. Start the Profile Wizard.
2. Click on the Show Profiles button in the Properties dialog box, as shown at the top of the next page.

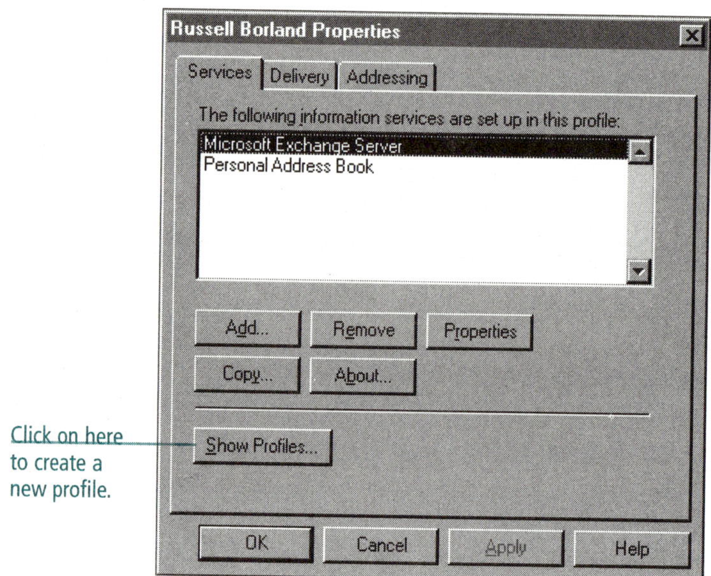

3. Click on the Add button.

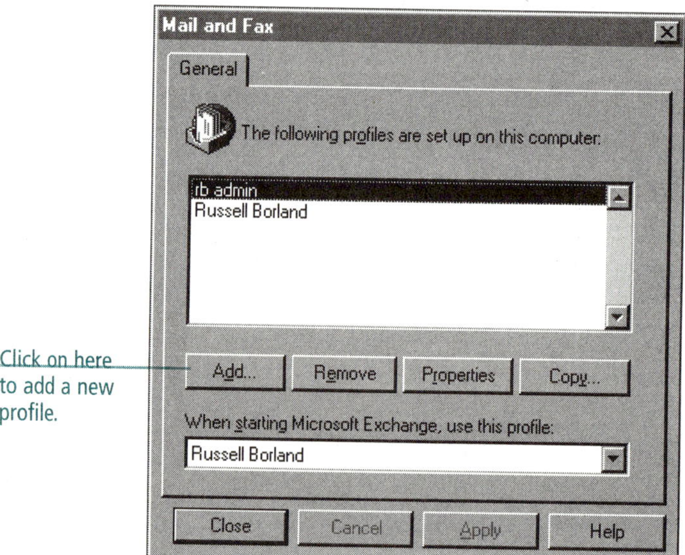

4. To include all the possible Exchange services, leave all the check boxes turned on, as shown in the illustration at the top of the next page. To omit a service, click on its check box to turn it off.

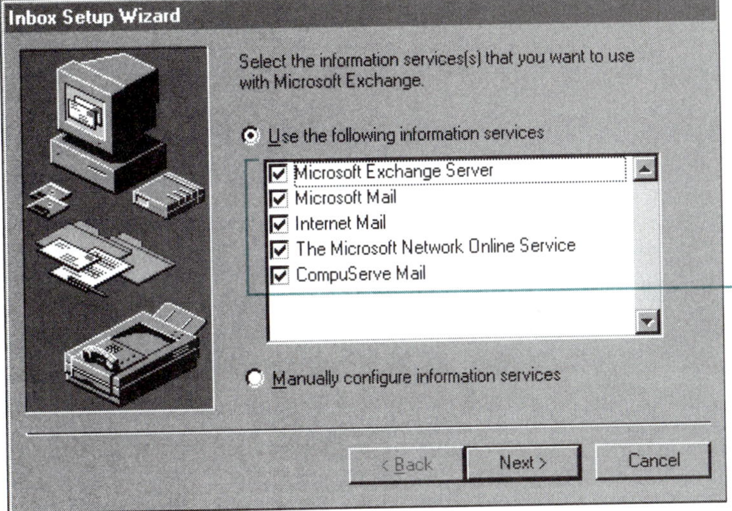

Click on these check boxes to turn off services you don't want in this profile.

Note If you think you really know what you're doing, you can click on the Manually Configure Information Services option and then select individual services and set them up the way you want. This book won't tell you all the things you need to know to take this path. You're better off letting Exchange supply the list and then selecting and omitting the services you want for each profile.

After selecting the services, click on the Next button.

5. Type a name for this profile, and then click on the Next button.

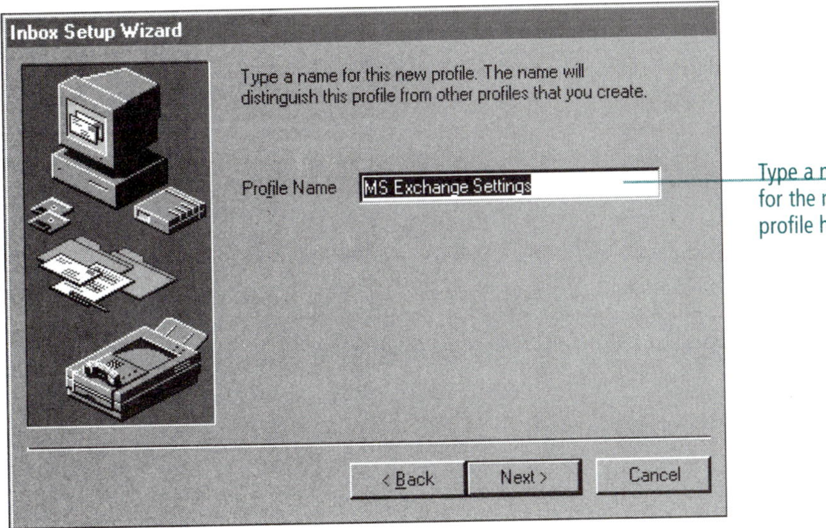

Type a name for the new profile here.

6. In the Microsoft Exchange Server box, type the name of your Exchange server. In the Mailbox box, type your mailbox name. If this is an additional profile for an Exchange server that you already use, you'll know the server name and mailbox name. If this is the first profile you are setting up, or if you have forgotten the information, you'll need to get the server name and mailbox name from your Exchange administrator.

Click on the Next button.

7. The dialog box shown at the top of the next page appears. If you are using a laptop that gets yanked free of the network when you leave your office, click on the Yes option. If your computer never leaves your office, click on the No option. Click on the Next button.

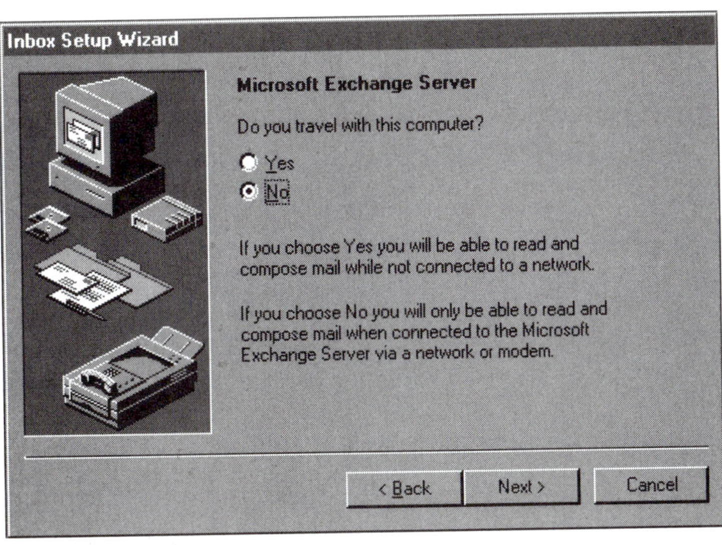

8. If you selected Microsoft Mail as part of this profile, type the path to your Microsoft Mail post office server. This post office is typically on your mail server for Microsoft Mail 3.2 and earlier versions, installed as part of Windows for Workgroups 3.11 or Exchange Mail in Windows 95.

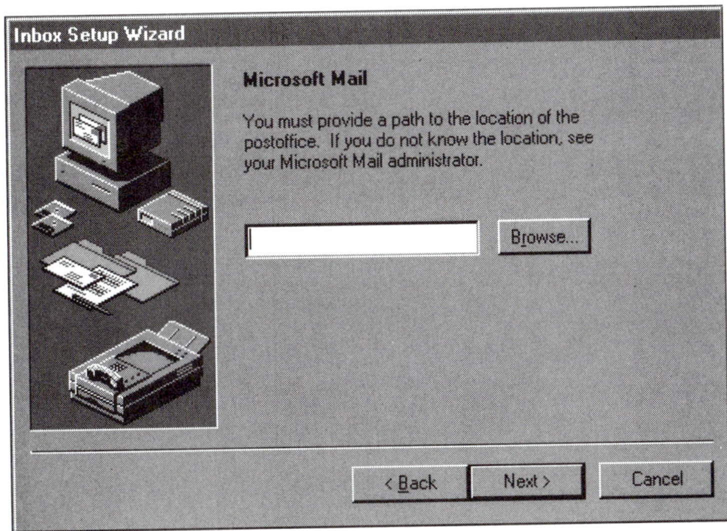

If you need assistance locating your Microsoft Mail post office server, try using the Browse button, which helps you browse the network. This will probably be useful only if you have some idea about the name of the server but are not sure about the exact spelling. After entering the server name, click on the Next button.

TIP If you get a message that the Profile Wizard can't find the server but you know the name is correct, click on the Next button to proceed without making the connection. You can make the connection later, when you start Exchange with this new profile.

If you are unable to connect to the Microsoft Mail post office for any reason, you'll be asked for your Microsoft Mail mailbox name and password on a single screen, instead of on two separate screens as described in step 9. Enter your mailbox name and password on this screen, and click on the Next button. Then skip to step 10.

9. The Profile Wizard displays a list of mailbox names in the post office, as shown here:

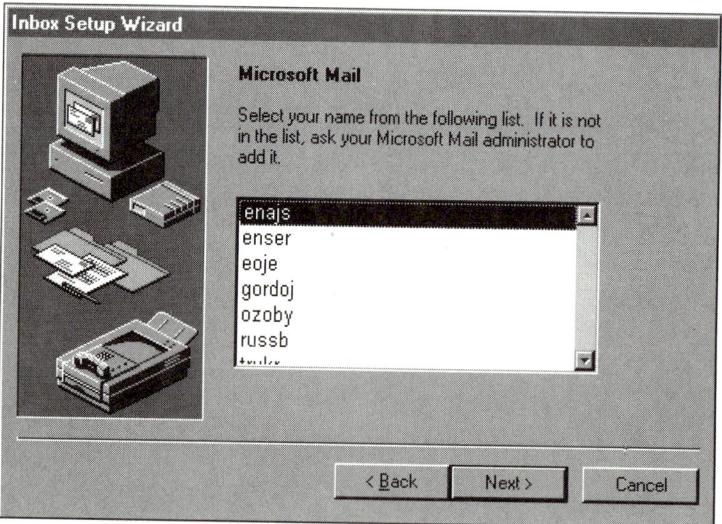

Select your mailbox name and click on the Next button. The Profile Wizard asks for your Microsoft Mail password.

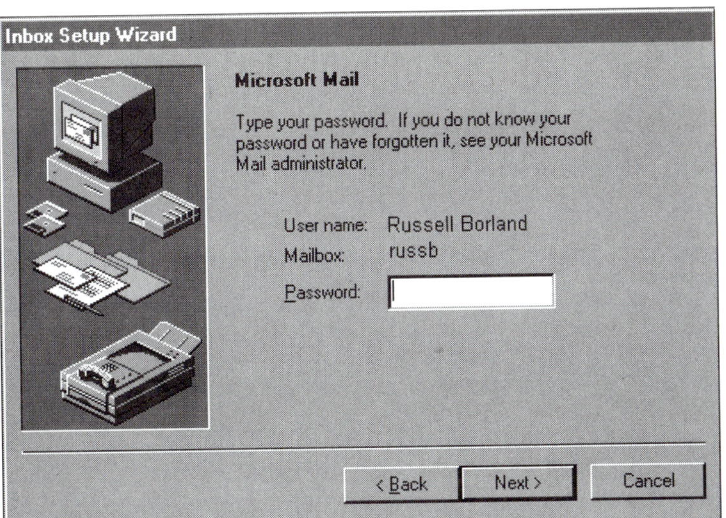

Type your Microsoft Mail password and click on the Next button.

10. If you have a personal address book set up already, type the path to it in the box. You can click on the Browse button to locate the address book rather than type a path name. (This is the only way to go if you have no idea what a path name is or how to type one.) If you don't have an address book set up yet, don't change the path name in the box. Click on the Next button.

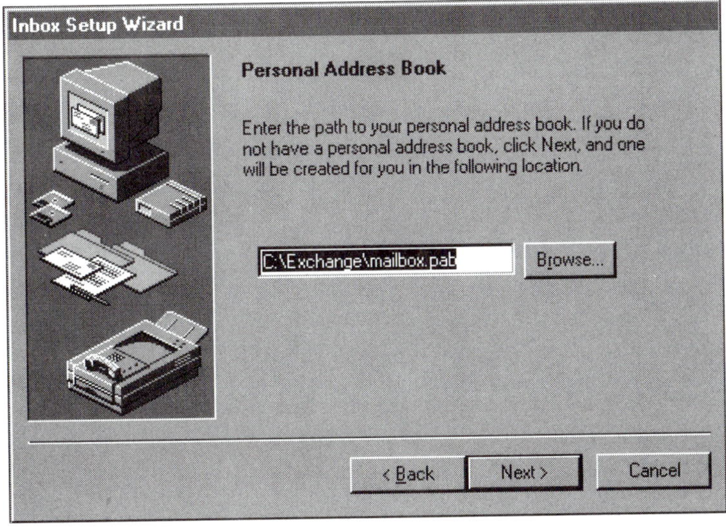

CHAPTER 4

11. Do you want Exchange to start every time you start Windows? If yes, click on the Add Inbox To The Startup Group option. If you want to start Exchange yourself (when you're good and ready), click on the Do Not Add Inbox To The Startup Group option. Click on the Next button.

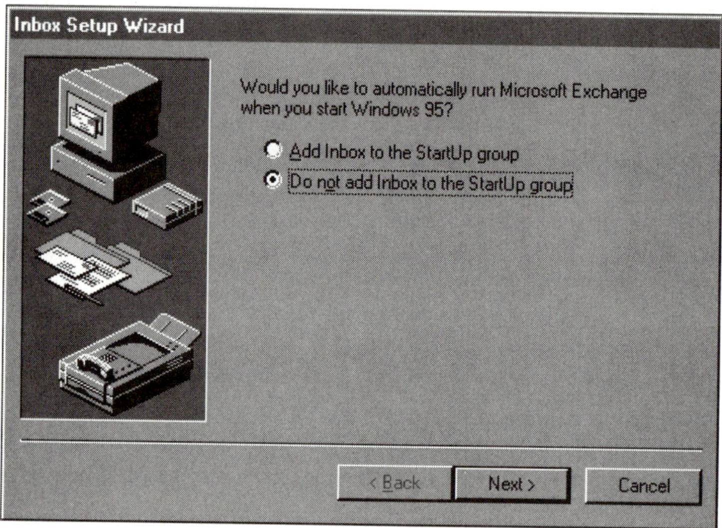

12. Check over the list of information services you have set up for this new profile, as shown in the dialog box at the top of the next page.

    If something is missing or if the profile contains a service you don't want in it, you can change the profile after you're finished. To do so, use the steps in "Who Are You Now? Changing a Profile," next.

13. Click on the Finish button.

Pretty easy, right? You can use the Profile Wizard to create profiles specific to each location from which you use Exchange: office, home, and away. Or you can set up profiles specific to different services you use in Exchange, such as Internet Mail, MSN, or CompuServe.

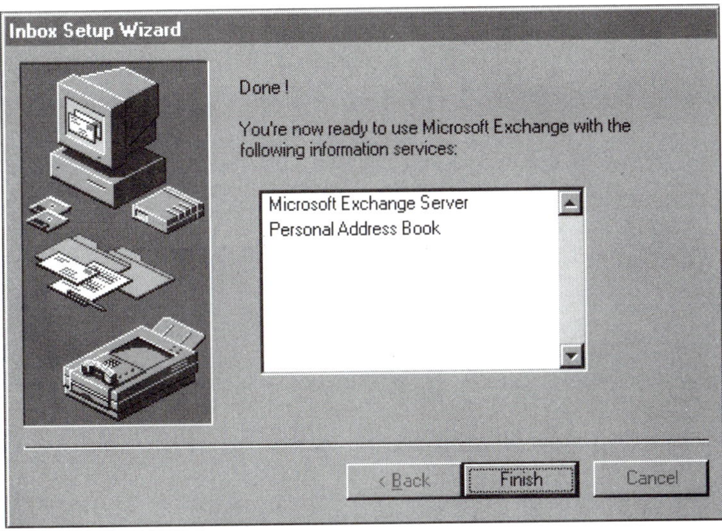

Who Are You Now? Changing a Profile

You signed up for a new online service and want to add it to one or more of your profiles. You bailed out of an online service that wasn't giving you what you wanted. Your profile is now out of date, so you want to update the online service information. Here's how you do it:

1. Start the Profile Wizard.
2. Click on the Show Profiles button.
3. Select the profile you want to change, and then click on the Properties button.

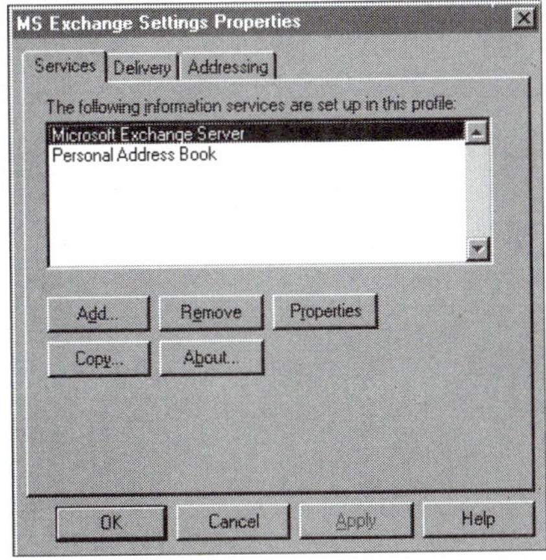

4. To add another information service, click on the Add button. To remove an information service, select it, and then click on the Remove button. If you want to see or change the properties of one of the services, select it, and then click on the Properties button.

5. To check or change the delivery properties, click on the Delivery tab. On the Delivery tab, you can change the location at which your mail is delivered and you can specify an alternate location at which to deliver mail if the first location is unavailable. If your profile includes two or more services that support mail having the same address type (for example, Exchange and Internet), you can specify the order in which those services should process outgoing mail.

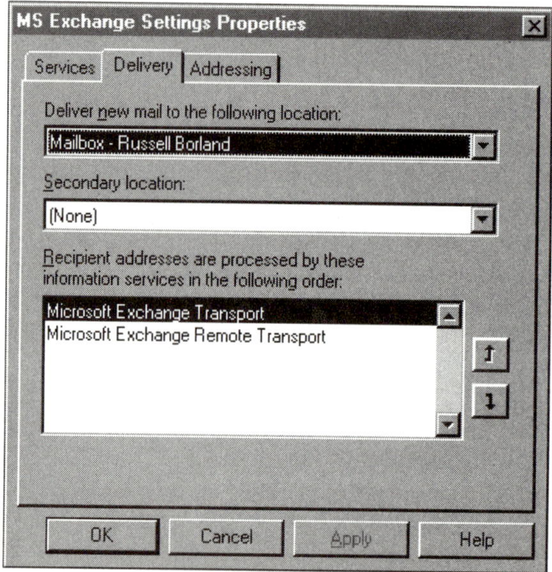

6. To check or change the Addressing properties, click on the Addressing tab. On the Addressing tab, you can specify which address list to display when you first open the address book, where to save new entries in your address book, and in which order to search address lists for recipient names.

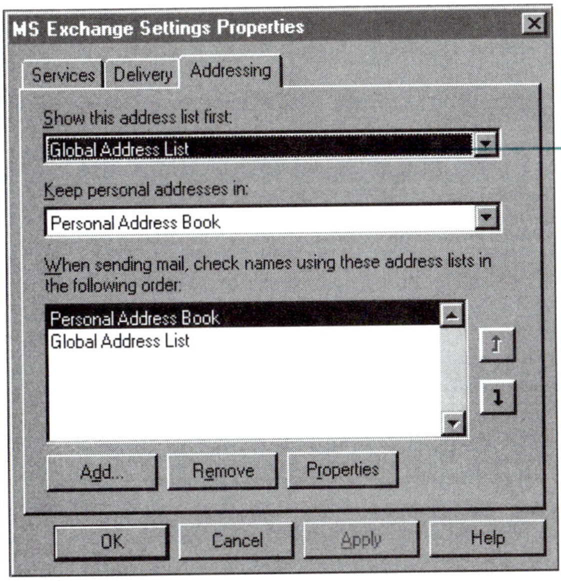

Select a different address book if you want a different address book to be your primary one.

7. Click on OK.
8. If you want to change another profile, repeat step 3 through step 7. Click on the Close button when you are finished.

Adding Fax to Exchange

Sending faxes is a popular form of communication. The trouble with a stand-alone fax machine is that you need to print your message before you can send it. If your computer has a fax modem installed, you can create your message on the computer and then use Exchange to send the fax to its destination.

Before you can add fax service to Exchange, you need to install your fax modem and accompanying software. Installing a fax modem can be a tricky process, so consult your operating system manuals for instructions on how to install your fax modem software. After you set up the fax modem software, take these steps to add fax service to an Exchange profile:

1. If you want to change your current profile, in Exchange, choose the Tools Services command.

   To change a profile other than the one you're using, start the Exchange Profile Wizard as described in the sidebar "Where's the Profiler?" on page 130. When the Properties dialog box appears, be sure that the name of the profile you want to change appears in the title bar. (To select a different profile, click on the Show Profiles button. Select the profile you want to change, and then click on the Properties button.) Be sure the Services tab is showing.

To add a profile, follow the steps in "Who Are You? Creating a Profile," on page 131.

2. Click on the Add button on the Services tab.

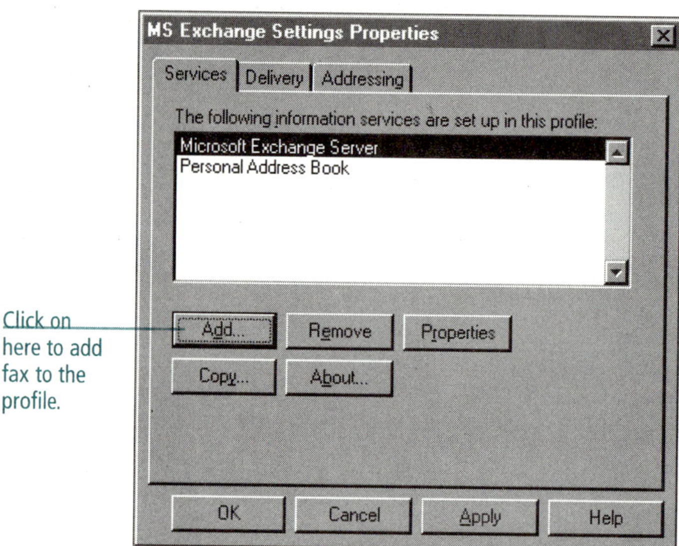

3. In the Add Service To Profile dialog box, select Microsoft Fax, and then click on OK.

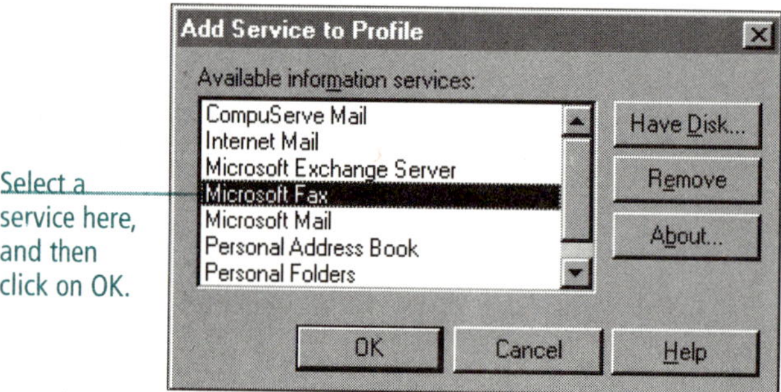

4. When you see a box that asks if you want to set up your fax modem for Exchange, click on the Yes button.

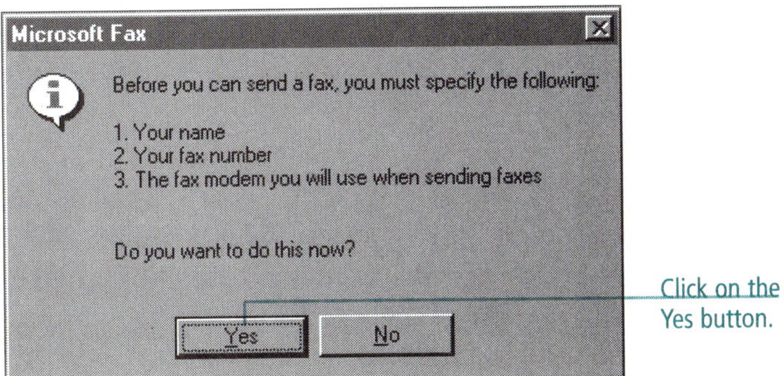

Click on the Yes button.

5. When the Microsoft Fax Properties dialog box appears, fill in as much of the information as you can. You *must* provide your fax number on the User tab.

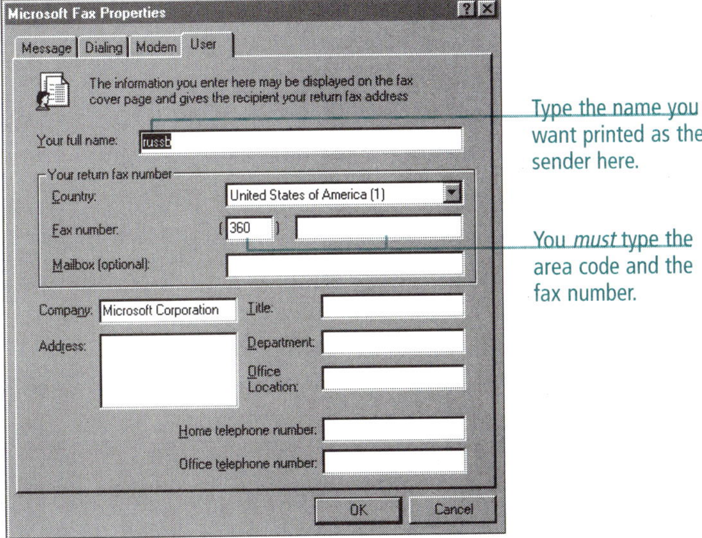

Type the name you want printed as the sender here.

You *must* type the area code and the fax number.

6. If you have more than one modem available to you, click on the Modem tab, select the modem you'll be using, and then click on the Set As Active Fax Modem button.

7. Click on the Dialing tab, and then click on the Dialing Properties button.

8. If you'll only send faxes from one location, you can set up the Default Location with the information that's needed. If you'll be sending faxes from several locations, click on the New button, type a location name, and then click on OK. Set up the information that's needed for this new location. Click on OK in the Dialing Properties dialog box.
9. If you will be dialing long-distance numbers within your area code, click on the Toll Prefixes button. In the Local Phone Numbers list, select a prefix in your area code that requires you to dial 1 plus the area code before you dial the number, and then click on the Add button. Repeat this step for each long-distance prefix that you will be dialing within your own area code.

TIP If most of the prefixes require you to dial 1 plus the area code first, click on the Add All button, and then remove the few prefixes that are local to your number. If you aren't sure about which prefixes are toll and which are toll-free, you can work around this when you set up a fax entry in your address book. See the steps for setting up a fax address beginning with step 1 on page 145.

---

10. Click on OK in the Toll Prefixes dialog box, and then click on the Message tab.
11. Select the time when you want your faxes to go out.
12. Select a message format.
13. Click on the Paper button to select the size of paper you want your fax transmitted as, the image quality, and the orientation of the fax image on the paper. When you're finished, click on OK.
14. If you don't want a cover page, click on the Send Cover Page check box to turn it off. If you do want a cover page, select the cover page you want to use.

    If you want to see what the cover page looks like or change it, click on the Open button. Or, if you want to create a new cover page of your own, click on the New button. In both cases, the Cover Page Editor starts up so that you can modify the existing cover page or create a new one.

    If you have cover page files available, you can click on the Browse button to open one of them for use.

15. When you're done setting fax properties, click on the OK button. If Exchange is running, you'll see a message that tells you that you can't use the service until you log off and restart Exchange. The next time you start Exchange, you can send faxes.

To send a fax, you must first set up a fax address. Then you simply send your message to that address. Exchange sends the message by fax rather than through the Exchange server mail transport.

To set up a fax address, take these steps:

1. In Exchange, click on the Address Book button on the Exchange toolbar.
2. In the Address Book, click on the New Entry button on the Address Book toolbar.
3. In the New Entry dialog box, select Fax, and then click on OK.
4. On the FAX - Address tab, type the name of the fax recipient in the Name To Show On Cover Page box.

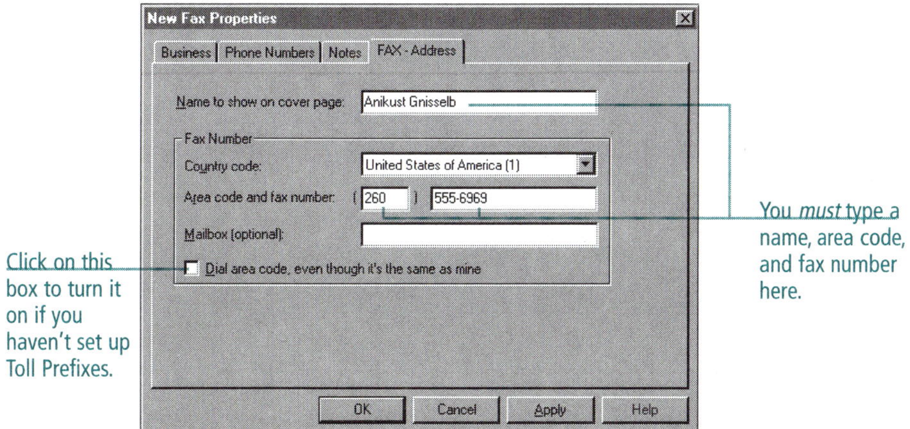

Click on this box to turn it on if you haven't set up Toll Prefixes.

You *must* type a name, area code, and fax number here.

5. In the Area Code and Fax Number boxes, type the area code and fax number of your fax recipient.
6. If the number is long-distance within your area code and you didn't set up a special toll prefix for it when you set up your fax properties, click on the Dial Area Code, Even Though It's The Same As Mine check box to turn it on.
7. Fill out any other information you want on the other tabs, and then click on OK.

Who Are You in This Place? Using a Different Profile

When you have more than one profile set up, you can select which profile to use when you start Exchange. You can tell Exchange to use a particular profile all the time, or you can tell Exchange you want to choose a profile each time you start Exchange.

To use the same profile all the time, do this:

1. In Exchange, choose the Tools Options command, and then select the General tab if necessary.

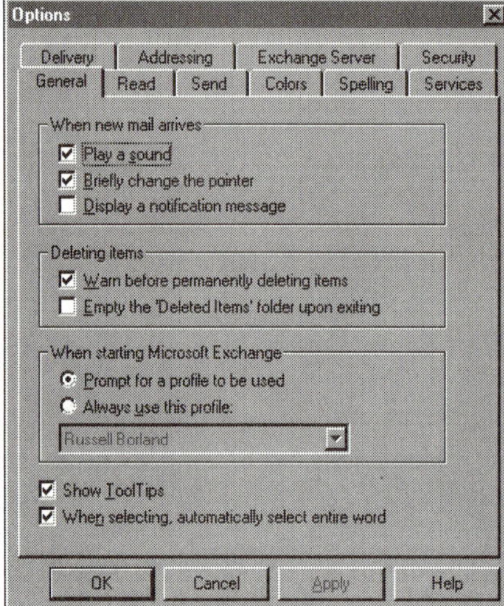

2. Select the Always Use This Profile option, and then select a profile to use.
3. Click on OK.

If you prefer, you can choose a profile at the start of each Exchange session. For this option, follow these steps:

1. In Exchange, choose the Tools Options command, and then select the General tab if necessary.
2. Select the Prompt For A Profile To Be Used option, and then click on OK.

Once the Prompt For A Profile To Be Used option is turned on, you choose a profile by selecting the profile name in the Choose Profile dialog box, which you'll see each time you start Exchange.

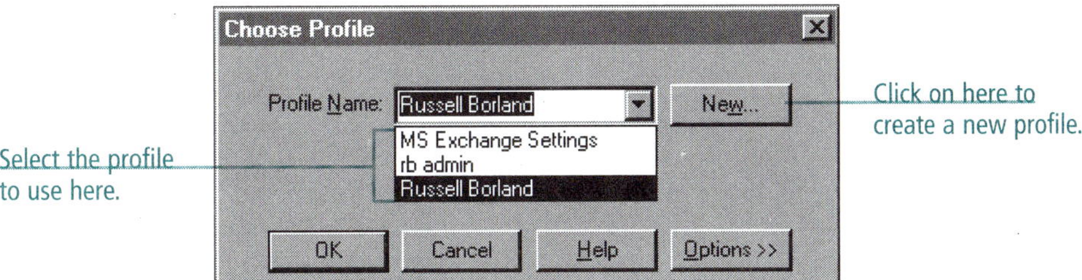

I'm Not That Me Anymore: Removing a Profile

So you moved to a new dwelling. It's in a different area code. You can edit one or more profiles, but maybe now you need only a couple of the profiles that you already have set up. To simplify your Exchange life, you can remove the unwanted and unnecessary profiles.

To remove a profile from Exchange, follow these steps:

1. Start the Profile Wizard.
2. Click the Show Profiles button.
3. Select the profile you want to remove.
4. Click on the Remove button.
5. When the Profile Wizard asks if you want to remove this profile, click on the Yes button.
6. Click on the Close button.

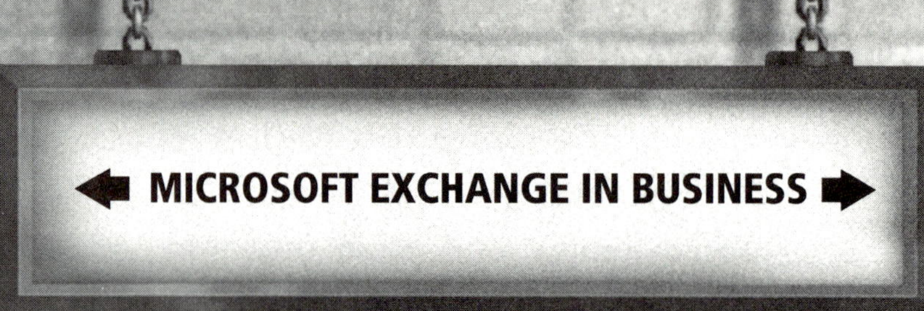
MICROSOFT EXCHANGE IN BUSINESS

PART 2

From time to time during the workday, you might find yourself wondering about ideas that relate to your work. These ideas could be of interest to some of your colleagues, and, rather than save your ideas for a meeting, you might prefer to dash off a note about your ideas and ask the others to respond.

A discussion forum provides an easy-to-use means of sharing ideas and responses with many people at once. People check the discussion forum when they have time and interest. This way, they don't have to be interrupted.

In this part of the book, you'll learn how to participate in a discussion, how to set up a discussion forum, how to add and remove participants, and how to control exchanges on a forum. You might not need or even have permission to perform the administrative actions associated with a discussion forum. But if you do have permission to start a discussion forum, you'll want to know how to administer it.

Discussion Forum

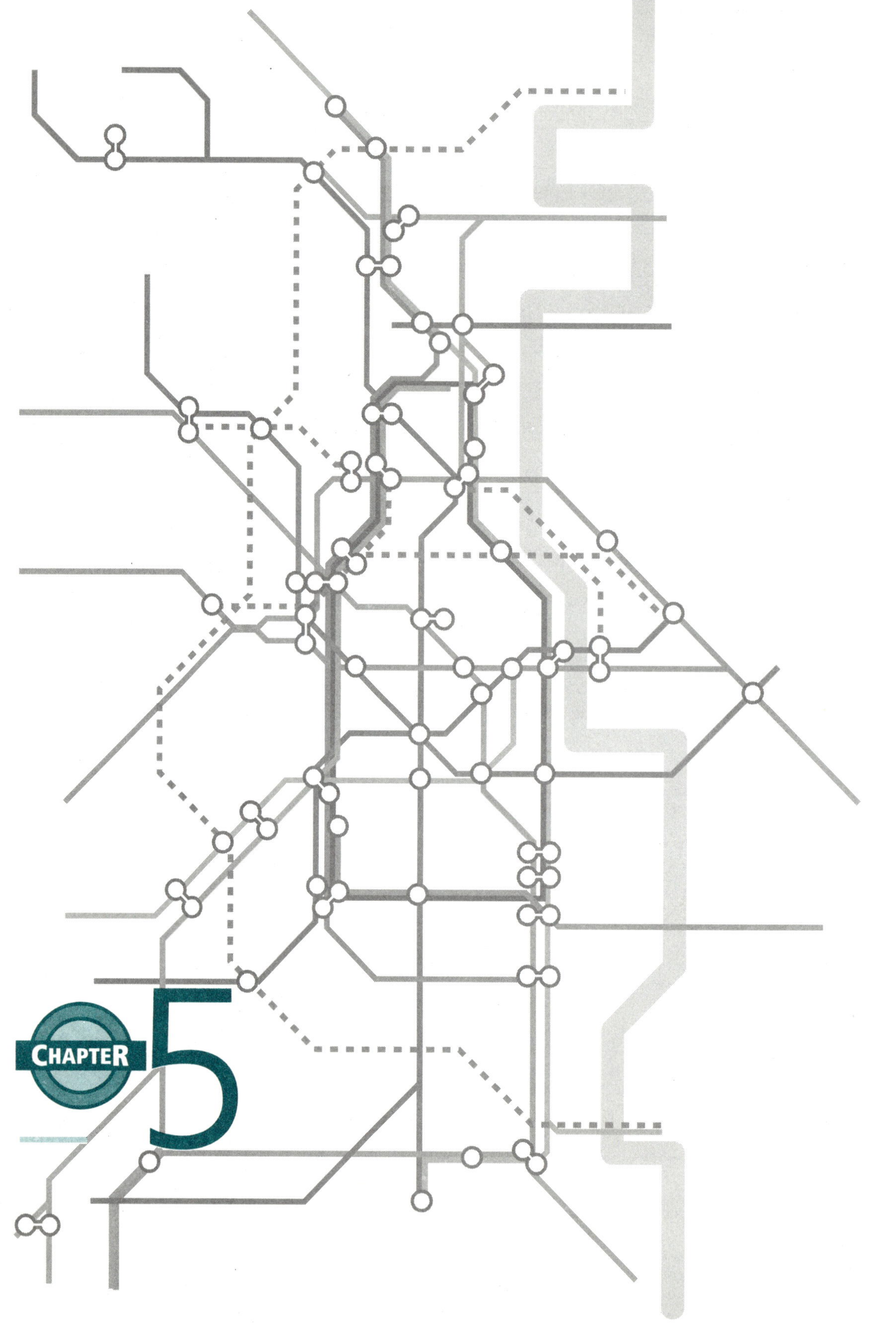
CHAPTER
5

Participating in a Discussion

Participation in a discussion forum entails several different actions. You'll certainly want to read the discussion as it has proceeded so far, and you might want to add your two-cents' worth. You might want to extract the original question and a selection of responses, and you might also want to limit what you read by filtering through only those messages that interest you. You'll learn how to do all these things in this chapter.

Scenes from This Chapter

A discussion forum is really just a use of a public folder. The participants in a discussion post messages in the folder, which can also be set up to receive all the e-mail messages that a project group sends to each other about a project. (See Part 3, "Project Information," for more about this use of a public folder.) The public folder becomes the repository of the e-mail discussions and contains the historical record for everyone to review and comment on.

To give some context to the various parts of a discussion forum, consider the following scenario. I'll use this scenario throughout this chapter as the basis for examples as well as for the steps you take.

Scenario

You've been asked to prepare a report about changes in your company's competitive landscape. To start out, you're trying to keep up with news about your company's business and its business rivals. Fortunately, your company librarian posts messages about new developments in a public folder on the Exchange server. So today you decide to look into this folder and see what's there.

As wonderful as it is that Exchange keeps all the messages and postings of a discussion forum in a public folder, you're faced with a mountain of material. Remember: All the messages and postings appear in the folder. Typically, you have permission to post and reply to messages and postings, but you have permission to delete only your own messages and postings. After a while, a folder can contain thousands of messages and postings about a wide variety of topics that pertain to the various interests of the forum members. How do you make any sense of this mountain? How do you find and follow a particular topic of discussion? You tease out a thread.

Teasing Out a Thread: Organizing a Discussion

A "thread" is a term used to label all the messages and postings about a single, particular topic in a discussion forum. For example, if you have a discussion forum for industry news, one thread might concern competitors,

another thread might be about the market for your organization's products or services, and still another thread might concern analysts' projections for sales.

Exchange gives you several ways to view the messages and postings in a discussion forum and to tease out the threads of a discussion. All of these methods are listed on the submenu that appears when you choose the View Personal Views command.

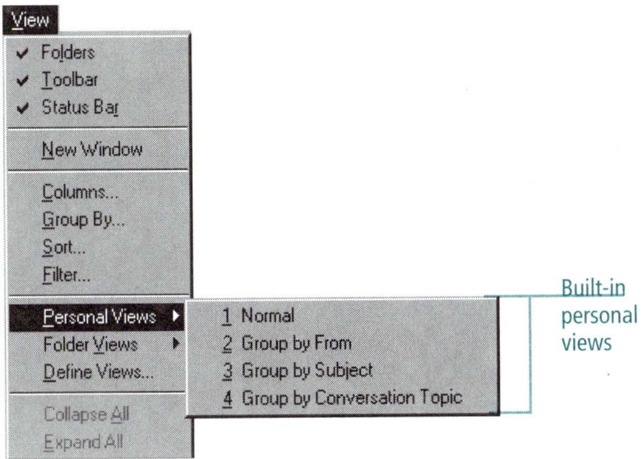

- Normal view displays all messages and postings without groupings; you also use this view to remove other groupings.

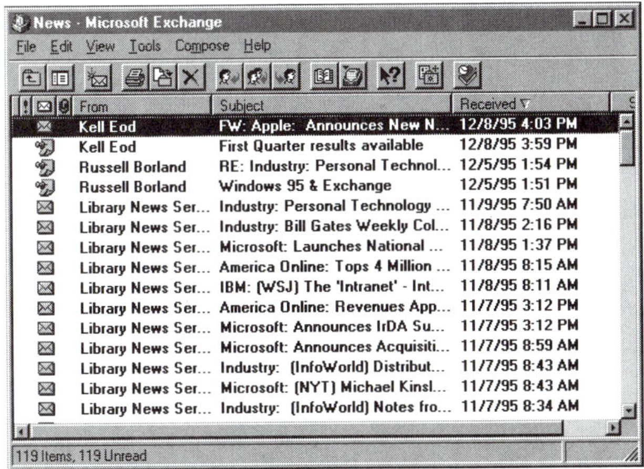

- Group By From organizes messages by the sender; use this view to group all the messages and postings from a particular person.

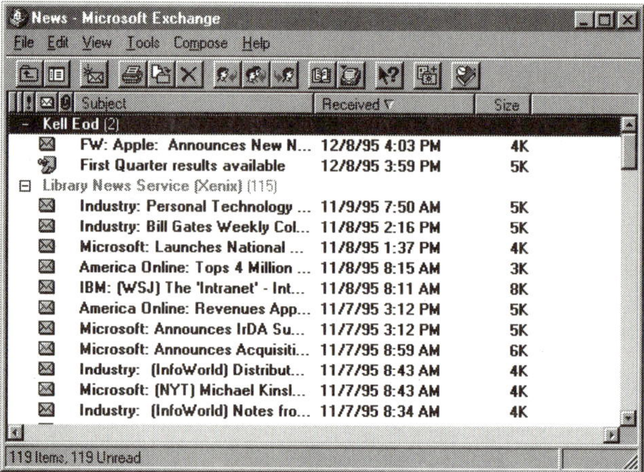

- Group By Subject groups messages and postings under headings taken from the Subject line; use this view to see a list of subjects in the folder.

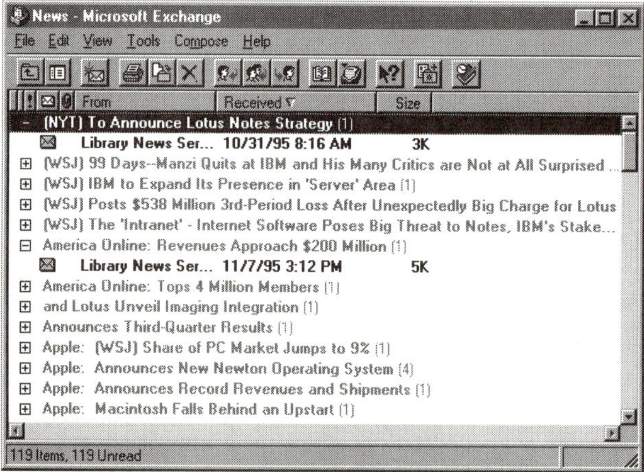

- Group By Conversation Topic groups postings by the Discussion line and groups messages by the Subject line; use this view

when the Discussion lines and Subject lines of postings aren't exactly the same, as they won't be for replies, for example. This view will let you follow a thread from beginning to end.

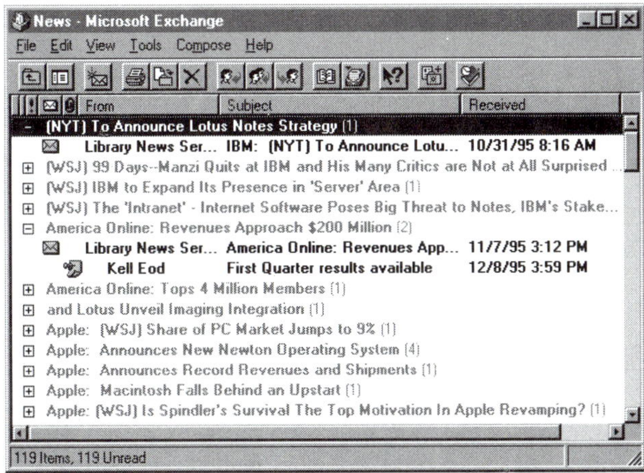

To group a discussion in any of the ways described above, do the following:

1. Open the public folder that contains the discussion forum you want to peruse.
2. Choose the View Personal Views command, and then select from the submenu the view that organizes the discussion the way you want it.

If the views Exchange provides don't satisfy you, Exchange makes it possible for you to add your own personal views.

Taking It Personal: Setting Up Personal Views

Maybe you like the groups Exchange gives you and maybe you don't. In either case, you might want to set up other groupings. You can do this by creating new personal views that change the number and types of columns and how messages and postings are grouped and sorted.

You can also apply a filter to view only messages that meet certain criteria. You can use any personal view in any folder.

To create a new personal view, do the following:

1. Choose the View Define Views command.

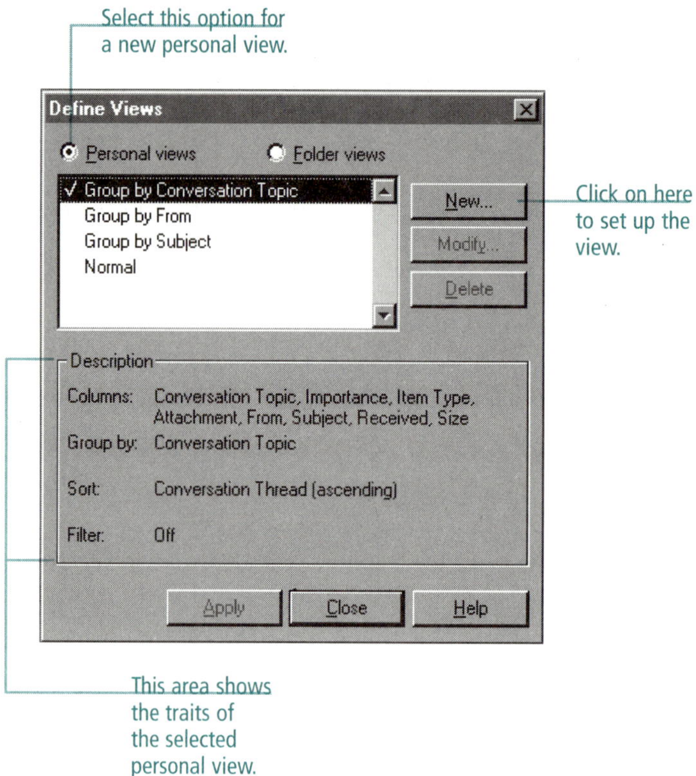

2. Select the Personal Views option.
3. Click on the New button. See the illustration at the top of the next page.
4. Type a name for this new personal view.
5. Click on the Columns button if you want to change the number and types of columns. (See "Columns Right, March: Changing Column Number and Order," on page 159, for details.)

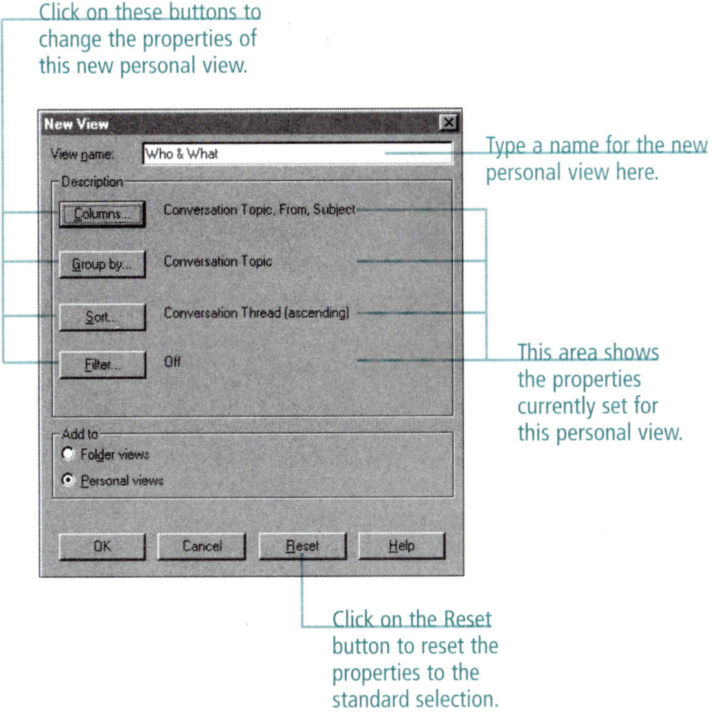
Click on these buttons to change the properties of this new personal view.
New View
View name:
Who & What
Description
Columns...
Conversation Topic, From, Subject
Group by...
Conversation Topic
Sort...
Conversation Thread (ascending)
Filter...
Off
Add to
Folder views
Personal views
OK
Cancel
Reset
Help
Type a name for the new personal view here.
This area shows the properties currently set for this personal view.
Click on the Reset button to reset the properties to the standard selection.

6. Click on the Group By button to change the grouping. (See "Teasing Out a Thread: Organizing a Discussion," on page 152, for details.)
7. Click on the Sort button to change the sorting order. (See "Sorting It Out in Other Ways," on page 160, for details.)
8. Click on the Filter button to set up a filter. (See "Filtering Discussions," on page 166, for details.)
9. Click on OK.
10. If you want to apply this personal view to the folder that is currently open, click on the Apply button.
11. Click on the Close button.

After you define a new personal view, you can switch to it by selecting its name from the submenu that appears beside the View Personal Views command, as shown in the illustration on the next page.

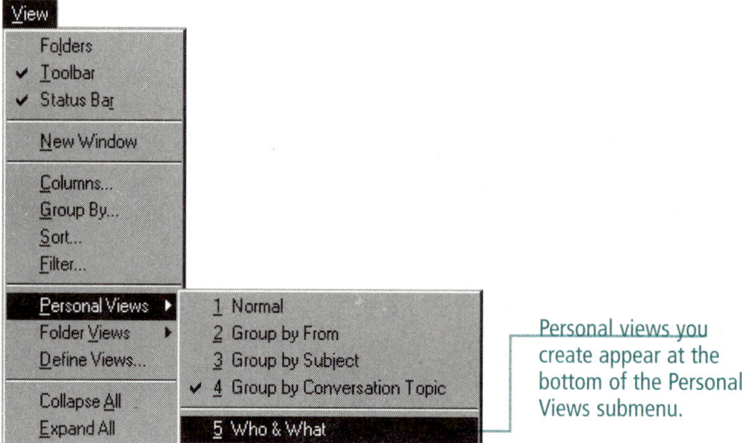

Personal views you create appear at the bottom of the Personal Views submenu.

Adjusting and Canceling Personal Views

If a personal view isn't quite right—for example, if all the columns you want aren't displayed—you can change it to suit you better. To change a personal view, do this:

1. Choose the View Define Views command.
2. Click on the Personal Views option.
3. Select the name of the personal view you created that you now want to change.

Note You can't modify the four views built into Exchange.

4. Click on the Modify button.
5. Change the personal view settings in the Modify View dialog box. You can even change the name. The Modify View dialog box looks the same as the New View dialog box shown on page 157; it just has a different title.
6. Click on OK, and then click on the Close button in the Define Views dialog box.

If you no longer have a use for a personal view, you can get rid of it:

1. Choose the View Define Views command.
2. Click on the Personal Views option.
3. Select the name of the personal view you created that you now want to delete.

4. Click on the Delete button. When Exchange asks if you're sure, click on the Yes button.
5. Click on the Close button.

Columns Right, March: Changing Column Number and Order

In addition to the column headings that are originally set up for Exchange, you can add (or remove) column headings to see other properties of the messages and postings in a public folder. For example, you might want to see a column for the keywords in postings; or the date messages were created; or the number of words, paragraphs, or pages—to list just a few of the possibilities.

To add a column to a folder, do the following:

1. Open the folder to which you want to add the column.
2. Choose the View Columns command.

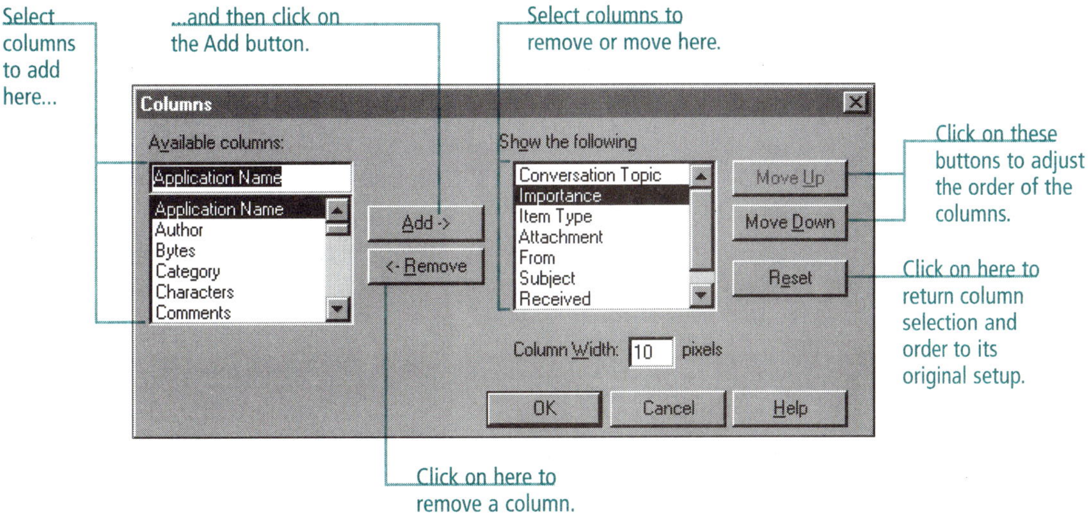

3. From the Available Columns list, select the column you want to add.
4. Click on the Add button.
5. If you want the new column to appear in a particular position, select the column's name in the Show The Following Columns box, and then click on the Move Up or Move Down button to move the column to its new position. The column name at the

top of the list appears as the leftmost column in the folder contents pane; the column name at the bottom of the list appears as the rightmost column.

6. Click on OK.

For more information about changing columns in folders, see "Window Options," on page 408.

Sorting It Out in Other Ways

In any personal view of a folder, including the built-in views, you can sort the messages, postings, and groupings by using the column headings at the top of the pane.

To sort the folder by a particular column in descending order (A to Z, newest to oldest, smallest to largest), click on the column heading. For example, to sort from the latest date to the oldest date, click on the Received column heading. To sort alphabetically by sender, click on the From column heading. The column heading shows an arrow pointing downward to show that Exchange uses this column for sorting and to show that the direction of the sort is descending.

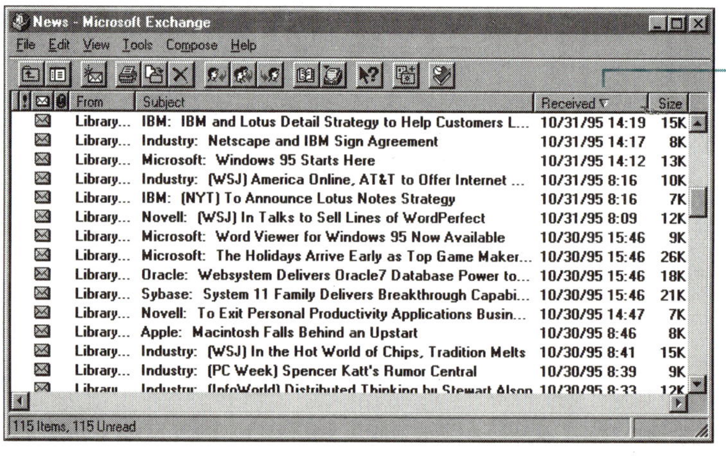

An arrow indicates that this column is used for sorting. A down arrow like this one means descending order (newest to oldest).

To sort the folder by a particular column in the opposite (ascending) order (Z to A, oldest to newest, largest to smallest), click on the column heading again. For example, to sort from the oldest date to the latest date, click on the Received column heading and then click on it again. The column heading shows an upward-pointing arrow, as seen in the illustration on the next page.

Note that the selected item in the folder stays visible in the pane even though it moves to a new position in the list.

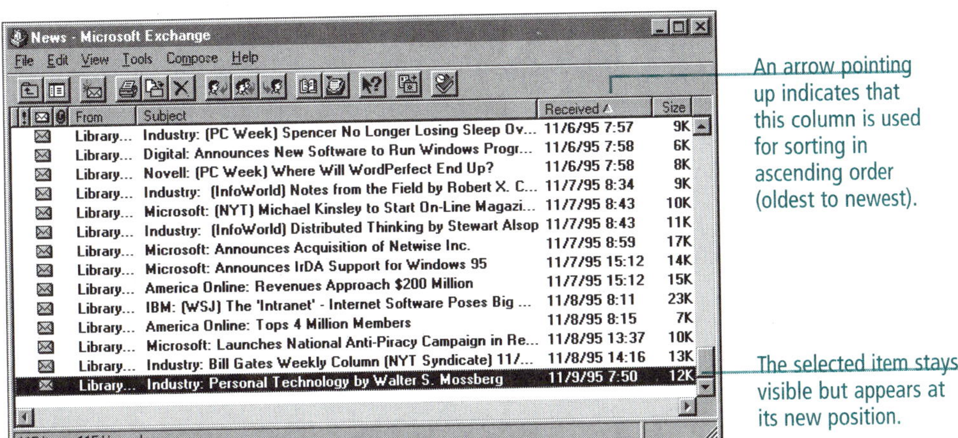

Following a Thread

After you sort out a discussion by teasing out the threads, you are ready to follow any of the threads from beginning to end.

To follow a thread, do this:

1. Organize the folder contents into threads by choosing the View Personal Views command, and then selecting Group By Conversation Topic from the submenu.
2. Scroll to locate the thread you want to follow, and then click on the plus sign to expand the thread.
3. Double-click on the first message or posting in the thread, and then read it.
4. Click on the Next button on the message or note window to see the next message or note in the thread.
5. When you've read all of the thread, click on the Next button. If the next thread is already expanded, Exchange opens the first message or posting in the next thread. If the next thread is not expanded, Exchange closes the message window and highlights the next thread in the message list pane. If you have read as much as you need before you reach the end of the thread, click on the Close box in the upper right corner of the message window.

Do You Have Permission?

All public folders can have a level of protection against vandalism and voyeurism. Some public folders are open and available to all Exchange users on your system. Some public folders are limited to people who have a special affiliation with the folder, such as a project team. Other folders might be available by subscription; that is, you sign up with the group whose conversations are kept in the public folder. And there are some public folders that you might be barred from seeing.

In general, you can read the contents of a folder if you can open the folder. Anytime you are restricted from a folder or some functions in a folder, Exchange lets you know that you're trying to trespass into forbidden territory. If you don't have permission to use a folder, you can't open it. If you don't have permission to post to a folder, you'll see an error message when you try to post—or the commands you need will be unavailable. If you don't have permission to move or delete folders or their contents, you'll see a message when you try.

To check the precise nature of your permissions, do the following:

If right-clicking is unavailable, select the folder and choose the File Properties command.

1. Right-click on the folder and choose Properties from the shortcut menu.
2. Click on the Summary tab and review your permissions.

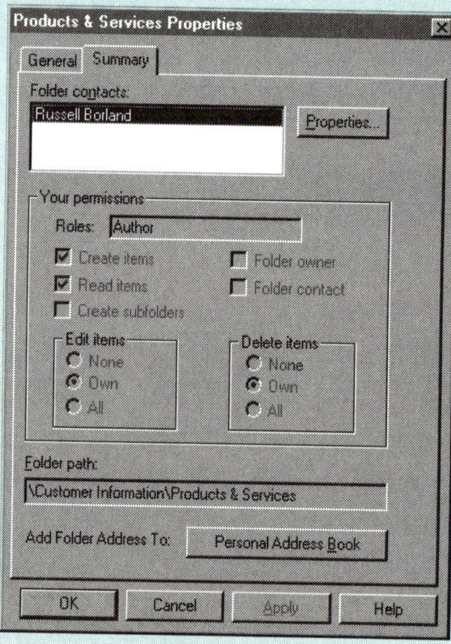

(continued)

Do You Have Permission? *(continued)*

3. When you're done, close the Properties dialog box.

After you review the level of your permissions, you can discuss changes you want to make with the folder contact listed on the Summary tab in the Properties dialog box.

Adding Your Voice to a Discussion

You have two ways to raise your voice and broadcast your views in a discussion: send a message or post a note. Both methods are similar to the methods you use to send a personal message, which are discussed in Part 1, "Personal Information." The major difference is that, in a group discussion, you address a message or a note to the group's public folder.

Before you can send a message to a public folder, you must add its name to your Personal Address Book. To do so, follow these steps:

1. Right-click on the public folder, and then choose Properties from the shortcut menu.
2. Click on the Summary tab, click on the Add Folder Address To Personal Address Book button, and then click on OK.

If right-clicking is unavailable, choose the File Properties command.

To send a new message to a discussion forum, follow these steps:

1. Click on the Compose button on the Exchange toolbar.
2. In the To box, type the folder's name, for example, *News*.
3. Type an appropriate subject line and then type the message you want to send.
4. Click on the Send button to the right of the message window's To line.

To send a reply message to an individual instead of posting a reply to the entire group, do this:

1. Open the folder that contains the item to which you want to reply, and then select the item.
2. Click on the Reply To Sender button on the Exchange toolbar. Exchange displays a standard reply window, shown at the top of the next page. This way, you can send private replies to note posters rather than announce your views over the public folder.

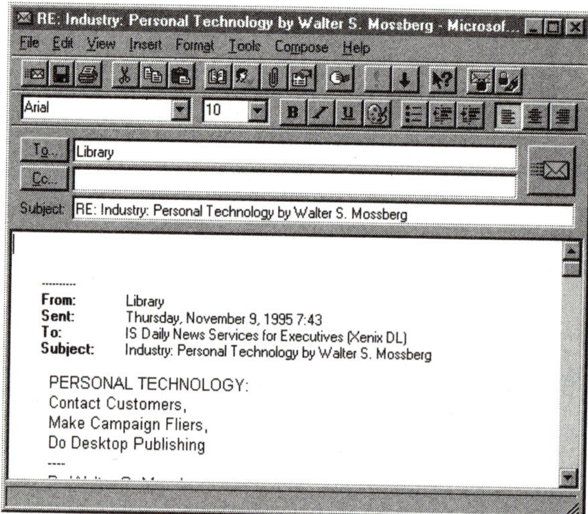

3. If you want to, change the To and Cc boxes in the message header to share your reply with a few extra people.
4. If you want to, alter the Subject line to make the point of your reply and the topic of discussion obvious.
5. Type your comments in the message area, and then click on the Send button to the right of the reply window's To line.

To post a new note, thereby creating a new thread, do this:

1. Open the public folder for the discussion group.
2. Choose the Compose New Post In This Folder command.

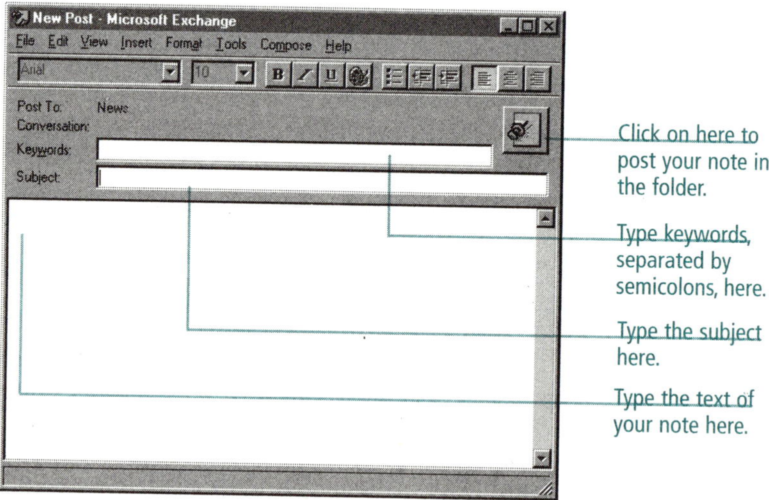

3. In the Subject line, type the topic of conversation. When you move to the message area, Exchange copies your Subject line to the Conversation line. The Conversation line will be used as the name of a new thread.
4. To assist you and others in grouping postings later, fill in the Keywords box with words that identify all the important points in your posting. If you want to enter two or more keywords, separate the keywords with semicolons.
5. Click on the Post button to the right of the Posted To line.

To post a response to a note, do this:

1. Open the public folder for the discussion group.
2. Select the note you want to respond to.
3. Choose the Compose Post Reply In This Folder command.

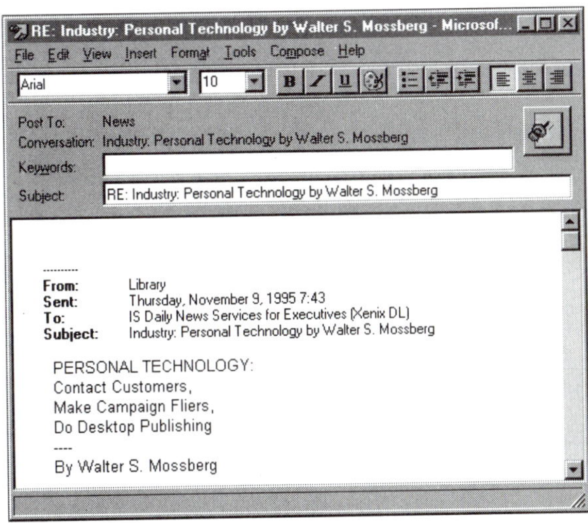

4. Type your reply in the message area.
5. If you want, you can add keywords that identify the points of your reply. You can also alter the Subject line to make the point of your reply and the topic of discussion obvious.
6. Click on the Post button to the right of the Posted To line.

Filtering Discussions

Discussion forums and public folders are notorious for capturing a wide variety of topics and interests under a (quite often barely) common umbrella. For example, you might find a public folder that contains postings of published articles about your company along with staff and management commentary on the articles. In all the swirl of postings, you might be interested only in what a particular person has to say, or you might want to see all that was said, but only after a particular date. You might also prefer to restrict the listing of folder contents to particular topics or conversations because you don't have an interest in other topics that end up in the folder.

When you want to restrict the list of messages and postings in a public folder in some particular way all the time, you can set up a filter. A filter screens out what you don't want to see and directs Exchange to list only those messages and postings that you do want to see.

A filter can screen out items on the basis of one general part of the messages and postings—such as senders' names—or on the basis of two or more parts, which makes the list more particular—and shorter.

To set up a filter, take these steps:

1. Open the folder in which you want to set up a filter. Exchange uses a filter only in the folder in which you set it up.
2. Choose the View Filter command.

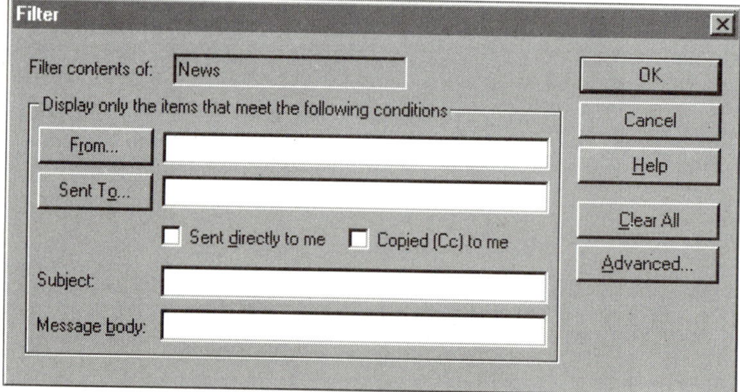

3. Set up the dialog box to tell Exchange what kinds of messages and postings you want to see in the folder. The fewer settings you make, the more messages you'll see. The more settings you make, the finer the filter. (And like a water filter, the finer the

filter, the purer the stream that comes through.) Consult the following table to decide what kinds of messages and postings you want to see.

Setting	What Stays
From	Shows only messages and postings from the people you list.
Sent To	Shows only messages sent to the people you list.
Sent Directly To Me	Shows only messages and postings with your name in the To box.
Copied (Cc) To Me	Shows only messages and postings with your name in the Cc box.
Subject	Shows only messages and postings whose Subject line contains the exact text you type in the Subject box.
Message Body	Shows only messages and postings that contain the text you specify somewhere in the message body.

Click on the Advanced button to display a dialog box that contains additional settings for filtering messages and postings. The table on the next page shows the additional filtering options you can set.

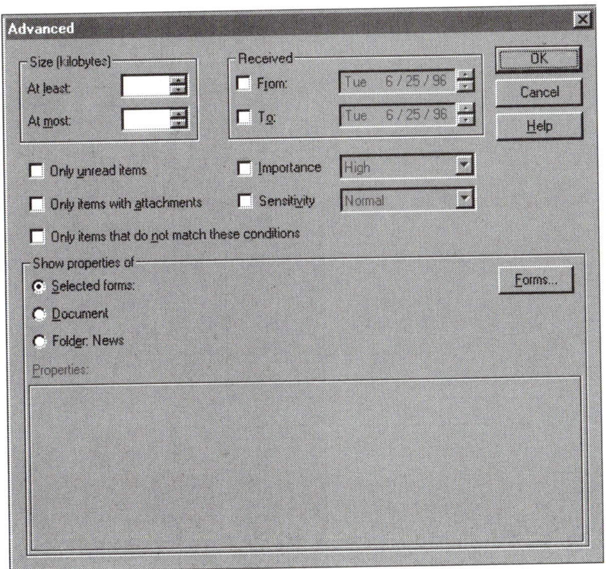

Setting	What Stays
Size	
At Least	Shows only messages and postings that are larger than the size you set.
At Most	Shows only messages and postings that are smaller than the size you set.
Received	
From	Shows only messages received after the date you set; to see messages between two dates, also set a To date.
To	Shows only messages received before the date you set; to see messages between two dates, also set a From date.
Only Unread Items	Shows only messages and postings you haven't yet read.
Only Items With Attachments	Shows only messages and postings that contain attachments.
Importance	Shows only messages and postings set to the specified level of importance—High, Normal, and Low.
Sensitivity	Shows only messages and postings with the specified level of sensitivity—Normal, Personal, Private, Confidential.
Only Items That Do Not Match These Conditions	Reverses all the settings in both the Filter and Advanced dialog boxes; for example, if you select the Only Unread Items option and this option, the folder shows only messages and postings that you have already read.
Show Properties Of	
Selected Forms	Allows you to filter based on fields in the forms you select with the Forms button. The fields will be displayed in the Properties area.
Document	Allows you to filter based on document properties. The fields will be displayed in the Properties area.
Folder	Allows you to filter based on fields in the custom forms associated with the folder whose name appears after the Folder label. The fields will be displayed in the Properties area.

4. Click on OK. (If you made any settings in the Advanced dialog box, click on OK in both the Advanced and the Filter dialog boxes.)

You can still sort and use personal views with the messages and postings that your filter lets through.

Adjusting and Canceling Filters

You can change filter settings at any time, and you can remove a filter so that you get the raw contents again.

To change a filter's settings, follow these steps:

1. Open the folder with the filter you want to change.
2. Choose the View Filter command.
3. Change the settings in the Filter dialog box, and then click on OK.

To remove a filter, take these steps:

1. Open the folder with the filter you want to change.
2. Choose the View Filter command.
3. Click on the Clear All button, and then click on OK.

Note The Clear All button also clears settings in the Advanced dialog box.

Doing It All at Once: Folder Views

Folder views allow you in one shot to set up, group, and sort the columns in a folder, and to set up a filter for a folder. Not only that, but you can also give each folder view a name so that you can switch to a different folder view to see a different set of messages and postings in a folder. A folder contact can set up a folder view, and folder views are available to all users of the folder.

To set up a folder view, take these steps:

1. Open the folder in which you want to set up a folder viewing scheme.
2. Choose the View Define Views command. See the illustration at the top of the next page.

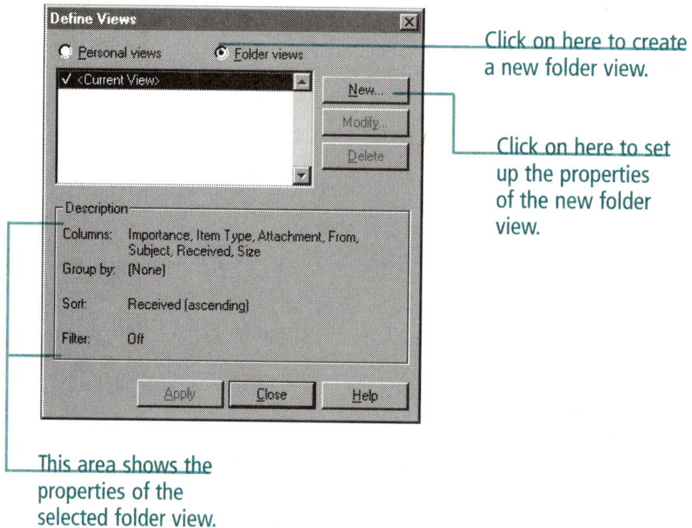

3. Click on the New button.

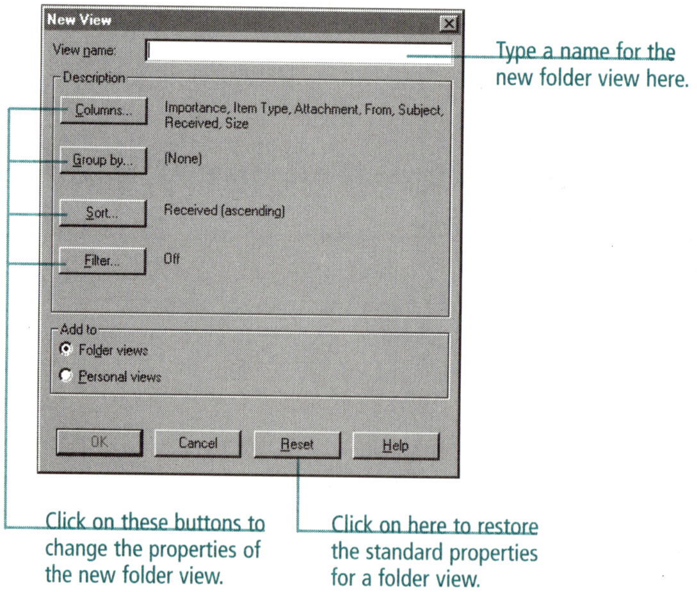

4. Type a name for this folder view. The name you choose should clearly indicate what the folder view shows because others will see this name.
5. Click on the Columns button if you want to change the number and types of columns. (See "Columns Right, March: Changing Column Number and Order," on page 159, for details.)
6. Click on the Group By button if you want to change the grouping. (See "Teasing Out a Thread: Organizing a Discussion," on page 152, for details.)
7. Click on the Sort button if you want to change the sorting. (See "Sorting It Out in Other Ways," on page 160, for details.)
8. Click on the Filter button if you want to set up a filter. (See "Filtering Discussions," on page 166, for details.)
9. Click on OK.
10. If you want to apply this folder view to the currently open folder, click on the Apply button.
11. Click on the Close button.

After you define two or more folder views, you can switch between views by selecting the view's name from the submenu that appears beside the View Folder Views command.

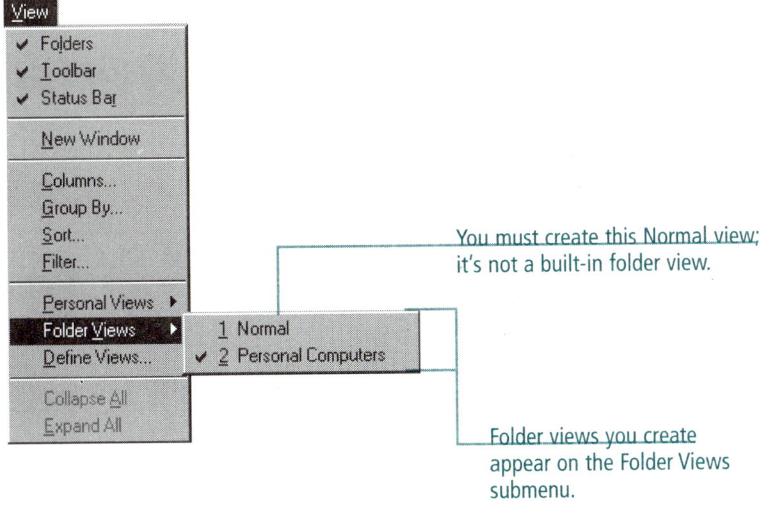

If you will want to return to the full view of a folder at some point, create a folder view named "Normal" or "Full" or some such name. You can instantly return to the full view any time you want by choosing the name from the View Folder Views submenu.

Adjusting and Canceling Folder Views

Just as with private views, if a folder view isn't quite right, you can change it so that it better suits your needs. To change a folder view, do this:

1. Open the folder with the folder view that you want to change.
2. Choose the View Define Views command.
3. Select the name of the folder view you want to change.
4. Click on the Modify button.
5. Change the folder view settings in the Modify View dialog box. You can even change the view name if you want.
6. Click on OK, and then click on the Close button in the Modify Views dialog box.

If you no longer have a use for a folder view, you can delete it.

1. Open the folder with the folder view that you want to delete.
2. Choose the View Define Views command.
3. Select the name of the folder view you want to delete.
4. Click on the Delete button. When Exchange asks if you're sure, click on the Yes button.
5. Click on the Close button.

CHAPTER
6

Setting Up a Discussion Forum

It starts with a friend or two passing messages back and forth about a topic of special interest. Then one friend forwards a message to another friend, who forwards it to two more friends, who forward it to two more friends. And so the circle of discussion expands until you find yourself in a group that has a common interest and whose members want to share information with the entire group at once. To make passing information within a group easier, you can set up a Microsoft Exchange discussion forum. In this chapter, you'll learn how.

Scenes from This Chapter

Caveat—Something to Be Aware Of

A discussion forum can solve a number of problems associated with using e-mail for group discussions. For example, unlike a regular group e-mail alias, which exposes members to every random discussion that surfaces in the minds of other group members, a discussion forum lets members sift through the information exchanged by the group when they have the time and inclination. But setting up thousands of discussion forums on a network can cause problems of its own—namely, clogging the network with traffic. Because of the problems that can arise from giving every Exchange user free and open license to create discussion forums, your network administrator might place controls on who can create them.

You might be the lucky duck who, at your own discretion, gets to set up public folders for a discussion forum, but it is more likely that you will be at the mercy of the Exchange administrator. In that case, after the administrator creates the public folder for you, he or she will make you the contact. Being the contact gives you extensive powers over how the public folder can be used, including (possibly) being able to create and set up subfolders, deciding who can and who can't participate in your discussions, and making your public folder a legal address for e-mail messages. The descriptions and procedures in the rest of this chapter assume in most cases that you are the contact for a public folder.

Scenario

A number of your cohorts like to share examples of unique, weird, awful, fun, distorted, and convoluted uses of language—statements by politicians and sportscasters, malapropisms by school children, accident reports, newspaper gaffes, and the like. While the interest in most of this information is ephemeral, from time to time people want to see a particular instance again, for a second laugh or to illustrate some point in a document they are preparing.

You and your friends decide to set up a discussion forum to collect examples of language use and abuse. For no particularly logical reason, we'll call this discussion forum *Word Fun*.

Setting Up the Discussion Forum Folder

In setting up a new discussion forum, a public folder must be created. In most cases, you ask the Exchange administrator to set up the folder, and then you, as folder contact, set up the rest of the characteristics of the folder.

Just in case you are lucky enough (or cursed enough) to have the right to create public folders, here's how you do that:

1. In the folder pane, click on the Public Folders icon.
2. Choose the File New Folder command.

3. Type a name for the new public folder, and then click on OK. When you create a new public folder yourself, you automatically become the owner and contact for the new folder.

Setting Properties for Your Discussion Forum

Once the public folder for your discussion forum is set up, you (as contact) can set up the properties that are appropriate to your discussion forum. You don't have to change any properties for the discussion forum to work as a repository of messages and postings, but changing a few of the properties will make it more useful and effective. For example, you can enter a description of the folder to let people know what it's all about and assign roles to participants of the discussion forum so that some participants have larger roles in the control of folder content.

To set folder properties, do the following:

1. In the folder pane, expand the Public Folders icon, if necessary, by clicking on the plus sign at the left of the icon.

If right-clicking is unavailable, select the discussion forum folder, and then choose the File Properties command.

2. Right-click on the discussion forum folder, and then select Properties from the shortcut menu.

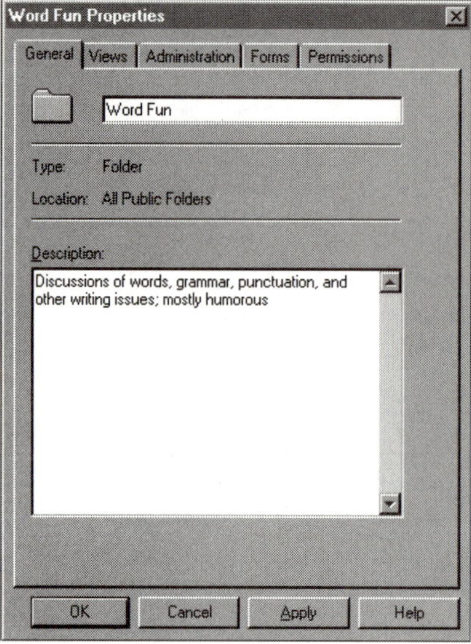

Note If the Properties dialog box has only a General tab and a Summary tab, you are not the contact for the selected public folder. Have your Exchange administrator set up the public folder for you—or have the administrator make you a contact for the folder.

3. On the General tab of the properties sheet, you can change the folder name if you want, and you can type a description that lets members know the nature of this discussion forum.

   For example, the description of the Word Fun folder could be:

   Discussions of words, grammar, punctuation, and other writing issues; mostly humorous

4. On the Views tab of the properties sheet, set up any folder views you want to make available for the participants to use when browsing the folder. For details about setting up folder views, see "Doing It All at Once: Folder Views," on page 169.

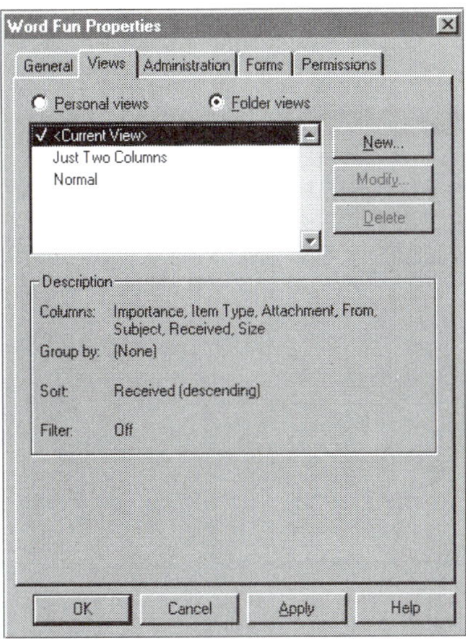

5. On the Administration tab of the properties sheet, set the initial view of the folder. (This selection matters only if you set up additional folder views on the Views tab.)

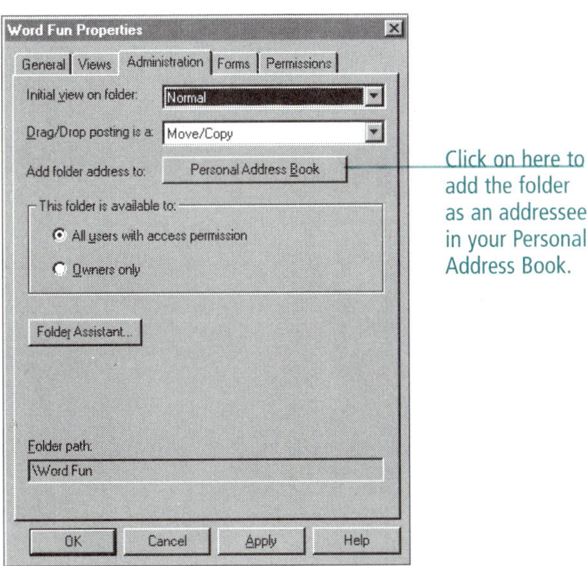

Leave the Drag/Drop Posting Is A box set to Move/Copy if you want a message that is dragged and dropped into the public folder to appear as if it is from the originator of the

message rather than from the person who dragged and dropped it. Change this box to Forward if you want such a message to appear as if it was forwarded to the public folder by the person who dragged and dropped it.

Initially, a new folder is available to all users to whom you give permission to open it (see step 7, on the next page). If you want to temporarily restrict the folder to its owners (and there can be one or many owners), click on the Owners Only button.

The Folder Path box shows the name of the folder as it will appear in your Personal Address Book if you click on the Personal Address Book button. When you click on this button, you can send messages directly to the folder.

For information about the Folder Assistant button, see "Adding and Removing Participants," on page 183, and Chapter 7, "Controlling Forum Exchanges."

6. On the Forms tab of the properties sheet, set up and select any forms you want to associate with the discussion forum. Chapter 9, "Setting Up Project Information Messages," and Chapter 12, "Collecting Customer Information," cover the creation of forms and their application to a public folder. Forms probably won't be necessary for a discussion forum. You're more likely to use forms for public folders that contain status reports or time cards or other such types of information.

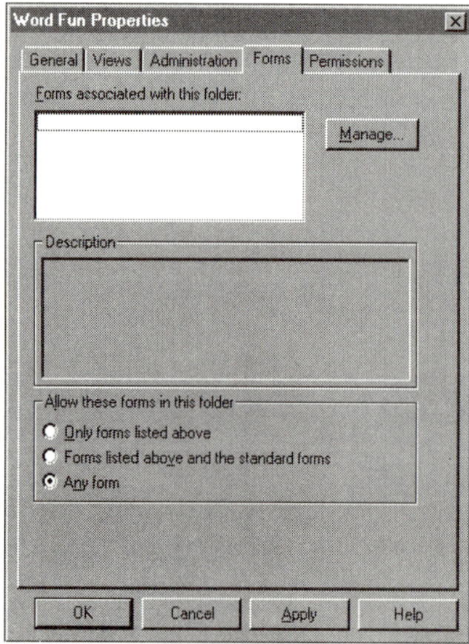

7. On the Permissions tab, you'll make your most dramatic changes. Notice that the tab has a "Default" entry with the role of Author. This means that anyone who isn't specifically added to the roster automatically has the role of Author. As an Author, a person can add new items, can read everything, and can edit and delete their own items. If you want most users of this folder to have a different role, change the Default role by clicking the down arrow at the right of the Roles dropdown list box and selecting a different role. Click the Help button to see a description of what each role allows a user to do.

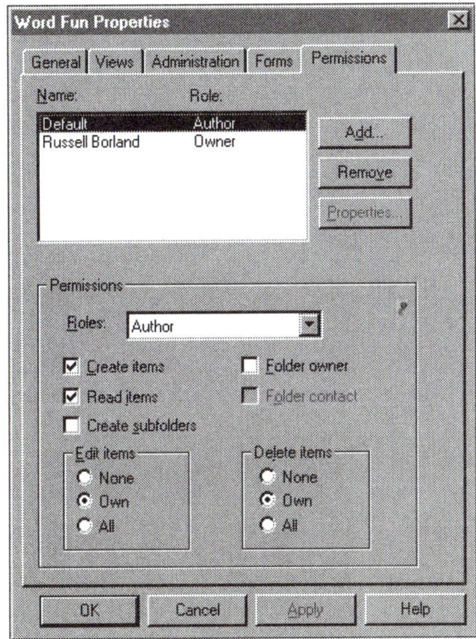

If the Default role is the one you want for most participants, all you have to do is add the participants who need special privileges. To do so, see "Adding a Participant," on page 184.

8. When you're finished changing the properties, click on OK.

Moving Information to the Discussion Forum Folder

When the folder is set up as you want it, it's time to put something in it. In due course, discussion participants will put messages and postings in the folder. They and you can put information in the folder in several ways:

- Move messages and postings to the folder
- Create a new posting in the folder
- Post a reply in the folder
- Include the folder name as a recipient of messages

You move a message or posting to a public folder in the same way that you move e-mail messages between your private folders. For details, consult "Moving Messages" on page 46. For information about how to create a new posting or to post a reply, see "Adding Your Voice to a Discussion" on page 163. For information about including the folder as a mail message recipient, read on.

Sending New Messages to a Discussion Forum

A discussion forum can receive mail messages just as if the discussion forum were a person on the Exchange system. There are a couple of ways to set this up. The first requires the intervention of the Exchange administrator; you can perform the second yourself.

To send mail to a discussion forum folder without relying on your administrator, do the following:

If right-clicking is unavailable, choose the File Properties command.

1. Open the discussion forum folder, right-click on the folder, and then select Properties from the shortcut menu.
2. Select the Summary tab. See the illustration at the top of the next page.
3. Click on the Add Folder Address To Personal Address Book button, and then click on OK.

From now on, when you consult the address book, you can find the discussion forum's folder name in your Personal Address Book.

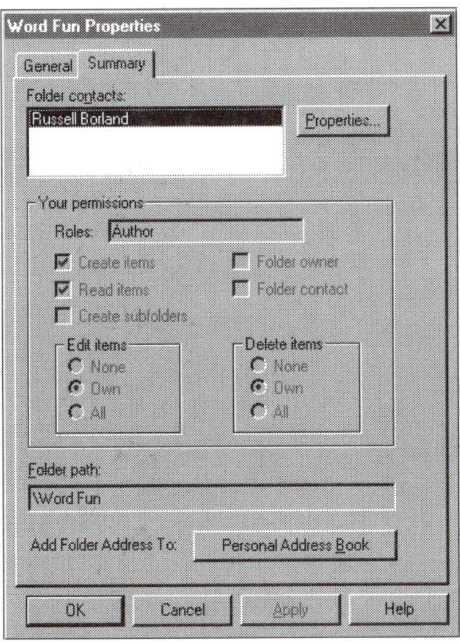

Let the Admin Do It

The trouble with adding the discussion forum folder to your Personal Address Book is that it's yours and yours alone. The other members of your group must also set up the discussion forum address in their personal address books if they want to send mail to the discussion forum folder.

Instead of having everyone add the discusson forum to their address books, you can ask your Exchange administrator to set up a distribution list in the Global Address List that includes the names of all the group members plus the name of the public folder to which you want messages to the group to also be sent.

Adding and Removing Participants

As people hear about a discussion forum from friends, they might want to join in the fun. As discussion forum participants tire of the "fun," they might want to resign from a discussion forum. Also, as people join your company or resign from it, you'll want to add or remove them as appropriate.

In general, unless you change the role of the Default member of a public folder (Author), anyone on your Exchange system can open, read, and add to the messages and postings in a discussion forum. If, however,

you decide that people must sign up for a discussion forum, you have some work to do to keep the folder's list of participants current. For those who want to join, you have to add their names. For those who want out, you have to remove their names. Maintaining the list of members and their permissions in a discussion forum comes down to a matter of control—who controls what and how much control does someone have.

Who's in Control?

In all cases, your Exchange administrator has total authority and can exercise complete control over a public folder. That's the nature of the Exchange administrator's position. Beyond that, folder contacts have equal control over the folder (with the probable exception, at your site, that contacts can't create new public folders willy-nilly).

If you are the contact for a public folder, you can grant additional permissions to participants by assigning them a special role or by modifying their current role so that it has additional powers.

Before we get to that, however, let's see how you go about adding and removing participants. To make these two processes clearer, let's say that you are the contact for the Word Fun public folder. You have changed the default role to None so that you have control over who can read items in the folder, who can add or delete items, and who can edit items. You decide that you want to add some people to the folder's list of contributors. (Later, you'll want to remove some of the contributors because they don't want to participate anymore.) And, you want to let one or two other participants have some additional powers in the administration of the folder.

Adding a Participant

Sirch Smit sends you a message: "Please add me to the Word Fun discussion." You're in a good mood, so you set about it like this:

If right-clicking is unavailable, select the folder, and then choose the File Properties command.

1. Right-click on the Word Fun public folder, and then select Properties from the shortcut menu.
2. Click on the Permissions tab, and then click on the Add button.
3. In the Add Users dialog box, find and select Sirch Smit, and then click on the Add button.

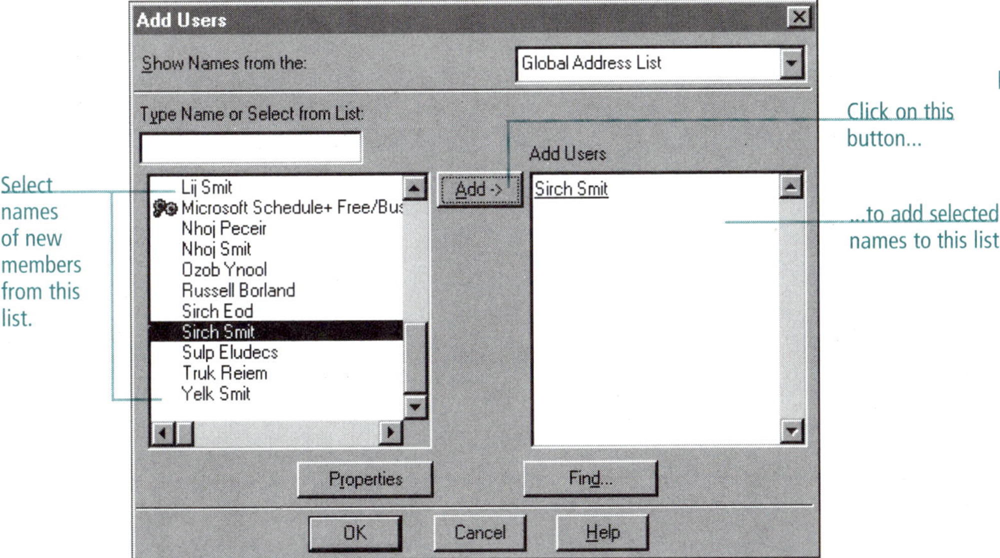

4. Click on OK. Notice that Sirch's name now appears in the name box. Sirch has been assigned the role of None because you set the default to None.
5. Select Sirch Smit, click on the arrow at the right end of the Roles box, and then select Author. Now Sirch can create items, read items, and edit and delete the items that Sirch puts in the folder.
6. Click on OK to finalize this change.

Removing a Participant

Gordo Jones sends you a message: "I'm sick and tired of these bizarre messages. I haven't got time for this anymore. Please remove me from this worthless discussion forum." You're nonplussed by Gordo's attitude, but you agree to remove Gordo from the discussion forum. Here's how you do it:

1. Right-click on the Word Fun public folder, and then select Properties from the shortcut menu.
2. Click on the Permissions tab.
3. Select Gordo Jones in the list, and then click on the Remove button.
4. Click on OK to finalize this change.

If right-clicking is unavailable, select the folder, and then choose the File Properties command.

These steps apply to someone who requests removal from the discussion forum or for someone who leaves the organization and must be removed to prevent Exchange from sending return messages that e-mail cannot be delivered to the (now) "unknown address." For cases in which more force is required, see "Handling Bad Manners," on page 193.

Granting Powers: Assigning Other Roles

When you add a participant to a discussion forum, a default role appears in the Roles box. Each role has specific privileges attached to it. You can change the role for each participant, and you can individually change the privileges of each participant.

You can, of course, turn on and off the privileges one by one in the Permissions section of the Permissions tab. If the resulting combination of powers is the same as one of the predefined roles, Exchange assigns that role to the selected participant. If the combination of privileges is different from any of the built-in roles, Exchange assigns Custom as the role. You won't see this role in the Roles list; it appears only when you change an assigned role in a way that doesn't match any of the preset roles.

The following table lists the roles and their respective privileges. (The role None is not listed because None has no privileges.) Following the table is an example of a custom role you might set up.

	Roles						
Privileges	Author	Contributor	Editor	Owner	Publishing Author	Publishing Editor	Reviewer
Create Items	✓	✓	✓	✓	✓	✓	
Read Items	✓		✓	✓	✓	✓	✓
Create Subfolder				✓	✓	✓	
Folder Owner				✓			
Folder Contact				✓			
Edit Items/None		✓					✓
Edit Items/Own	✓				✓		
Edit Items/All			✓	✓		✓	
Delete Items/None		✓					✓
Delete Items/Own	✓				✓		
Delete Items/All			✓	✓		✓	

Example of a Custom Role

Suppose that you have a participant, Ense Rodnev, whose assigned role is a Reviewer. As you can see in the table above, a Reviewer can read items but can't do anything else. Now you decide that Ense is to be the keeper of the public morals as well as of company security. To perform this role properly, Ense needs to be able to delete items that shouldn't be in the public folder, regardless of how limited the membership. You need to customize Ense's role as a reviewer, but you don't want to give Ense more power than Ense really needs.

Here's what you do:

1. Right-click on the Word Fun public folder, and then select Properties from the shortcut menu.
2. Click on the Permissions tab.

If right-clicking is unavailable, select the folder, and then choose the File Properties command.

Select the member's name to change the member's role.

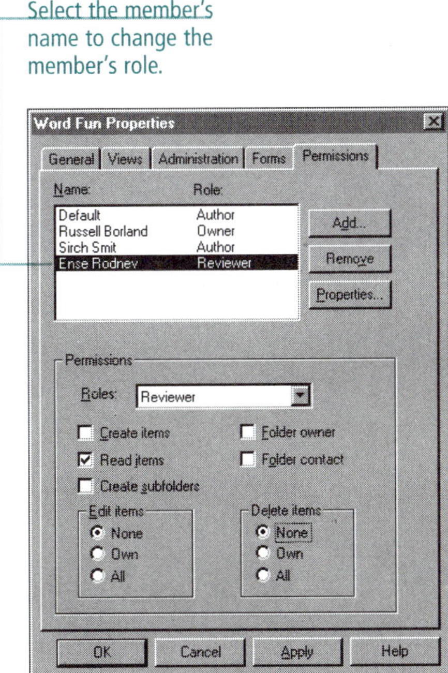

3. Select Ense Rodnev in the list, and then click on the All option under Delete Items. Ense's role now becomes Custom.

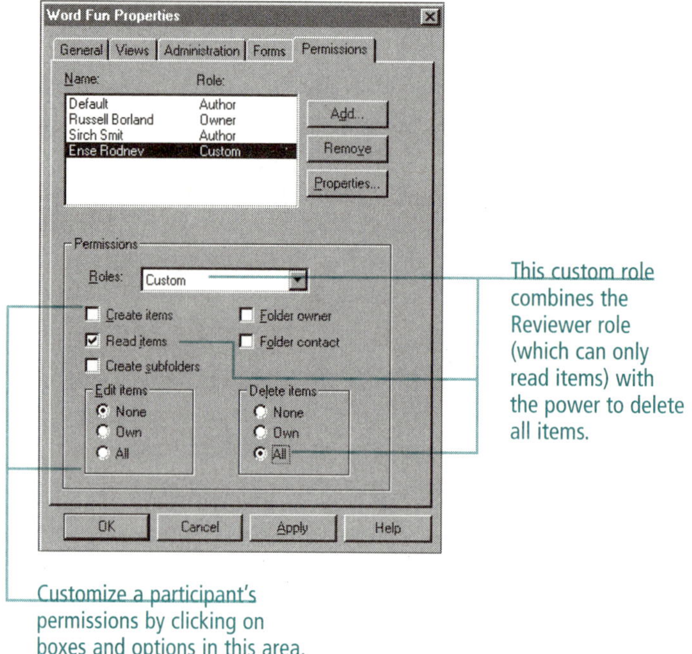

This custom role combines the Reviewer role (which can only read items) with the power to delete all items.

Customize a participant's permissions by clicking on boxes and options in this area.

4. Click on OK to finalize this change.

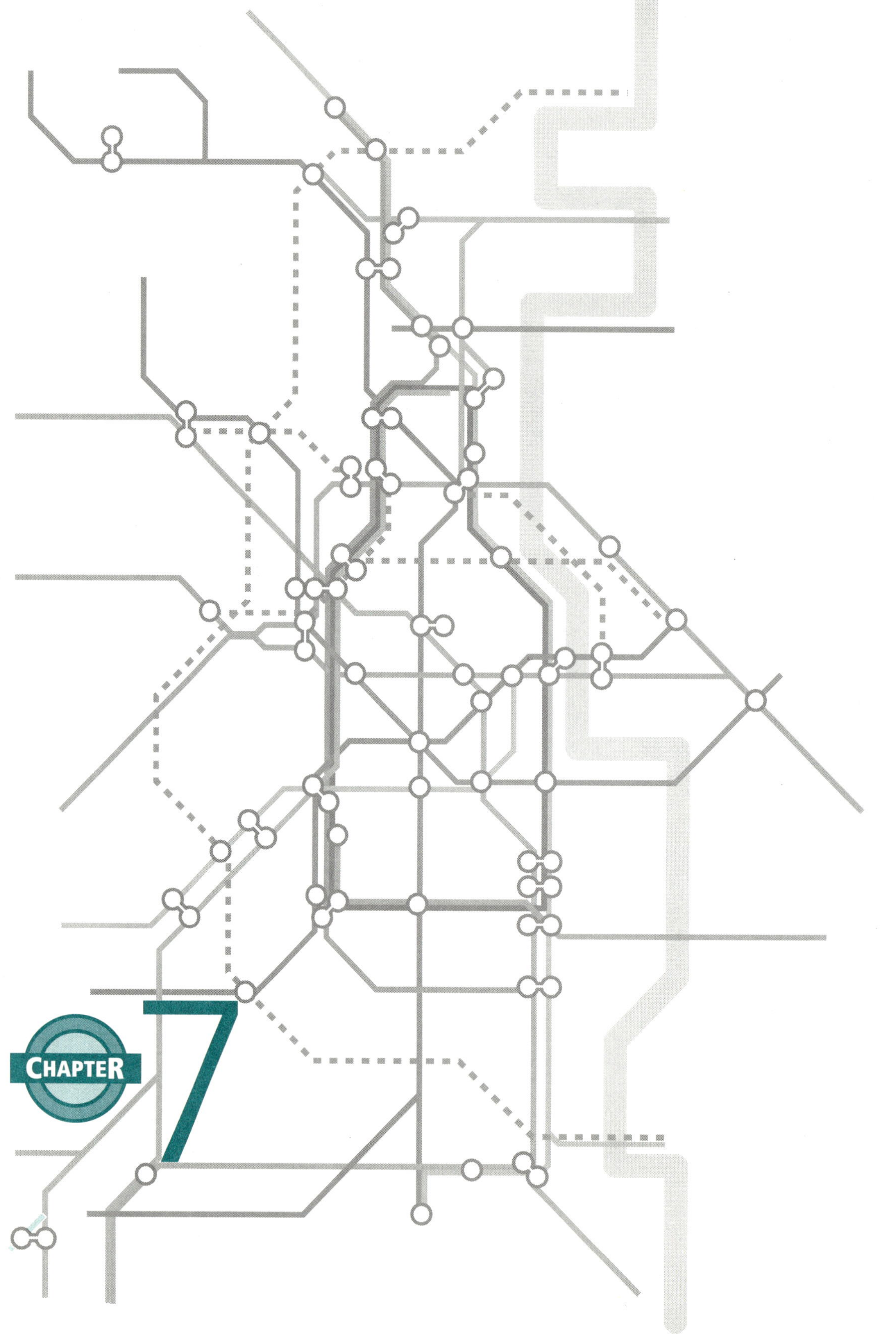
CHAPTER
7

Controlling Forum Exchanges

One of the amazing things that happens occasionally when people conduct electronic exchanges is a drop in courtesy. Some people simply lose their manners when they aren't talking face-to-face. Bad manners, insensitive and abusive discussions, and socially unacceptable messages and documents can find their way into your discussion forum. At times like these, the discussion forum moderator needs to step in and remind participants to mind their manners and, if necessary, remove offending materials from the forum. In this chapter, you'll learn how to control exchanges on a discussion forum.

Scenes from This Chapter

Caveat—Something to Be Aware Of

The following descriptions and actions apply to a discussion forum's owner (often called the "moderator")—the person who has control of the discussion forum. If you are not the moderator, you might not be able to remove inappropriate materials from a discussion forum. You can, however, make the forum moderator and other participants aware of instances of bad manners.

Because a discussion forum is considered a "company resource," your company has both the right and the obligation to ensure that the "resource" is being used according to company policy and applicable laws, statutes, and regulations. A company that allows discussion forums can face criminal and civil penalties as a result of the misdeeds of discussion forum participants. Many companies are content to let discussion forum participants and moderators set and enforce the proper guidelines for discussion forum exchanges. Still, the company is ultimately responsible and so retains the right to shut off any discussion forum it deems inappropriate. This is not an endorsement of censorship. It's a fact of the business, social, political, and legal considerations a company faces at this time.

Scenario

A participant in the Word Fun discussion forum starts posting messages and documents that contain racist, sexist, and otherwise socially unacceptable language. There's nothing fun about the material the participant posts. You remind all the participants that such materials are not only unacceptable but are potentially dangerous and legally actionable for a participant who posts such materials, for the forum moderator, and for the company for "allowing" such behavior. You must delete the inappropriate postings, remove the participant from Word Fun forum, and give several reminders not to post such material again.

Handling Bad Manners

Most of the discussion forums I've seen are in organizational settings. In many ways, the members of the discussion forum are pretty keen about upbraiding forum members who display "bad manners"— obscene, prejudicial, distasteful, hateful, spiteful, or other offensive messages and postings. On occasion, however, some people just won't take the hint from their peers, and the forum's moderator needs to intervene. The moderator's intervention can take several forms:

- A private message from the moderator or another organization official reminding the offender of the guidelines for good manners.
- A message from the moderator or another organization official broadcast to all members reminding them of the guidelines for good manners.
- Removal of the offender from the list of those privileged to participate in the forum and removal of the offender's messages and postings from the public folder. (See "Removing Inappropriate Exchanges," on page 197.)
- Blocking messages and postings from known offenders. This is a very radical and forceful step to take; details follow.

> **Note** You can block messages only for folders for which you are the owner or contact.

Blocking Known Offenders

You have three ways to deal with messages from participants who offend the standards of conduct for a discussion forum:

- Set up Exchange to send an automatic reply to the offender.
- Automatically move messages and postings from the offender to another folder.
- Automatically return messages and postings to the offender.

If right-clicking is unavailable, select the public folder, and then choose the File Properties command.

To set up any one of these methods, do the following:

1. Right-click on the public folder, and then select Properties from the shortcut menu.
2. Click on the Administration tab, and then click on the Folder Assistant button.

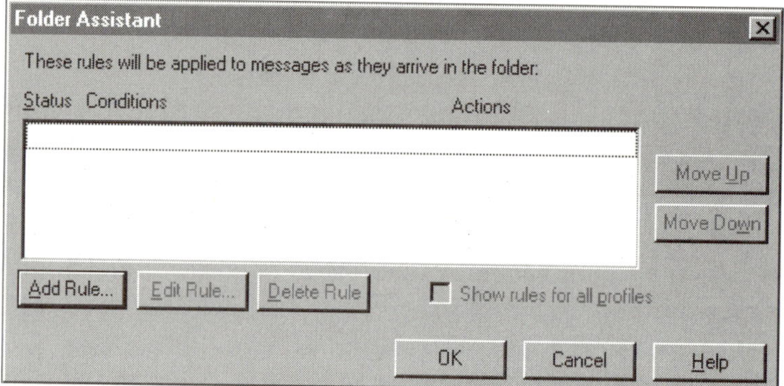

3. Click on the Add Rule button. The Edit Rule dialog box appears.

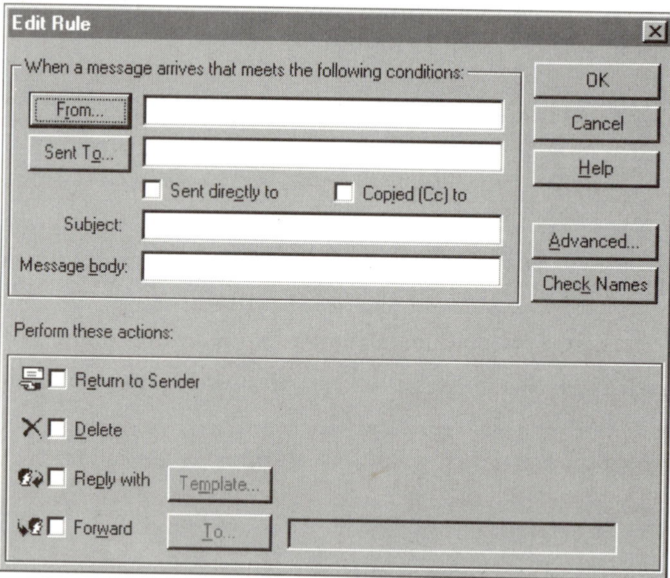

4. In the From box in the Edit Rule dialog box, type the name of the person whose messages and postings you want to reply to automatically. Alternatively, you can click on the From

button to select names in the Choose Sender dialog box, which is similar to an address book dialog box.

Note If you don't specify names in the From box and don't set up any other rules, Exchange will perform the specified action on all messages sent to the folder.

5. In the area labeled Perform These Actions, choose the options you want to use:
   - To send an automatic reply to the offender, select the Reply With check box (a check mark appears), and then click on the Template button.

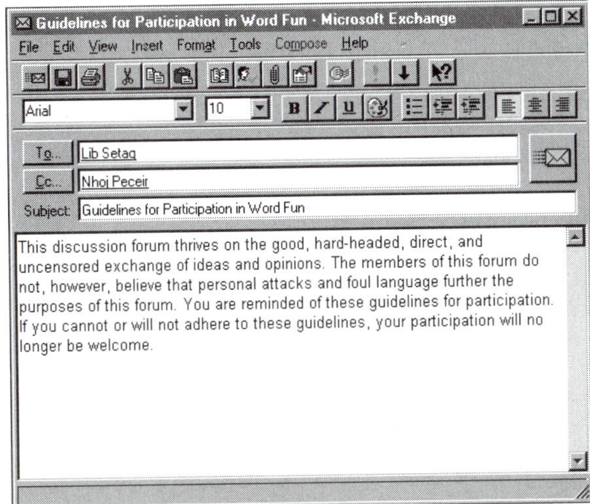

If you want the reply to be sent to others besides the individual originator, type the names of the additional recipients in the To or Cc boxes. Also type a Subject line and an appropriate message, such as:

> This discussion forum thrives on the good, hard-headed, direct, and uncensored exchange of ideas and opinions. The members of this forum do not, however, believe that personal attacks and foul language further the purposes of this forum. You are reminded of these guidelines for participation. If you cannot or will not adhere to these guidelines, your participation will no longer be welcome.

If you are blocking an offender's messages, your reply message might be stronger, such as:

> Because of repeated offenses against the members of this discussion forum, your messages and postings are no longer welcome. We have set up a mechanism for preventing your messages from appearing in our public folder, and we are returning all your messages unposted.

Close the message window and click on the Yes button to save changes when prompted.

- To automatically forward messages and postings to another folder, select the Forward check box (a ✔ appears), and then click on the To button.

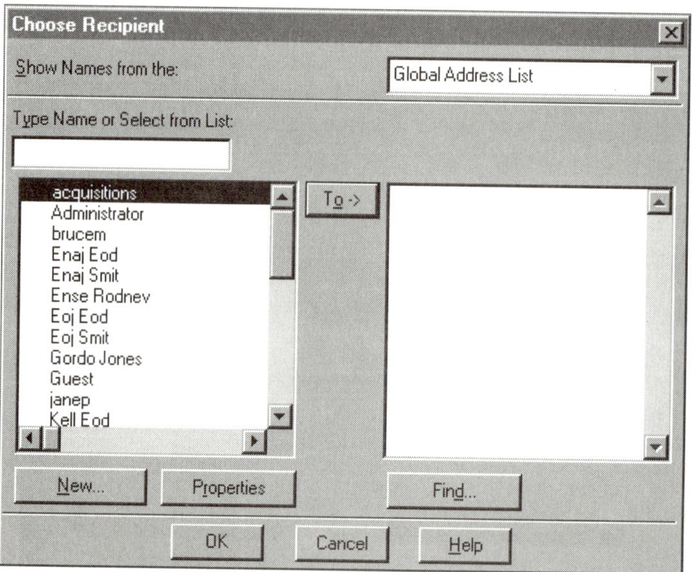

Select the recipients to whom you want to forward the incoming messages. You can also forward messages and postings to other folders. Click on OK in the Choose Recipient dialog box.

- To automatically return messages and postings to the sender, make sure all other boxes are unchecked, and then select the Return To Sender check box (a ✔ appears).

6. Click on OK in the Edit Rule dialog box. If you want to add more rules, click on the Add Rule button again. If you want to change a rule, select the rule, and then click on the Edit Rule button. If you want to get rid of a rule, select the rule, click on the Delete Rule button, and then click on the Yes button to confirm that you want to delete this rule.
7. Click on the Close button in the Folder Assistant dialog box, and then click on OK in the Properties dialog box.

Removing Inappropriate Exchanges

If you are the contact (Owner) or Publishing Editor of a discussion forum, you have the power to delete inappropriate exchanges from the public folder. If you are the contact (Owner), Editor, or Publishing Editor of a discussion forum, you have the power to edit inappropriate exchanges in the public folder.

You'll want to delete exchanges that contain no value. You might want to edit exchanges that contain some value for members of the discussion forum but which also contain inappropriate content. You, your organization, and the discussion forum members will have to decide what content is inappropriate.

To delete inappropriate exchanges, do the following:

1. Select the messages and postings you want to remove.
2. Click on the Delete button on the Exchange toolbar.

To edit inappropriate exchanges, follow these steps:

1. Double-click on the icon for the message or posting.
2. Delete or change the inappropriate content in the Subject line and message area of the message or posting and in the Keywords box of a posting.
3. Click on the Close box in the upper right corner of the message or posting window.
4. Click on the Yes button to save the changes you've made to the message.

MICROSOFT EXCHANGE IN BUSINESS

PART 3

One of the greatest headaches of working on any project is keeping track of project information. During the course of a project, there's a constant need to define task lists and assign tasks to team members, to track the progress of each task (or part of a task), and to monitor overall project progress. You also need to manage schedules, keep track of decisions, and set up meetings.

Microsoft Exchange provides several tools that you can use to manage a project and to review and share information about its progress. For collecting and sharing information, you set up a public folder for the project. For easy mail connections among project team members, you set up a group name. You can schedule regular and special meetings of the project team, and you can assign and schedule tasks for team members and then check on the progress of individual tasks or of the overall project. In this part, you'll learn how to use Exchange and Schedule+ to share and control project information.

Project Information

CHAPTER
8

Setting Up a Project Folder

Now you've got a project to manage. Never mind that you might be the only member of the project team or that the team includes some of your fellow jokers. The project team is going to create lots of information—mail messages, memos, art, meeting notes, and who knows what else. To share all the project information, you set up a public folder in which you'll keep the artifacts created during the project's course. In this chapter, you'll learn how.

Scenes from This Chapter

Scenario

You're working for a company that develops and sells games, both physical games (board games, for example) and electronic games. Your project team has to create a new game.

You have decided on a game idea (which you're calling Bozo Bit—at least for the time being), and now you need to create the game structure, develop and write the rules and strategies, and package the game. These diverse tasks require several people to be working on the project and, in some cases, several people on each task. You need to assign, track, and collect the efforts of each team member as well as manage the progress of the project as a whole.

As your team starts to develop the new game, you and the other team members send messages and post reports, memos, and notes about your thoughts and research to a project folder that is set up to share information about the project.

As you post messages and other documents to the project folder, your team compiles a historical record of the game's development. Any team member can refer to the record at any time. In addition, as the need arises, sales and marketing teams can refer to your project folder to understand the background and development of the game as a basis for an effective marketing and sales campaign.

Creating the Project Folder

To set up a new project folder, you need to create a new public folder. In most cases, you must have permission from the Exchange administrator to set up a public folder, or you have to ask the Exchange administrator to set up the folder for you. For a project folder, the administrator will make you—the project manager—the folder contact. Then, as folder contact, you set up the rest of the folder's characteristics.

In case you have permission to create public folders on your Exchange system, here's how you do it:

1. Click on the All Public Folders icon.
2. Choose the File New Folder command. The New Folder dialog box appears, shown on the next page.

3. Type a name for the new public folder (such as *Bozo Bit*), and then click on OK.

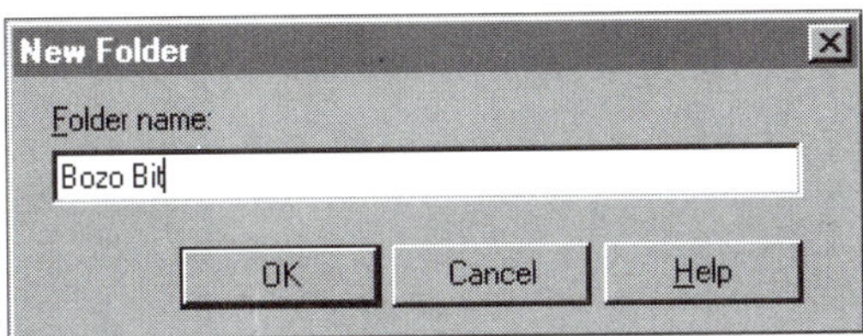

Once the public folder for your project is set up, you need to set up your project folder with appropriate properties. These include the following:

- *Subfolders.* Follow the steps listed above to create subfolders, but click on the project folder (Bozo Bit) in step 1 and type a name for a subfolder in step 3. You might, for example, set up subfolders for project status, project documents, project deliverables, miscellaneous project information and messages, and the project budget, among other categories that come to mind.
- *Permissions.* Give permissions to the project team members to create and read items in the folder. (See "Setting Up a Roster of Team Members," next.)
- *Message templates and forms.* Create project message templates and other forms for collecting, storing, and retrieving project information. (See "Creating a Project Report Form," on page 228, and "Creating a Project Message Template," on page 256.)

Setting Up a Roster of Team Members

Putting together a roster of team members who can use a project folder is a fairly straightforward task. Basically, you have to select the names of the team members from the Address Book and give them the proper permissions. You will also be responsible for removing the names of lapsed team members—people who are no longer associated with the project and who no longer need to visit or use the project folder.

Adding New Members to a Project Folder

To add team members' names to a project folder and give them the proper permissions, do the following:

If right-clicking is unavailable, click on the public folder, and then choose the File Properties command.

1. Right-click on the project folder, and then select Properties from the shortcut menu.
2. Click on the Permissions tab. Notice that the tab has a "Default" entry with the role of Author. This means that people who aren't explicitly added to the list of permissions will have the role of Author. Having the Author role means a person can add new items to the folder, read everything in the folder, and can edit and delete items he or she contributes.

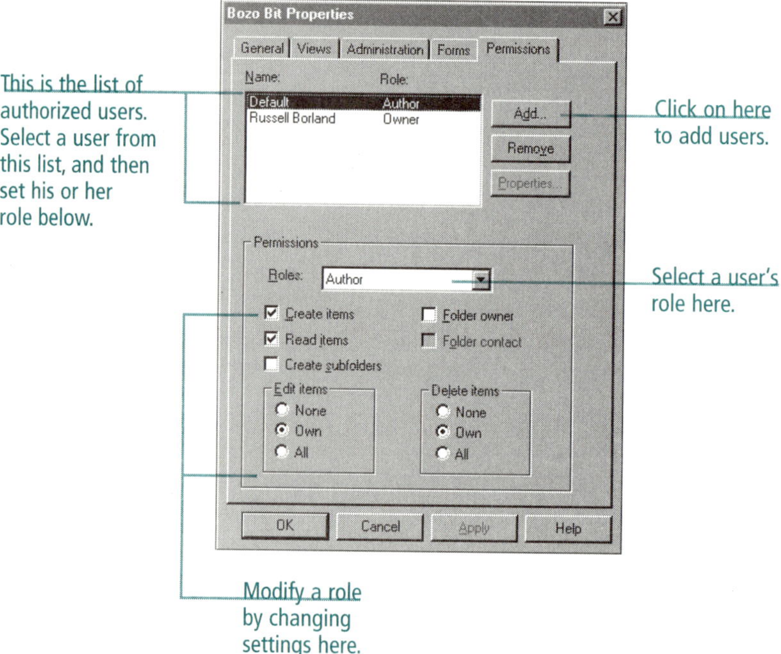

3. Click on the Add button.
4. In the Add Users dialog box, find and select the names of the people who are members of the project team. Hold down Ctrl as you click to select more than one name at a time.

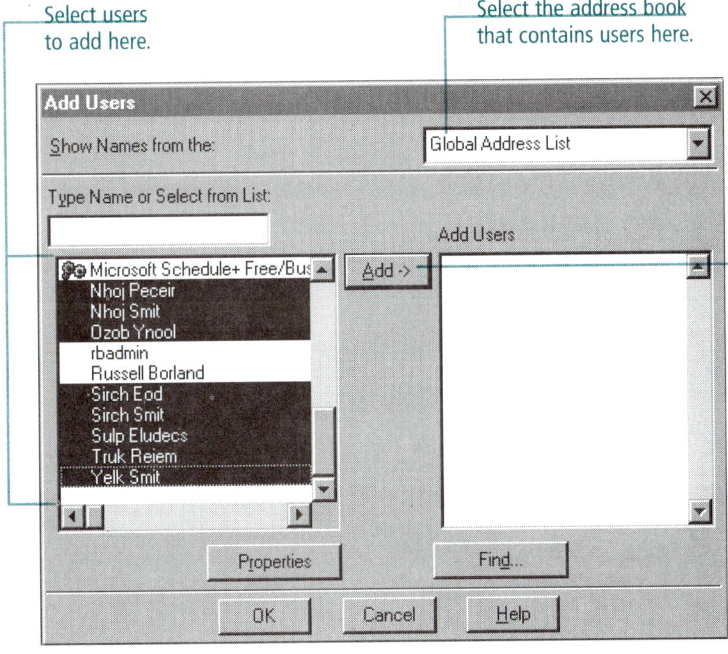

5. Click on the Add button, and then click on OK. The names now appear in the dialog box and are assigned the role of Author.
6. If you want some team members to have more permissions than the Author role grants, select each name, and then use the check boxes and other options in the Permissions area either to select a different role or to specify the additional permissions you want to give to the person. If the combination of permissions matches one of the roles set up in Exchange, Exchange automatically assigns that role. If the combination of permissions doesn't match a standard role, the role is listed as Custom.

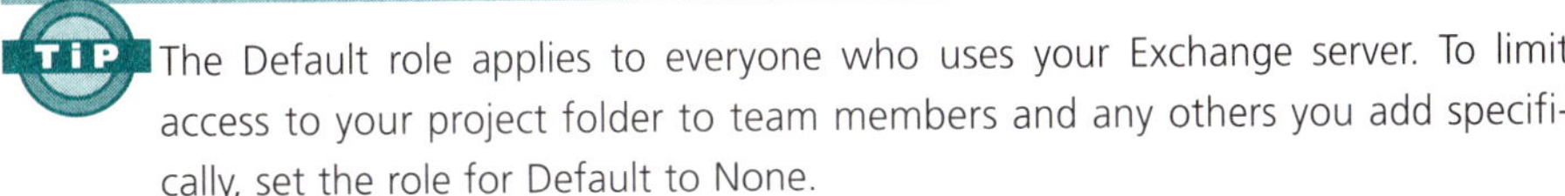

The Default role applies to everyone who uses your Exchange server. To limit access to your project folder to team members and any others you add specifically, set the role for Default to None.

7. When you're done adding members and setting their permissions, click on OK in the project folder properties sheet.

Removing Lapsed Members from a Project Folder

Well, Sirch Eod is off the team and no longer needs to use the project folder. Maybe Sirch moved to another department, or maybe you threw Sirch off the team and now want to block further access to the project folder. In either case, you need to remove this lapsed member from the project folder; you need to retract permissions. Here's what you do:

If right-clicking is unavailable, click on the public folder, and then choose the File Properties command.

1. Right-click on the project folder, and then select Properties from the shortcut menu.
2. Click on the Permissions tab.
3. Select Sirch Eod in the list, and then click on the Remove button.
4. Click on OK to finalize this change.

Adding Materials to the Project Folder

A project folder, like other public folders in Exchange, can contain mail messages and postings as well as various files, such as Schedule+ files, documents from a word processor, spreadsheets from a spreadsheet program, or art from a drawing or graphics program. For each of these types of materials—a message, a posting, and a file—you use a different method to add the material to the project folder. But for all three methods and types of materials, certain conditions must be met so that a public folder works well as a project folder:

- Each member of the project team must have permission to create and read items in the project folder. In most cases, the Author role is sufficient. In some cases, you might want certain members of the project team to have the Editor, Publishing Author, or Publishing Editor role. You might also want someone else to have the Folder Contact role in case you or another project manager aren't available.
- The views of the folder should always include the Item Type column so that you can tell if the item is a mail message, a posting, or a file.
- You'll probably always want to know who the author of an item is, so be sure to include the From column in the folder views.

- You'll also probably want to know the date an item was put in the folder. Include the Received column to show this.

The Item Type, From, and Received columns are part of the standard view of a folder. You don't have to change the view to get them. If you do decide to change the view, however, you should probably retain these three columns.

Adding Mail Messages to a Project Folder

You can add mail messages to a project folder either by moving or copying a message to the folder or by sending the message directly to the folder. These methods are essentially the same methods you use to work with mail messages in other public folders.

To move or copy a mail message to a project folder, do the following:

1. Open the folder that contains the message you want to move to the project folder.
2. Expand the Public Folders folder to display the project folder you will be moving the message to.
3. To move the message, simply drag the message to the project folder. To copy the message, hold down the Ctrl key as you drag the message to the project folder.

Before your team can send messages directly to a project folder, the folder needs to be set up to receive them. There are three ways to do this:

- Have the Exchange administrator set up an account for the project folder so that the folder's name appears in the Address Book. Team members can then select the folder's name as an addressee, just as they would select the name of a person.
- Have the Exchange administrator include the project folder in the project's group name (project distribution list), which appears in the Address Book. Then any message sent to the entire project team is also sent to the project folder.
- Have each team member add the project folder name to his or her Personal Address Book. This method does not require that the Exchange administrator add an Exchange account for the project folder. To add the project folder name as an address in each team member's Personal Address Book, have *every* team member take the steps on the following page.

If right-clicking is unavailable, click on the public folder, and then choose the File Properties command.

1. Right-click on the project folder, and then select Properties from the shortcut menu.
2. Click on the Summary tab.

Note You will see the Summary tab only if you are not a contact or owner for a public folder. If you are a contact or owner for a public folder, click on the Administration tab.

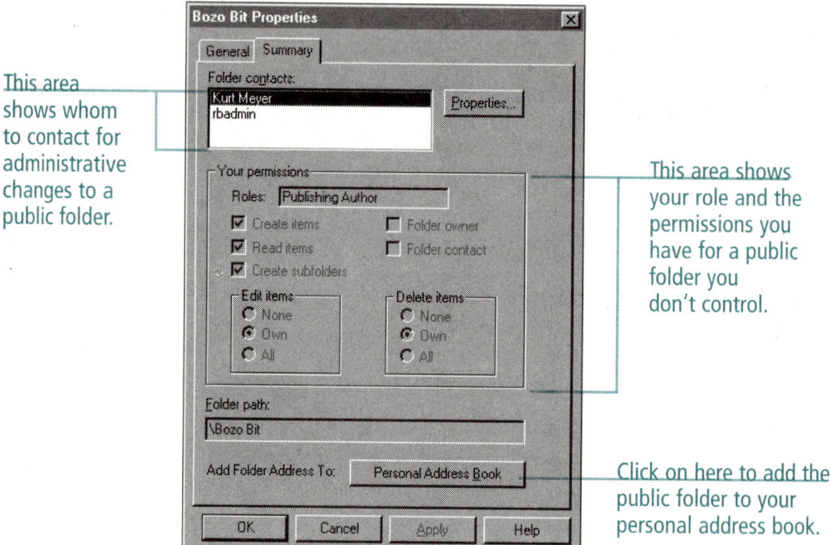

3. Click on the Personal Address Book button, and then click on OK.

After you've set up a project folder to receive messages directly, you can include its name (or the project group name if you had the Exchange administrator set up the project folder as part of the project group name) in the To box or the Cc box when you compose, forward, or reply to a message. Exchange sends the message to the project folder in the same way it sends the message to other team members.

Adding Postings to the Project Folder

As another way to add new information to a public folder, you can either post a notice for a new topic or post a response to a previous posting.

To post a new notice in a public folder, follow these steps:

1. Choose the Compose New Post In This Folder command.

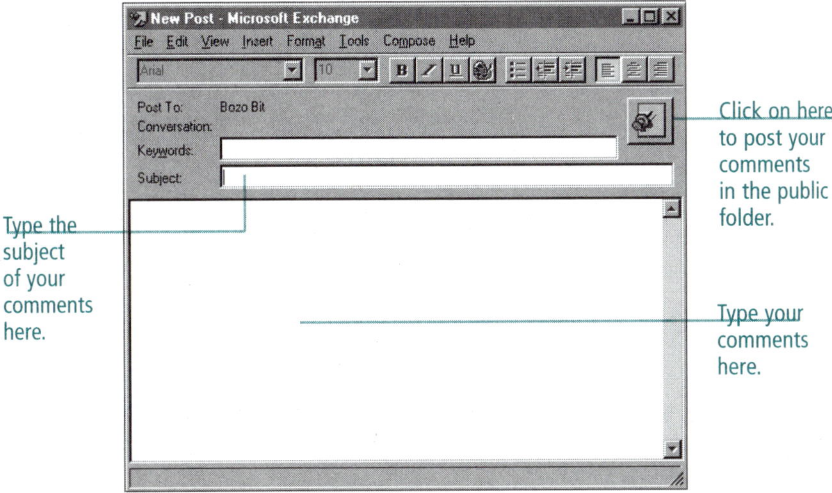

2. Type the topic of your posting in the Subject box, and then type your note.
3. Click on the Post button.

To respond to a posting, do this:

1. Choose the Compose Post Reply In This Folder command.

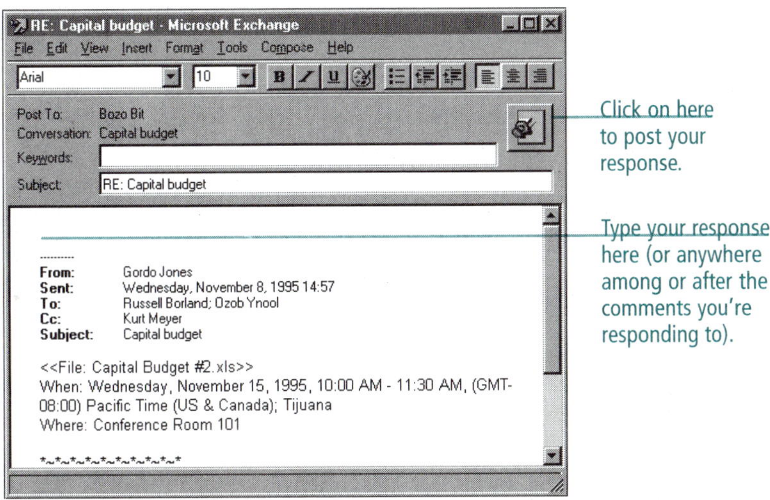

2. Type your reply.
3. Click on the Post button.

Note If you select a posting, the Compose Reply All command is *not* available. If you select a message, the Compose Reply All command *is* available. For both cases (posting or message), you can post a reply posting, send a reply message to the poster or sender, or forward the message or posting.

Adding Files to a Project Folder

Every Exchange folder can contain files. You don't have to wrap a file in a message and send the message to the project folder; you can put the naked file in the project folder for all to see and read. Adding files to a project folder is one operation that you *cannot* perform directly from Exchange. Instead, you have to use the file system (Windows Explorer, Windows Program Manager, or a My Computer window) and Exchange together.

To put files in an Exchange folder, follow these steps:

1. Open the project folder in Exchange.
2. Open a window that shows your file system—for example Windows Explorer or Windows File Manager—and find the file you want to put in the project folder.
3. Arrange the file system window and the Exchange window so that you can see both of them at the same time.

Drag a file from the Explorer window to the public folder's message pane in the Exchange window.

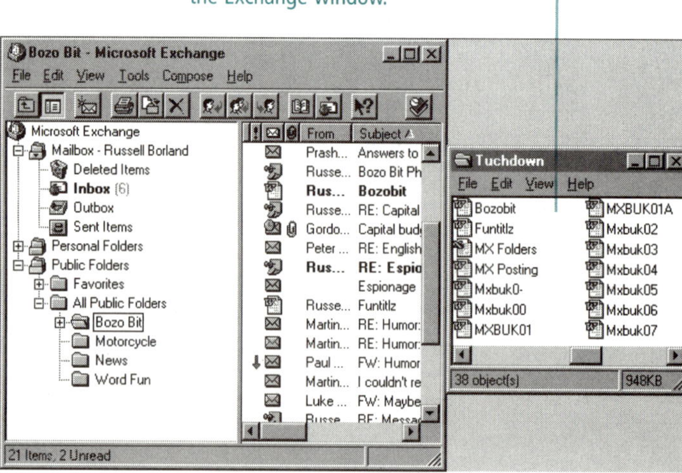

4. Drag the file's icon from the file system window to the project folder's message pane in the Exchange window.

Note This procedure copies the file to the public folder; it does not remove the file from the file system.

Finding Materials in the Project Folder

Most projects generate a lot of materials—messages, schedules, task lists, and descriptive documents. After a while, the project folder can get mighty full. Setting up subfolders for various types of information, tasks, and project phases can help bring some order to the mass of materials, but even subfolders can get full. If you have lots of subfolders—and even sub-subfolders—finding the information you want or need can be quite difficult. Pulling together information from several subfolders to review or to work on some part of a project that doesn't have its own subfolder can take up valuable time.

If you're able to rely on another project team member or an assistant to collect information for you, you can assign the task and go do something else until the materials are ready. Exchange, however, includes some tools you can use to find the materials you want, and these tools are generally faster, more accurate, and more efficient than the fastest human assistant (although not nearly as good company, perhaps). The tools Exchange provides for finding materials in a folder are the Find command, various views of the materials, and filters.

Searching Folder Contents

Exchange provides a Find command to help you locate items in a folder. The Find command works for any Exchange folder, including public folders you use for a project.

To locate specific items in a project folder, do the following:

1. Right-click on the folder you want to look in, and then choose Find from the shortcut menu. The Find dialog box appears.

If right-clicking is unavailable, click on the public folder, and then choose the Tools Find command.

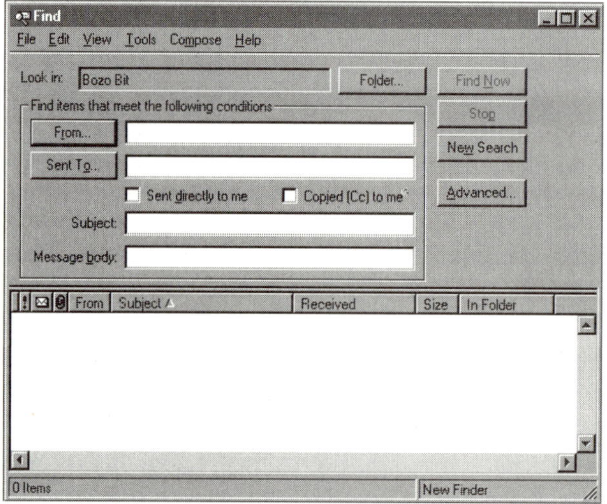

2. Type or select the types of information you want to locate. For more ways to find information, click on the Advanced button, set up the Advanced dialog box, and then click on OK. If you want to look in a folder other than the one that's currently open, you can click on the Folder button, select a different folder, and then click on OK in the Find Items In Folder dialog box.
3. Click on the Find Now button. Exchange displays the messages, postings, and files that match the criteria you set up in the Find and Advanced dialog boxes. If none of the items shown fits your needs, click on the New Search button and set up different criteria.

You can open any of the found items directly from the Find dialog box by double-clicking on the item.

Grouping and Filtering Folder Contents: Choose Your View

As with other public folders in Exchange, you can organize and define views of the items in a project folder. You can change the way the items are grouped, or you can set up a view of the folder to change the order and number of columns and the way items are sorted. You can also apply filters to a project folder to sort out the messages, postings, and files the folder contains.

To group the items in a project folder, do the following:

1. Open the project folder.
2. Choose the View Personal Views command, and then select the view from the submenu that organizes the discussion the way you want it organized.

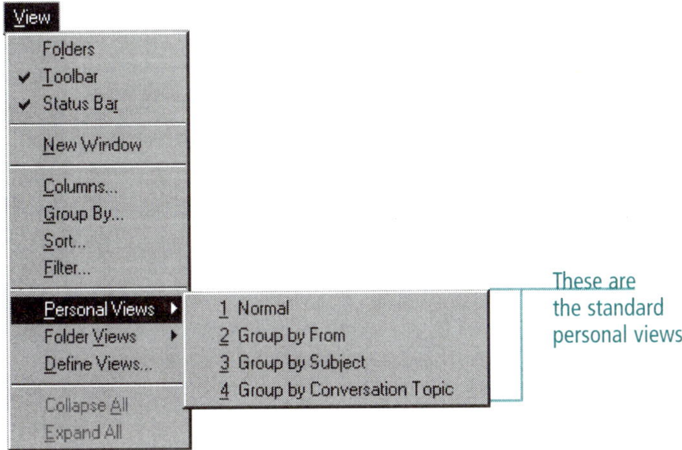

The following table lists the choices and what they do for you.

View	Effect on folder contents
Normal	Displays all items without groupings; use this view to remove groupings created by choosing other views.
Group By From	Groups items by sender; use this view to find all the items from a particular person.
Group By Subject	Groups items under headings taken from the Subject line; use this view to see a list of subjects in the folder.
Group By Conversation Topic	Groups postings by the Discussion lines and groups messages and files by the Subject lines; use this view when the Discussion lines and Subject lines of postings aren't exactly the same, as they won't be for replies, for example.

Setting Up a Personal View

If you need to view the items in a project folder other than by using one of the standard views provided by Exchange, you can do this by creating a personal view of the folder's contents. You can use your new personal view in any folder.

To create a personal view, do this:

1. Choose the View Define Views command.
2. Click on the Personal Views option.
3. Click on the New button.
4. Type a name for this new personal view.
5. Use the options in the Define Views dialog box to set up the view you need. You can change the number and types of columns, change the grouping, change the sorting, and set up a filter, if you want to use one.
6. Click on OK.
7. If you want to apply this personal view right away to the folder you're currently viewing, click on the Apply button.
8. Click on the Close button.

After you define a new personal view, you can switch to it by selecting its name from the submenu that appears beside the View Personal Views command.

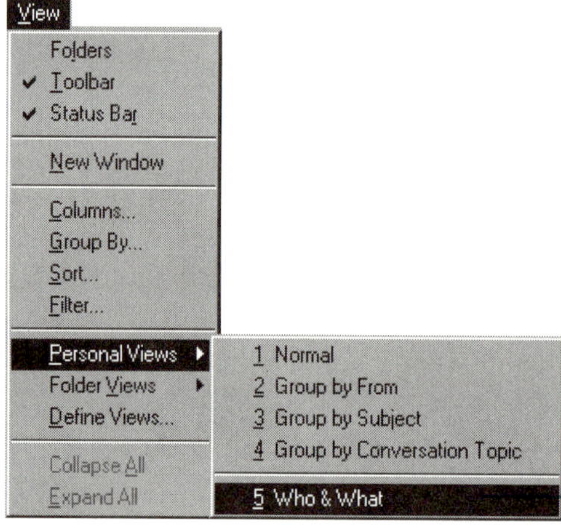

Personal views you create appear at the bottom of the Personal Views submenu.

For more information about defining personal views, see "Columns Right, March: Changing Column Order," on page 159, and "Sorting It Out in Other Ways," on page 160.

Filtering Folder Contents

When you want to restrict the list of items in some particular way *all the time,* you can set up a filter. A filter screens out what you don't want to see and directs Exchange to list only those items you do want to see. A filter can screen items on the basis of one general part of the items—such as the senders' names—or on two or more parts, which makes the resulting list more particular—and shorter. In addition to senders' names, you can filter on the basis of criteria such as whether an item was sent directly to you or on a portion of the text in the Subject box or in the body of the message. Using advanced filter options, you can sort out items with attachments, items received within a specified period, and so on. (For information about all the fields you can use to create a filter, see "Filtering Discussions," on page 166.)

To set up a filter, take these steps:

1. Open the project folder. Exchange uses a filter only in the folder in which you set it up.
2. Choose the View Filter command.

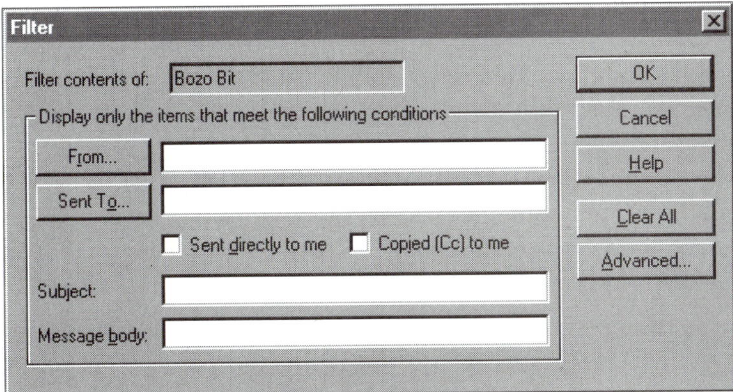

3. Set up the Filter dialog box to tell Exchange what kinds of items you want to see in the folder. The fewer settings you make, the more items you'll see. The more settings you make, the finer the filter.

4. Click on OK. (If you made any settings in the Advanced dialog box, click on OK in both the Advanced dialog box and the Filter dialog box.)

You can still use personal views with—and sort on—the messages and postings that your filter lets through.

Acting on Folder Contents

As materials come into a project folder, you might want to let your team members know what's new. To do this, you can set up a folder rule so that team members are notified automatically when new materials (or new materials of a particular type) are added to the project folder.

For other types of information, you might want some other kind of action to take place when new contents appear in the project folder. You can set up rules for other actions, too.

Setting Up Notices for New Contents

You can set up your project folder to notify you or any and all team members when new items come into the folder. If you've set up your project folder as part of the team group name in the Address Book, you won't need to notify team members about new messages; they'll see them in their own inboxes at the same time as they appear in the folder. But postings and the additions of files to the folder won't usually appear as messages in the team members' inboxes unless you set up the folder to do that.

Let's suppose that when a team member adds a file to the project folder, you want the entire team to know about it. To let them know, you set up a reply that is sent automatically when new documents are put in the folder. Here's how:

If right-clicking is unavailable, click on the public folder, and then choose the File Properties command.

1. Right-click on the project folder, and then choose Properties from the shortcut menu.

Note You can set up automatic notices for folders for which you are the owner or contact.

2. Click on the Administration tab, and then click on the Folder Assistant button.

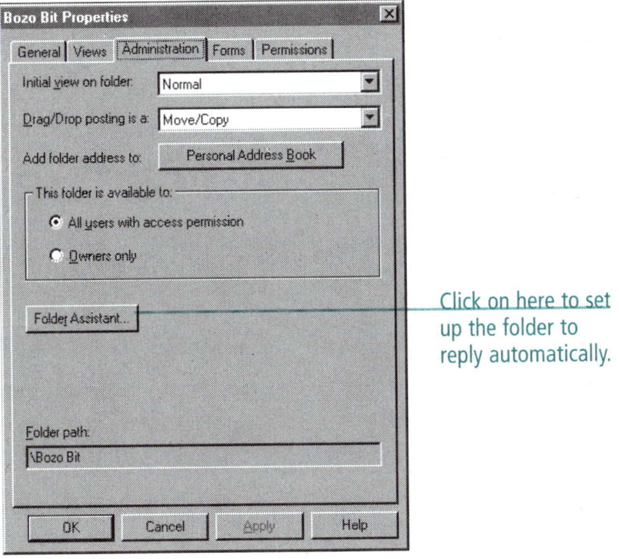

3. Click on the Add Rule button in the Folder Assistant dialog box.

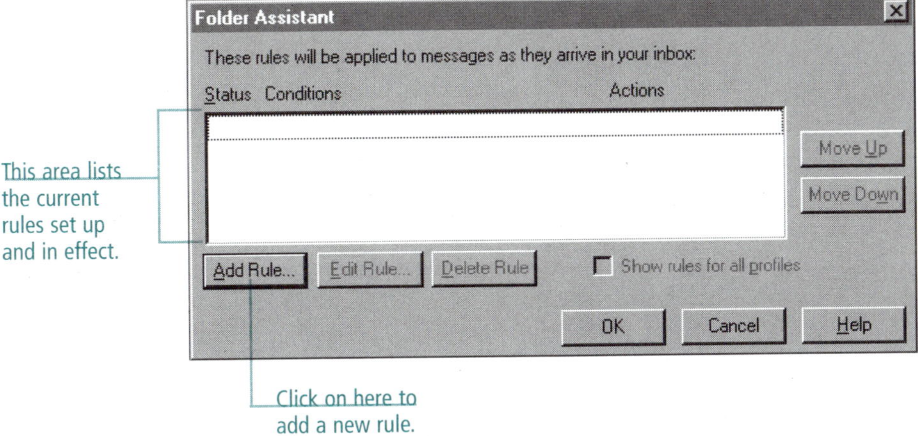

4. Select the Reply With check box in the Edit Rule dialog box, shown at the top of the next page, and then click on the Template button. The Reply Template window appears as shown at the bottom of the next page.

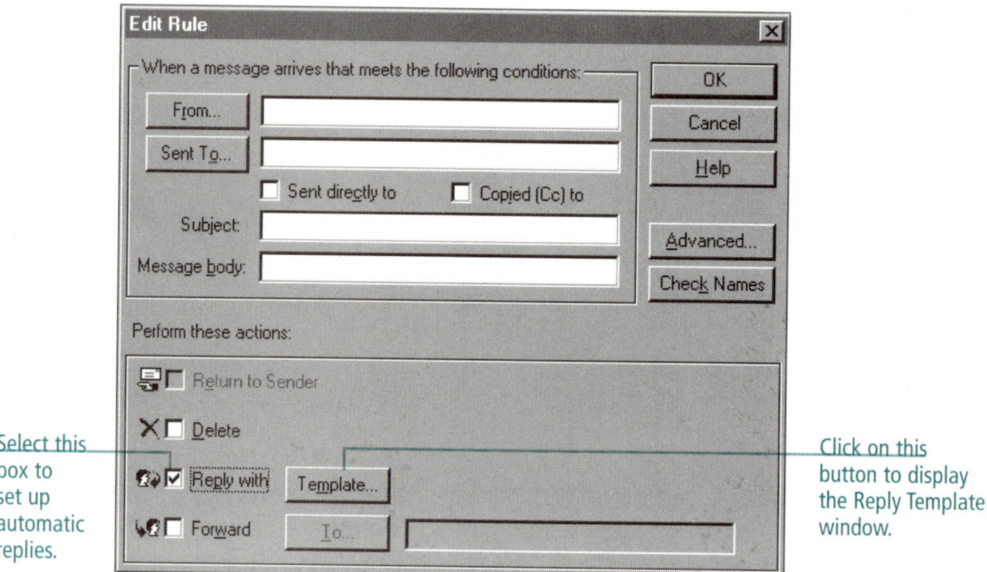

5. In the To box (seen below), type the group name of your project team. You can also add names to the Cc box.
6. Leave the Subject box blank. Exchange will insert the standard "RE:" plus the name of the new document when it sends the automatic message.
7. In the message area, type a standard message, such as:

   This document is now available in the project folder.

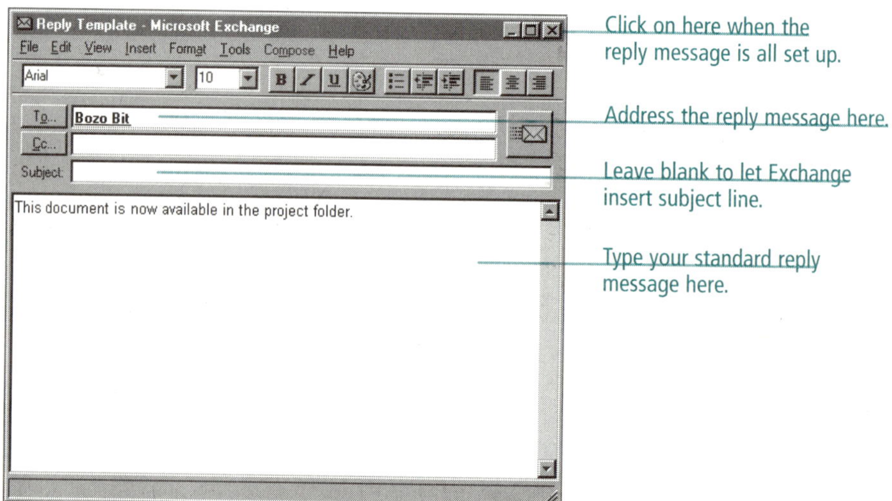

8. Close the Reply Template window, and then click on the Yes button to keep your changes.
9. In the Edit Rule dialog box, click on the Advanced button. The Advanced dialog box appears.
10. Under Show Properties Of, click on the Document option.
11. Fill in one or more of the document properties that you want to trigger an automatic message.

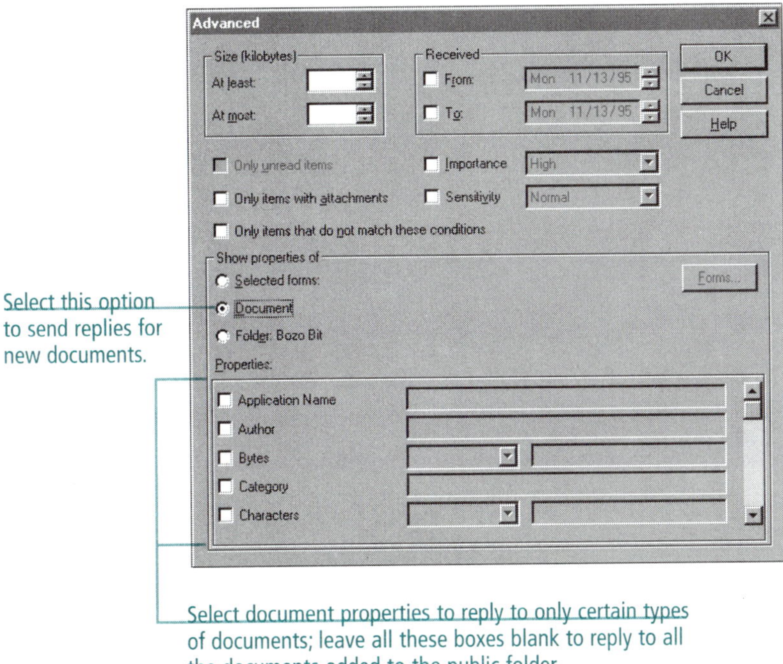

Select this option to send replies for new documents.

Select document properties to reply to only certain types of documents; leave all these boxes blank to reply to all the documents added to the public folder.

For example, if your team creates all of its files in Microsoft Word, you could type that in the Application Name box. If you use various applications for creating project documents, you'd need to set up a separate rule for each application.

You can also use the authors' names as a trigger. For multiple names, type a semicolon between names, like this:

Russell Borland;Ense Rodnev

If you want to reply automatically to all incoming documents, leave the document properties area blank.

12. Click on OK in the Advanced dialog box. If Exchange asks whether you want this rule to apply to all incoming messages, click on the Yes button to accept this filter. Click on the No button and then repeat step 11 to limit replies to a narrower selection of messages, postings, or documents.
13. Click on OK in the Edit Rule dialog box, click on OK in the Folder Assistant dialog box, and then click on OK in the Properties dialog box.

Setting Up Automatic Forwarding of New Folder Contents

One of the setups you can arrange in your project folder is to forward items to people when the items are placed in the folder. Here's what you do:

If right-clicking is unavailable, click on the public folder, and then choose the File Properties command.

1. Right-click on the project folder, and then choose Properties from the shortcut menu.
2. Click on the Administration tab, and then click on the Folder Assistant button.
3. Click on the Add Rule button.
4. In the Edit Rule dialog box, click on the Forward box, and then type a name in the To box or click on the To button to select the name or names for the To box.

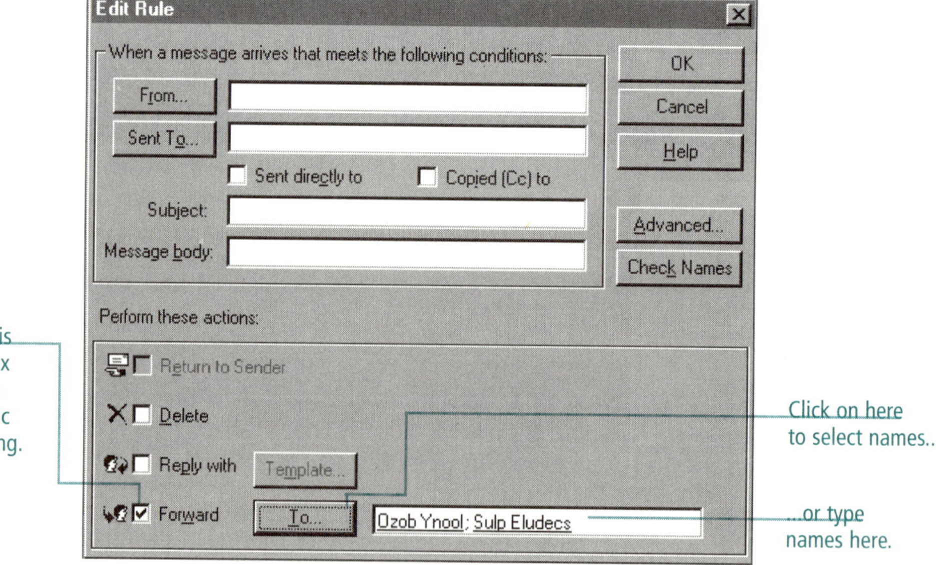

5. Click on the Advanced button.
6. Under Show Properties Of, click on the Document button.
7. Fill in one or more of the document properties that you want to trigger an automatic message.

   For example, you can specify that documents of a certain type, say Microsoft Word documents, get sent to the project's editor. You could set up another rule to have spreadsheets sent to the budget analyst. You can also use the document author's name to direct the document to a particular team member. To specify multiple author names, type a semicolon between them.

   If you want to forward all incoming documents automatically, leave all the document properties blank.
8. Click on OK in the Advanced dialog box. If Exchange asks whether you want this rule to apply to all incoming messages, click on the Yes button to accept this filter. Click on the No button and then repeat step 7 to limit replies to a narrower selection of messages, postings, or documents.
9. Click on OK in the Edit Rule dialog box, click on OK in the Folder Assistant dialog box, and then click on OK in the Properties dialog box.

Now whenever a team member adds a document to the project folder, Exchange automatically forwards a copy of the document to the Inbox of the people whose names you put in the To box in step 4 above.

Removing Materials from a Project Folder

When some message, posting, or file no longer needs to be in a project folder, you (as folder contact) can discard it quite easily. Team members with the Folder Owner or Publishing Editor role can also delete items added by other team members. Remember, of course, that each team member assigned the Author role can delete items she or he put in the folder but not items put there by other team members.

To remove materials from a project folder, do this:

1. Click on the folder to open it.

2. Select the messages, postings, and files that you want to remove. To remove more than one item at a time, hold down the Ctrl key as you click on the items you want to remove.
3. Click on the Delete button on the Exchange toolbar.
4. Click on the Yes button to permanently remove the selected items.

Note Items you delete from a public folder don't go to the Deleted Items folder. That's why you're asked to confirm that you want to permanently delete the items.

Archiving Project Folder Contents

From time to time during a project—and certainly at the end of a project—you'll want to archive materials in the project folder. You can do this to keep a record of what you did and how you did it and at the same time clean out space on your Exchange server for your next project.

Exchange provides no direct way to archive a project folder, but you have a couple of choices for how to archive information nonetheless. To archive a project folder, you can do the following:

- Move or copy items from a project folder to a personal folder.
- Save the items in a file of some kind.
- Drag the items to a folder on your file system (using Windows Explorer, Windows File Manager, or a My Computer window).

Note It would be most uncommon if your Exchange administrator did not regularly back up your Exchange server, so in most cases you can be sure that the contents of your project folder are safely backed up. You can create your own archive copy for the convenience of having the file readily available when you need it.

Archiving in a Personal Folder

Your project folder, like other public folders, lives on the Exchange server, not on your personal computer's hard disk. Personal folders live on your personal computer's hard disk.

One way to archive a project folder is to copy items from the public folder to a personal folder. To do this, follow these steps:

1. Create a subfolder in your Personal Folders folder and give it the same name as the project's public folder.

2. Open the project's public folder and select all the items.
3. Drag the items to the folder you created in your Personal Folders folder.

Once the project folder items are in your personal folders, you can make a backup copy of your PST file. Your PST file usually is called MAILBOX.PST. You can also copy your PST file to a network server that is regularly backed up.

Archiving in a File

This method of archiving is a bit odd. You might expect that Exchange would have a command that specifically backs up, archives, saves, or exports folders to some kind of file. But NOH-oh-oh! So, instead of archiving a folder, you archive the items in the folder to some kind of file.

Now I know that "some kind of file" sounds pretty vague, but as you might guess, there's a reason; namely, you can, in one specific case, archive a folder to three different kinds of files. In all other cases, you have only one choice for the type of file.

- If you select only *one* message or posting in a folder, you can save that item as Text Only, as Rich Text Format, or as Message Format.
- If you select two or more messages or postings, you can save the selected items *only* as Text Only.
- If you select a single document file and choose the File Save As command, you see a standard Save As dialog box, just as if you were working in the application that created the document in the first place.

Note By the way, you probably won't need to "save" document files in the project folder. You probably have copies of those files on your hard disk already.

- If you select a file and any other item, the File Save As command is disabled.

  So you've got two choices:

  - Select each message or posting and save it in either Rich Text Format or Message Format. This might take quite a while because a project can generate a lot of items.

- Select a group of messages and postings (which could mean all the messages and postings) and save them all at once in one text file.

In all cases, the steps are the same.

1. Open the project's public folder.
2. Select the item or items that you want to save.
3. Choose the File Save As command.

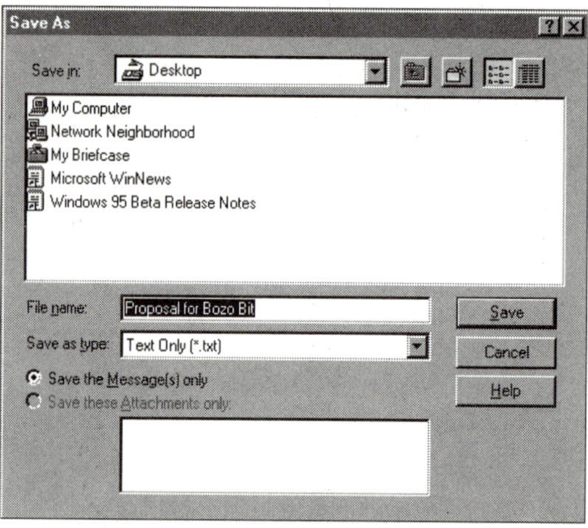

4. Switch to the disk and folder in which you want to store the items you're saving.
5. In the File Name box, type a name for the new file that will contain the items you're saving.
6. In the Save As Type box, select the format for the file. Remember that in most cases, you'll probably have only one choice: Text Only.
7. Click on the Save button.

Archiving in the File System

Here is the best and the brightest, even if the most indirect, way to archive project folder items—drag them to the file system! You can use a disk on your personal computer or on a computer anywhere on the network.

Here's what you do:

1. Open the project folder.
2. Select all the items in the folder (or at least the items that you want to archive).
3. Open the Windows Explorer window (or the Windows File Manager or the My Computer window) and switch to the disk and folder in which you want to archive the project folder items.
4. Drag the project folder items to the folder on your file system.

Copies of each message, posting, and file that you selected in the project folder are saved as separate files with names taken from the subject line or the filename of the items.

Removing a Project Folder

After you archive a project folder (see "Archiving Project Folder Contents," on page 222), you're ready to remove the folder. Removing a project folder after the project is finished is good for security reasons and also helps to save space on your Exchange server.

To remove a project folder, follow these steps:

1. Click on the folder you want to remove.
2. Click on the Delete button on the Exchange toolbar.
3. Click on the Yes button to confirm that you want to remove the folder and all its contents. This will also delete any subfolders the project folder might contain.

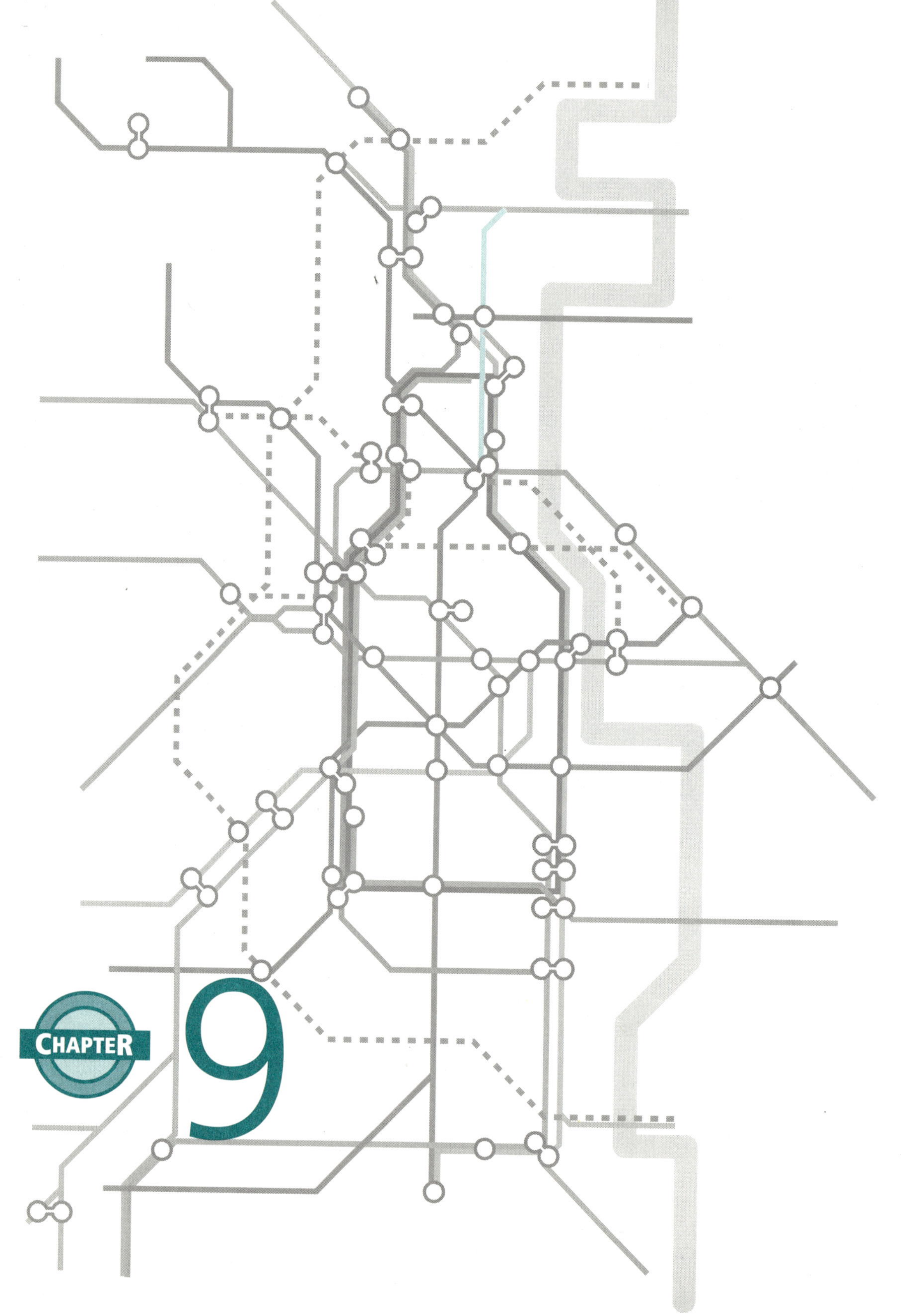
CHAPTER
9

Setting Up Project Information Messages

As a project progresses, the fur starts to fly. Team members begin to pass notes and reports about this, that, and the other thing. Although an occasional personal or nonessential message might get through, more often than not team members will use Microsoft Exchange to share important information about the project. For status and progress reports, a standard form can help team members organize information and share it in a common format. For information about certain tasks, it can be handy to have a standard message template. In this chapter you'll learn how to create a project report form and a project message template.

Scenes from This Chapter

Scenario

Some of the information that your team shares regularly about the Bozo Bit project fits properly within a standard message format. Some information is best suited to a form that you create to share the information. For example, each team member is responsible for reporting project status or project problems. You might want to create a standard form for their reports and for passing on information about features and quirks of the game you're creating.

Using Exchange, you create some message templates for your team to use to share information, and you create forms for standard reports. You have no way, other than a leader's coercion and peer pressure, to enforce use of the message templates and forms. But if you create templates and forms that are well suited to the task, your team members will probably use them gladly—they'll like the forms for convenient reporting and for receiving information from others in a standard format.

Note A project group name in the Global Address List can assist your team in its communications by making it easy to send messages to the entire group. In addition, a project group name makes it easy to set up a team meeting with Schedule+. You'll read more about scheduling a team meeting in Chapter 10, "Scheduling Project Meetings." The most efficient and the preferred way to set up a group project name is through your Exchange administrator. You send a request to the server administrator, who then sets up and maintains the project name.

Creating a Project Report Form

An important activity of managing every project is letting team leaders and team members know what you have accomplished. A project report gives you the credit you deserve for the good work you've done and lets others know if the pieces they need from you are ready to integrate with their work. Taken together, project reports that you prepare give an overall picture of the project's progress.

While you can (and probably will) use the Schedule+ To Do List to adjust the percentage completed for the tasks you have to work on, a project report often provides information that can't be reduced to a simple number. Your team leaders and team members want to know what problems you have encountered and what solutions you have devised. Team members want to know if they can use your solutions to solve similar problems that they encounter in their own tasks. Also, team members want to know what problems you have had so that they can watch for related ones in their work.

A standard form makes reporting and reviewing project status easier for everyone on the project team. In this section, you'll create a project report form using the Exchange Forms Designer wizard. The project report form will contain an area to specify the task you're reporting about, the percentage completed, the problems you encountered, the solutions you devised, the next phase of work you're undertaking, the approximate date you'll finish the task, and any other information about your work that your team members need to know.

Note The Microsoft Exchange Forms Designer is an additional component of Exchange that is not installed by default. In order to create forms, you must first install the Exchange Forms Designer. Check with your Exchange administrator for the location of the Exchange Forms Designer files and the installation procedure. You should also note that you can create a form and add it to a personal folder, but you can't add the form to a public folder unless you have Owner permission.

To create a project report form to use with the Bozo Bit project, take these steps:

1. Choose the Tools Application Design command, and then choose Forms Designer from the submenu.

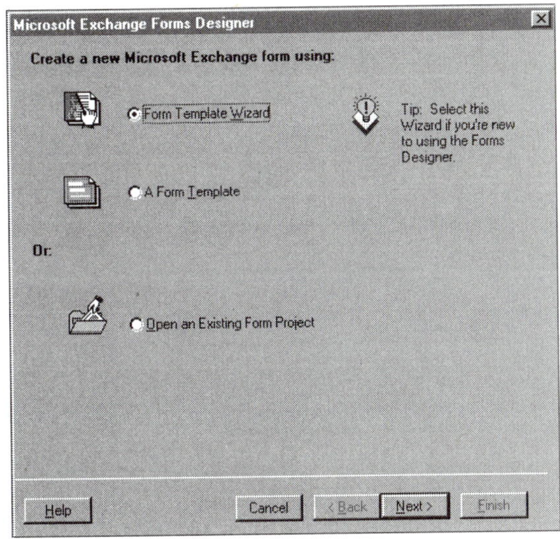

2. Select the Form Template Wizard option, and then click on the Next button.

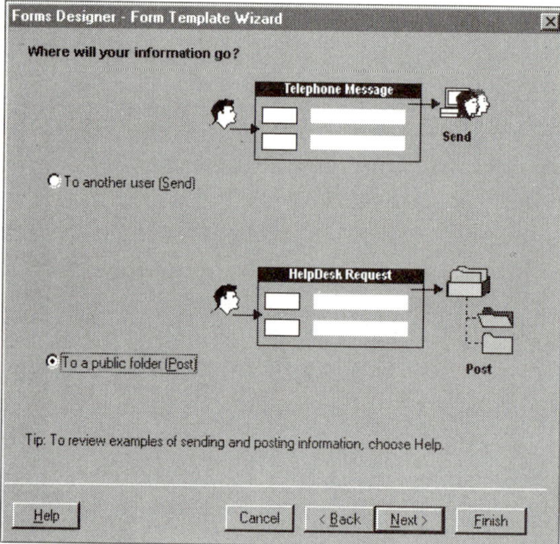

3. Select the To A Public Folder (Post) option, and then click on the Next button.

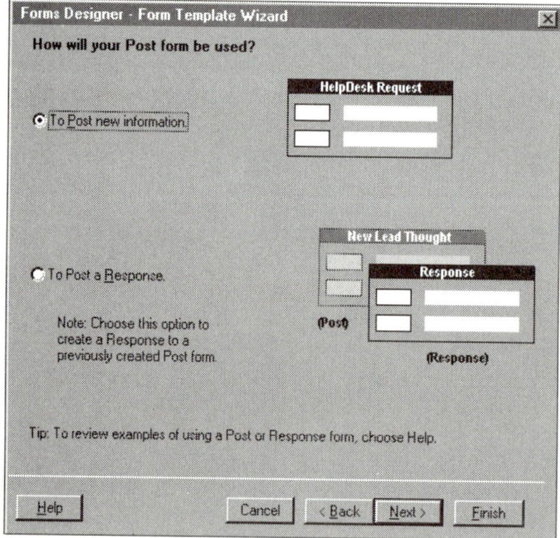

4. Select the To Post New Information option, and then click on the Next button.

Note Because this form is used to report rather than to comment, you need a form for new postings, not a form for posting responses.

---

5. Select the One Window option.

   Selecting the One Window option for this example means that the layout of the form will be the same for composing a report and for reviewing one. If you want to review the information using a layout different from the one used to collect the information, you would select the Two Windows option instead.

   Click on the Next button.

Forms Designer - Form Template Wizard
Do you want one window or two windows in your form?
One window
Design the same window to compose and read information.
Compose / Read window
Two windows
Design one window to compose and the other to read information.
Compose window
Read window
Tip: To review examples of designing a one or a two window form, choose Help.
Help
Cancel
< Back
Next >
Finish

6. Type a name for your form, such as *Project Report*, and a description of the form, such as *Use this form to report your progress, problems, and solutions for a task.*

CHAPTER
9

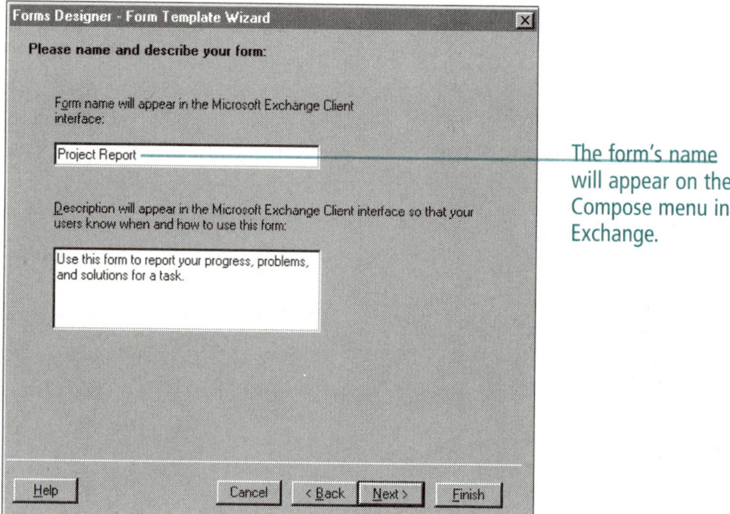

The form's name will appear on the Compose menu in Exchange.

Click on the Next button to see the last panel of the Form Template wizard.

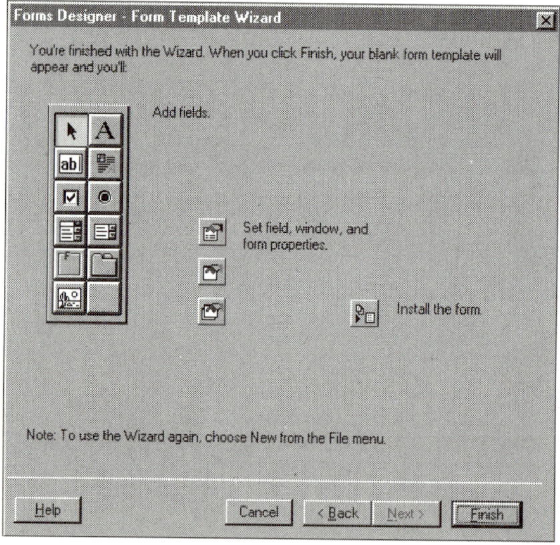

7. From this panel, you can go back to a previous panel (to change a selection) or click on the Finish button when you're ready to add the pieces of the form to the outline you've set up with the Form Template wizard.

   When you click on the Finish button, you see the Microsoft Exchange Forms Designer window, with its menus and toolbars, as shown here:

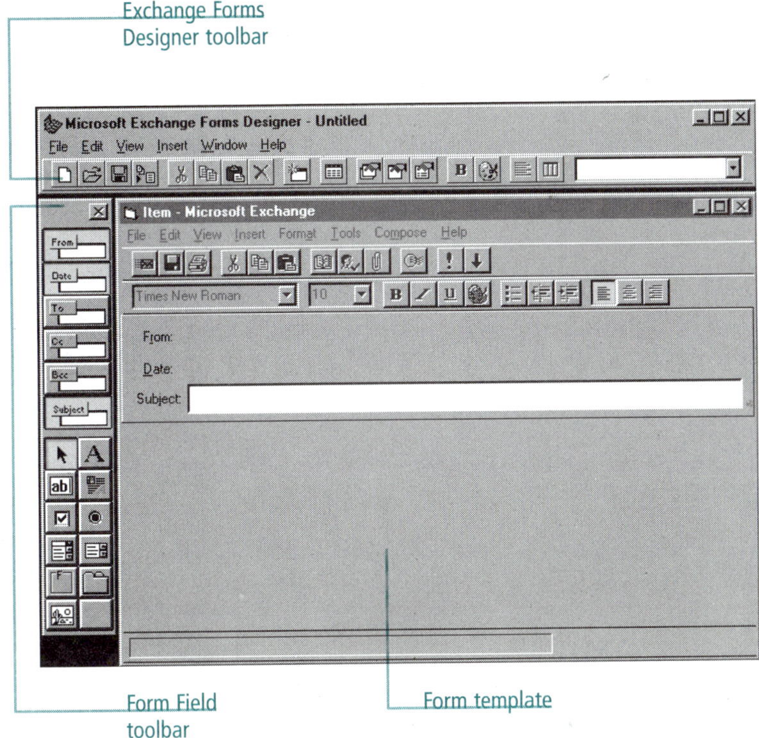

You have now set up the basic template for the project report form. To complete the form, you'll perform the following tasks:

- Place fields on the form
- Set the properties of the fields
- Set the properties of the form
- Set the properties of the form window

- Install the form
- Add the form to the Bozo Bit public folder

Placing Fields on the Project Report Form

As mentioned earlier, we want the project report form we're designing to contain the following fields:

- Task name
- Percentage completed
- Problems encountered
- Solutions devised
- Next phase of work
- Approximate finish date for the task
- Other notes

To add these fields to the project report form template, follow these standard steps for each field:

1. Click on the button on the Field toolbar for the type of field you want to place on the form. You can use the tooltips to identify the field type for each button.

Placing, Moving, and Sizing Fields

When creating a form, you need to place, move, and size fields appropriately. To move and size a field box you use move and size handles, which appear at the corners and on the borders of the field boxes. When you first place a new field, place it away from the edges of the window or tab, and then move it into position after you size it. It's easier to place and size a field when all of the sizing handles and the move box are visible. If you place a field too close to an edge, you might not be able to grab the sizing handles or the move box. When you need to move a field box, rest the mouse pointer on the move box in the upper left corner of a field. The mouse pointer changes into a hand with a pointing index finger.

Drag the move box to move the field. Alternatively, press and hold down the mouse button anywhere within a field. The mouse pointer changes to a hand. Drag the field to move it. Using the move box allows you to move the caption and field separately.

2. Click on the form template to place the field.
3. Delete the default caption for the new field and type a new caption.
4. Size and move the field box as needed.

For the project report form we're creating, these standard steps translate to the following:

1. Click on the To Field button on the Field toolbar.
2. Click on the Cc Field button on the Field toolbar.
3. Click on the Tab Field button on the Field toolbar, and then click on the template to place the tab field. The Form Designer places a four-tab tab field on the form.
4. Click on the caption for the first tab in order to edit it. Type *Status.*
5. Click on the second tab, and then click again to edit the caption. (This is not the same as a double-click.) Type *Problems.*
6. Click on the third tab, click again, and then type *Solutions.*
7. Click on the fourth tab, click again, and then type *Notes.*
8. Move and size the tab field, if necessary, to fill up the lower half of the form template.

Your form should now look something like this:

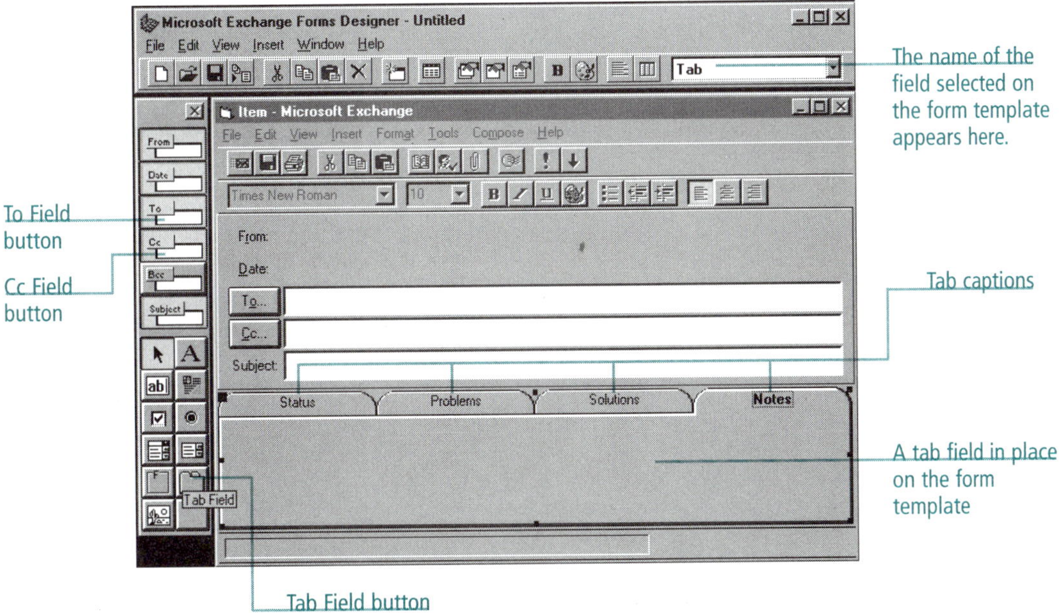

By placing a tab field on the form, you provide plenty of space for typing descriptions of problems and solutions as well as other notes without crowding the form or making it too large. Now you're ready to add fields to the tabs. To do that, follow these steps:

1. To add a field for tasks to the Status tab, click on the Status tab, click on the ComboBox Field button on the Field toolbar, and then click to place the new field in the upper left corner of the form message area, as shown here:

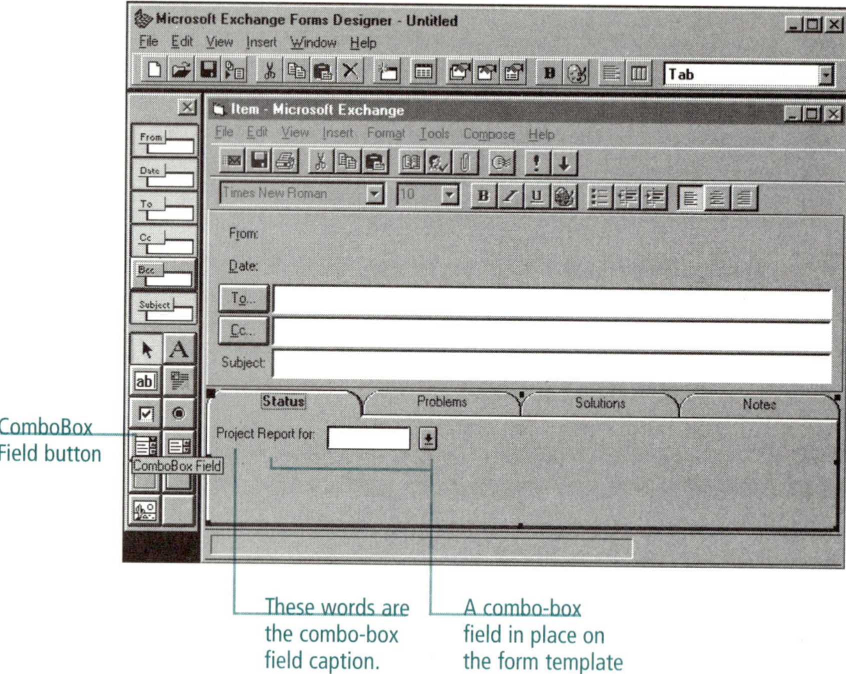

2. Type *Project Report for:* in the Caption box of the combo-box field and press Enter. Move and size the field as appropriate.
3. To add the field for the percentage completed, click on the Entry Field button on the Field toolbar, and then click to the right of the combo-box field on the form template.

4. Type *Percent Complete* in the Caption box of the entry field, and then press Enter. Move and size the field as appropriate.

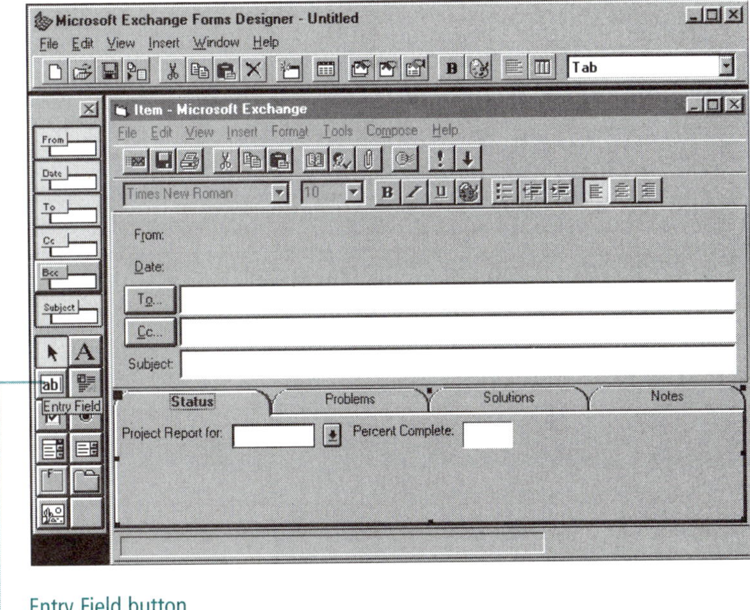

Entry Field button

5. To add the other two fields to the Status tab (fields for the estimated completion date and the next phase of the project), follow step 3 and step 4 again: click on the Entry Field button on the Field toolbar, click on the Status tab to place the field, type a caption (*Finished By* for the estimated completion date, and *Next Phase* for the next phase of the project), press Enter, and size and move the fields as needed. You'll want to make the entry box for Next Phase fairly large.

   The Status tab should now look something like the figure at the top of the next page.

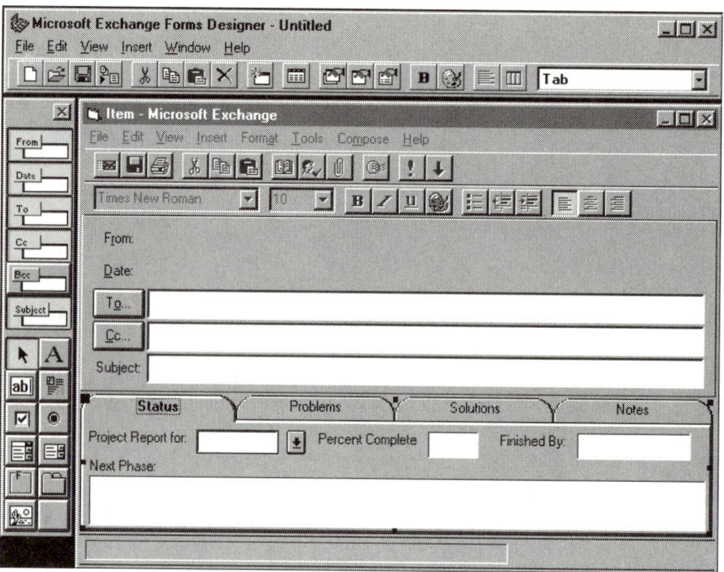

6. Click on the Problems tab, click on the Entry Field button on the Field toolbar, click on the upper left corner of the Problems tab to place the field, delete the caption, and move and size the field box to fill the tab, covering the caption placeholder. Because the tab itself contains a label for the only field on the tab, you don't need a caption for the field on the tab.

You can select the entry field on the Problems tab, copy it to the Windows clipboard, and then paste it onto the Solutions and Notes tabs. When you paste a copied field, Forms Designer lets you know that the field you're pasting has the same name as a field that's already part of the form. You'll see a dialog box with a button labeled Rename To Be Unique. Click on this button to complete the placement of the field.

The Problems tab should look something like the figure at the top of the next page.

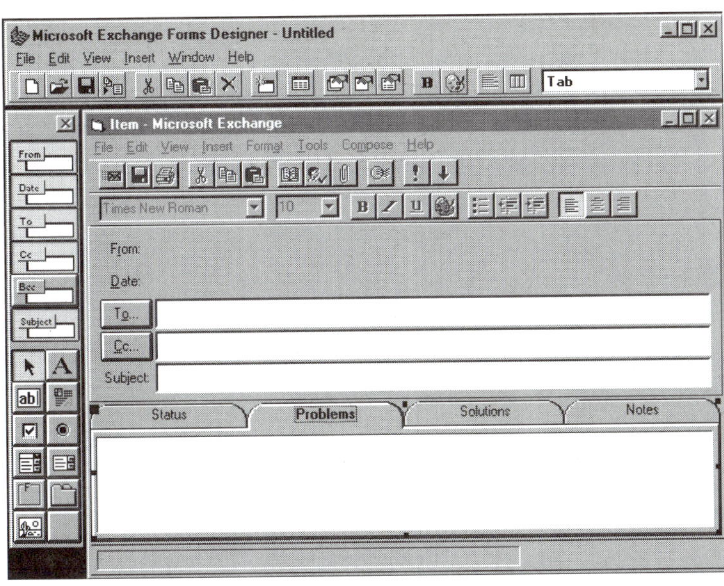

7. Repeat step 6 for the Solutions and the Notes tabs. These two tabs should look similar to the Problems tab.
8. Click on the Save button on the Forms Designer toolbar, select the Efdforms folder in the Exchange folder, type a name for the form (such as *PROJREPT*), and then click on OK.

Now you need to set the properties of each of the fields you placed on the project report form.

Setting the Properties of the Project Report Form Fields

Every type of field that you can place on a form has a set of properties. For each type of field, Forms Designer provides a dialog box that shows the properties for that field. Each field properties dialog box typically has three tabs: General, Format, and Initial Value. We won't run through all the field property dialog boxes and tabs here, but you'll get a sense of how to work with field properties by following the steps for setting properties for the three types of fields (tab, combo-box, and entry) that you have placed on the project report form. In any of the field properties dialog boxes, you can click on the Help button for specific information about the contents of the dialog box.

Setting Tab Field Properties

In general, a tab field provides a background for other fields on the form. Tabs give you a way to design a form that requires a number of fields (including large ones) without crowding or enlarging the form itself.

Even so, tab fields do have properties, and you might want to experiment with them a bit. To set tab field properties, perform the following steps:

1. Click on the surface of the tab to select the tab field. You'll know you have selected the tab field when sizing handles appear along the top, bottom, and side borders.
2. Click on the Field Properties button on the Exchange Forms Designer toolbar. The properties buttons on the toolbar are shown in Figure 9-1.

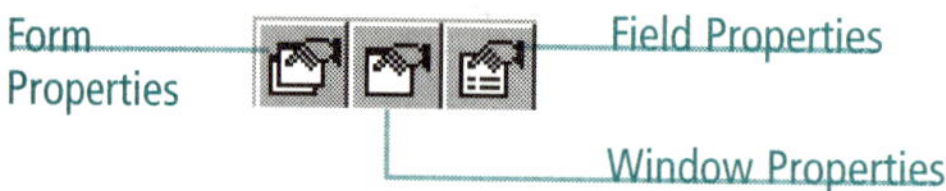

Figure 9-1

The three properties buttons on the Forms Designer toolbar

3. On the General tab, delete the text *Caption* from the Field Caption box. Because each tab in the tab field carries a label, the tab field itself doesn't need a caption. If it had one, it would likely cause confusion.

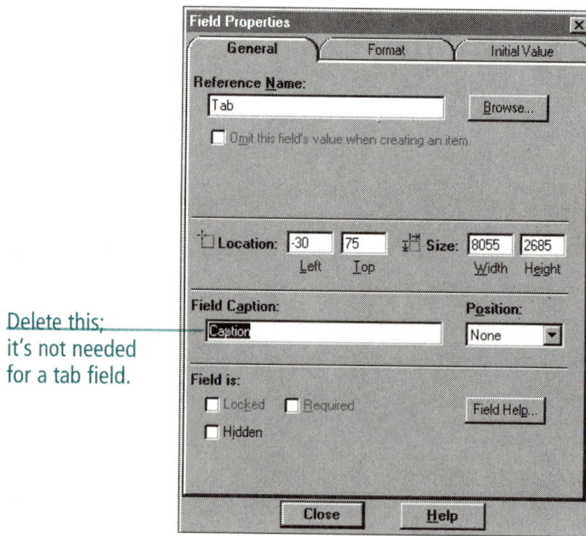

4. If you want, you can play around with the size and position of the tab field by changing the values in the Location and Size boxes. The values are measured in twips (there are 1440 twips in an inch).
5. Click on the Format tab in the Field Properties dialog box.

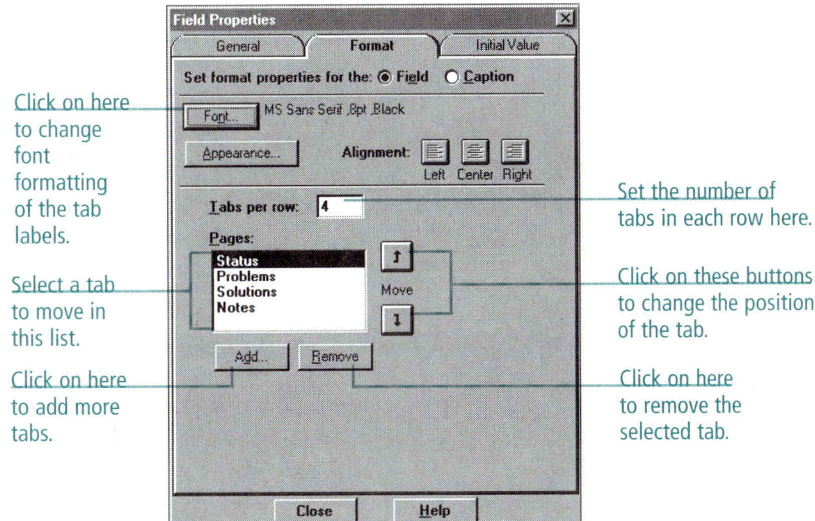
Field Properties
General
Format
Initial Value
Set format properties for the: Field Caption
Font...
MS Sans Serif ,8pt ,Black
Appearance...
Alignment:
Left Center Right
Tabs per row: 4
Pages:
Status
Problems
Solutions
Notes
Move
Add...
Remove
Close
Help
Click on here to change font formatting of the tab labels.
Select a tab to move in this list.
Click on here to add more tabs.
Set the number of tabs in each row here.
Click on these buttons to change the position of the tab.
Click on here to remove the selected tab.

Most often, you'll use the Format tab to change a tab field after you place it on a form. Forms Designer always places a four-tab tab field on a form when you use the Tab Field button on the Field toolbar. Suppose, however, that you want only two or three tabs? Or suppose that you want eight tabs? The Format tab is where you can change the number of tabs and their order and arrangement.

For our project report form, we don't need to change the tab setup. But the MS Sans Serif font is kind of dull, don't you think? So let's change it to Desdemona, boldface, maroon color. To do this, click on the Font button, change the font properties in the Font dialog box, and then click on OK. The tab labels now appear with boldface Desdemona in maroon.

If you want to you can alter the order of the tabs by selecting a tab's name in the Pages list and clicking on the Move buttons. You can change the number of tabs per row to two. This arrangement gives you longer tabs to click on when you're using the form. You'll probably want to change the number of tabs per row only when you have a large number of tabs to fit on one form.

CHAPTER
9

6. Click on the Initial Value tab. But wait! What don't you see? Tab fields have no values, so they also have no initial values. You'll find out about initial values with combo boxes, in the next section.
7. Click on the Close button.

Setting Combo-Box Field Properties

I had you use a combo box for the task name so that you could report on a variety of tasks by using the same form, or even use the form for reporting on tasks in other projects. As with a tab field, a combo-box field has its own Properties dialog box with General, Format, and Initial Value tabs. The Initial Value tab is probably the most important because that's where you set up the list of choices that appear in the combo-box list.

To set properties for a combo-box field, perform the following steps:

1. Click on the combo-box field.
2. Click on the Field Properties button on the Exchange Forms Designer toolbar (shown earlier in Figure 9-1, on page 240).
3. On the General tab, select the Required option. You want team members to fill in this field so that you know for which task they're giving you a report.

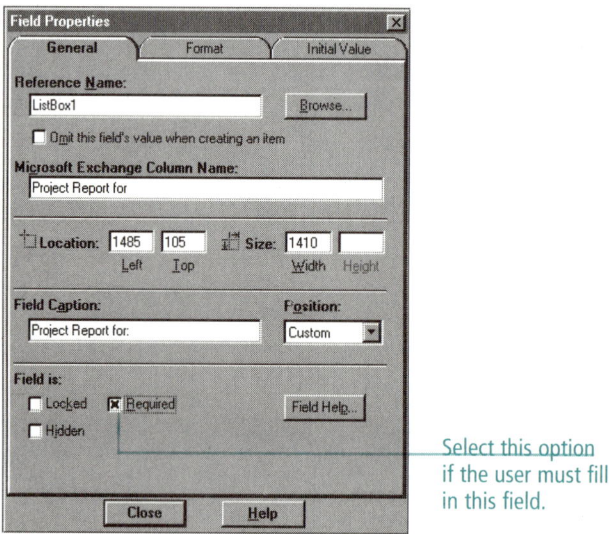

Select this option if the user must fill in this field.

Notice the vertical position (Location, Top) of the combo-box field. By entering these same numbers on the General tab of the Field Properties dialog boxes for the two entry fields to the right of the combo-box field, you can align the top of all three fields. Doing this will make your form look more polished.

4. Click on the Format tab of the Field Properties dialog box for the combo-box field, and then select the Field option at the top of the tab.

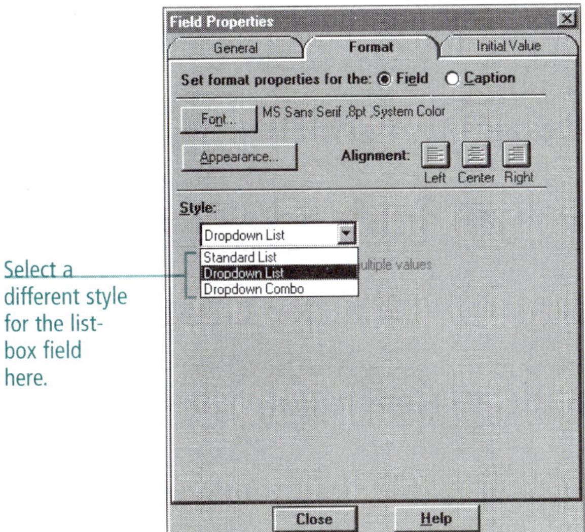

Select a different style for the list-box field here.

5. Until this point, you've been working with a combo-box field. A combo box gives you a list to choose from, plus a box in which users can type any old thing. Well, maybe you don't want that. Maybe you want to give them a set list to choose from, and that's it—no fanciful, exotic task names allowed! To change the combo box to a straight dropdown list, select Dropdown List from the Style box.

   If you want to change the font properties of the list or the caption, select the Field or the Caption option, depending on which element you want to change, and then click on the Font button, select the font properties you want to use, and finally click on OK.

6. Click on the Initial Value tab.

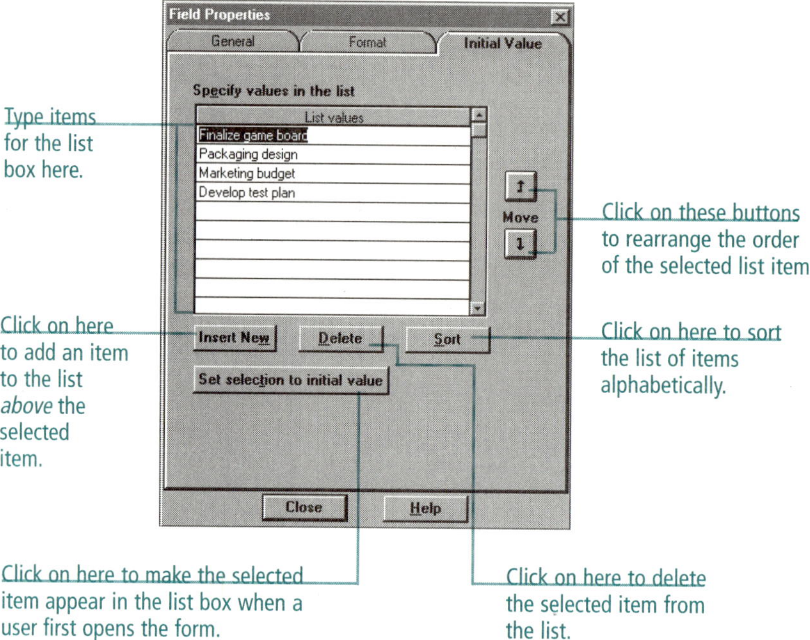
Field Properties
General
Format
Initial Value
Specify values in the list
List values
Finalize game board
Packaging design
Marketing budget
Develop test plan
Move
Insert New
Delete
Sort
Set selection to initial value
Close
Help
Type items for the list box here.
Click on these buttons to rearrange the order of the selected list item.
Click on here to add an item to the list *above* the selected item.
Click on here to sort the list of items alphabetically.
Click on here to make the selected item appear in the list box when a user first opens the form.
Click on here to delete the selected item from the list.

7. On the Initial Value tab, type the names of the tasks for which you want team members to use this project report form. Type the first task name on the first line, press the Tab or down arrow key to move to the next line, type the next task name, and so on.
8. If you want a particular task name to appear in the list when the form is opened—for example, if several members of your team are working on specific aspects of a critical task and you'll receive reports from each of them—select the task's name in the List Values list, and then click on the Set Selection To Initial Value button. The selected task's name now appears in boldface.
9. If you want or need to arrange the task names so that they appear in a more logical order, you have a couple of choices. If you want the list in alphabetic order, click on the Sort button. If you want the list sorted according to some other logic, select the task name you want to move, and then click on one of the Move buttons.
10. Click on the Close button.

Note You won't see the values in the list until you use the form.

Setting Entry Field Properties

In entry fields, form users can type whatever they want. (Well, you at least hope they type something appropriate!) The project report form we've been building has entry fields for describing the next phase of the task, for documenting problems and solutions, and for typing notes. The project report form also has an entry field for the percentage completed and one for the approximate finish date.

I'll walk you through how to set the properties for one of the entry fields and provide a table that shows you appropriate settings for the other entry fields. You can repeat these steps using the settings in the table to set the properties for the other entry fields on the project report form. The Problems, Solutions, and Notes fields don't require any changes.

To set the properties for the Percent Complete entry field, follow these steps:

1. Click on the Status tab, and then click on the Percent Complete entry field.
2. Click on the Field Properties button on the Exchange Forms Designer toolbar (as shown in Figure 9-1, on page 240).
3. On the General tab, click to select the Required option. Then click on the Format tab and select the Field option.

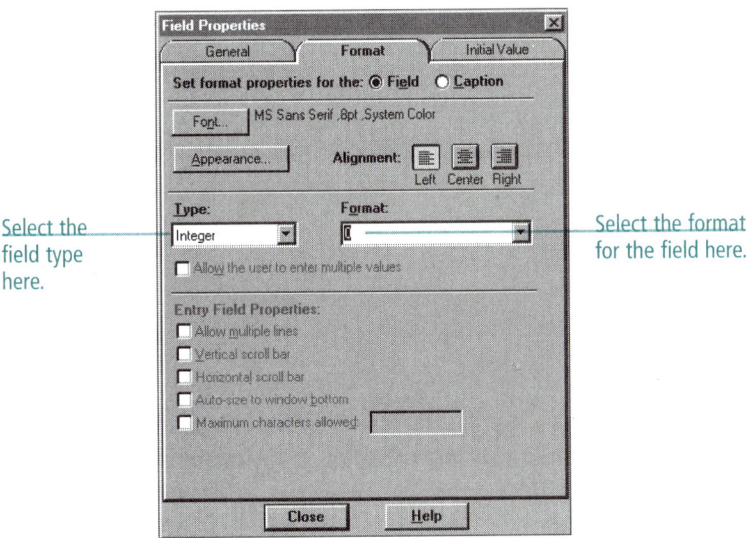

4. A percentage is usually an integer (some people call an integer a "whole number"), so select Integer from the Type list. By selecting the appropriate type, you control the kind of information a user can enter in a field. In this case, selecting Integer requires a user to enter a meaningful number rather than some unwanted text, such as "I Don't Know."
5. From the Format list, select 0 (that's zero). This sets the format of the number a user enters in this field.
6. Click on the Initial Value tab. Because every project task starts with none of it completed, the initial value for the Percent Complete entry field should be zero. You can either type a zero in the list or leave the list blank, which puts no initial value in the Percent Complete entry field.
7. Click on the Close button, and then click on the Save button on the Forms Designer toolbar.

For the other entry fields on the project report form, follow step 1 through step 7 in the previous procedure (in step 1 you need to click on the tabs for Problems, Solutions, and Notes as appropriate) and set the properties as shown in the following table:

Field caption	General tab	Format tab	Initial Value tab
Finish by	Click on the Required box.	Click on the Field button, and then select Date from the Type list.	(none)
Next Phase	Click on the Required box.	No changes.	(none)
Problems, Solutions, and Notes	No changes.	No changes.	(none)

Setting the Properties of the Project Report Form Itself

Just as each field on a form has properties, so does the form itself. For basic forms such as the project report form you're creating here, many of the properties are unimportant. All the same, a few properties are worth your consideration now in case you want to change them.

To set the properties of the project report form, take these steps:

1. Click on the Form Properties button on the Exchange Forms Designer toolbar (shown in Figure 9-1, on page 240).

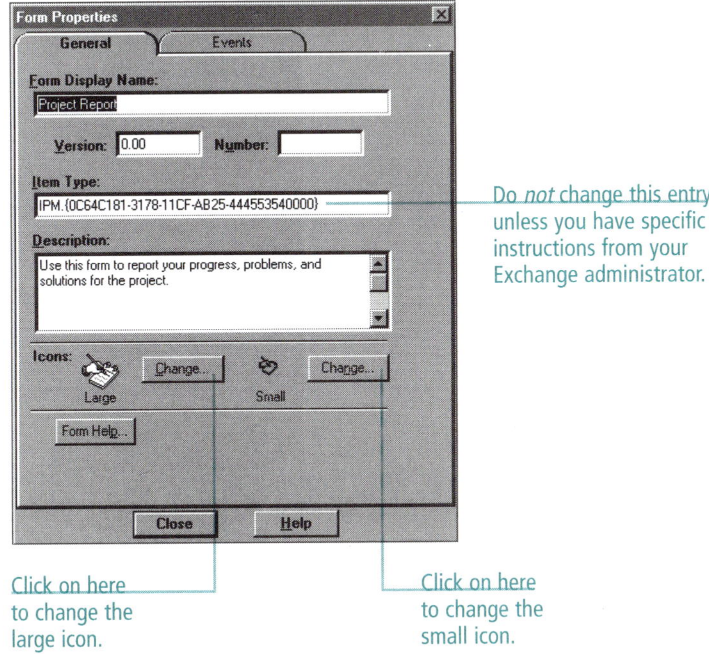

Do *not* change this entry unless you have specific instructions from your Exchange administrator.

Click on here to change the large icon.

Click on here to change the small icon.

The major properties that might interest you on the General tab are Form Display Name, Description, Large Icon, and Small Icon. Notice that the Form Display Name and the Description boxes show the text you typed when you set up the form template with the Form Template wizard.

Do not change the text in the Item Type box. Unless you're a whiz-bang Windows 95 programmer (or understand how to construct an Item Type entry), you'll create trouble for yourself if you mess around with the entry in the Item Type box.

2. If you want to change the information in the Form Display Name or the Description box, edit the existing entries or enter new ones. You'll also want to type entries in these boxes if you did not enter information for them while you were using the Form Template wizard.
3. To change the Large Icon, click on the Change button to the right of the large icon symbol.
4. In the Select Icon dialog box, select the disk and folder that contains icon files. The Icons folder (which is a subfolder of the Efdforms folder, a subfolder of the Exchange folder) contains icon files designed specifically for the Exchange Forms Designer. Select the file for the icon you want to use, and then click on OK.

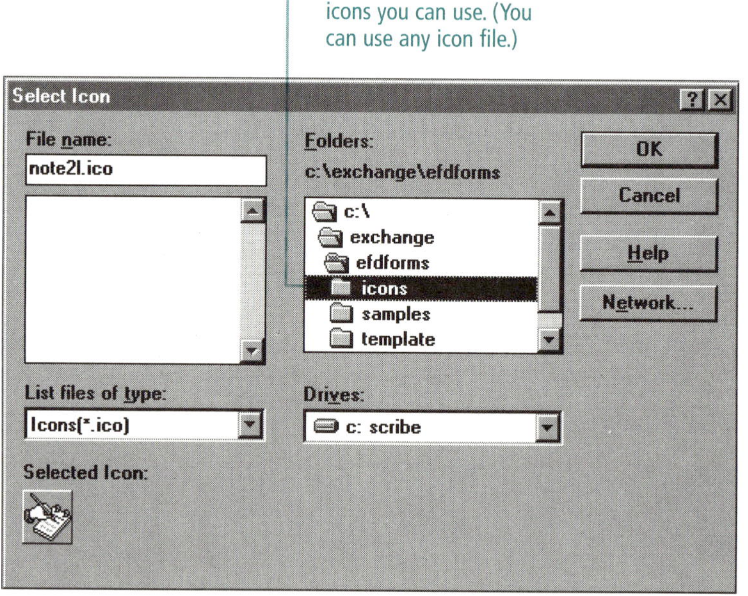

TIP In the Icons folder, icon files that use L in their names are large icons. Large icons will appear in the Exchange Forms Manager. (See "Adding the Project Report Form to the Bozo Bit Public Folder" on page 253.) Icon files that contain S in their names are small icons. Small icons will appear in the Exchange message list pane.

5. To change the Small Icon, click on the Change button to the right of the small icon symbol, and then repeat step 4.
6. The project report form doesn't require any changes on the Events tab, so click on the Close button. (You can use the Events tab to cause a form to be displayed whenever a user executes a specific command.)

Setting the Properties of the Project Report Form Window

Because Exchange forms appear in windows (even Exchange forms for the Macintosh appear in what Apple Computer calls "windows"), you can use the Exchange Forms Designer to set properties for the form window. Some of the window properties can add spiff to your form.

To set the properties for the project report form window, take these steps:

1. Click on the Window Properties button on the Exchange Forms Designer toolbar (shown in Figure 9-1, on page 240), and then click on the General tab.

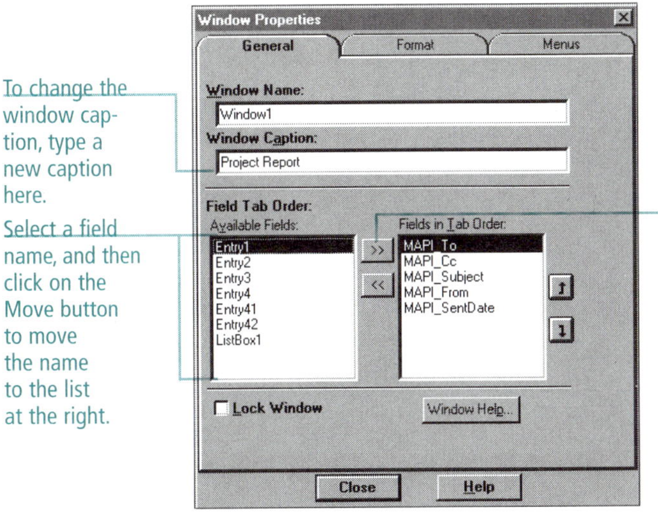

To change the window caption, type a new caption here.

Select a field name, and then click on the Move button to move the name to the list at the right.

This is the Move button; click on here to move the selected field name from the list at the left to the list at the right.

2. If you don't want to use the default window caption, you can change the caption in the Window Caption box. (The window caption appears in the title bar of the form window.)
3. Use the Field Tab Order area to arrange the order in which a user moves from field to field on the form by using the Tab key. In the Available Fields list, select the field you want a user to be able to tab to, and then click on the Move button—the button with the double chevron (>>) pointing to the right. The field name appears in the Fields In Tab Order list. Repeat this procedure until all the fields you want are in the Fields In Tab Order list.
4. If you need to change the tab order of the fields, select a field in the Fields In Tab Order list, and then click on the Up or Down button to rearrange the order of the fields.

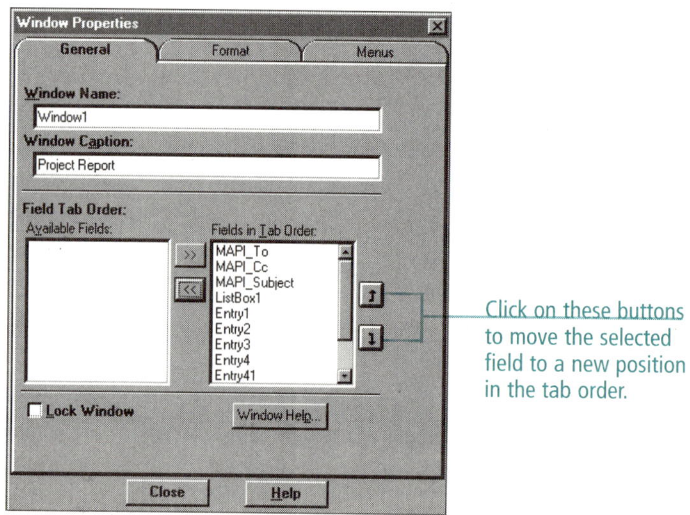

Click on these buttons to move the selected field to a new position in the tab order.

5. Click on the Format tab.

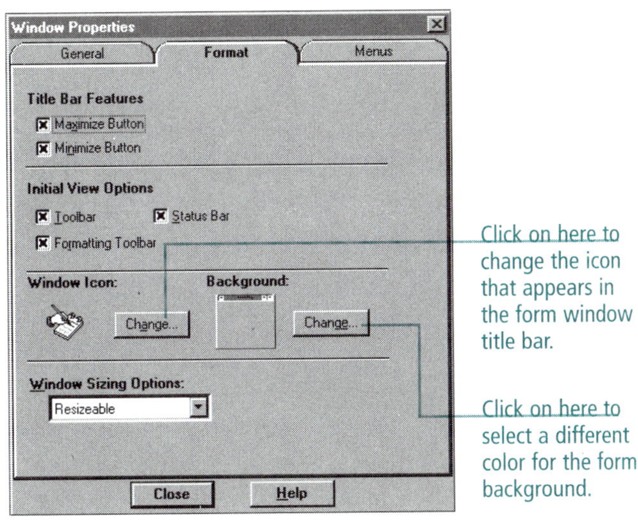

6. You can use options on the Format tab to set properties such as window sizing options, view options, and features of the window's title bar. You can also change the window icon. If you want a different window icon, click on the Change button beside the window icon symbol. You'll find icon files in the Icons folder inside the Efdforms folder inside the Exchange folder.
7. If you want the form background to be a color other than gray, click on the Change button beside the Background preview, select the color from the Color dialog box, and then click on OK. The Background preview shows you the color you selected. If, as in the case of the project report form, most of the message area is covered with fields (in this case a tab field), you won't see much of the background color on the form.
8. For now you don't have to worry about the Menus tab, so click on the Close button, and then click on the Save button on the Exchange Forms Designer toolbar. If this is the first time you have saved the form, choose a filename and folder in which to store your form, and then click on OK.

Your project report form is now set up and ready to install.

Installing the Project Report Form

After you create a form, you have to install it. In this case, "install" means that the Exchange Forms Designer converts all the pieces and parts of the form to Visual Basic program code and then compiles the form so you can use it. Until the Forms Designer performs this process, you cannot use the form.

To install the project report form, do the following:

1. Click on the Install button on the Exchange Forms Designer toolbar.

2. You'll see several message boxes and windows appear and disappear, including the title panel for Visual Basic For Microsoft Exchange Server. Just wait. Eventually you'll see the Set Library To dialog box, which looks like this:

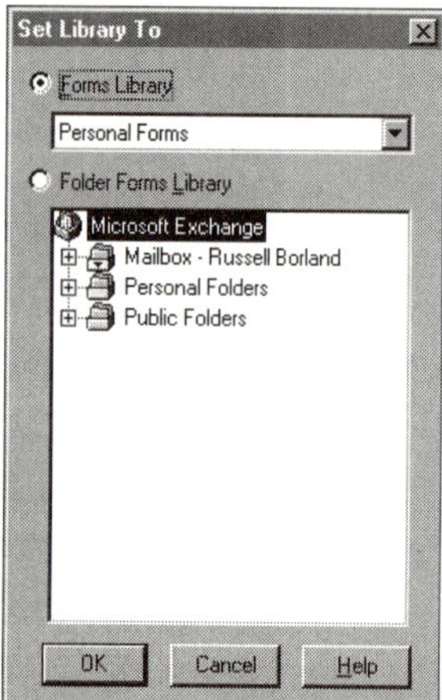

3. Click on OK. (We'll associate the form with a public folder in the next section.) You'll then see the Form Properties dialog box, which shows a summary of the form properties you set during form development. The Form Properties dialog box looks like the figure at the top of the next page.

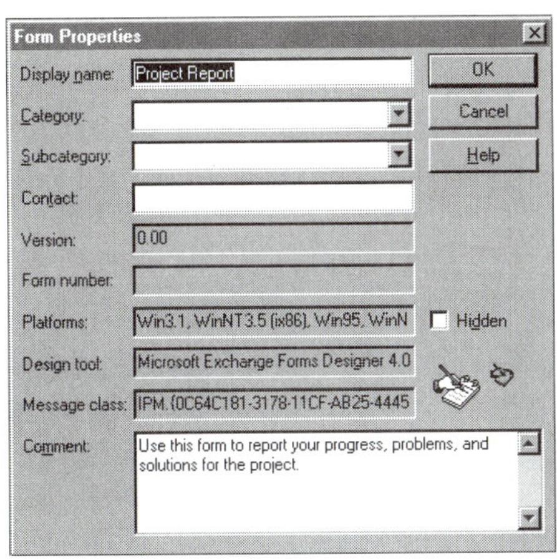

Note You must have Owner permission in order to add a form to a public folder.

4. Change the Display Name and the Comment boxes, if you want. The display name appears in the Forms Manager dialog box as well as on the Compose menu. Then click on OK.
5. When all the action stops, click on the Save button on the Exchange Forms Designer toolbar, and then choose the File Exit command to close the form and exit the Exchange Forms Designer.

   You're now ready to add the form to the Bozo Bit public folder.

Adding the Project Report Form to the Bozo Bit Public Folder

The purpose of creating a form is to use the form with folders. In this case, the form was designed primarily to work with the Bozo Bit public folder for reporting about project tasks. After you create and install the form, it's time to put the form to work.

To add the project report form to the Bozo Bit public folder, do this:

1. In Exchange, right-click on the Bozo Bit folder, and then select Properties from the shortcut menu.
2. Click on the Forms tab, and then click on the Manage button.

If right-clicking is unavailable, select the Bozo Bit folder, and then choose the File Properties command.

3. In the Forms Manager dialog box, click on the Set button above the list box at the left.

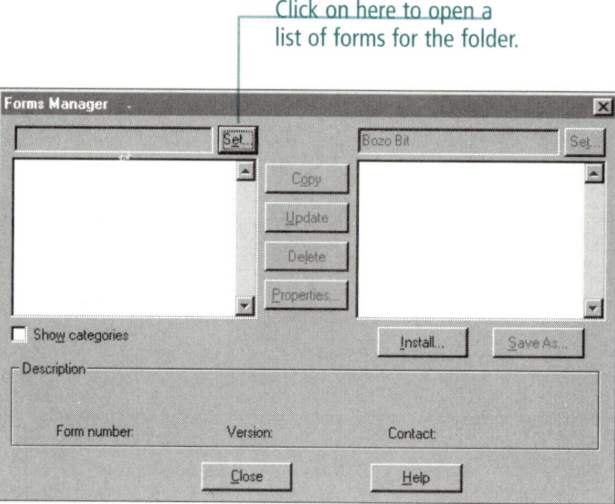

4. Once again you see the Set Library To dialog box. Click on OK. The label "Personal Forms" appears above the list box at the left, and Project Report appears in the list.
5. Click on Project Report, and then click on the Copy button. Exchange indicates that it is copying the form. When Exchange is finished, Project Report appears in the list at the right, under Bozo Bit.

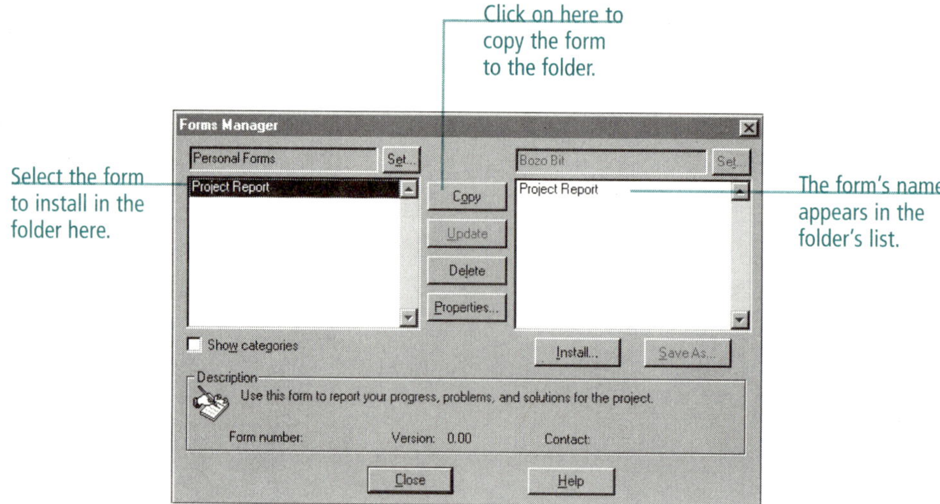

6. Click on the Close button.
7. On the Forms tab in the Bozo Bit Properties dialog box, decide which forms you'll permit team members to use in the Bozo Bit folder. Click on one of the buttons in the Allow These Forms In This Folder area. Usually, you'll want to let team members use the standard forms as well as the project report form (and any other forms you create for the folder). You might require team members to use only the forms you set up if you want to regulate how information is sent to the folder and how it appears. Because we want team members to send mail messages and replies to the folder, we have to let them use the standard forms.
8. After you decide which forms you'll permit team members to use, click on OK.

You can now use the project report form to send a project report to the Bozo Bit public folder.

Using the Project Report Form

Now that you've set up the project report form in the Bozo Bit folder, it's ready to use. Better than that, when you open the Bozo Bit folder, a command for the project report form appears at the bottom of the Compose menu.

To use the project report form to put a project report in the Bozo Bit folder, do the following:

1. Click on the Bozo Bit folder.
2. Click on the Compose menu.

3. Click on the New Project Report command. You'll see a message telling you that Exchange is installing the form on your computer. After a bit, the project report form appears, as shown next.

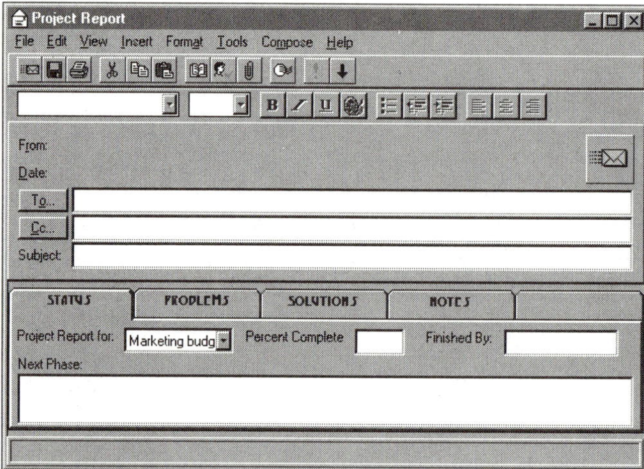

4. Fill in the project report form.
5. Click on the Post button to the right of the From field.

You should now (or shortly hereafter) see your project report in the Bozo Bit folder. The posting in the message list pane displays the small icon you set up when you were developing the form.

Note To edit a form after you have created it, choose the Tools Application Design command in Exchange, and then select the Forms Designer command from the submenu. On the first screen of the Exchange Forms Designer wizard, select the Open An Existing Form Project option, and then click on the Next button. Select the disk and folder that contains the form, select the form you want to edit, and then click on OK.

After editing the form, you will again have to set properties, install the form, and associate it with the public folder in order for the changes to take effect.

Creating a Project Message Template

In addition to creating forms for various types of information and messages, you can set up a message template. You use message templates with the WordMail tools in Exchange. To make this work, you need to have Microsoft Word installed and you must have selected the option to use Word as an electronic mail editor when you installed Word. If you do have Word installed and you turn on the WordMail tools, you can use Word to create your messages. Exchange gives you some

formatting—such as color, indention, alignment, and bullets—but by using Word to create messages, you can use tables, formulas, fields, and Word's wealth of formatting features when composing a message.

To turn on the WordMail tools, take these steps:

1. Choose the Compose WordMail Options command.

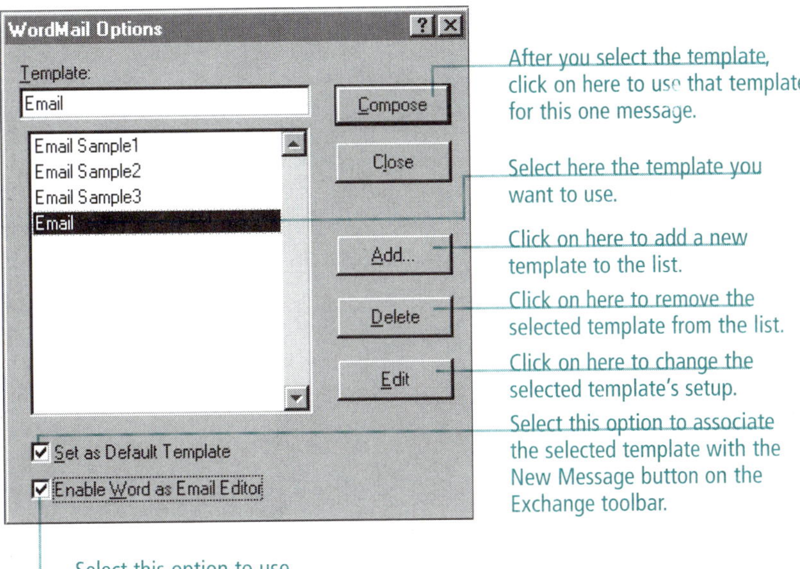
WordMail Options
Template:
Email
Email Sample1
Email Sample2
Email Sample3
Email
Compose
Close
Add...
Delete
Edit
Set as Default Template
Enable Word as Email Editor
After you select the template, click on here to use that template for this one message.
Select here the template you want to use.
Click on here to add a new template to the list.
Click on here to remove the selected template from the list.
Click on here to change the selected template's setup.
Select this option to associate the selected template with the New Message button on the Exchange toolbar.
Select this option to use Word to compose messages.

2. Select the Enable Word As Email Editor option.
3. Select the template you want to use. (For information about adding templates, see "Adding a WordMail Template," next).
4. If you want to use the selected template to compose most of your messages, select the Set As Default Template option.
5. If you want to compose a new message now, click on the Compose button.

   If you aren't ready to compose a new message, or if you want to compose a reply or forward a message, click on the Close button.

After you turn on the WordMail option, each time you compose a new message or reply to or forward a message, you'll see a window that looks much like your Microsoft Word window, with a few added toolbar buttons, as shown here:

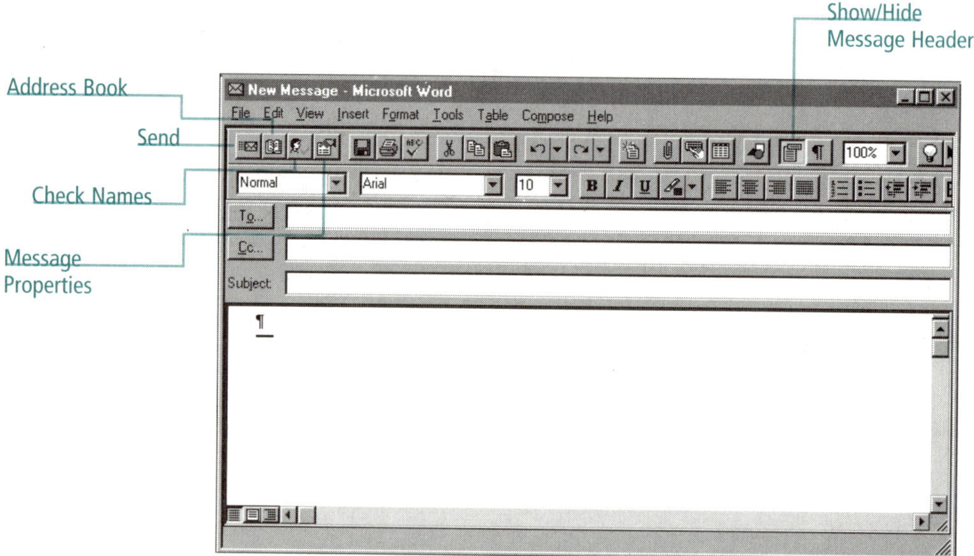

The WordMail Options dialog box lists several templates all ready to use. These templates are relatively plain. If you want a template that suits your purposes better, you can either edit one of the standard templates or create an entirely new one.

Adding a WordMail Template

If you use Word regularly, you have, no doubt, a number of templates. Word itself comes with a variety of ready-made templates, and you can add any Word template you have to the list in the WordMail Options dialog box. Here's how to do it:

1. Choose the Compose WordMail Options command.
2. Click on the Add button.
3. In the Add dialog box, open the folder that contains the template you want to add to your WordMail list.
4. Select the template. You can select only one template at a time.

5. Click on the Add button.
6. To add more Word templates to your WordMail Options, repeat step 2 through step 5.
7. When you're finished adding templates, select the template you want to use most often.
8. Select the Set As Default Template option.
9. Be sure the Enable Word As Email Editor box is checked, and then click on the Close button.

TIP If you want to create a Word template specifically for sending Exchange messages, create the template in Word, and then add it to the list in the WordMail Options dialog box in Exchange.

Editing an Existing WordMail Template

You can change the setup of any WordMail template at any time. To do so, take these steps:

1. Choose the Compose WordMail Options command.
2. Select the template you want to edit.
3. Click on the Edit button. Exchange starts Word and opens the template file.
4. Edit the template, and then save the changes.
5. Close the Word document window and exit Word.

The altered template is now ready to use with WordMail. To select the template, follow the steps described in "Switching to a Different WordMail Template," next.

Switching to a Different WordMail Template

You might have various WordMail templates set up for different purposes. When you want to use a template other than the WordMail template you usually use (the default template), do this:

1. Choose the Compose WordMail Options command.
2. Select the template you want to use.
3. If you're ready to compose a new message, click on the Compose button. Exchange displays a new message form based on the template you chose.

If you aren't ready to compose a new message, click on the Close button.

If you want to forward a message or compose a reply by using a different template, take these steps:

1. Choose the Compose WordMail Options command.
2. Select the template you want to use.
3. Click on the Set As Default Template box.
4. Click on the Close button.
5. Select the message you want to forward or reply to.
6. Click on either the Reply button or the Forward button on the Exchange toolbar.

Note If this is a one-time shot for a reply or forwarded message, you'll want to reset the default WordMail template to the one you use most often after you send the reply or forwarded message.

CHAPTER
10

Scheduling Project Meetings

Have you ever worked on a project that didn't require meetings? Impossible! Meetings are a part of every team project. Scheduling a meeting for a group of people is usually problematic, but Schedule+, the scheduling program that comes with Microsoft Exchange, eases the pain. You can schedule regular meetings in particular rooms, schedule special meetings, change meetings, and cancel meetings. You can also keep a record of your meetings and the information shared during them as part of a project archive.

Scenes from This Chapter

Scenario

For the health and welfare of team pride, cohesion, and spirit, you decide to set up a schedule of regular team meetings. Development of the Bozo Bit game is going along fine, but meeting once a week will help the team stay in touch. Your idea is that during these meetings, team members can share questions, problems, answers, and solutions from the preceding week and make plans for the week to come.

From time to time, you also find it necessary to call a special meeting; that is, a meeting outside the regular day and time. Perhaps an issue has come up that needs immediate attention, or you've just been given another million dollars of development funds and you and the team need to figure out how to respond. You might also find (don't we all?) that you need to change the day and time of a meeting, whether it's the regularly scheduled meeting or a special meeting. And sometimes, just now and then, you might want or need to cancel a meeting for any number of legitimate (and occasionally illegitimate) reasons.

After your project is completed (many months from now, of course), you might want to archive the project scheduling and tasks as a record of your travails, as a tool for analyzing how the project went, and as a reference for planning your next wonderful game.

Scheduling a Regular Meeting

To keep the project running efficiently, you decide that a weekly team meeting is in order. During the meeting, team members can share the progress they have made during the past week and discuss the project at large. The regular weekly meeting will also be the time when the project team coordinates its efforts for the coming week, setting priorities and identifying important questions to resolve.

You decide that you'd like to start the week off with a bang. You want to make sure the entire team is on the same page, and you want to give a pep talk to motivate them through the coming week. You decide that first thing Monday morning is a good time for the regular team meeting, say at 9:00 A.M.

To schedule a regular team meeting, start Schedule+, and then follow these steps:

1. Jump to the date for the first regular Monday team meeting.
2. Select from the beginning time tag (9:00 A.M.) to the end time tag (10:00 A.M.) along the left side of the appointment slots, as shown here:

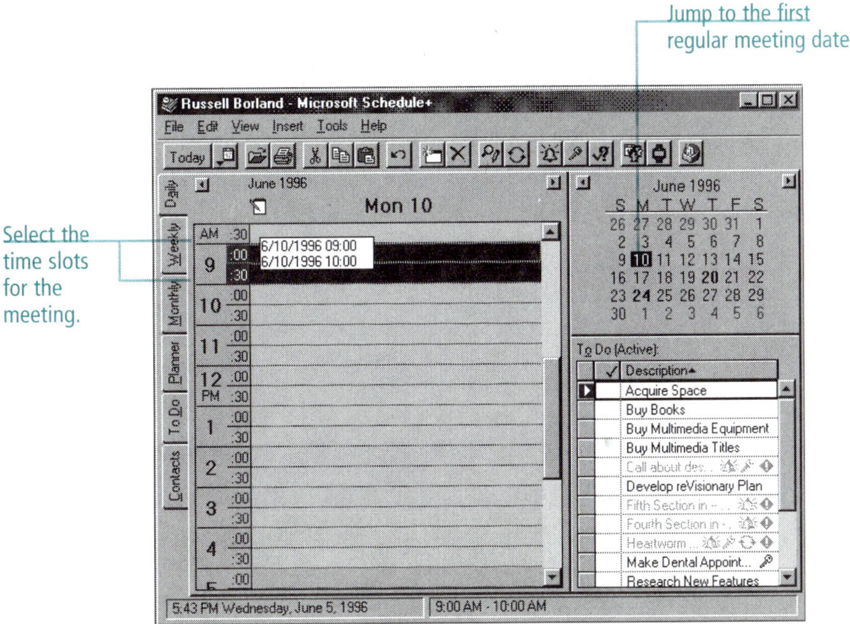

3. Click on the Recurring button.

4. Type a name for the appointment in the Description box (for example, *Bozo Bit Team Meeting*) and the location in the Where box (for example, the name or number of a conference room).

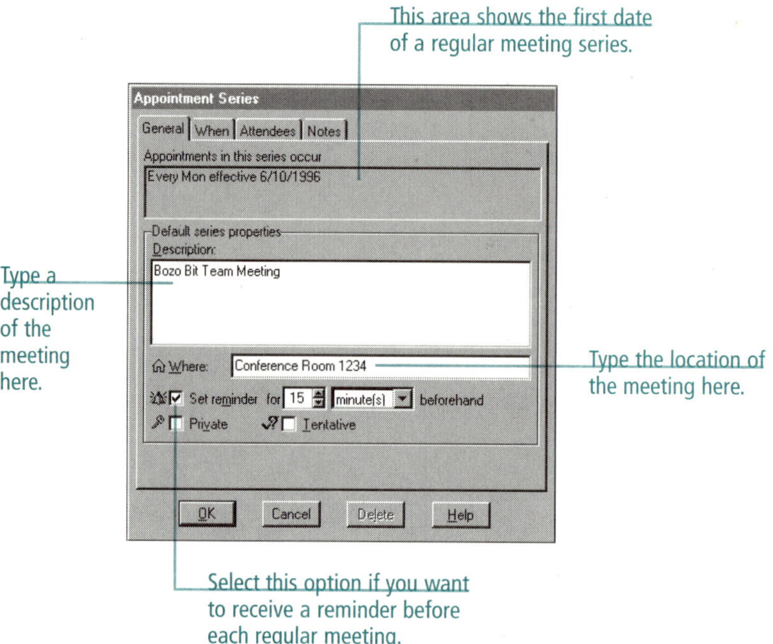

5. Set the advance notice time to remind you when it's time to go to the meeting.

Note When attendees accept this meeting in their appointment books, Schedule+ uses their standard advance notice, not yours.

6. Click on the When tab, and then select the Weekly interval for the appointment.
7. Set the number of weeks between occurrences to *1*.
8. If these regular team meetings will end at a specific date, click on the Until box. A box for the end date appears. Set the end date. If you don't know yet when the regular meetings will stop (in other words, if you don't yet know when the project will be finished), leave the Until box turned off.
9. If you want to jot down some notes about the regular team meetings (for example, a list of regular agenda items), click on the Notes tab, and then type your notes.

Note The only way to see notes you type for an appointment is to edit the appointment. To do so, right-click on the appointment, select Edit Item from the shortcut menu, and then click on the Notes tab. (If right-clicking is unavailable, choose the Edit Edit Recurring command, and then select Appointments from the submenu.) Select the regular meeting for which you want to see the notes, and then click on the Edit button. In the Appointment Series dialog box, select the Notes tab.

10. Click on the Attendees tab.

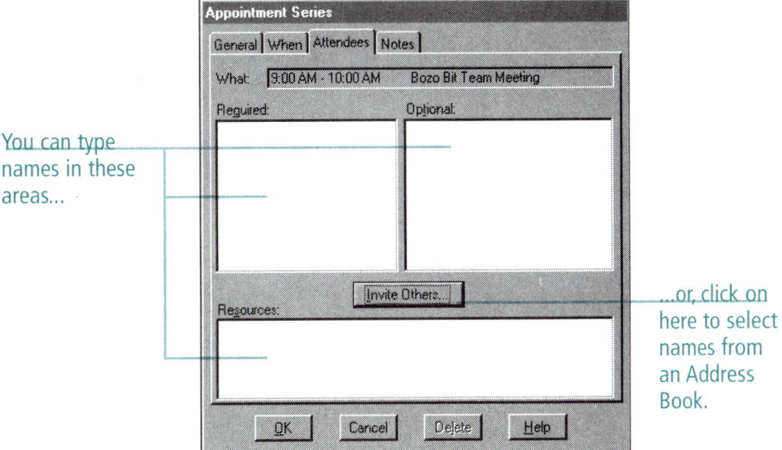

11. In the Required box, type the names of the people who must attend the meeting. Separate multiple names using a semicolon. If you have a distribution list already set up for your team, you can simply type the name of the distribution list.

Using the Meeting Attendees Dialog Box

Rather than type the names of people whom you are inviting to a meeting, you can select them in a dialog box that looks a lot like the Address Book. To select names of people and resources, click on the Invite Others button. You see the Meeting Attendees dialog box, shown on the top of the next page.

(continued)

Using the Meeting Attendees Dialog Box *(continued)*

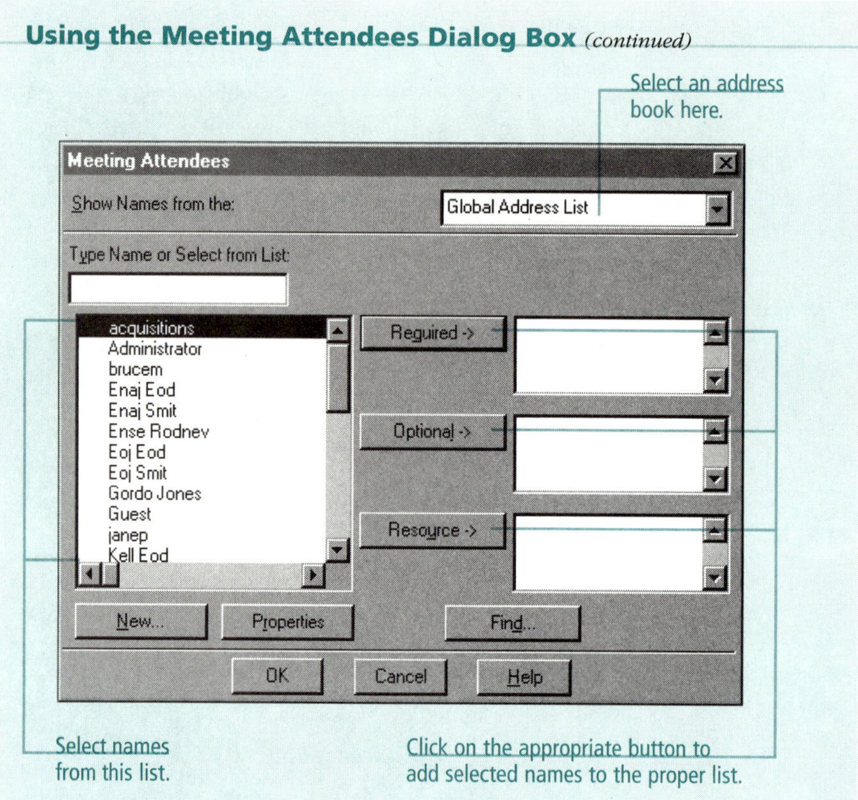

Select each name, and then click on the button for the category of that person or resource. For example, to invite Enaj Eod as a required attendee, select Enaj Eod from the list on the left, and then click on the Required button. Enaj Eod then appears in the Required box on the right. Click on OK when you've selected all your attendees.

12. In the Optional box, type the names of the people who might be interested in the meeting, but whose schedule need not be free for the meeting to be set up.
13. In the Resources box, type the names of the conference room, the audiovisual equipment, computers, and so on that you want to use for this meeting.

    If your Exchange administrator is wise, conference rooms will be listed in the Global Address Book. This makes it easy to

see when the conference rooms are free and to schedule the room as an "attendee." Just select the conference room you want from the Address Book. The same goes for other resources, such as audiovisual equipment or computers. These, too, can be listed in the Address Book and scheduled for meetings, the same as people can be. (Of course, conference rooms and other resources can't send a reply themselves. Generally, someone is assigned to monitor requests for the resources and send a reply as to availability.)

14. Click on OK in the Appointment Series dialog box. Schedule+ displays a meeting request form, which you send to each of the invitees. Here's a sample meeting request:

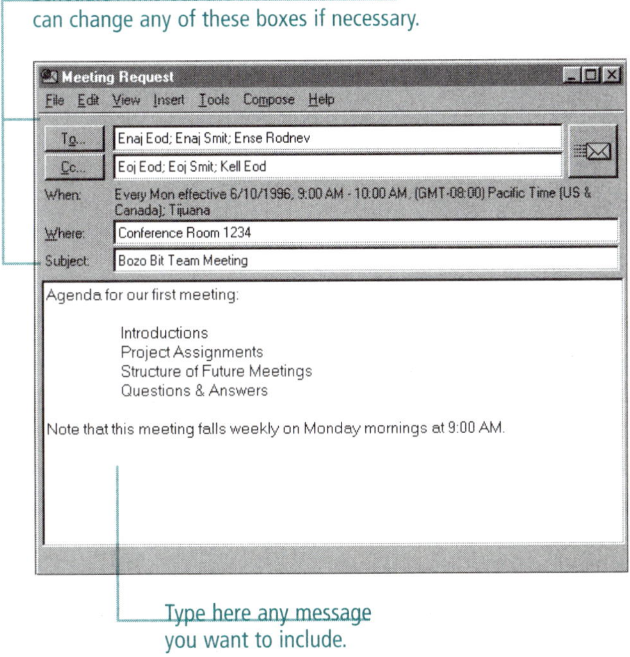

15. Type any message you want to send with the meeting request, and then click on the Send button beside the To and Cc boxes.

Jump to subsequent dates of the regular meeting to see a team meeting set for the duration of the project (or until the end of time, if you didn't set an end date).

Scheduling a Special Meeting

All projects seem to have emergencies, times when the team needs to have a meeting right now! (As British spies call it, a "crash meeting.") You might have some important new information that affects this week's work and can't wait until the next regular meeting. You might have a company-wide announcement that you've been asked to convey to your group *today*. Or you might just want to celebrate a birthday, an anniversary, or a particular triumph by a team member. In any case, you need to meet soon—or at least sooner than the next regular meeting.

To set up a specific meeting, follow these steps:

1. Switch to the date of the meeting.
2. In the time scale, select from the start time to the end time of the meeting.
3. Type a name for the appointment.
4. Click on the Edit button on the Schedule+ toolbar.

5. Click on the Attendees tab, and then click on the Invite Others button.
6. In the Meeting Attendees dialog box, select the names of the team members and any others that need to come to the meeting. If you have a distribution list already set up for your team, you can simply select the name of the distribution list.
7. Click on the Required button.

Note You might also want to let your boss or others know that you have called the meeting. In this case, select the names of these people and click on the Optional button.

8. Select a conference room for the meeting, and then click on the Resource button.
9. When you have selected the attendees, click on OK in the Meeting Attendees dialog box.

10. Click on the Planner tab. Schedule+ checks the appointment books of all the invitees and shows you if any of them, including the conference room, already have something scheduled for that time.

    If some team members are busy during the time you've scheduled, you can use your prerogative as team leader to schedule the meeting at that time and ask them to change their other appointments, or you can select a different time. For this, you can click on the AutoPick button, which jumps to the next available time slot when all resources and required attendees are free.

11. Click on OK in the Appointment dialog box.
12. Schedule+ displays an Exchange message window containing a meeting request form. Type any message you want to send with the meeting invitation, and then click on the Send button.

Receiving and Responding to a Meeting Request

When someone invites you to a meeting, you receive an Exchange message containing a meeting request form, something like this one:

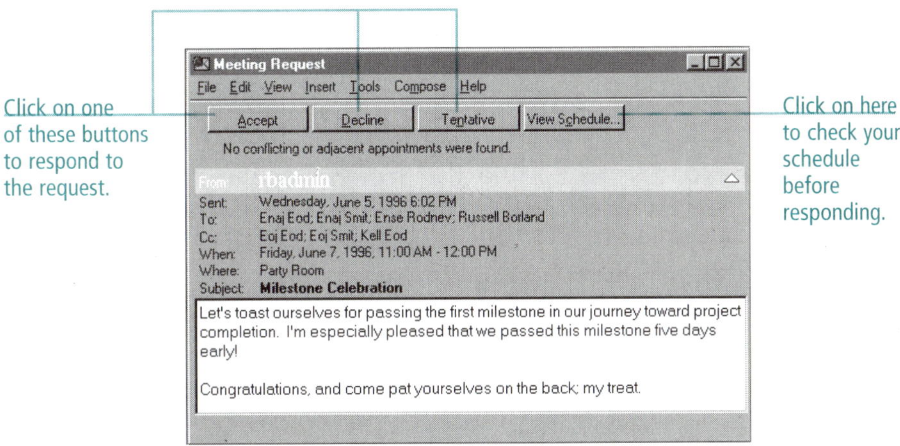

You open the message the same as you do any other Exchange message. Then, you respond to the meeting request form, as follows:

1. Click on one of the three buttons at the top of the message header—Accept, Decline, or Tentative. If you're not sure which button to click on, click on the View Schedule button to switch to your appointment book and check your schedule before responding. When you're ready to respond, press Alt+Tab to return to the meeting request form.
   - Click on the Accept button to return a message to the sender that states "Yes, I will attend." Schedule+ also adds the meeting to your appointment book. If you have some other appointment scheduled at the same time, Schedule+ lets you know and asks if you want to schedule the meeting anyway. Click on the Yes button to add the appointment alongside your previously scheduled appointment. Click on the No button to return to the original meeting request form.
   - Click on the Tentative button if you might attend the meeting but you're not yet sure. Schedule+ adds a tentative meeting to your appointment book and sends a message to the sender that states "I might attend."
   - Click on the Decline button to reject the appointment and to send a message to the sender that states "No, I won't attend."
   - After you click the button for your response, you see an appropriate message form, as shown here:

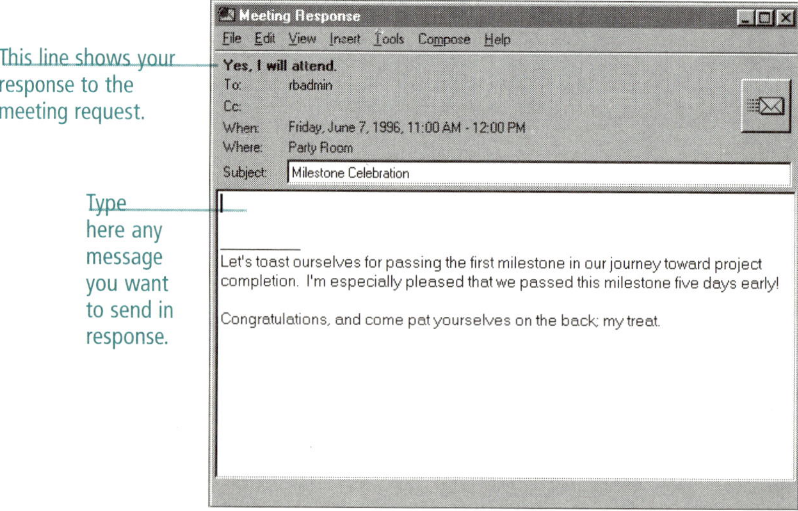

Who's Coming and Who's Not?

After you send a meeting request, you'll usually receive responses from each person and resource contact (the person responsible for the resource's schedule) to whom you sent your meeting request. As the responses come in, Schedule+ records the answer. Rather than having to open each message to check who's coming and who's not, you can switch to Schedule+ to view the list of those you invited and see if they are coming, aren't coming, might come, or have not yet sent their RSVP. Here's how:

1. Select the appointment, and then click on the Edit button on the Schedule+ toolbar.
2. Click on the Planner tab.
3. Check the Attendees box in the lower right corner of the Planner tab.

Attendees with a check mark beside their names have accepted your request for a meeting. Attendees with an X beside their names have declined your request for a meeting. Attendees with a question mark beside their names have given their tentative acceptance. Attendees with an envelope beside their names have not yet responded to your request. After checking the status of the invitees, you can send a reminder to the people from whom you need a response.

2. Type any comments you want to add to your return message, and then click on the Send button.

Changing a Meeting

The best laid plans of mice and men go awry sometimes. Even though you carefully schedule your regular meetings—and even more carefully schedule your special meetings—sometimes something comes up and you've got to change the meeting time, place, or date.

Changing special meetings isn't much of a problem. You simply change the date, time, or place, and Schedule+ asks if you want to notify the attendees of the changes. Of course you do—well, don't you? (Or is this change some kind of prank?)

Changing one meeting in a series of regular meetings is the same as changing a special meeting. Changing your regular meeting to always occur at a different time or place takes some different steps.

Changing a Special Meeting or One in a Series of Meetings

Sometimes you'll have to move a special meeting or one of your regular meetings to a different time or day. Sometimes the meeting has to be longer than originally set, and sometimes, if you're truly lucky, a meeting can be shortened.

Moving a Special Meeting or One in a Series of Meetings

When you have to move a special meeting or one of your regular meetings, you've got two choices. You can always use the Edit Move command, but as long as the meeting's original and new times are both visible on the screen, you can also drag the meeting to a different time or date.

To move a meeting by dragging it, do the following:

1. Select the meeting, and then position the mouse pointer in the top or left border of the meeting. The mouse pointer becomes a four-headed arrow.
2. Drag the meeting to the new time or date.

Drag the top or left border to move the meeting's start time.

If the time is earlier or later than the time bands shown on the screen, drag the meeting into the border of the time bands. Schedule+ scrolls the time bands. (This feature works better for moving to an earlier time than a later time.)

If the meeting is rescheduled for a new day this week, click on the Weekly tab, and then drag the meeting horizontally to the new date and time.

You can display as many as seven days in Weekly view. Use the View Number Of Days command to select the number of days to see in Weekly view.

If the meeting is next week or next month or any time beyond the current week, you need to use the Edit Move Appt command.

To move a meeting with the Edit Move Appt command, follow these steps:

1. Select the meeting.
2. Choose the Edit Move Appt command.
3. In the Move Appointment dialog box, set the new time or new date or both, and then click on OK.

Tailoring a Meeting: Longer or Shorter

So you have set up a special meeting to discuss the Bozo Bit project. The night before, two team members corner you and say they want to report on a breakthrough in development, something you hadn't planned on discussing. Everyone who needs to hear about this will be gathered anyway, so you agree, but now the meeting must be longer. Or, what happens if a team member reporting on a new aspect of the game's design suddenly takes ill? You decide to forgo discussing that item on the meeting's agenda, so now the meeting can be shorter. Here's what you do:

1. Position the mouse pointer on the bottom border of the meeting. The mouse pointer becomes a two-headed arrow.
2. Drag the bottom border up to shorten the meeting. Drag the bottom border down to lengthen the meeting.

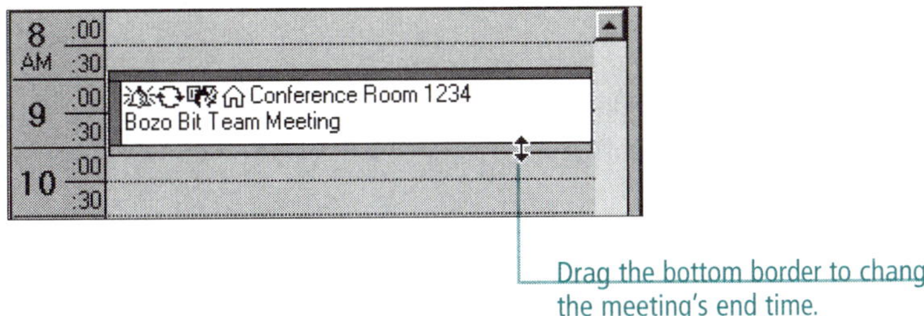

Drag the bottom border to change the meeting's end time.

TIP If you prefer, instead of dragging a meeting to a new time or duration or choosing the Move Meeting command, you can simply edit the properties of the meeting, as follows:

1. Select the meeting.
2. Click on the Properties button on the Schedule+ toolbar.
3. Change the meeting times and date in the Properties dialog box.
4. Click on OK.

Changing Further Occasions of a Regular Meeting

For various reasons, your regular meeting time and day aren't working with the rhythms of the project. You originally set up the regular meeting for 9:00 A.M. Monday morning, but the project rhythms make Wednesday afternoon a better time for your project team to meet. So now you need to move the regular meeting to the new day and time. Here's how you do that:

1. Choose the Edit Edit Recurring command, and then select Appointments from the submenu.
2. In the Recurring Appointments dialog box, select the regular meeting you want to move, and then click on the Edit button.
3. In the Appointment Series dialog box, select the When tab, and then select the check box for the day of the week on which you now want to meet (Wednesday).
4. Select the check box for the day you were meeting (Monday) to cancel that day. If you don't cancel the previous meeting day, you'll have a regular meeting two days a week.
5. Adjust the Start and End times for the new meeting.
6. Make any other changes to the meeting properties in the dialog box. (For example, if you need to change the place of the meeting, do so on the General tab.) Click on OK when you've finished.
7. When Schedule+ asks if you want to notify the meeting participants about the change, click on the Yes button. Schedule+ sends a message to the attendees about the new meeting day and time.
8. In the Recurring Appointments dialog box, click on the Close button.

Canceling a Meeting

Well, sometimes you just don't need this or that meeting after all. Maybe you want to skip a week or two of the regular team meeting (and let everyone get some work done). Or, you're finished! You don't need a regular team meeting anymore. In all these cases, you cancel the meeting or put the regular team meeting out to pasture.

Canceling One or Several in a Series of Regular Meetings

From time to time, you might decide to forgo the regular meeting—a week here, a week there, or a couple of weeks in a row. Canceling one regular meeting in a series is easy: You simply cancel the meeting you're not going to hold. Here's how:

1. Click on the regular meeting you want to cancel.
2. Click on the Delete button on the Schedule+ toolbar.
3. Schedule+ asks if you want to delete all occurences of the meeting. Click on the No button.
4. When Schedule+ asks if you want to notify the meeting participants about the change, click on the Yes button. Schedule+ creates a message in a message window. Add any text you want, and then click on the Send button to send a message to the attendees that the meeting has been canceled.
5. Repeat step 1 through step 4 to cancel additional occurrences of the regular meeting.

Canceling a single meeting from a series doesn't affect the other regular meetings at all.

Canceling All Further Occasions of a Regular Meeting

When you no longer need to hold a regular meeting, you can remove the appointments for it from your calendar. Schedule+ gives you two ways to do this. If you know in advance when the series of regular meetings will end, you simply give the series an end date. If you don't know until the last meeting that you won't be meeting anymore on a regular basis, you simply cancel the series.

To set an end date for a series of regular meetings, do this:

1. Choose the Edit Edit Recurring command, and then select Appointments from the submenu.

2. Select the regular meeting you want to change, and then click on the Edit button.
3. Click on the Until box. A box for the end date appears.
4. Set the end date, and then click on OK.

   If the end date has passed already, Schedule+ marks the series Finished in the Recurring Appointments dialog box. The evidence of the meetings remains in your schedule.

To cancel a series of regular meetings and remove a record of them from your schedule, do this:

1. Choose the Edit Edit Recurring command, and then select Appointments from the submenu.
2. Select the regular meeting you want to cancel, and then click on the Delete button.
3. When Schedule+ asks if you want to delete all occurrences of the meeting, click on the Yes button.
4. When Schedule+ asks if you want to notify the meeting participants about the change, click on the Yes button. Schedule+ creates a message in a message window. Add any text you want, and then click on the Send button to send a message that the rest of the regular meetings have been canceled.

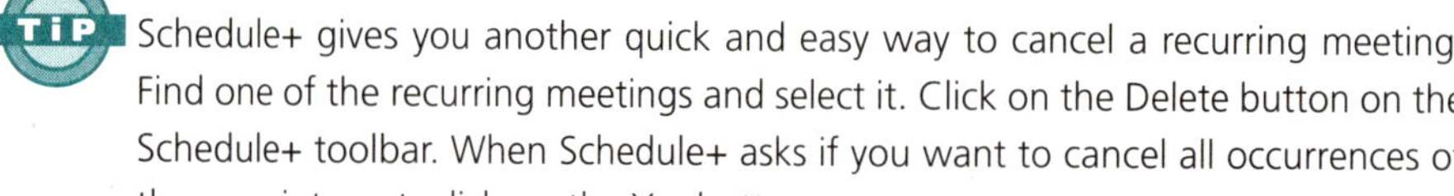

TIP Schedule+ gives you another quick and easy way to cancel a recurring meeting. Find one of the recurring meetings and select it. Click on the Delete button on the Schedule+ toolbar. When Schedule+ asks if you want to cancel all occurrences of the appointment, click on the Yes button.

Canceling a Special Meeting

After all the gyrations you've gone through to set up a special meeting, if it turns out that it just isn't going to come off (or that you don't really need the meeting), you can cancel it. Here's how:

1. Click on the meeting.
2. Click on the Delete button on the Schedule+ toolbar.

3. When Schedule+ asks if you want to notify the meeting participants about the change, click on the Yes button. Schedule+ creates a message in a message window. Add any text you want, and then click on the Send button to send a message to the attendees that the meeting has been canceled.

Archiving Project Scheduling

After you've completed a project, you might want to keep a permanent record of the schedule. This record can be useful for analyzing project progress and for planning your next project. Schedule+ gives you a way to save a project schedule in an archive file.

To archive a project schedule, do the following:

1. Choose the File Archive command.

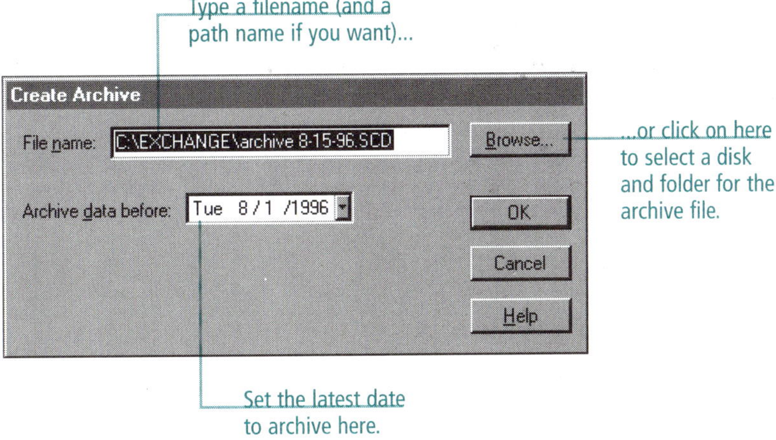

2. Select the range of dates you want to archive.
3. If you don't like the filename Schedule+ makes up, type a new name for the archive file.
4. If you want to change the disk or folder in which Schedule+ will store the archive file, click on the Browse button, select the place for the archive file, and then click on the Open button.

5. Click on OK in the Create Archive dialog box.

If you later need to recover the archived schedule information, follow these steps:

1. Choose the File Open command, and then choose Archive Or Project Schedule from the submenu.
2. Select the disk and folder in which you stored the archive file.

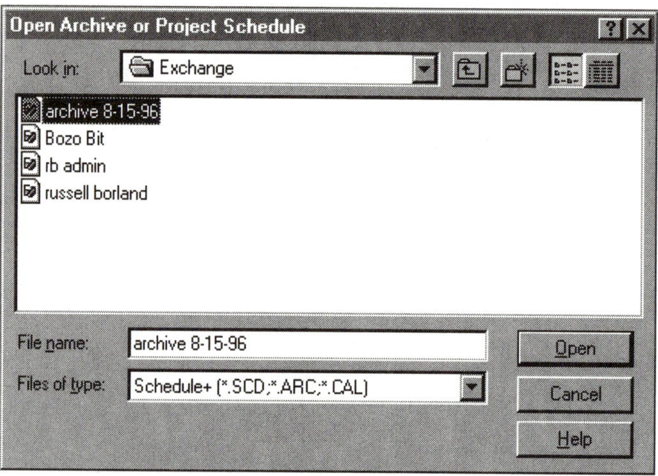

3. Select the archive file, and then click on the Open button.

CHAPTER
11

Setting Up and Tracking Project Tasks

Everybody needs to know what to do. In Microsoft Schedule+, you can schedule tasks and assign tasks to team members. You can then track the progress of individual tasks or parts of tasks. In this chapter, you'll learn how to set up and track project tasks.

Scenes from This Chapter

Scenario

The members of the Bozo Bit team each have their individual tasks to perform. As project team leader, you want to set up the various tasks, assign them to the appropriate team members, and track the team's progress toward completing each task.

As project development moves along, you decide to do away with some of the tasks, either because of time and budget constraints or because the original task changed or became unnecessary. Also, as you watch the team work together, you might need to reassign a task—for example, if you happen to lose a team member, if you gain a team member who can take over one or more tasks, or if you need to balance tasks better among the team members.

Giving a Project Its Own Appointment Book

If you expect to work on a project for a reasonably long period of time, you might find it beneficial to set up a separate appointment book for the project. You still control this appointment book, but it contains only the appointments, tasks, and contacts that pertain to the particular project. None of your personal or other business scheduling crowds the appointment book.

You'll want to share the appointment book you create with your team members so that they can check the task list and report their progress toward completing their tasks. To make the appointment book available to your team members, put it into a special project folder in which team members are allowed to edit all items.

To create a separate appointment book for your project, start Schedule+, and then follow these steps:

1. Choose the File New command.
2. Type a name for the new appointment book, for example, *Bozo Bit.*
3. Select a disk and folder in which you want to temporarily store this appointment book. In Windows 95, you can store the appointment book on the Desktop, which makes it easy to put the appointment book into the project folder.
4. Click on the Save button.

Next, you'll need to create a subfolder for the schedule only. Set the permissions of the schedule folder to give each team member permission to edit all items. For information about creating a subfolder, see "Creating the Project Folder," on page 202. For information about setting folder permissions, see "Setting Up a Roster of Team Members," on page 203. To put the appointment book in the schedule folder, take these steps:

1. Open the schedule folder.
2. Drag the icon for the appointment book (.SCD) file into the schedule folder.
3. Delete the copy of the appointment book file from the temporary location you used in the previous procedure.
4. Send a message to the team members with the name of the project file and its folder location.

To open the project schedule, team members double-click on the project schedule file icon in the schedule folder.

Team members can now use the project appointment book in all the same ways they use their personal appointment books.

Note If you open a Schedule+ file in a public folder, Exchange might warn you when you exit Exchange that you still have an open document, even if you have closed all open documents. In this case, click on OK to close the message. Exchange will exit.

Setting Up a Project Name

You can set up a project name in your Schedule+ To Do List so that you can list the tasks related to that specific project. If you are using a separate project appointment book, you can use phases and parts of the project as project names within the project appointment book, and then set up tasks under these categories. This approach enables you to break down the project work into more manageable and measurable pieces. You can set up tasks in your To Do List without setting up a project name (in which case all the tasks fall under the project name None), but I'd suggest that you set up at least one project name for the tasks you need to assign or track.

To set up a project name, do the following:

If right-clicking is unavailable, choose the Insert Project command.

1. Click on the To Do tab to display the To Do List.
2. Right-click anywhere in the To Do List, and then choose New Project from the shortcut menu. The project dialog box appears, as shown on the next page.

3. Type the name of the project, for example, *Bozo Bit*. Remember, if you're using a project appointment book, you might want to create names for phases or elements of the project—for example, Marketing, Sales, Advertising, Production, Distribution, and so on.
4. If this project is more important than your other daily tasks, set the Priority box higher than the standard priority 3.
5. Click on OK.

You can create a new project when you set up its first task. To do so, type the project name in the Project box of the Task dialog box. For details of setting up a task, see the next section.

Scheduling a Task

When you have a project name set up, you are ready to set up the tasks that are part of the project. Although you can set up a task, assign it to someone (or to several someones), and set up a time and effort "budget" for the task all at once, we'll look at these three parts of a task separately. (For information about assigning a task, see "Assigning Tasks to Team Members," on page 289. For information about budgeting task time and effort, see "Tracking Task Progress," on page 292.)

To set up a task, follow these steps:

1. Click on the To Do tab to display the To Do List.
2. Right-click on the project name, and then choose New Task from the shortcut menu.

If right-clicking is unavailable, select the project, and then choose the Insert Task command.

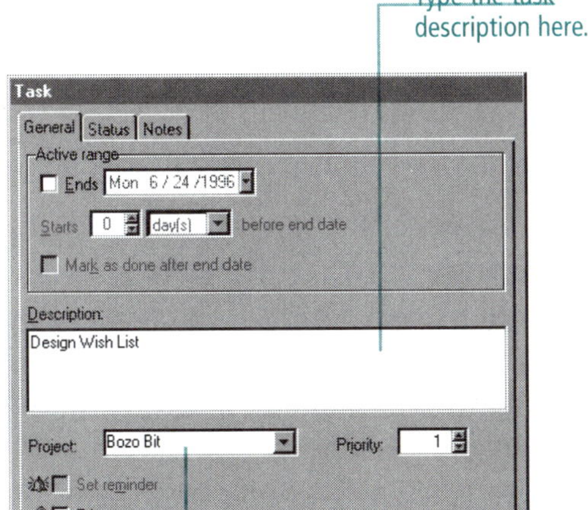

3. Type a name for the task.
4. Fill in the other information for the task—for example, its priority—and then click on OK.

Task Appointments, Appointed Tasks

Let's say that as part of your project assignment, you have to attend a meeting to gather information from an engineer, report your progress to your team members, and then give a demonstration to an executive manager. Or, on another occasion you have an appointment and need to prepare for it somehow—write a report, create a presentation, or conduct research.

For both ways—setting up an appointment from a task and setting up a task from an appointment—you can use two special commands in Schedule+. You can also use the mouse to set up an appointment from a task.

(continued)

Task Appointments, Appointed Tasks *(continued)*

To set up a task from (or for) an appointment, do the following:

1. On one of the appointment tabs (Daily, Weekly, or Monthly), find and select the appointment for which you want to set up a related task.
2. Select the appointment, choose the Insert Related Item command, and then choose Task From Appointment from the submenu.
3. Fill out and adjust the Appointment dialog box that appears, making sure you've selected the correct project, and then click on OK.

To set up an appointment from (or for) a task, do this:

1. On the To Do tab or in the Active To Do List on the Daily tab, find and select the task from which you want to set up an appointment.
2. Select the task, choose the Insert Related Item command, and then choose Appt From Task from the submenu.
3. Fill out and adjust the Appointment dialog box that appears, and then click on OK.

Schedule+ displays no obvious connection between an appointment and a task, even when you set one up from the other following the procedures above. The one bond between them that you can count on is the description. The description for an appointment that you set up from a task shows both the task name and its project name. The same doesn't apply to tasks set up from appointments because appointments don't have projects. You can use two methods to ensure that you know the connection between appointments and tasks. First, you can make sure the description shows the relationship. Second, you can add notes to the Notes tab for both the appointments and tasks that are related. To add notes to the Notes tab, select the appointment or task, choose the Edit Item command, click on the Notes tab, type your notes, and then click on OK.

(continued)

Task Appointments, Appointed Tasks *(continued)*

As an alternative to using the Appt From Task command, you can use the mouse by doing the following:

1. In the Active To Do List on the Daily or Weekly Schedule tab, find and select the task from which you want to set up an appointment.
2. Drag the task from the Active To Do List to the appointment time slot.
3. Click on the Edit button on the Schedule+ toolbar, fill out and adjust the Appointment dialog box, and then click on OK.

You can only drag tasks to set appointments from the Active To Do List, not from the To Do tab. For future tasks that don't appear on the Active To Do List, use the Appt From Task command.

For a more complete view of the Active To Do List, add the Weekly Schedule tab to your appointment book. This tab shows appointments at the top and the Active To Do List at the bottom. You can then drag active tasks to set appointments.

Assigning Tasks to Team Members

Without someone to perform a task, the task simply won't get done. So, with tasks set up, it's time to assign tasks to team members so that they can start working—and the project can move forward.

To assign a task to a team member, you make that person the contact for that task. The contact is the team member who manages the task and reports the progress on the task in the project To Do List. If you find later that one team member is overloaded with tasks, you can assign a different team member as the task contact.

You can create an archive record of project tasks after the project is complete. To learn about archiving the project task schedule, see "Archiving Project Scheduling" on page 279.

Assigning a Team Member as a Task Contact

To assign a team member as a task contact, follow these steps:

If right-clicking is unavailable, select a task, and then click on the Edit button on the To Do List toolbar.

1. Right-click on the task, and then choose Edit Item from the shortcut menu.
2. Click on the Status tab.

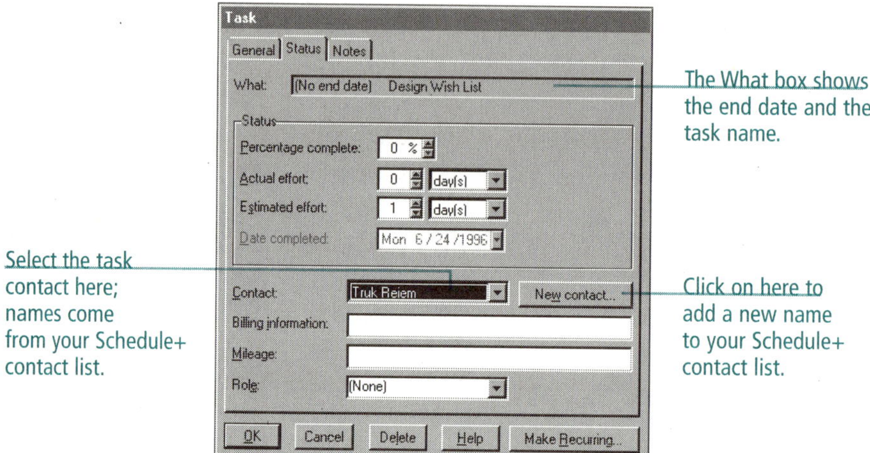

3. From the list in the Contact box, select the name of the person you want to assign as contact for the task or add a new contact as described next.

Adding Contact Names

When you first begin to assign contacts to tasks, the list in the Contact box might contain only the name None. If that's the case, you need to add names. Also, if the contact is someone who's not in your Schedule+ contact list already, you'll need to add the new name to the list before you can list the name as the contact.

To add a new contact name, do this:

If right-clicking is unavailable, select a task, and then click on the Edit button on the To Do List toolbar.

1. Right-click on the task for the new contact, and then choose Edit Item from the shortcut menu.
2. Click on the Status tab, and then click on the New Contact button.

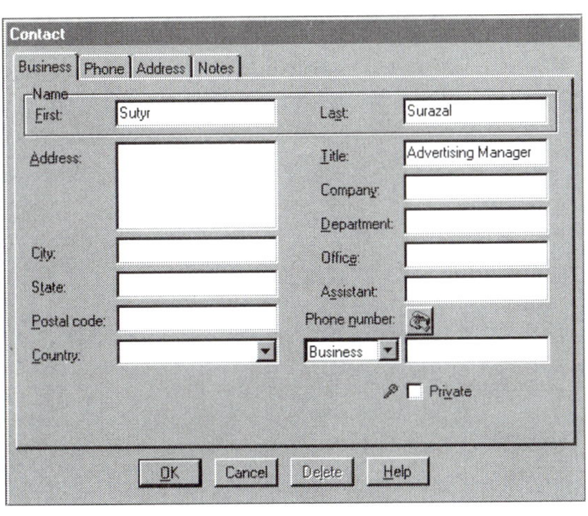

3. Fill in the name of the contact. You can also enter any other information you have or want to record for this contact. Then click on OK.
4. The new contact name now appears in the Contact box. If this is the name you want, click on OK. If not, select a different name from the list in the Contact box, and then click on OK.

Reassigning a Project Task to a New Contact

If you have contact names set up already, changing the contact name is easy. It's even easier if you also set up a Contact column in the To Do List. (See "Setting Up Columns of Task Information," on page 295.)

To change the contact for a task when you don't have a Contact column, use the same steps you use for assigning a contact the first time. (See "Assigning a Team Member as a Task Contact," on page 290.)

To change the contact for a task when you have a Contact column in the To Do List, follow these steps:

1. Click on the Contact name for the task.
2. Click on the down arrow button, and then select a new name from the list. If the name you want isn't in the list, you'll have to add a new contact name, as described in "Adding Contact Names," on page 290.

Tracking Task Progress

Besides setting up tasks and giving them due dates, you can also keep track of the progress of each task as the team member assigned to it moves toward completing the task. For budgeting purposes, you can also set an estimated time and effort for each task. With all this information filled in, you can then get a picture of the overall progress of the project.

To track task and project progress, you'll do these things:

- Set time and effort estimates for each task
- Set and review the percentage complete for each task

Setting Task Estimates

Setting time and effort estimates for a task gives you the basis for budgeting the task. As you work through the task, you can compare actual time and effort with the estimates you set to see if you need to adjust your estimates and your budget. After you complete a task, you can use the figures for the actual time and effort for planning another similar project.

To set the time estimate for a task, do this:

If right-clicking is unavailable, select a task, and then click on the Edit button on the To Do List toolbar.

1. Right-click on the task and choose Edit Item from the shortcut menu.
2. Click on the General tab.
3. Click to place a check in the Ends box, click on the down arrow button beside the date shown, and then select the task end date from the calendar. (Click the right or left arrow button at the top of the calendar to move forward or backward one month.)
4. In the Starts box, set the amount of time you need for this task. For example, if this task should take two weeks, the Ends and Starts boxes would look something like the figure at the top of the next page.

You can view and adjust the time and effort estimates more easily if you add their columns to the To Do List page. With the columns displayed, you can click the column for a task and adjust the setting without opening a dialog box. To set up these columns and others, see "Setting Up Columns of Task Information," on page 295.

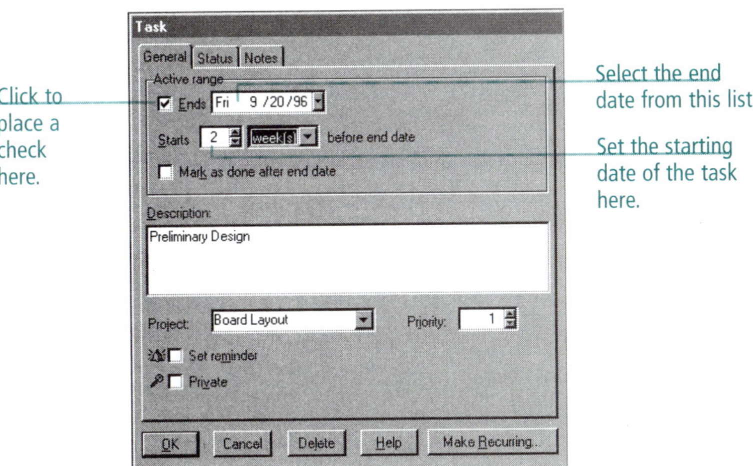

The estimated effort is the amount of time you plan to spend on the task over the course of the estimated time. For example, if you will be devoting 2 hours per work day to the task, and the estimated time is two weeks, the estimated effort would be 10 hours.

To set up the estimated effort for a task, do the following:

1. Right-click on the task, and then choose Edit Item from the shortcut menu. (If right-clicking is unavailable, select a task, and then click on the Edit button on the To Do List toolbar).
2. Click on the Status tab.

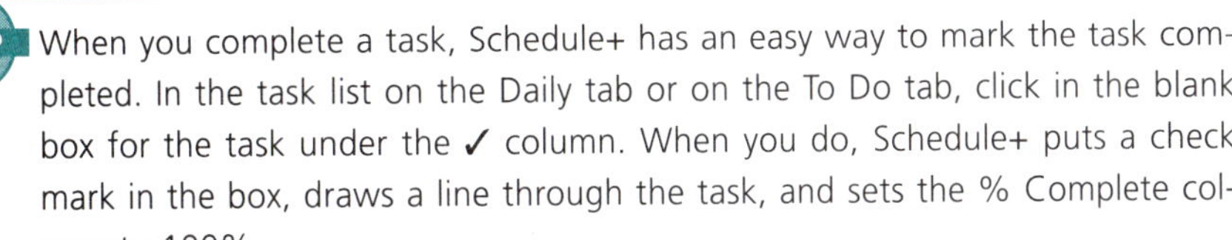

TIP When you complete a task, Schedule+ has an easy way to mark the task completed. In the task list on the Daily tab or on the To Do tab, click in the blank box for the task under the ✓ column. When you do, Schedule+ puts a check mark in the box, draws a line through the task, and sets the % Complete column to 100%.

3. In the Estimated Effort boxes, set the amount of time you need for this task. For example, if this task should take 10 hours, the Estimated Effort boxes would look something like the figure at the top of the next page.

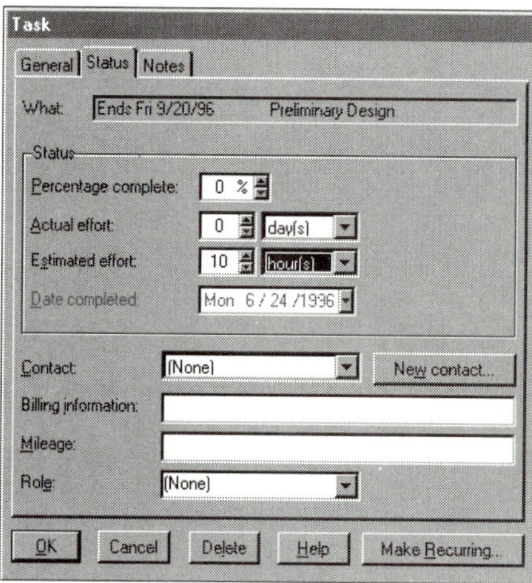

Tracking Task Progress

To review and set the progress of an individual task, do this:

If right-clicking is unavailable, select a task, and then click on the Edit button on the To Do List toolbar.

1. Right-click on the task, and then choose Edit Item from the shortcut menu.
2. Click on the Status tab.
3. Adjust the number in the Percentage Complete box, and then click on OK.

TIP Schedule+ shows the % Complete column in the To Do List as part of its standard set up. (To save space, this column might display only part of the word "Complete"; for example, you might see only % C....) The entry for a task in the % Complete column shows you at a glance how much of a task has been completed. This number is completely manual; that is, you or the contact must manually change the number. It doesn't change itself over time (with one exception—discussed next).

The % Complete column also makes it easy to adjust the percent complete. Simply click on the current percentage, and then either type or scroll to the percentage as it should be for the current status of the task. If you turn on the Mark As Done After End Date and set an end date on the General tab of the Task dialog box, Schedule+ automatically sets the percent complete to 100% on the day after the end date you set.

Worlds of Views: Columnbining, Grouping, Sorting, and Filtering Tasks

The To Do List in Schedule+ can display lots of information. Organizing the information in ways that make sense is an important part of managing projects, team members, and tasks. Schedule+ gives you various ways to control your view of the To Do List:

- Selecting the number of columns of information you see and arranging their order
- Grouping tasks
- Sorting tasks
- Filtering tasks

All of these methods of controlling your view of the To Do List interact. What you see on the To Do List tab depends on the combination of the settings you select for columns, grouping, sorting, and filtering. It's almost impossible to describe, at least in fewer than several dozen pages, how all the combinations look. In effect, you'll have to experiment with the combinations to come up with the ones that suit your purpose in any given situation.

Setting Up Columns of Task Information

In the To Do List, as well as on the other tabs of a Schedule+ appointment book, you can set up a large number of columns to show information about each entry on a tab. On the To Do List tab, you have a column available for each of the pieces of information you set up for each task. Initially, the To Do List shows columns for Done, Description, Priority, Due Date, % Complete, and Project. You can add to this list of columns, take away any of the columns, and rearrange the order of the columns to suit your working style, task needs, and organization's culture. Also, to help you view the information more efficiently and effectively, you can adjust the width of the columns to show more of the information in a column or to fit more columns within the width of the To Do List display.

Adding and Removing Columns of Task Information

Schedule+ provides 16 columns that you can use to show information for each task in the To Do List. At first, the To Do List shows a "typical" selection. (Microsoft decided what was "typical.") In addition to the "typical" list, Schedule+ provides three other built-in selections of columns: All, Few, and Description Only. The Description Only selection shows you only the task description that you typed in the Description box on the General tab of the Task dialog box. The following table lists all the column names you can display and which columns appear in the Few and Typical selections. The column titles are listed in the order in which Microsoft organized them in Schedule+, but you can change the arrangement of columns, as described in "Rearranging Columns," on page 298.

All Columns	Few Columns	Typical Columns
Completed	✓	✓
Description	✓	✓
Priority	✓	✓
End Date	✓	✓
Duration		✓
% Complete		✓
Date Completed		
Actual Effort		
Estimated Effort		
Project		✓
Billing Information		
Contact		
Notes		
Mileage		
Role		
Creator		

To change the number of columns to one of the built-in selections, choose the View Columns command, and then choose the column display option you want from the submenu.

To customize the columns displayed, do the following:

1. Right-click on one of the column buttons, choose Columns from the shortcut menu, and then choose Custom from the submenu. (If right-clicking is unavailable, choose the View Columns command, and then choose Custom from the submenu.)

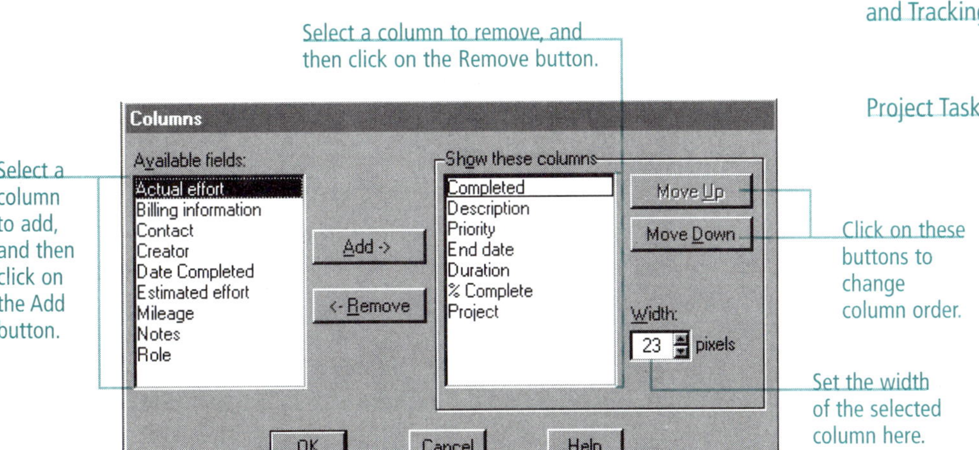

Figure 11-1
The Columns dialog box

2. To add a column, select it in the Available Fields list, and then click on the Add button.

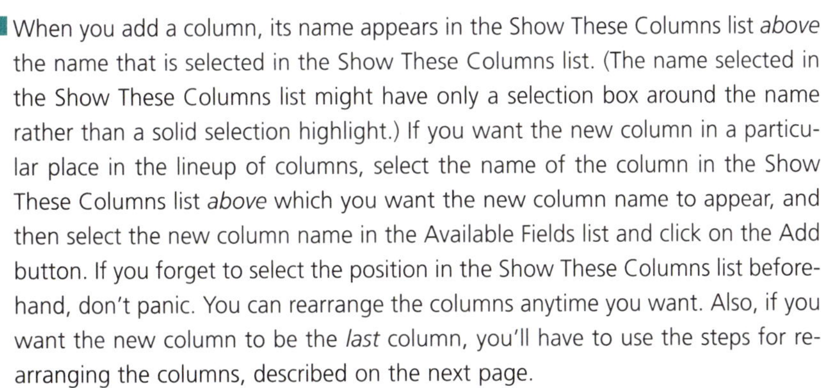

TIP When you add a column, its name appears in the Show These Columns list *above* the name that is selected in the Show These Columns list. (The name selected in the Show These Columns list might have only a selection box around the name rather than a solid selection highlight.) If you want the new column in a particular place in the lineup of columns, select the name of the column in the Show These Columns list *above* which you want the new column name to appear, and then select the new column name in the Available Fields list and click on the Add button. If you forget to select the position in the Show These Columns list beforehand, don't panic. You can rearrange the columns anytime you want. Also, if you want the new column to be the *last* column, you'll have to use the steps for rearranging the columns, described on the next page.

3. To remove a column, select it in the Show These Columns list, and then click on the Remove button.
4. When you have added the columns you want to see and removed the columns you don't need, click on OK.

Note No matter in which list the solid selection highlight appears, the Add button adds the column selected in the Available Fields list, and the Remove button removes the column selected in the Show These Columns list. The lists in the Columns dialog box each have a selection. In one list or both lists you might see only a selection box around a column name. The name surrounded by a selection box or highlighted is the selected column name.

Rearranging Columns

Microsoft decided the order in which columns should appear for the built-in selections. You might prefer a different order. Also, if you set up a custom selection of columns, you might have added the columns without first selecting the positions you wanted for them. Or, you might want a new column to be the last column. In all of these cases, you need to rearrange the column order in the Columns dialog box, which is shown in Figure 11-1 on page 297.

To rearrange the column order, do this:

If right-clicking is unavailable, choose the View Columns command, and then choose Custom from the submenu.

1. Right-click on one of the column buttons, choose Columns from the shortcut menu, and then choose Custom from the submenu.
2. In the Show These Columns list, select the column you want to move, and then click on the Move Up or Move Down button.

   Note Even if you select a name in the Available Fields list and click on the Move Up or Move Down button, the name selected in the Show These Columns list moves. In this case, the name selected in the Show These Columns list might have only a selection box around the name rather than a solid selection highlight.

3. When you have arranged the columns as you want them, click on OK.

Changing Column Width

Whenever the information for a column is wider than the column, you see the first part of the information followed by an ellipsis (...). Likewise, if the column heading is wider than the column, you see the first part of the column heading followed by an ellipsis. If this bugs you, you can widen the column to see all the information it displays or to see the complete column name.

But widening columns can put you in a quandary: with wide columns, you can't see as many columns on the To Do List tab at the same time. You have to scroll to see the columns that are out of view to the right, and then scroll back to see the columns that were moved to the left. In this case, you might want to narrow the columns to see more columns at once. (You understand, of course, that if you've set up many columns or chosen the All selection of columns, you will most likely need to scroll the task list horizontally in any case.)

Schedule+ gives you two ways to change the width of columns. You can drag the column borders with the mouse, or you can set specific column widths in the Columns dialog box.

To change column width with the mouse, do this:

1. Position the mouse pointer on the border at the right of a column heading, as shown here:

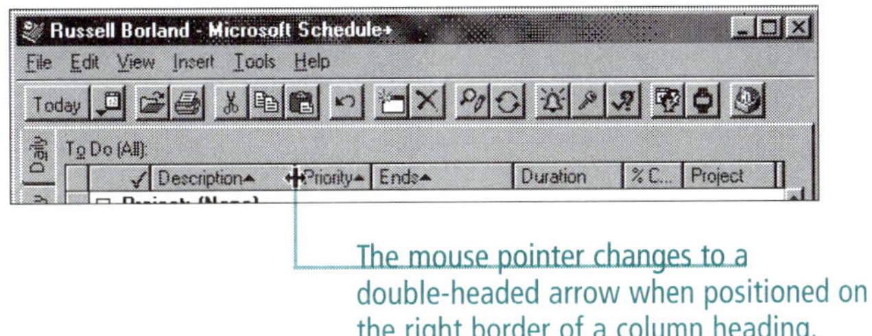

The mouse pointer changes to a double-headed arrow when positioned on the right border of a column heading.

2. Drag the column border to the right to widen the column. Drag the column border to the left to narrow the column.

If you're going to adjust the width of several columns, start with the leftmost column first, and then work your way to the right. Changing one column's width doesn't change any of the other columns' widths.

To change column width in the Columns dialog box, do this:

1. Right-click on one of the column buttons, choose Columns from the shortcut menu, and then choose Custom from the submenu.
2. In the Show These Columns list, select the name of the column you want to adjust.
3. In the Width box, set the width of the column.

If right-clicking is unavailable, choose the View Columns command, and then choose Custom from the submenu.

Note The column width is measured in pixels, which means the number of dots on the computer screen. The width of a pixel varies with the resolution of the screen. On higher-resolution screens, pixels are smaller than on lower-resolution screens.

4. To adjust other columns, repeat step 2 and step 3.
5. When you have adjusted the widths of all the columns you want to change, click on OK.

Grouping Tasks

A grouping of tasks separates one set of tasks from other sets. For example, the standard grouping of tasks in Schedule+ is by project, as shown here:

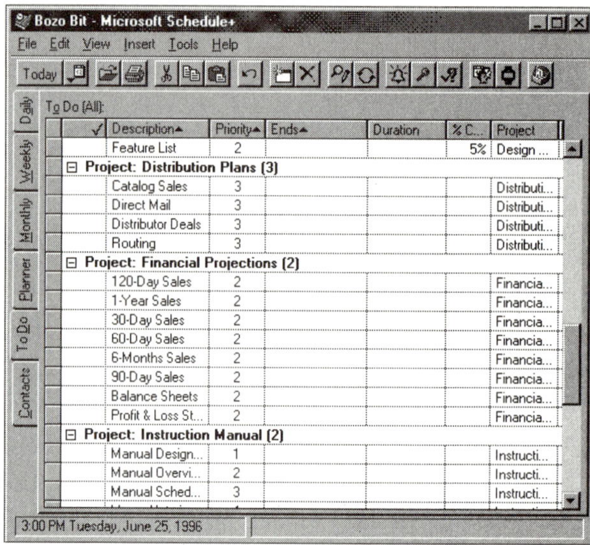

You can group tasks various ways. Your choices are:

- No groupings. All the tasks appear in a single, undivided list, sorted according to the sorting scheme you select. (See "Sorting Tasks," on page 302, for details.)
- One group. Tasks appear within their associated group. The project grouping is the most common, but you might prefer priority or due date groupings.
- Two or more groups. Tasks appear in subgroups under groups or other subgroups. For example, you could group tasks by project, then by priority, and then by end date. Each grouping shows a label in the To Do List, as shown in Figure 11-2.

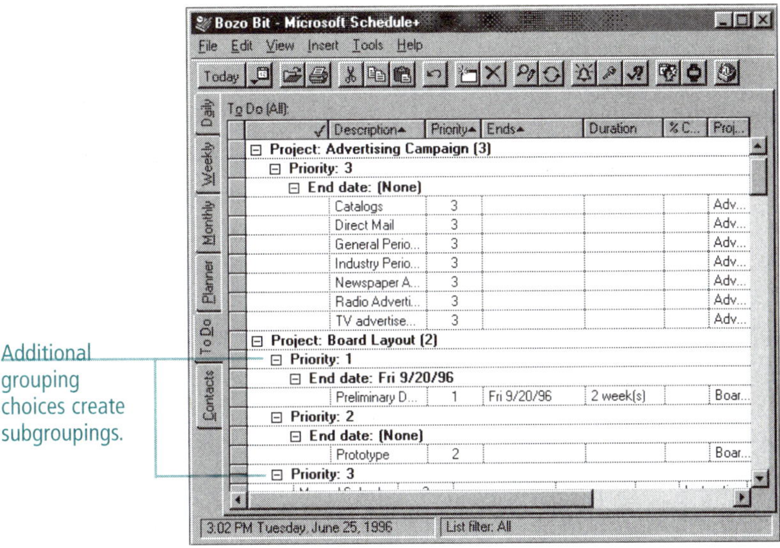

Additional grouping choices create subgroupings.

Figure 11-2
The To Do List with three groupings—project, priority, and end date

To change the way tasks are grouped in the To Do List, follow these steps:

1. Right-click on a column heading, and then choose Group By from the shortcut menu.

If right-clicking is unavailable, choose the View Group By command.

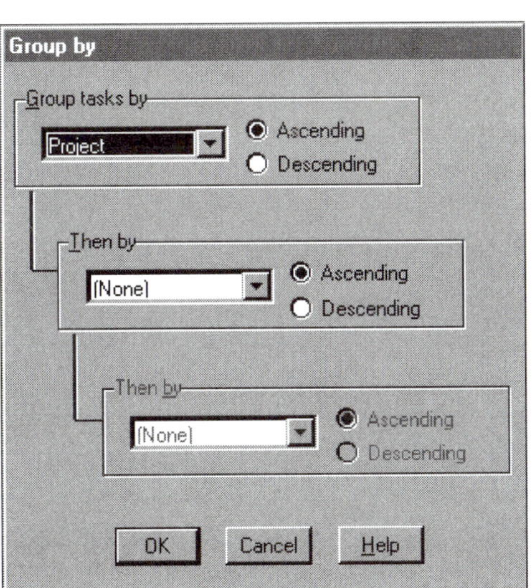

2. Select a grouping from the Group Tasks By list. If you want the first grouping to be Project, don't change the selection in this box. The list contains all possible ways to group tasks, regardless of whether you have all the columns displayed on the To Do List tab.
3. If you want a second grouping, such as Priority, select the grouping from the first Then By box. If you leave the Then By box set to None, you can't select a grouping from the second Then By box.
4. If you want a third grouping, such as End Date, select the grouping from the second Then By box.
5. For each grouping, choose either the Ascending or the Descending option. Ascending order is alphabetical, earlier to later dates, or higher to lower priority—"higher" means the lower number or letter. Descending order is the opposite of ascending.
6. When you have set up the groupings you want, click on OK.

Sorting Tasks

You can sort tasks using any column of information you have displayed. For example, you might want to sort the tasks according to percent complete, by due date, by team member, by priority, or by another column.

Schedule+ sorts within groups. If the column you're using to sort the task list contains no information for particular items, those items appear at the top of the group when you sort in ascending order. Items without information appear at the bottom of the list when you sort in descending order.

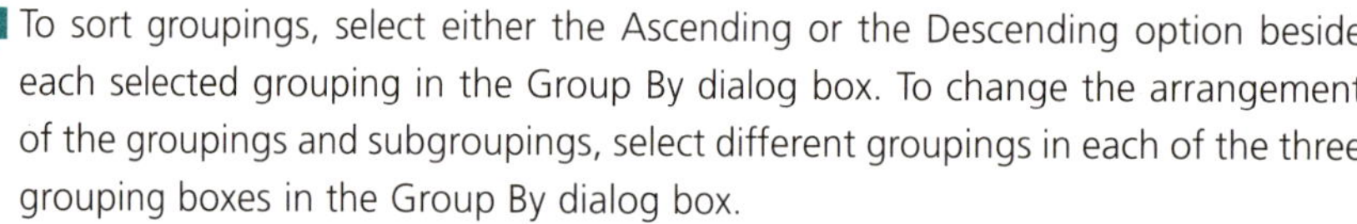

TIP: To sort groupings, select either the Ascending or the Descending option beside each selected grouping in the Group By dialog box. To change the arrangement of the groupings and subgroupings, select different groupings in each of the three grouping boxes in the Group By dialog box.

Schedule+ gives you two ways to sort tasks: with the mouse and with the View Sort command. You can sort by up to three sorting keys. (A sorting key is the column of information you want to use to sort the lists.)

For a multiple-key sort (two or three sorting keys), Schedule+ sorts the tasks with the first sorting key, then by the second sorting key, and then by the third sorting key.

Schedule+ also provides a Sort Now command and an AutoSort command. (See "Sort Now and AutoSort," on page 304, for details.)

Mouse Sorting

With the mouse, you can sort tasks using any column you have displayed in the To Do List in either ascending or descending order. To sort tasks in ascending order, click on the heading of the column you want to use to sort the tasks within their groups. To sort tasks in descending order, hold down the Ctrl key while you click on the heading of the column you want to use to sort the tasks within their groups.

To use the mouse to sort tasks by more than one sorting key, click on the heading of the *last* column you want to sort by, then on the heading of the *second* column you want to sort by, and finally on the heading of the *first* column you want to sort by. For example, if you want to sort by project, then by priority, and then by the ending date, click on the Ends heading, then on the Priority heading, and then on the Project heading.

Sorting with the View Sort Command

To sort the To Do List with a column that isn't displayed, follow these steps:

1. Choose the View Sort Command

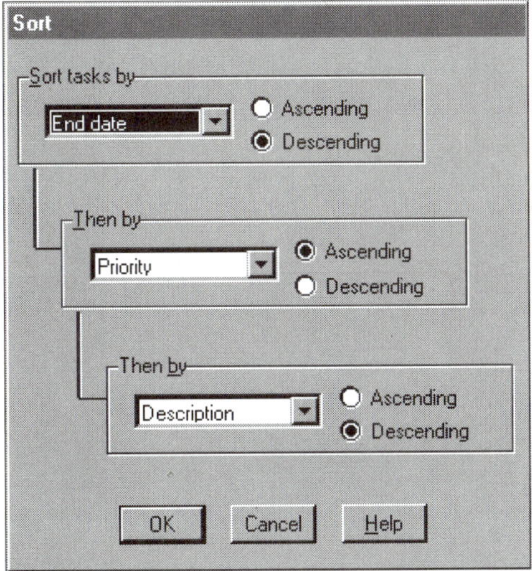

2. In the Sort Tasks By box, select the category you want to use to sort the tasks. The list contains all the possible columns, whether or not you have them displayed on the To Do List tab.
3. Select the sort order for the Sort Tasks By box by clicking on the Ascending or the Descending option.
4. For a second sort key, select the category you want to sort by in the first Then By box, and then select the sort order by clicking on the Ascending or the Descending option.
5. For a third sort key, select the category you want to use in the second Then By box, and then select the sort order by clicking on the Ascending or the Descending option.
6. Click on OK.

Sort Now and AutoSort

By default, sorting the list of tasks by using column headings (mouse clicking) or the View Sort command is a one-time event that you direct Schedule+ to perform. If you then change some of the information for a task, add a new task, or delete a task, the list is not sorted automatically. For these occasions, Schedule+ provides the Sort Now command.

The Sort Now command performs a one-time sort using the settings in the Sort dialog box. You can, however, turn on the AutoSort option, which causes Schedule+ to sort the task list as soon as you enter new information, add a new task, or remove a task.

To perform a one-time sort using the settings in the Sort dialog box, right-click on a column heading, and then choose Sort Now from the shortcut menu. (If right-clicking is unavailable, choose View Sort Now.)

To turn on AutoSort, right-click on a column heading, and then choose AutoSort from the shortcut menu. (If right-clicking is unavailable, choose View AutoSort.)

When you turn on AutoSort, you see a check mark beside the command name on the View menu and on the shortcut menu. To turn off AutoSort, choose the AutoSort command again.

Filtering Tasks

A filter sets up a screening process that lets some tasks show up and keeps others hidden. The value of a task filter is to give you an unobstructed and uncluttered view of the tasks you want to see, and of only those tasks. This limited view makes it easier to analyze the tasks without interference from irrelevant tasks and task information.

If right-clicking is unavailable, choose the View Filter command.

Schedule+ provides six built-in filters for tasks and one additional choice that affects each of the six filters. These six filters all appear on the submenu of the Filter command.

To set up a task filter, take these steps:

1. Right-click on a column heading, and then select Filter from the shortcut menu.
2. From the submenu, select the filter you want to use. (See Table 11-1 for descriptions of the filters.) Or, turn on or off the Include Tasks With No End Date option.

Whichever filter you select, its name appears in the status bar at the bottom of the To Do List tab.

Task Filter	Effect on Task List	Effect of turning off the Include Tasks With No End Date option
All	Shows all tasks.	Hides all tasks without an end date.
Upcoming	Shows tasks with end dates that have not yet arrived; hides overdue tasks, completed tasks, and tasks without end dates.	No effect.
Active	Shows all tasks without end dates, tasks with end dates that are past their start dates, and overdue tasks; hides tasks that have been completed.	Hides active tasks without an end date.
Not Yet Completed	Shown only tasks that have not been completed.	Hides not-yet-completed tasks without an end date.
Completed	Shows only tasks that have been completed.	Hides completed tasks without an end date.
Overdue Tasks	Shows only tasks that are still not completed after their end date.	No effect.

Table 11-1
Task Filters, their effect on the task list, and the effect of the Include Tasks With No End Date option on the filter

MICROSOFT EXCHANGE IN BUSINESS

PART 4

Whatever work your business or organization does, or even if you work independently and privately, keeping records of your customers (however loosely you might define that term) is important. You have contacts—people you work with in one way or another—and you need to record their names, addresses, and phone numbers as well as other vital information. You might also want to keep track of the birthdays and anniversaries of special people.

The Microsoft Exchange Address Book, public folders, and the Schedule+ Contacts tab give you plenty of space for recording your customer information. The chapters in this part dramatize the ways you can use these tools for collecting customer information, for working the information over, and for storing information you prepare for customers and then finding it and sending it to them.

Information at Work

CHAPTER
12

Collecting Customer Information

In this chapter you'll learn how to use the Microsoft Exchange Address Book and the Schedule+ Contacts tab to collect information about customers and suppliers. You'll also learn about how you can use public folders and forms in Exchange to help you keep track of the information you collect.

Scenes from This Chapter

The Exchange Address Book and Schedule+ Contacts tab give you ample space to record facts about your contacts—the people you meet and work with. But most business and organizational contacts go beyond bare facts. When you do business with a customer, you'll want to record other pertinent information about that customer as well. These records can include the date, time, and place of contact, the gist of the conversation, and any action items that you or the contact agreed to perform. For these kinds of information you need a contact report.

If the business relationship is set up in a formal contract, you'll not only want a record of the contract, but you'll also want to make the contract available to all those in your organization who might need to consult it—legal, finance, sales, marketing, manufacturing, distribution, and so on.

In this chapter, you'll find information about the following actions:

- How to set up contact information in the Exchange Address Book and on the Schedule+ Contacts tab
- How to set up a public folder for customer information
- How to set up forms for company profiles and for contact reports
- How to fill out the forms you set up and post the forms to a public folder
- How to store, make available, and display details of customer contracts using folder views

Contact Information

Both the Exchange Address Book and the Schedule+ Contacts tab give you a place to record and store information about contacts. These tools overlap quite a bit, but each can store information about contacts in a unique way.

Exchange Address Book

You use the Exchange Address Book primarily to record e-mail addresses for your contacts. If a contact doesn't have an e-mail address, you can't record contact information in the Address Book. In this case, you'll have to rely on the Schedule+ Contacts tab.

Note If you have Microsoft Fax at Work set up and installed in an Exchange profile, you can add fax numbers to the Address Book entires for your customers. For information about adding Microsoft Fax at Work to an Exchange profile, see "Adding Fax to Exchange," on page 141.

To record contact information in the Exchange Address Book, take these steps:

1. Start Exchange, and then click on the Address Book button on the toolbar.

2. Click on the New Entry button on the Address Book toolbar.

3. Select the appropriate entry type, and then click on OK.

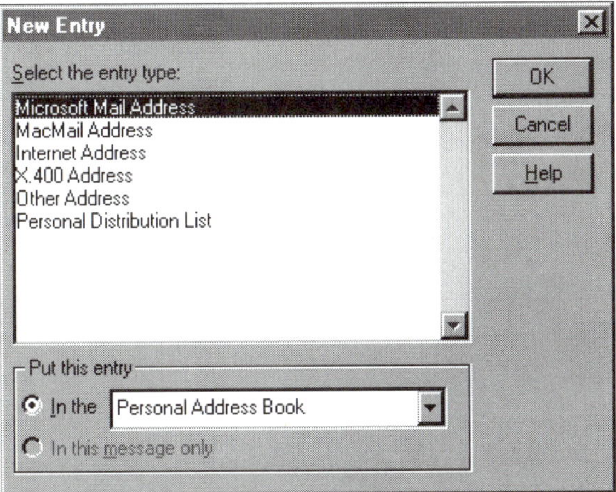

4. Fill in the display name, e-mail address, and e-mail type. (The number of fields and their labels on the New-Address tab vary depending on which entry type you specify in the preceding step.)

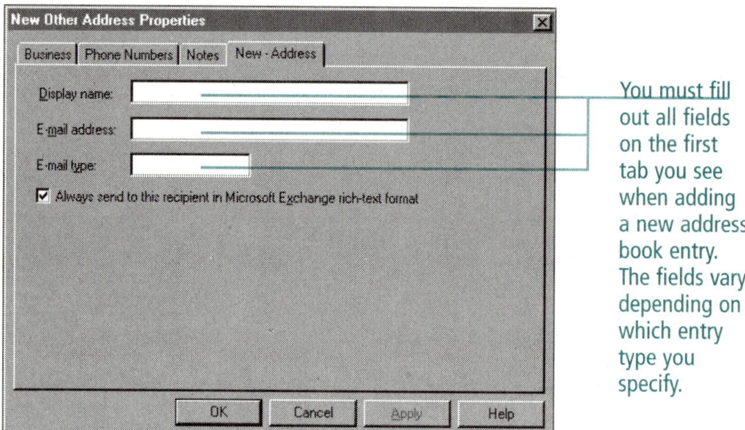

5. Click on the Business tab, and then fill in the information you have about the contact—first and last name, business address, title, company, department, office, and assistant. You can also add phone numbers on this tab, but it's easier to add them on the Phone Numbers tab, described on the next page.

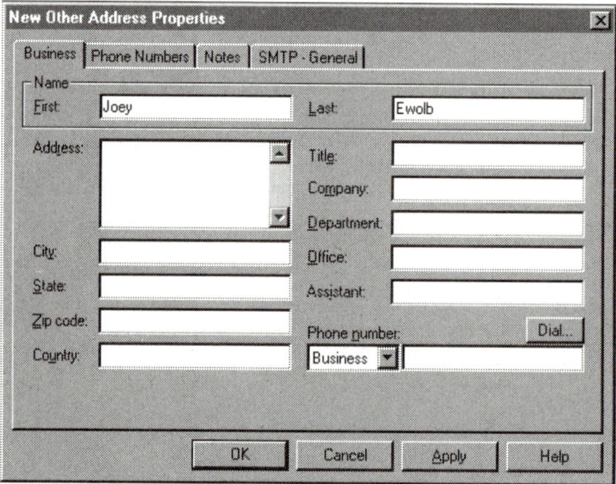

Figure 12-1

The Exchange Address Book Business tab

6. Click on the Phone Numbers tab, and fill in the phone numbers you have for the contact—business numbers, an assistant's number, a fax number, mobile phone, pager, and home phones.

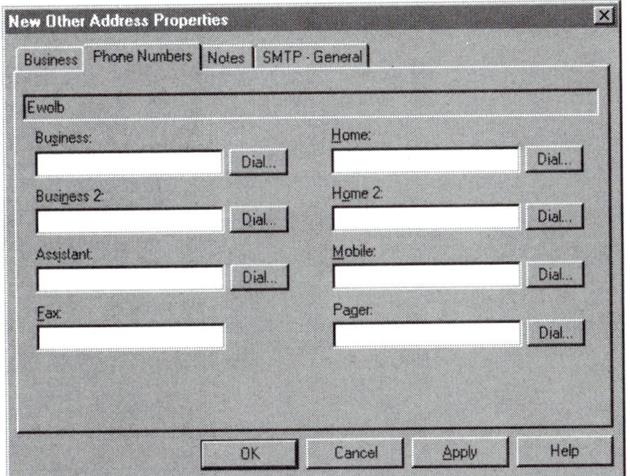

Figure 12-2
The Exchange Address Book Phone Numbers tab

7. If you want to record other information about this contact—the business relationship, a contract number, the type of goods or service that you supply or that the contact supplies to you, click on the Notes tab and record the information there.
8. Click on OK to add this contact to your Exchange Address Book.

Schedule+ Contacts Tab

You can use the Schedule+ Contacts tab to record information for contacts who don't have an e-mail address and for those contacts for whom you want to record information other than that stored in the Address Book.

One other advantage of listing contacts in Schedule+ is that you can use the information to set up letters, envelopes, and mailing labels in Microsoft Word.

To record contact information on the Schedule+ Contacts tab, take these steps:

1. Start Schedule+, and then click on the Contacts tab.
2. Choose the Insert Contact command.

3. Click on the Business tab, and then fill in the appropriate information.

   The Schedule+ Business tab looks the same as the Business tab in the Exchange Address Book, shown in Figure 12-1 on page 312, but it also contains a check box for marking the contact Private. Click on this box for personal contacts.

4. Click on the Phone tab, and then fill in all the phone numbers you have for this contact.

   The Phone tab in Schedule+ is the same as the Phone Numbers tab in the Exchange Address Book, shown in Figure 12-2 on page 313, except that the Dial buttons show a telephone icon instead of the word *Dial*.

5. Click on the Address tab, and then fill in the contact's home address and other personal information (the contact's spouse's name and the contact's birthday and anniversary).

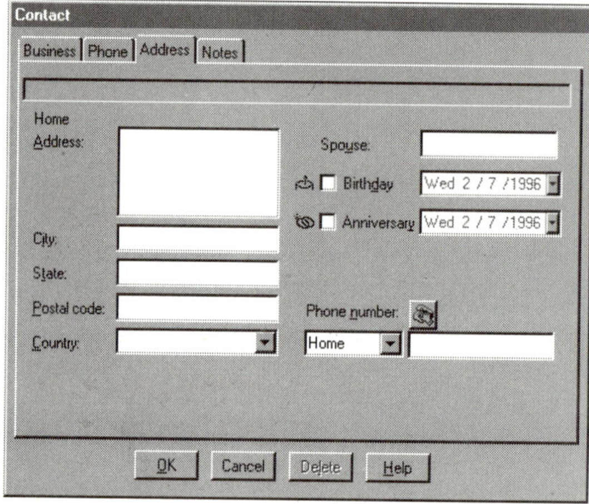

6. If you want to record other information about this contact, click on the Notes tab and record the information there. For example, you might include directions to your contact's home or place of business.

7. Click on OK to add this contact to your Schedule+ Contacts tab.

Note Exchange provides no direct way to transfer information between an entry in your Exchange Address Book and your Schedule+ Contacts tab. You can copy and paste the information, but you might find it easier to type the information you need in both places.

Creating Public Folders for Customer Information

Using public folders in Exchange is an easy and efficient way to collect and provide access to customer information. When you create a public folder for customer information, you'll do at least two important tasks: create the folder and some subfolders for storing the information and select the forms you want coworkers to use for working with customer information—collecting it, reviewing it, modifying it, and even deleting it when it's no longer useful. In this section, we'll cover both these topics.

Before you can select forms to use in a folder, however, you need to create them. We'll work through setting up some forms that can be useful for collecting customer information in "Designing Customer Information Forms," on page 319. After you set up the forms, you might want to return to the steps in this section for information on how to select the forms for the folder.

To create the public folder for customer information, follow these steps:

1. In the Exchange folder pane, click on the All Public Folders folder.
2. Choose the File New Folder command.

Note You must have permission to create a public folder. If you don't, contact your Exchange administrator and request a public folder for your purposes. If you need to rely on your Exchange administrator to create the public folder, skip to step 4. Your Exchange administrator should give you permission to create subfolders within the new folder by yourself.

3. Type the name for the folder—for this example, type *Customer Information*—and then click on OK.
4. Click on the new Customer Information folder.
5. Choose the File New Folder command to create a subfolder.

6. Type the name for the subfolder—*Company Profiles*—and then click on OK.
7. Repeat step 5 and step 6 to create subfolders named *Contact Reports* and *Contract Information*.

The public folders are now ready to receive customer information. If you have documents or messages that you want to add to these folders, copy the documents or messages to the Customer Information folder or to the appropriate subfolder.

To copy messages to the Customer Information folder (or one of its subfolders), do this:

1. Click on the folder that contains the messages you want to copy to one of the public folders.
2. Right-click on the message you want to copy, and then select Copy from the shortcut menu.

If right-clicking is unavailable, select the message, and then choose the File Copy command.

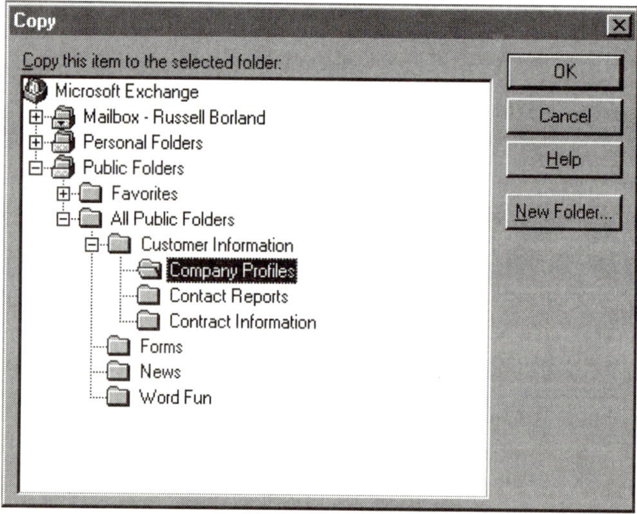

3. Select the folder in which you want to put the copy, and then click on OK.

Note You can move messages rather than copy them. To move a message, either select Move from the shortcut menu, choose the File Move command, or drag the messages to the new folder.

To copy documents to the Customer Information public folder (or one of its subfolders), do this:

1. Set up the Exchange window and the Windows Explorer (or Windows File Manager) window side by side.
2. In the Explorer or File Manager window, open the folder that contains the document you want to copy to the public folder.

Note Before you can install a form in a public folder, as shown next, you have to create it (or somebody has to create it). For help with creating forms for collecting customer information, see "Setting Up the Sample Company Profile Form," on page 320, and "Contact Reports," on page 326. As you'll see in these topics, you can also add a new form to a public folder when you first create it.

3. Drag the document to the public folder in the Exchange window.

To select the forms you want people to use in a public folder, take these steps:

1. Right-click on the public folder and select Properties from the shortcut menu.
2. Click on the Forms tab.

If right-clicking is unavailable, click on the public folder, and then choose the File Properties command.

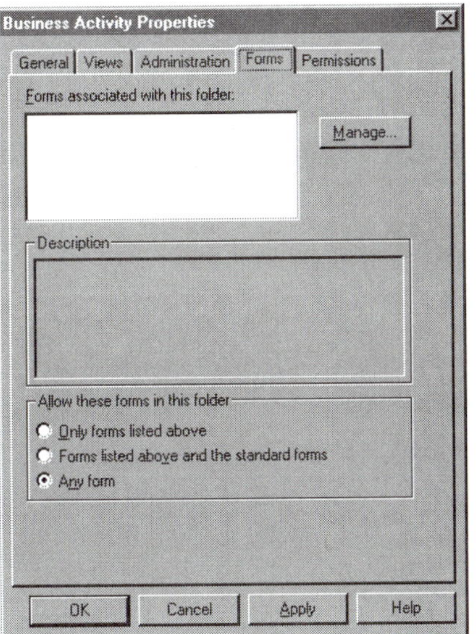

3. Click on the Manage button.

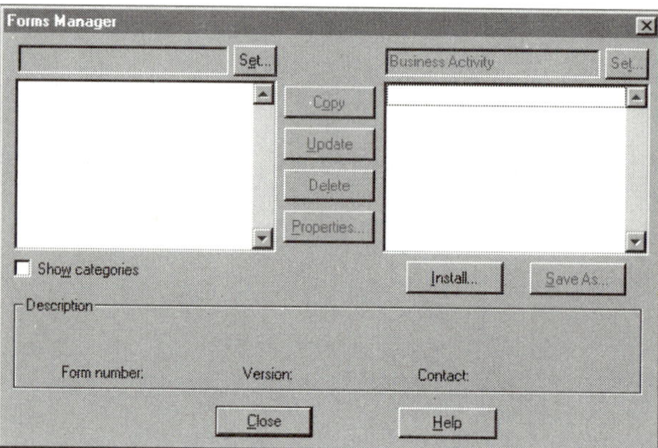

4. Click on the Set button.

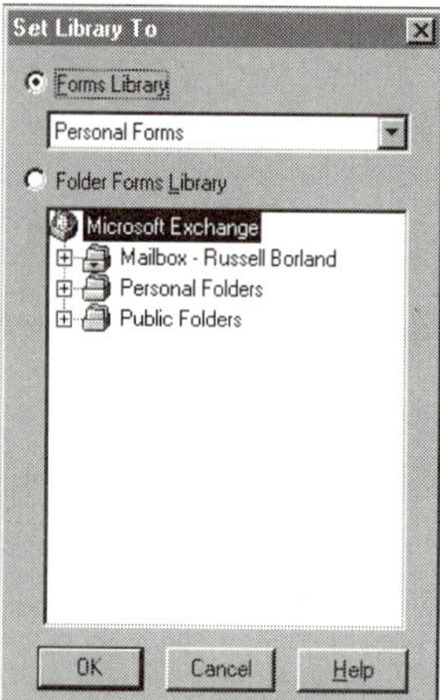

5. In the Set Library To dialog box, select the folder in which you stored the form, and then click on OK.
6. In the list at the left of the Forms Manager dialog box, select the forms you want to add to the public folder, and then click on the Copy button. The names of the forms now appear in the list at the right of the dialog box.
7. Click on the Close button.

Designing Customer Information Forms

Three of the more important pieces of information that you'll collect about customers are facts about customers (company profiles), contact reports (reports of meetings and phones calls with customers), and contract information (the terms and conditions that govern business transactions with the customer). Later in this section, you'll install a sample form that comes with the Exchange Forms Designer into a related public folder. This sample form can be used for recording company profiles. Then you'll modify the company profile form and make it a contact report and install it into another public folder. Later in this chapter in "Designing Views for Document Information," on page 335, you'll set up a public folder with special columns, groupings, and folder views for displaying information from customer contracts.

Note The Exchange Forms Designer is an additional component of Exchange that is not installed by default. In order to create forms, you must first install the Exchange Forms Designer. Exchange Forms Designer is not available for the Macintosh. Forms created using Windows 95, Windows 3.1, or Windows NT cannot be used on a Macintosh.

Starting the Exchange Forms Designer

For each form you'll work on in the following sections, start the Exchange Forms Designer in one of the following ways:

- From Exchange, choose the Tools Application Design command, and then choose Forms Designer from the submenu.
- From Windows 95, click on the Start button, select Programs, select Microsoft Exchange from the submenu, and then select Microsoft Exchange Forms Designer from the submenu.
- From Windows 3.1 or 3.11 and Windows NT, double-click on the Microsoft Exchange Forms Designer icon in the Microsoft Exchange group window.

Note You don't have to start Exchange to work with the Forms Designer. When the Forms Designer needs Exchange, it starts Exchange for you.

When the Exchange Forms Designer starts, you'll see the first panel of the Forms Template Wizard, shown here:

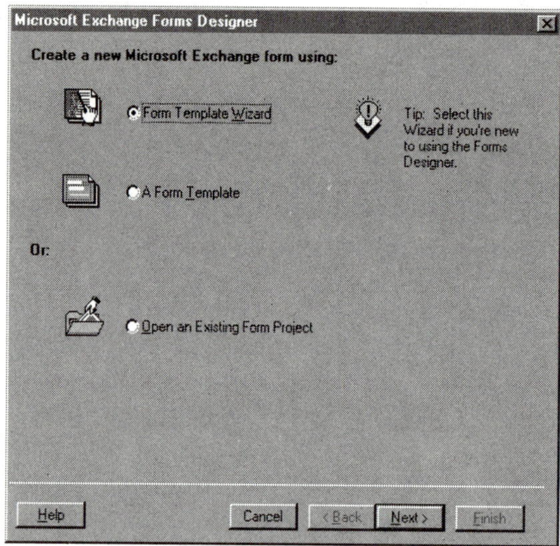

Continue with the steps listed in the following sections for setting up a company profile form or a contact report form, whichever type of form you want to create. (You will need to create a company profile form in order to work through the examples in Chapter 13.)

Setting Up the Sample Company Profile Form

When you're working with a customer, it's always a good idea to know something about the customer's company. With this information at hand, you can treat your customer like a friend rather than simply as a revenue source.

In this section, you'll learn how to open, modify, and save the sample Company Profile form that comes with the Exchange Forms Designer. Then you'll install the form in the Company Profile public folder you created earlier. This exercise will show you the simplest way to set up a

ready-made form in a public folder. You will probably want to make a few changes, however, because the form has some fields with built-in lists of responses that probably don't match your needs.

Opening the Sample Company Profile Form Template

The first step in setting up the sample Company Profile form is opening it. To do so, follow these steps:

1. Start the Exchange Forms Designer in one of the ways described in "Starting the Exchange Forms Designer," on page 319.
2. Click on the Open An Existing Form Project option, and then click on the Next button.
3. In the Open dialog box, switch to the Custrack folder. The Custrack folder is a subfolder in the Samples folder, which is a subfolder in the Efdforms folder, which in turn is a subfolder in the Exchange folder.

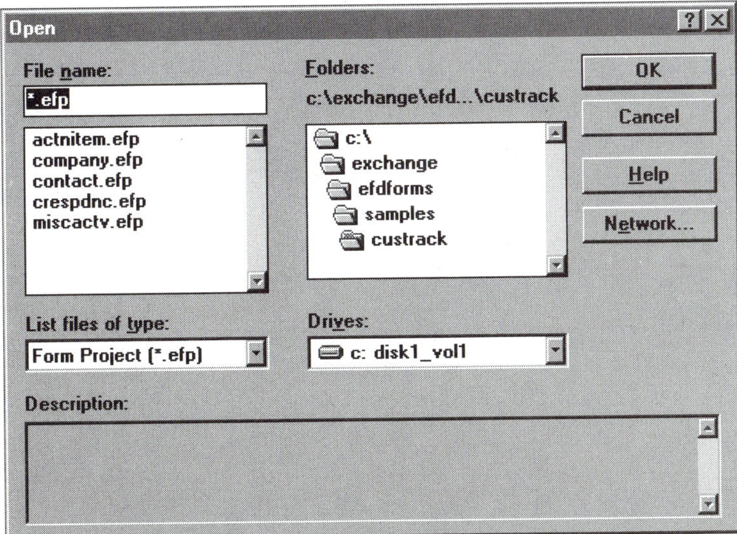

Figure 12-3

The Open dialog box in the Exchange Forms Designer

Note The Open dialog box is the same dialog box you see when you choose the File Open command or click on the Open button on the Exchange Forms Designer toolbar.

---

4. Select Company.efp, and then click on OK. Here's the form template you see.

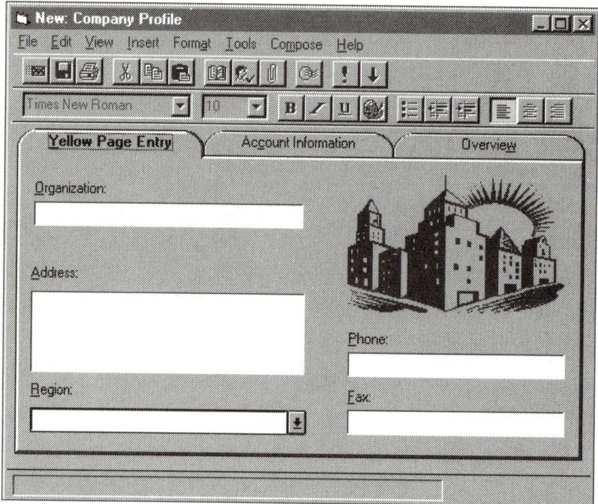

Figure 12-4

The first tab on the Company Profile form template

Peruse the form, and check out its various tabs and fields.

Modifying the Company Profile Form Template

Several fields on the Company Profile form have preset lists of responses that might not fit your needs. Here are three fields for which you might want to change the possible responses:

- The Region field on the Yellow Page Entry tab has entries titled Northern, Eastern, Southern, and Western in its Initial Value list. You might have more or fewer regions in your organization, or you might divide your customers by different geographical units—states or local areas, for example.
- The Manager field on the Account Information tab has only three names in its Initial Value list—Brian, Terry, and John. You'll want to change these to match the names of the account managers in your organization.
- The Status field on the Account Information tab has four settings in its Initial Value list—Lead-Unqualified, Tier 1-High Priority, Tier 2-Medium Priority, and Tier 3-Low Priority. Your organization

might describe the status of an item differently. For example, it might use a system of discounts or names that reflect a business relationship.

To modify the items in these fields, take the following steps:

1. Click on the Region field on the Yellow Page Entry tab, and then click on the Field Properties button on the Exchange Forms Designer toolbar.

2. Click on the Initial Value tab.

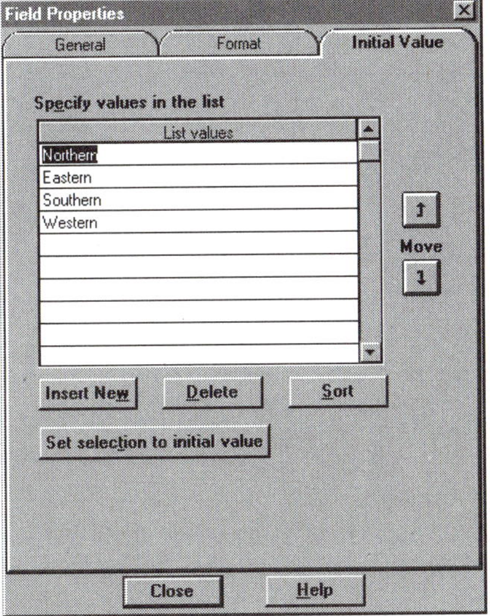

3. To add a region name, select the name of the region above which you want the new name to appear, and then click on the Insert New button.
4. Type the new region name.
5. Repeat step 3 and step 4 to add more region names.

6. If you want to delete a region name, select it, and then click on the Delete button.
7. If you want the region names listed alphabetically, click on the Sort button.

Note The names appear in the dropdown list on the form in the order they appear on the Initial Value tab.

8. If you want to reorder the region names, select a name, and then click on the Move buttons to move the name up or down in the list. Repeat this step for each region name you want to move.
9. Click on the Close button.
10. Click on the Account Information tab, click on the Manager field, click on the Field Properties button on the toolbar, and then click on the Initial Value tab.
11. Change the names in the list by using the techniques described earlier in step 3 through step 8.

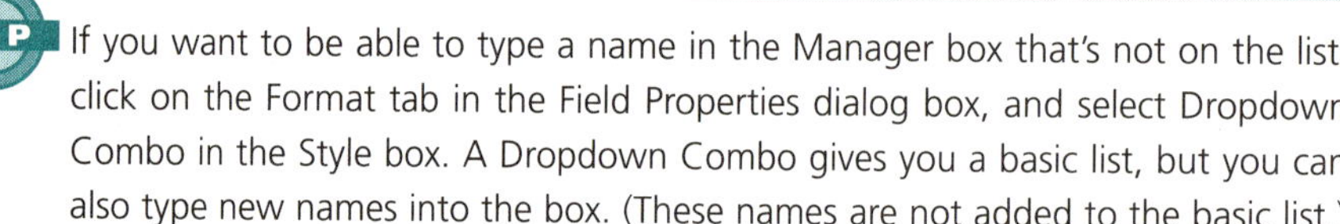

If you want to be able to type a name in the Manager box that's not on the list, click on the Format tab in the Field Properties dialog box, and select Dropdown Combo in the Style box. A Dropdown Combo gives you a basic list, but you can also type new names into the box. (These names are not added to the basic list.)

12. Click on the Close button.
13. Select the Status field on the Account Information tab, click on the Field Properties button on the toolbar, and then click on the Initial Value tab.
14. Adjust the status labels in the list by using the techniques described earlier in step 3 through step 8 above.
15. Click on the Close button.
16. Choose the File Save As command, type a unique name for the form template—for example, *CompProf*—and then click on OK. This step preserves the original Company Profile form template in addition to the modified form template.

Installing the Company Profile Form

After you have saved the changes you made to the Company Profile form, it's time to create the new form from the template you modified. This

process involves compiling the new form and then adding the form to the folder in which you want to use it.

If Exchange isn't running and you select a folder as the storage place for the form, Exchange Forms Designer starts Exchange. If you select a public folder or any other folder that you use only online, you'll have to connect to your Exchange server before Exchange Forms Designer can install the form in that folder. For offline folders, including Personal Folders and Favorites that are set up for work offline, you can install the form without connecting to your Exchange server. Exchange Forms Designer then installs the form in the folder and shuts down Exchange automatically.

To install the Company Profile form, take these steps:

1. Click on the Install button on the Exchange Forms Designer toolbar.

2. Wait and watch. Exchange Forms Designer starts Visual Basic for Microsoft Exchange Server. The visual basic code for the form is compiled, and then you see the Set Library To dialog box, shown in Figure 12-5.

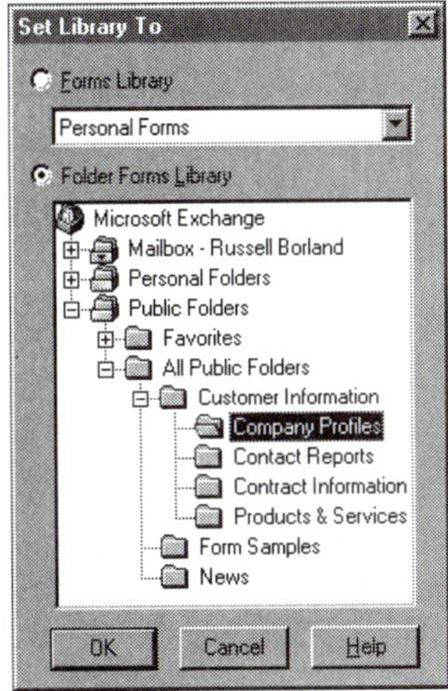

Figure 12-5
The Set Library To dialog box

3. To install this form in the Company Profile folder, expand the Public Folders folder, expand the All Public Folders folder, expand the Customer Information folder, select the Company Profile folder, and then click on OK.

Store a form in a personal folder if you will want to install it in several folders. If you'll be using this form in only one folder, install it there. Also, remember that you must have the proper permissions to store a form in a public folder.

4. When the Form Properties dialog box appears, check the settings for the Display Name box and the Comments box. When the Form Properties dialog box is set up as you want it, click on OK.
5. When the Exchange Forms Designer window reappears, quit Exchange Forms Designer.
6. If Exchange isn't running, start it.
7. Open the Company Profile public folder. Click on the Compose menu. You'll see the New Company Profile command at the bottom of the menu.

The Company Profile form is now ready to use. See "Filling Out the Company Profile Form," on page 334, for the steps you take to fill out and post this form.

Contact Reports

In a contact report you record the customer's name and organization, the date of contact with a customer, the type of contact—such as a call, meeting, e-mail, fax, letter, or package—the customer's type of business, the gist of this contact, any action items, and any orders the customer placed with you. You might also want to keep notes about the nature and character of the organization and the individual you are dealing with.

In this section, you'll learn how to modify the sample Company Profile form you worked with earlier to collect contact information. Some of the fields on the Company Profile form are useful, and you'll keep those. You'll remove the fields you don't need for a contact report and add other fields that you do need. This exercise should serve as a model for modifying (or creating) a contact report that suits your organization.

Opening the Sample Company Profile Form Template

The first step toward modifying the sample Company Profile form to make it a contact report is to open it. To do so, take these steps:

1. Start the Exchange Forms Designer in one of the ways listed in the section "Starting the Exchange Forms Designer," on page 319.
2. Click on the Open An Existing Form Project option, and then click on the Next button.
3. In the Open dialog box, switch to the Custrack folder. The Custrack folder is a subfolder in the Samples folder, which is a subfolder in the Efdforms folder, which in turn is a subfolder in the Exchange folder. Refer to Figure 12-3, on page 321, for an illustration of the folder structure.
4. Select Compprof.efp (or whatever name you chose in step 16 on page 324), and then click on OK. You'll see the form template you adjusted in the preceding section.

Note If you didn't perform the exercise in the preceding section, open the Company.efp file. Before you modify this sample form, you'll probably want to follow the steps in "To change the form properties," on page 329.

Making the Company Profile Form a Contact Report

To modify the Company Profile form so that you can use it as a contact report, you'll need to perform the following tasks:

1. Modify the form's tabs.
2. Delete the picture and add fields.
3. Change the form properties.
4. Change the window properties.

The next sections provide specific steps for each of these tasks.

To modify the tabs. Let's change the tab names, add a new tab, and change the tab layout to better suit our idea of a contact report. To do so, take these steps:

1. Click on the Yellow Page Entry tab, and then click on the Field Properties button. Click on the Format tab, select the Field option, double-click on &Yellow Page Entry in the Pages list box, type *&Contact* in the Edit Tab Caption dialog box, and then click on OK.

The ampersand (&) in a field name indicates that the letter that follows will appear underlined on the form. An underlined letter indicates which key you press while holding down the Alt key to jump directly to the field.

2. Double-click on Ac&count Information, delete the ampersand, type an ampersand to the left of the "I" in Information, and then click on OK.
3. Click on the Add button, type *A&ctions*, and then click on OK.
4. Select A&ctions, and then click on the down arrow button to move A&ctions to the bottom of the list.
5. Type *2* in the Tabs Per Row box, and then click on the Close button. The form template should now look like this:

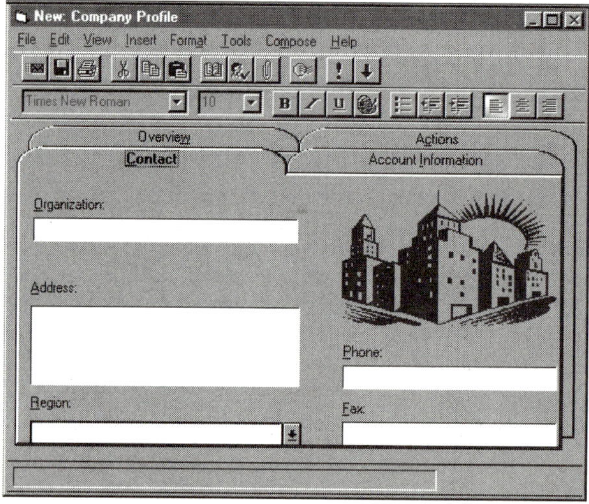

To delete the picture and add fields. To delete the picture from the Contact tab and to add the fields you need on the Contact and Actions tabs, take these steps:

1. Click on the Contact tab, click on the picture in the upper right corner of the tab, and then click on the Delete button on the Exchange Forms Designer toolbar.

2. Click on the Date Field button on the Field toolbar to insert a date field for the date of the contact report.
3. Click on the ListBox Field button on the Field toolbar, and then click in the space from which you deleted the picture in step 1.
4. Double-click on the list box you just inserted to display the Field Properties dialog box.
5. On the General tab, type *ContactType* in the Reference Name box, type *ContactType* in the Microsoft Exchange Column Name box, type *Type of Contact:* in the Field Caption box, and then select the Required check box.
6. Click on the Format tab, and then select Dropdown List in the Style box.
7. Click on the Initial Value tab, type *Call, Meeting, E-mail, Fax, Letter,* and *Package* in the list, and then click on the Close button.
8. Click on the Overview tab, click a second time (*not* a double-click) on the Overview caption, type *&Gist of Contact:*, and then press Enter.
9. Click on the Actions tab.
10. Click on the RichEntry Field button on the Field toolbar, and then click in the upper middle of the Actions tab.
11. Type *Action Items:* in the caption box and press Enter.
12. Click on the Field Properties button on the Exchange Forms Designer toolbar, click on the General tab, type *ActionItems* in the Reference Name box, and then click on the Close button.

To change the form properties. You'll want to change the display name of this form from Company Profile to Contact Report and change the description of the form to fit a contact report. You also need to change the setup of form events. To perform these tasks, take these steps:

1. Click on the Form Properties button on the Exchange Forms Designer toolbar.

2. On the General tab, type *Contact Report* in the Form Display Name box.

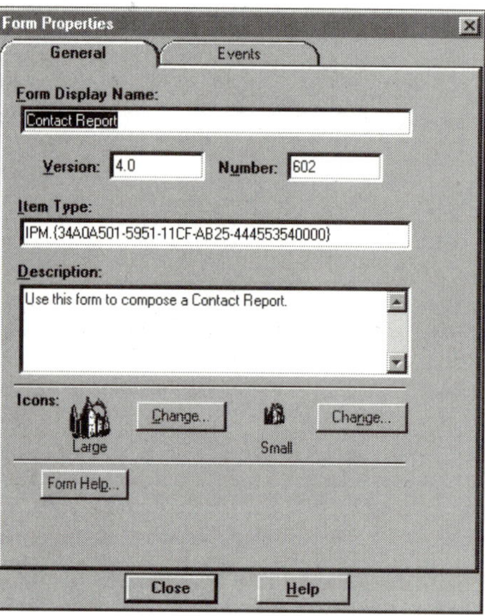

3. In the Description box, change the description to read *Use this form to compose a contact report.*
4. Click on the Events tab.

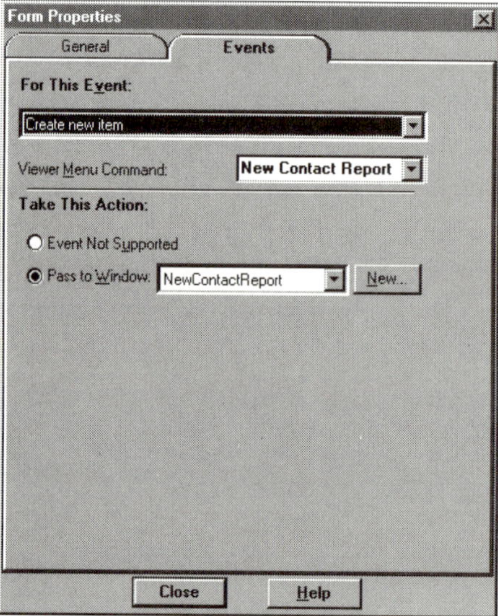

5. In the For This Event list, select Open Submitted Item.
6. Click on the New button.

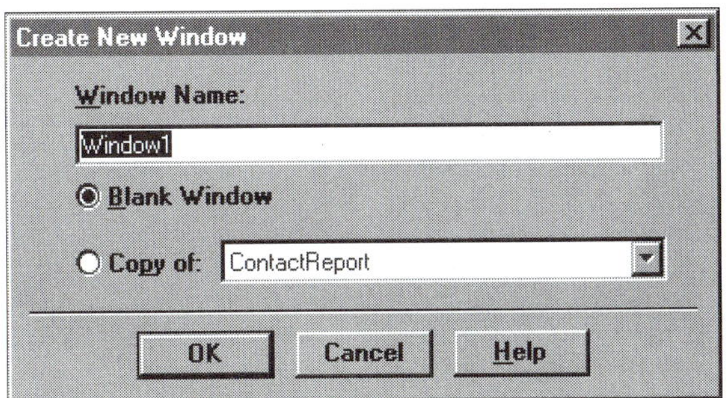

7. In the Window Name box, type *ContactReport*, select the Copy Of option, and then click on OK.

> **Note** Exchange Forms Designer doesn't permit spaces in the window name you type. If you type a space, it simply doesn't appear in the Window Name box.

8. In the For This Event list, select Print Submitted Item, and then select ContactReport in the Pass To Window box.
9. In the For This Event list, select Create New Item.
10. In the Viewer Menu Command box, type *New Contact Report*, and then click on the Close button.

To change the window properties. The window name and window caption for this form are still set up for a company profile. You'll want to change their text, and you'll want to arrange the tab order of the new fields to assist the users of your form. To perform these tasks, take these steps:

1. Click on the Window Properties button on the Exchange Forms Designer toolbar.

2. On the General tab, type *NewContactReport* in the Window Name box; type *New: Contact Report* in the Window Caption box.

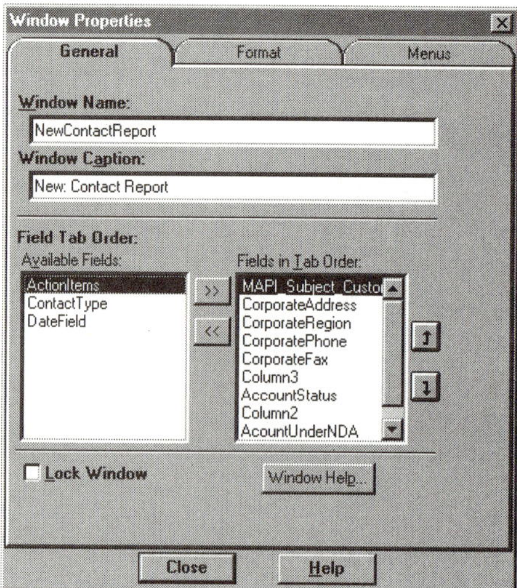

3. In the Available Fields list, select the ContactType field, and then click on the right pointing chevron (>>) button. Repeat this step for the ActionItems field. You don't need (or want) to put the Date field in the tab order because that field can't be modified.
4. Adjust the tab order of the fields so that the form's users can move through the fields in the proper order. Move the ContactType field below the CorporateRegion field, and move the ActionItems field to the bottom of the list. To change the order, select the field you want to move, and then click on the up or down arrow button to move the field one position.
5. Click on the Format tab, and then select Resizeable in the Window Sizing Options box.
6. Click on the Close button.
7. Choose the File Save As command, type a unique name for the form—for example, *ContactR*—and then click on OK.

Installing the Contact Form

After you have saved your Contact Report form template, it's time to create the form from the template. This process, called *installing* the form, involves compiling the form and then adding the form to the folder in which you want to use it.

To install the Contact Report form, take these steps:

1. Click on the Install button on the Exchange Forms Designer toolbar.

2. Wait and watch. Exchange Forms Designer starts Visual Basic for Microsoft Exchange Server. The visual basic code for the form is compiled, and you see the Set Library To dialog box, shown in Figure 12-5, on page 325.
3. To install this form in the Contact Reports folder, expand the Public Folders folder, expand the All Public Folders folder, expand the Customer Information folder, select the Contact Reports folder, and then click on OK.
4. When the Form Properties dialog box appears, adjust the settings for the Display Name box and the Comments box, if necessary. When the Form Properties dialog box is set up as you want it, click on OK.
5. When the Exchange Forms Designer window reappears, quit Exchange Forms Designer.
6. If Exchange isn't running, start it.
7. Open the Contact Reports public folder. You'll see a New Contact Report command at the bottom of the Compose menu.

The Contact Report form is now ready to use. See "Filling Out the Contact Report," on page 334, for the steps you take to fill out and post this form.

Using Forms to Collect Customer Information

Using the forms you've set up for the Company Profile and Contact Reports folders is very similar to creating a message in Exchange. There are some differences, of course, but the following steps shouldn't seem mysterious or unfamiliar.

To use a form installed in a folder, take these steps:

1. Open the folder—either Company Profile or Contact Report.
2. From the Compose menu, choose the command for the form. The command appears at the bottom of the menu.

> **Note** The Compose menu contains the New Message command, which you use to create an e-mail message. Because you use a form to create a special type of message, it's logical to find commands for forms on the Compose menu, too.

3. Fill out the form. See "Filling Out the Company Profile Form," next, and "Filling Out the Contact Report Form," at the bottom of this page, for more information.
4. Click on the Post button to send the information to the public folder.

Filling Out the Company Profile Form

In this table, you'll find specific instructions for filling out each field in the Company Profile form.

Field	Instructions
Organization	Type the name of the organization.
Address	Type the address of the organization.
Region	Select a region name from the list.
Phone	Type the phone number.
Fax	Type a fax number, if a fax number is available.
Manager	Select the name of the account manager from the list, or type a name that's not on the list if you made this field a Dropdown Combo.
Status	Select the account status from the list.
Type	Select the label that best describes the type of business the organization engages in.
Under Nondisclosure Agreement	Select this check box if the organization has signed a nondisclosure agreement. If not, leave this box turned off.
Overview	Type a description of the purpose, function, business, and success of the organization. Add any information pertinent to your organization's dealings with this customer.

Filling Out the Contact Report Form

In the table on the next page, you'll find specific instructions for filling out each field in the Contact Report form.

Field	Instructions
Date	Exchange fills in the date automatically when you post the contact report.
Organization	Type the name of the contact's organization.
Address	Type the address of the contact's organization.
Region	Select a region name from the list.
Type of Contact	Select the type of contact from the list.
Phone	Type the phone number for your contact.
Fax	Type a fax number for your contact, if a fax number is available.
Manager	Select the name of the account manager from the list, or type a name that's not on the list if you made this field a Dropdown Combo.
Status	Select the account status from the list.
Type	Select the label that best describes the type of business the organization engages in.
Under Nondisclosure Agreement	Select this check box if the contact has signed a nondisclosure agreement. If not, leave this box turned off.
Gist of Contact	Type a description of the purpose, tone, mood, and success of the contact.
Action Items	Enter a record of any action items that you will perform for the contact and that the contact will perform for you. Also type any orders your contact gave you for goods or services.

Designing Views for Document Information

Viewing and sorting information contained in the documents you store in a public folder is as important as knowing which types of documents are in the folder or who created the documents. In a folder you use to store documents that contain customer information—for example, customer contracts—wouldn't it be helpful to sort that folder using information such as the customer's name, a purchase order, the name of a product, or the contract's total dollar amount?

Contracts are formal legal documents that set out the basis of a business relationship and its transactions. There is no substitute for the contract itself. For this reason, keeping contracts in a public folder (perhaps with limited permissions) is a handy way to make the contracts readily available to those who need to consult them. (For information about the steps you take to copy documents into a public folder, see the procedure at the top of page 317.

As an aid to analyzing the value of a contract and other information the contract contains, you can set up columns in the public folder to view the details of a contract. You can also set up several folder views that group those details together. From these groupings, you can analyze the value and effect of the contracts.

However, before you take these steps to organize the Contract Information folder that you set up earlier in this chapter, you need to prepare your contract documents.

Preparing the Contract Documents: Setting Up Custom Document Properties

To view document information in a folder, Exchange uses document properties. Most applications provide some standard document properties such as Author or Subject. These built-in document properties are available as column headings in Exchange.

Many applications designed for Windows 95 also support custom document properties. Custom properties are based on information you define in a document. For this scenario, I've used Microsoft Word for Windows 95 to create a model contract document that uses Word bookmarks to define information such as the contract's purchase order number, the customer's name, product names, and the contract amount. (You could use other Microsoft Office for Windows 95 applications, for example Microsoft Excel, to create similiar sorts of documents, such as invoices, work orders, or sales reports.) Here's an example of one of the contracts—they all look the same.

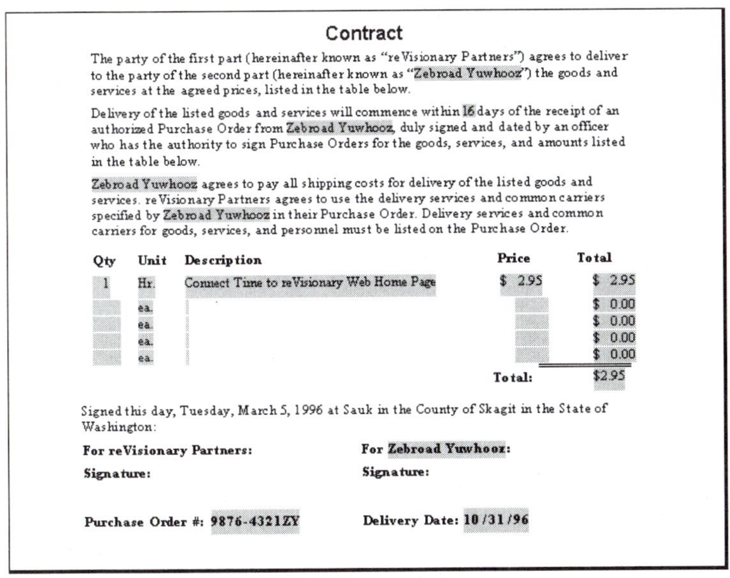

Contract

The party of the first part (hereinafter known as "reVisionary Partners") agrees to deliver to the party of the second part (hereinafter known as "Zebroad Yuwhooz") the goods and services at the agreed prices, listed in the table below.

Delivery of the listed goods and services will commence within 16 days of the receipt of an authorized Purchase Order from Zebroad Yuwhooz, duly signed and dated by an officer who has the authority to sign Purchase Orders for the goods, services, and amounts listed in the table below.

Zebroad Yuwhooz agrees to pay all shipping costs for delivery of the listed goods and services. reVisionary Partners agrees to use the delivery services and common carriers specified by Zebroad Yuwhooz in their Purchase Order. Delivery services and common carriers for goods, services, and personnel must be listed on the Purchase Order.

Qty	Unit	Description	Price	Total
1	Hr.	Connect Time to reVisionary Web Home Page	$ 2.95	$ 2.95
	ea.			$ 0.00
	ea.			$ 0.00
	ea.			$ 0.00
	ea.			$ 0.00
			Total:	$2.95

Signed this day, Tuesday, March 5, 1996 at Sauk in the County of Skagit in the State of Washington:

For reVisionary Partners: | **For Zebroad Yuwhooz:**

Signature: | **Signature:**

Purchase Order #: 9876-4321ZY | **Delivery Date: 10/31/96**

To set up custom document properties for viewing document information, follow these steps:

1. In Word, create a new document, and enter the text you use in a typical customer contract. For example, you might include, among other information, spaces for the contract's date, the customer's name, a purchase order number, a list of products the contract covers, and the total dollar amount of the contract.
2. Highlight the contract's date (or another of the contract's details that you want to see in Exchange), and then choose the Edit Bookmark command.
3. In the Bookmark Name box, type a name for the bookmark (such as *Date*), and then click on the Add button.

Note If you use Microsoft Word's form fields, the fields have their own bookmark names. You don't have to set bookmark names separately.

4. Repeat step 2 and step 3 to define the other information you want to view in Exchange. If you want to, you can use the bookmark names and property names listed in Table 12-1, on the opposite page, as a guide.

TIP If you save the documents with the customer's name as the filename and you only have one document per customer, you can keep the Subject column in the Show The Following list. Exchange uses the filename of documents for the Subject property. If you do this, you don't have to create a custom column for the Client property shown in Table 12-1.

5. Choose the File Properties command, and then click on the Custom tab.

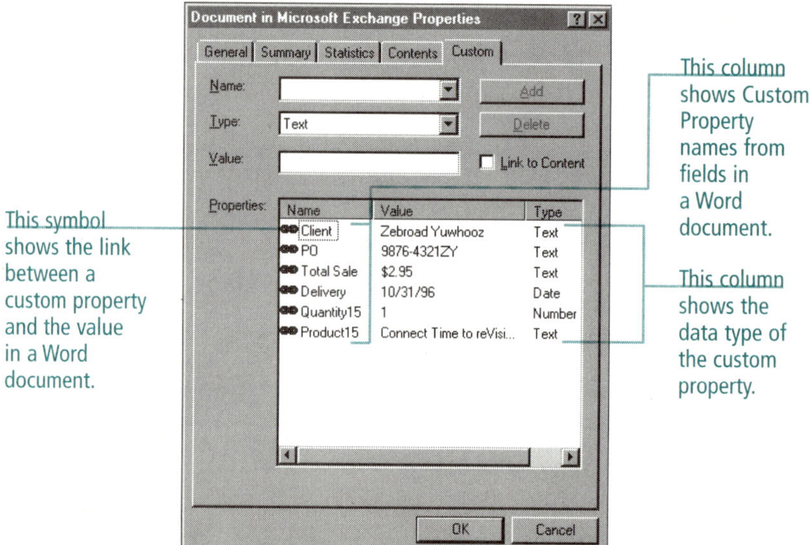

This symbol shows the link between a custom property and the value in a Word document.

This column shows Custom Property names from fields in a Word document.

This column shows the data type of the custom property.

6. In the Name box, type a name for the property, for example *Contract Date*.
7. Turn on the Link To Content check box.
8. In the Source box, select the bookmark name related to this property. In this case, the source of the contract date property is the bookmark name Date.

Note When you set up a custom property with a link to content in the document, Word automatically selects the type of property in the Type box. You can't change this.

9. Click on the Add button.
10. Repeat step 6 through step 9 to name the other custom properties you want to use.
11. Click on OK, and then save the document.

Bookmark Name	Property	Type of Information
Date	Contract Date	Date of the contract
Customer	Client	Customer's name
PO	Purchase Order	Customer's purchase order number
Amount	Total Sales	Total amount of purchases
Product1	Journal of reVisionaries	Product name

Table 12-1
Sample custom properties in Microsoft Word and their related bookmark names

When you have set up documents with custom properties, copy the documents to the Contract Information public folder. To do so, see the procedure at the top of page 317.

Setting Up Columns for the Contract Information Folder

At other places in this book, you'll find information about changing the number and arrangement of columns in a folder. What you're going to learn now is how to set up custom columns—columns that aren't listed in the Available Columns list of the Columns dialog box.

To set up custom columns in the Contract Information folder, take these steps:

1. Open the Contract Information folder.
2. Choose the View Columns command.
3. Remove all the column names from the Show The Following list.

4. In the Available Columns box, type one of the custom property names you created in your contract document. (Use one listed in Table 12-1, if you used those properties.) Click on the Add button.

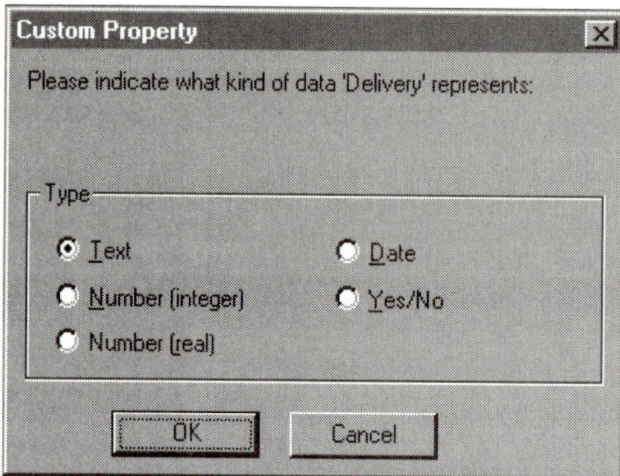

5. When the Custom Property dialog box appears, select the appropriate option for the property's data type, and then click on OK. Here are the data types for the properties listed in Table 12-1.

Property	Data Type
Contract Date	Date
Client	Text
PO	Text
Total Sales	Text
Journal of reVisionaries	Text

6. Repeat step 4 and step 5 for all the custom properties.
7. In the Show These Columns box, arrange the columns in the order in which you want to see them.
8. Click on OK.

You should now see the columns that you set up and information in the columns for the contract documents. You are now ready to set up views for the Contract Information public folder.

Defining Views Around Your New Columns

As you'll notice after you have set up and arranged a large number of columns, you have to scroll horizontally to see all the information. Also, in a folder that contains a large number of documents, it's not always easy to see all the information about one document at a glance. You can create views that group and sort the information in various ways. You can also create views that display only some of the columns while hiding others. And you can create views that filter out contracts that don't contain certain types of information. These are the tricks you'll learn in the following sections.

Note If you are the owner or contact for a public folder, you can set up folder views, instead of personal views. A folder view is available for use by all Exchange users who have access to the folder in which the view is created. To create a folder view, follow the instructions in these sections, but select the Folder Views option instead of the Personal Views option in the Define Views dialog box.

Before you start defining special views, however, you should create a view that shows all the columns. By creating this full view, you will be able to quickly return to a full display of all the columns. (The Normal personal view will discard all your custom columns.)

To create a full view, follow these steps:

1. Open the Contract Information folder.
2. Choose the View Define Views command.
3. Click on the Personal Views option, select Normal, and then click on the New button.
4. Type a name for the full view, such as *Full.*
5. Add all the column names from the Available Columns list.
6. In the Available Columns box, type one of the custom property names you created in your contract document. (Use one listed in Table 12-1 on page 339, if you used those properties.) Then, click on the Add button.
7. When the Custom Property dialog box appears, select the appropriate option for the property's data type, and then click on OK.
8. Repeat step 5 and step 7 for all the custom properties.
9. Be sure the Group By button displays None next to it. If not, click on the Group By button, select None in the Group Items By box, and then click on OK.

10. Be sure the Sort Items By button displays Client (or Subject) in ascending order next to it. If not, click on the Sort By button, select Client (or Subject) in the Sort Items By box, select the Ascending option, and then click on OK.
11. Be sure the Filter button displays Off next to it. If not, click on the Filter button, click on the Clear All button, and then click on OK.
12. Click on OK in the New View dialog box, and then click on Close in the Define Views dialog box.

On the submenu of the View Personal Views command, you should now see Full listed. Whenever you want to return to the full view of the folder contents, choose Full from the submenu.

Defining Views for Grouping and Sorting

Grouping items in a folder places similar items together under a heading. You can collapse a group to hide the items listed under the heading and expand a group to see what it contains. To make it easy to group items under certain headings, you can create views. Here's what you do to set up a view for groupings in the Contract Information folder:

1. Open the Contract Information folder.
2. Choose the View Define Views command.
3. Select the Personal Views option, select Full, and then click on the New button.
4. Type a name for the new group view. See Table 12-2, on the next page, for some suggestions for view names.
5. Click on the Group By button.
6. In the Group By box, select the column name for the type of grouping you want to set up. Table 12-2 lists some suggestions.
7. Click on the button for the sorting direction you want the groups to appear in. Remember that Ascending lists names alphabetically, numbers from smaller to larger, and dates from earlier to later. Descending order lists the groups in the opposite order.
8. If you want to see subgroups, select the columns you want to use in the Then By boxes, and then select a sorting order. If you don't want subgroups, select None in both Then By boxes.
9. In the Then Sort By box, select the column you want to use to sort items under the lowest level of grouping.
10. Click on OK.

11. If you want to reduce the number of columns, click on the Columns button. Follow step 4 and step 5 listed in "Defining Views for Hiding Columns," next, for reducing the number of columns.
12. If you want to set up a filter for this view, click on the Filter button. Follow step 6 through step 9 listed in "Defining a View for Filtering," on page 345, for setting up a filter.
13. Click on OK in the New View dialog box.
14. Repeat step 3 through step 13 to create additional personal views for grouping.
15. Click on Close in the Define View dialog box.

On the submenu of the View Personal Views command, you should now see commands for the views you have created. Choose that view's name from the submenu to group the folder's contents.

View	Group By	Then By	Then By	Then Sort By
Total Sales	Total Sale-Descending	None	None	Client-Ascending
Client	Client-Ascending	None	None	Delivery-Ascending

Table 12-2
Example groupings for views for the Contract Information public folder

Defining Views for Hiding Columns

For some business activities that use the Contract Information folder, you might want to set up views that hide a majority of the columns. By hiding columns, a viewer can concentrate on specific information contained in only a few columns.

To set up views for displaying only a few columns, take these steps:

1. Open the Contract Information folder.
2. Choose the View Define Views command.
3. Click on the Personal Views option, select Full, and then click on the New button.
4. Type a name for the new view. See Table 12-3, on the next page, for some suggestions.
5. Click on the Columns button.

6. Remove all the column names *except* those you want to see in the folder, and then click on OK.
7. Click on OK in the New View dialog box.
8. Repeat step 3 through step 7 for other column arrangements.
9. Click on Close in the Define Views dialog box.

Now when you want to see only some of the columns in the Contract Information folder, simply select the name of the appropriate folder view from the submenu of the View Personal Views command.

View	Show These Columns
Sales By Client	Client, Total Sale
Contract Date By Client	Contract Date, Client
Client and PO	Client, PO, Contract Date

Table 12-3

Columns for views that display only a few columns in the Contract Information public folder

Defining a View for Filtering

A view set up with a filter can sometimes be a very useful tool. You can screen out items you don't want to see and have Exchange display only those items that match conditions you set. Unfortunately, in a public folder that contains only documents or mostly documents, a filter is a little less useful, particularly if all of the documents were created with the same application (as all of my sample contract documents were created with Microsoft Word). The problem stems from not being able to select custom properties as a means of filtering. Even after you set up custom columns, the properties don't show up in the Advanced Filter dialog box. Still, there are a few situations where a filter might be helpful to you.

If different people prepare the contract documents, for example, you could create a filter to see all the contracts prepared by a specific person. Here's what you do to set up a filter for a specific author:

1. Open the Contract Information folder.
2. Choose the View Define Views command, and then select the Personal Views option.
3. Click on the New button.
4. Type a name for the view.

5. Click on the Filter button, and then click on the Advanced button.
6. Click on the Document button.
7. Click on the Author box, and then type the name of the person who prepared the contracts you want to see.
8. Click on OK in the Advanced dialog box, and then click on OK in the Filter dialog box.
9. If you want to reduce the number of columns, click on the Columns button. Remove all the column names *except* those you want to see in the folder.
10. If you want to set up groupings, click on the Group By column. Follow the steps listed in "Defining Views for Grouping and Sorting," on page 342, to set up groupings.
11. If you want a special sorting scheme associated with this filter, click on the Sort button. Then, in the Sort By box, select the column you want to use for sorting and also select the sort direction.
12. When you've finished setting up the view, click on OK in the New View dialog box, and then click on Close in the Define View dialog box.

Now when you want to see only the documents by that particular author in the Contract Information folder, simply select the name of the appropriate folder view from the submenu of the View Personal Views command.

Sorting the Contract Information Folder

When you want to look at the dates of the contracts or at one of the other contract details you've defined as a custom property, you can perform a simple sort of the Contract Information folder. Take the following steps to sort the Contract Information folder using contract details:

1. Open the Contract Information folder.
2. Choose the View Personal Views command, and then choose Full from the submenu.
3. Click *twice* on the column you want to sort by, for example, the Contract Date column. The first click sorts the column in ascending order, placing the earliest date at the top of the list. The second click sorts the column in descending order, which places the latest date at the top of the list.
4. To sort by other contract details, click on the column for that property.

CHAPTER
13

Working Over Customer Information

In this chapter you'll read about the ways to locate customer information, whether it's with a straight search or with grouping, filtering, sorting, or some combination of these methods. You'll also read about how to change the information you find and even (alas and alack) how to delete customer information that no longer has any meaning to your organization.

Scenes from This Chapter

CHAPTER 13

In Chapter 12, you learned several ways to collect and store information about customers. But even as you collect customer information, it seems that the one constant about customers is that the information you have about them changes. After all, if you sell a customer another order, that customer's business activities with you have changed, right? Even in the middle of a transaction, a customer might change an order—order more units or another type of good or service, change a delivery date, or even (dread the thought) cancel part or all of an order. As you ship orders to a customer, you might need to ship part of an order, which means you have to record what was shipped when and what more you need to ship. What about customer contacts? Aren't your contacts at a customer's organization frequently changing? People are promoted, or they resign or retire, so you need to be able to easily find and update your records for that customer.

After a while, you can collect a flood of information about customers. When you need to find some specific piece of information, you've got a lot of wading to do. Microsoft Exchange gives you several tools for lowering the water level in the pool so that you can fish out the details you need more quickly with less diving and less effort.

A straight eyeball search of customer information is most effective when there isn't much information to search. But because your organization is very successful and has hundreds of customers with whom you've conducted thousands of transactions—you do recognize your organization in this description, don't you?—you need a better way. You don't need to waste your time, effort, and patience scanning every item in a public folder trying to find the one or two or three pieces of information you need. You might "blink" one of the items (look at it and not recognize it—you know, brain fade). And if you're looking for all the information about one customer, which could entail hundreds of items, you want to be able to extract only those items and not be bothered with interference from the other thousand or so.

Note Most of the tasks I describe in this chapter rely on the sample forms for customer information that are created and discussed in Chapter 12. If you want to follow the tasks in this chapter most effectively but haven't yet worked through Chapter 12, you should do that now.

Finding Customer Information

Exchange gives you a tool for locating the information you want to see. With this tool—the Find command—you can tell Exchange what pieces of information the items you want have in common, and then Exchange finds them for you.

To use the Find command to locate specific pieces of information, take these steps:

1. Right-click on the folder you want to search, and then choose Find from the shortcut menu.

If right-clicking is unavailable, click on the folder you want to search, and then choose the Tools Find command.

Click on here to switch to a different folder.

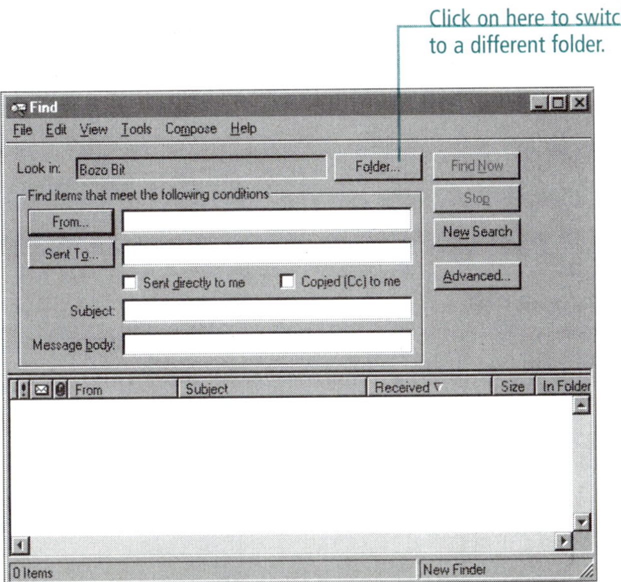

2. Fill in the blank boxes in the Find dialog box with the specific information that the items you want to find have in common. You can select criteria such as a sender's name, the subject line, and others.

If you want to search a different folder, click on the Folder button in the Find dialog box, select another folder, and then click on OK. The Find Items In Folder dialog box appears.

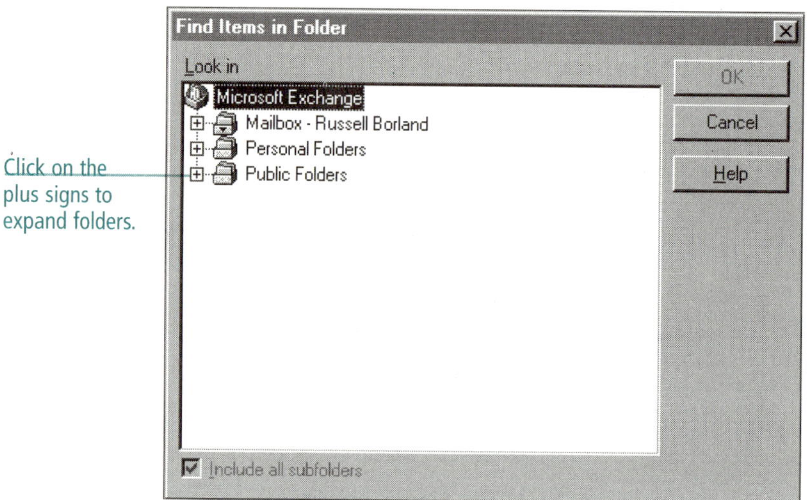

Click on the plus signs to expand folders.

3. If you need additional criteria for finding the items you want, click on the Advanced button in the Find dialog box, fill out the Advanced dialog box, and then click on OK.

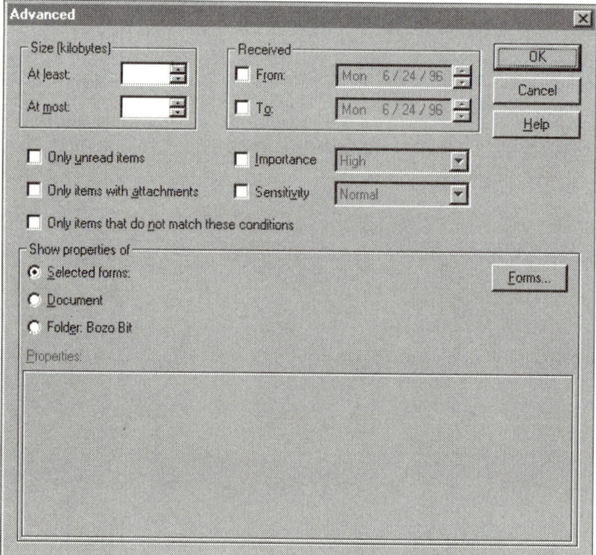

Note The Find and Advanced dialog boxes look very much like the Filter dialog box. For additional help with filling out these two dialog boxes, see "Filtering Customer Information," on page 352.

4. Click on the Find Now button. Exchange searches the folder and displays at the bottom of the dialog box the items that match the criteria you set up.

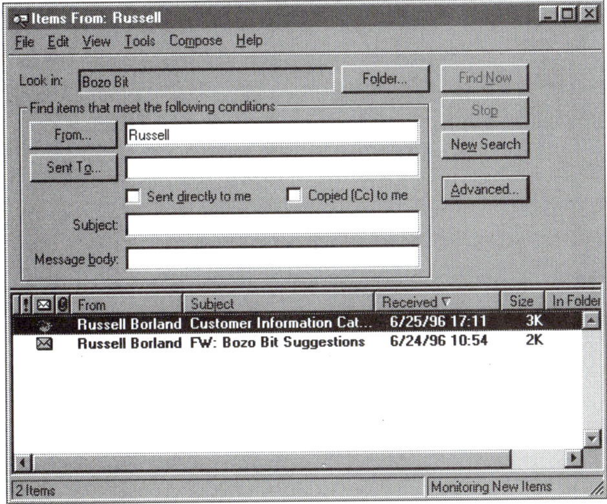

Note When Exchange finds items, the title bar of the Find dialog box displays Items, the name of the first option you selected in the Find or Advanced dialog box, and the criterion you used for that option.

5. If you want to look at the contents of a listed item, double-click on it.
6. If you want to refine the list so Exchange will display fewer items, add more search criteria in the Find and Advanced dialog boxes, and then click on the Find Now button again.
7. If you want to conduct an entirely new search, click on the New Search button, fill out the dialog boxes, and then click on the Find Now button.

You can use the Find command to search the entire contents of a public folder or only some of its contents. When you filter the items in a public folder, Exchange searches only items that the filter displays in the message list pane. Items are listed in the order they appear in the message list pane. If you group or sort the items a special way, Exchange follows the structure of the grouping or sorting to find items that match the search criteria you set up. For this reason, it's a good idea to filter, group, and sort before you use the Find command. (You don't have to take this advice; the Find command works fine on unfiltered and ungrouped items.)

Filtering Customer Information

Suppose you want to see all the contact reports for a customer named reVisionary Partners. The contact reports you want to see are mixed in with contact reports for your other hundreds of customers. Rather than simply finding the contact reports one by one with the Find command (or your naked eyeball), why not list those specific reports and only those reports? That's what a filter is for.

You set up a filter to tell Exchange that you want to see the items in a folder that fit a certain description. When you apply the filter, Exchange displays only those that fit the description. To see how a filter works, take the following steps. They set up a filter that shows only the contact reports for reVisionary Partners in the Contact Reports public folder.

Note For instructions on creating the Company Profiles and Contact Reports public folders referred to in this section, see "Creating Public Folders for Customer Information," on page 315.

1. Click on the Contact Reports public folder. (You might first have to click on the plus sign beside the Public Folders folder, then click on the plus sign beside the All Public Folders folder, and then click on the plus sign beside the Customer Information public folder.)

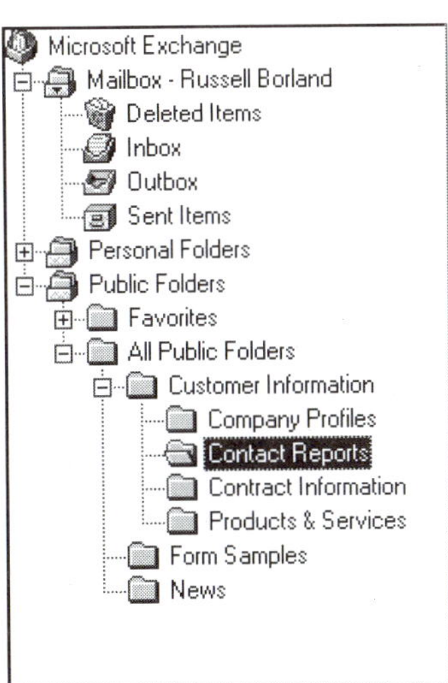

2. Because you'll probably use this filter only a few times, we'll set up a temporary filter. Choose the View Filter command.

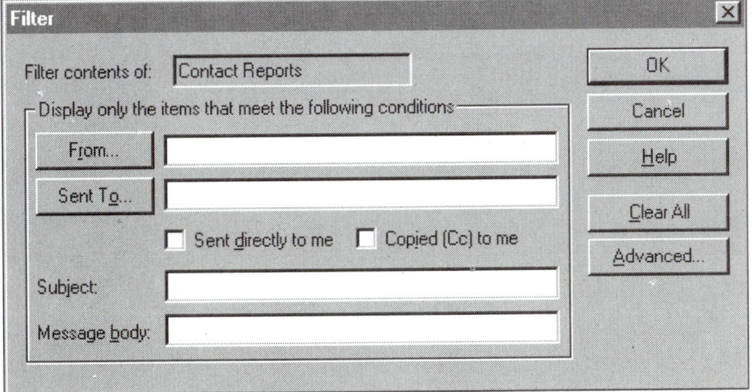

3. Click on the Advanced button.
4. In the Advanced dialog box (shown on the next page), in the Show Properties Of area, click on the Folder: Contact Reports option.

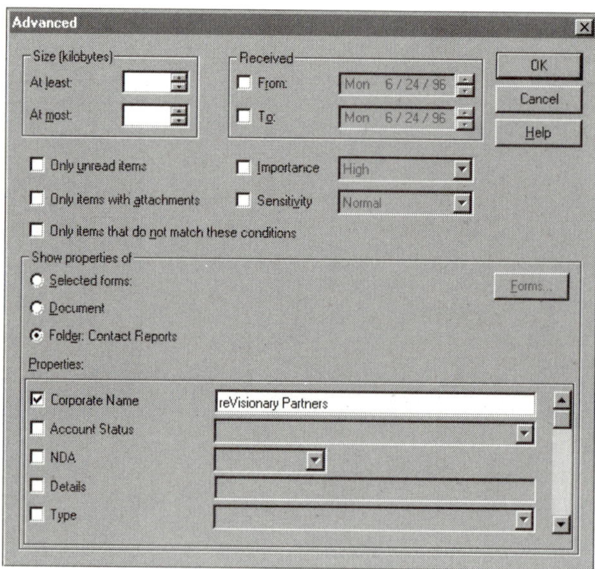

5. Select the Corporate Name check box in the Properties area, type *reVisionary Partners* in the corresponding text box, and then click on OK.
6. Click on OK in the Filter dialog box.

The Contact Reports folder now shows you contact reports for only reVisionary Partners. You can group and sort these contact reports in any way that suits your information needs.

To reset the Contact Reports public folder to display all the contact reports, do the following:

1. Click on the Contact Reports public folder.
2. Choose the View Filter command.
3. Click on the Clear All button, and then click on OK.

You'll now see the entire list of contact reports in the Contact Reports public folder.

Grouping Customer Information

Another way to find the information you want to review about various customers is to group items within a folder in some way. With the Group command, you can use any column of information that you have set up

in the folder as the grouping agent. For example, on a company profile form you might have a field for the region of each company to which you sell your product. If you want to see the various locations of your customers for an analysis of your customer distribution, you can group customers by their region.

To set up this grouping, you'll perform two tasks. First you'll adjust the column setup for the folder. Second you'll set up a grouping by region. Because this grouping is a complex setup, we'll make it a personal view. By doing so, you give yourself an easy way to return the folder to Normal view, showing all the company profiles in the folder.

Note For instructions on creating a form that includes the Corporate Region field referred to in this section, see "Setting Up the Sample Company Profile Form," on page 320.

To set up a personal view such as this, follow these steps:

1. Click on the Company Profiles public folder. (You might first have to click on the plus sign beside the Public Folders folder, then click on the plus sign beside the All Public Folders folder, and then click on the plus sign beside the Customer Information public folder.)

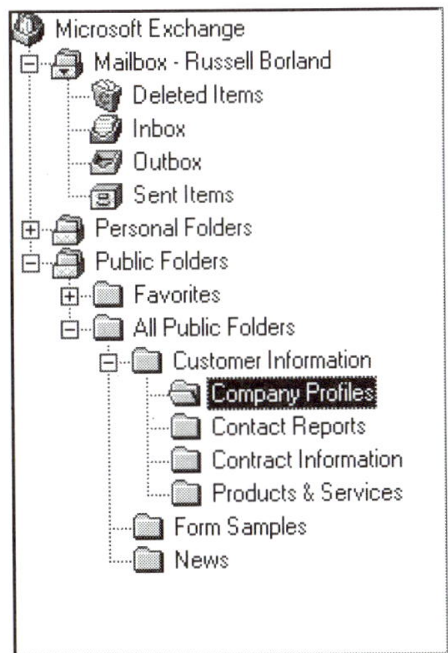

2. Choose the View Define Views command.

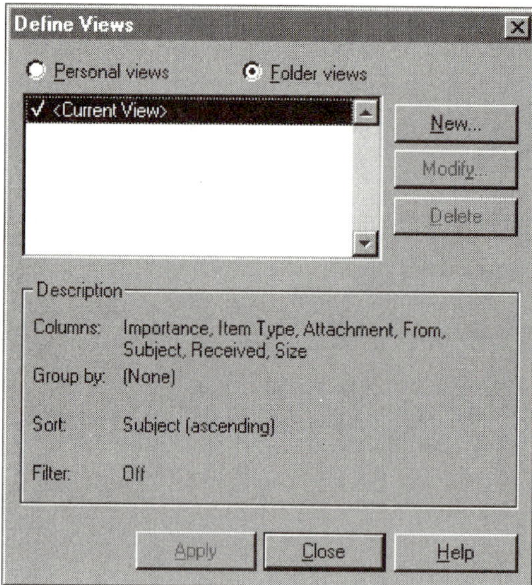

3. Select the Personal Views option.
4. Click on the New button.

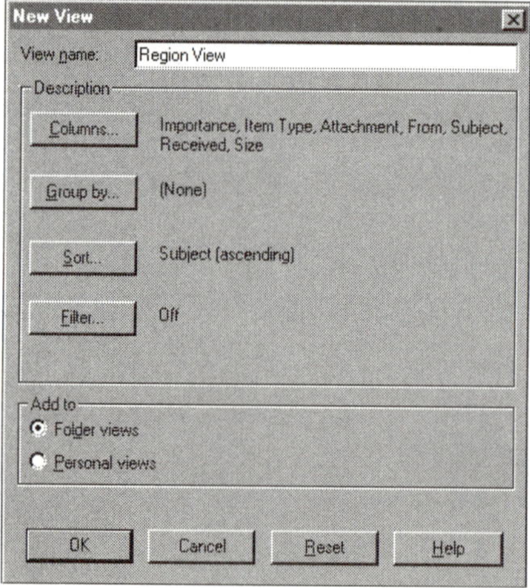

5. Type a name for this view (for example, *Region View*), and then click on the Columns button.

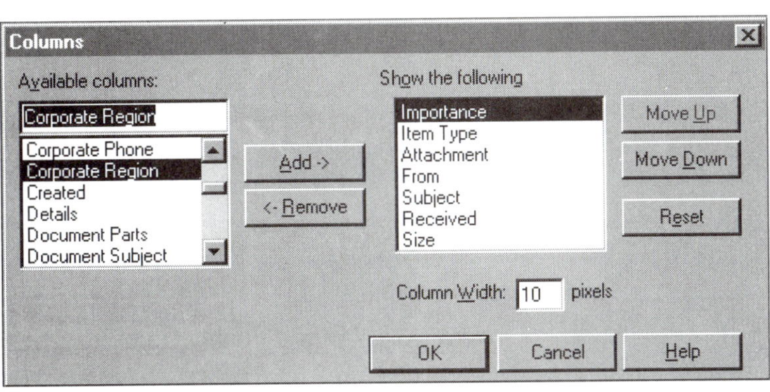

6. From the Available Columns list, select Corporate Region, and then click on the Add button. Corporate Region now appears in the Show The Following list.
7. If you want to remove a column from view, select the column's name in the Show The Following list, and then click on the Remove button. Repeat this step for any other columns you want to remove.
8. Click on OK, and then click on the Group By button in the New View dialog box.

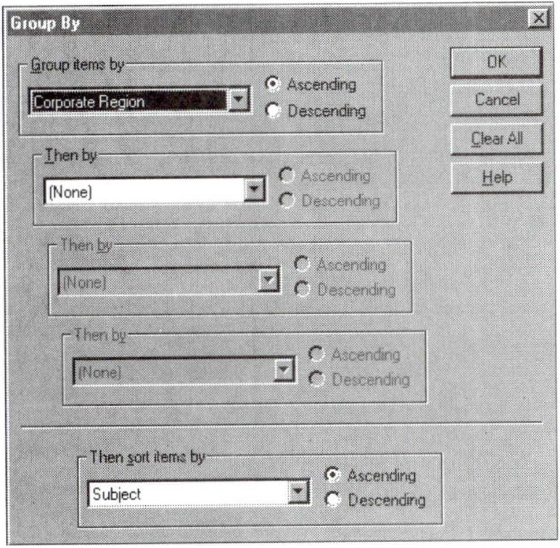

9. In the Group Items By box, select Corporate Region, and then click on OK.

You cannot select the same column for both Group By and Sort. If you try to do this, Exchange displays a message telling you that you can't. If, for example, sorting is already set up for Corporate Region and you try to set Group By to Corporate Region, you'll see a finger-wagging message. In that case, change the sort field first, and then change the Group By field.

10. Click on OK in the New View dialog box.
11. In the Define Views dialog box, click on the Apply button, and then click on the Close button.

You'll now see the region names listed with plus signs beside them. To see the items for a region, click on the plus sign next to that region. The plus sign changes to a minus sign and the items are displayed.

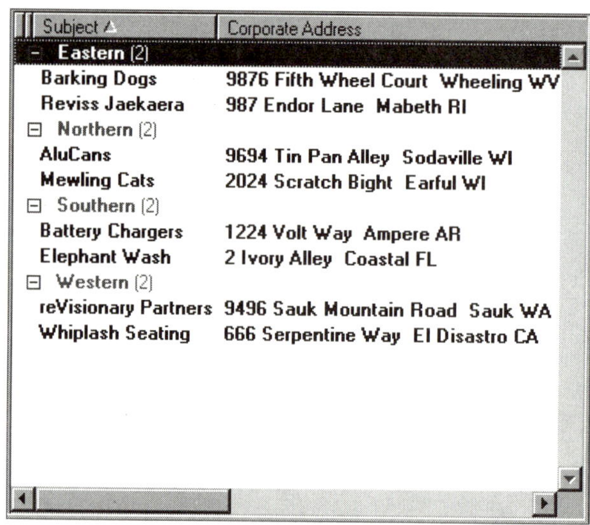

To hide the items for a region, click on the minus sign beside the group name. To return the folder to Normal view, choose the View Personal Views command, and then choose Normal View from the submenu.

Sorting Customer Information

There are as many ways to sort items in a public folder as there are columns for the information the items contain. All of the properties of a message and of documents, as well as all of the fields on forms used in a public folder, are available as column headings in the message list pane when that public folder is open. To sort the information by any one of these columns is an easy matter after you set up the column in the message list pane.

Note For instructions on creating the Who field and the Company Profile form referred to in this section, see "Setting Up the Sample Company Profile Form," on page 320.

For example, suppose you want to sort customer profiles by the names of the managers in your organization who serve those accounts. To do this, you'll add the Who column to the Company Profiles public folder ("Who" is the column name for the Account Manager field on the Company Profile form), and then you'll sort the items in the folder by the managers' names.

To set up a column for the account manager in the message list pane, take these steps:

1. Click on the Company Profiles public folder. (You might first have to click on the plus sign beside the Public Folders folder, then click on the plus sign beside the All Public Folders folder, and then click on the plus sign beside the Customer Information public folder.)
2. Choose the View Columns command.
3. From the Available Columns list, select Who, and then click on the Add button.
4. If you want to remove a column from view, select the column's name in the Show The Following list, and then click on the Remove button. Repeat this step for any other columns you want to remove.
5. Click on OK.

To sort the items in the Company Profiles public folder by account manager, all you need to do is click on the Who column heading.

Changing Customer Information

It's a simple matter to change the information in any item in a folder. Information in a form used in a folder is no different. Here's what you do:

1. Double-click on the item you want to change.
2. Change the information the way you want.
3. Close the item.
4. Click on Yes when Exchange asks if you want to keep the changes.

You won't be able to change items that are read-only on a form. The Company Profile form created in Chapter 12, for example, has one window for composing a message and a second window for reading a message; fields that are modifiable in the compose window are read-only in the read window. This prevents anyone from changing the information on the form after it is posted in the folder, but you can still copy it. If you find a form with incorrect information in a read-only field, copy the information to a new form, correct the information, post the new form, and then delete the old form.

Archiving and Deleting Customer Information

When a customer is no longer a customer and never will be again, you probably don't need to keep information about that customer in your active files. You might archive the information for legal and business purposes, but you don't need it cluttering up your public folder of information about active customers.

Archiving Records in a Public Folder

When a customer becomes inactive, archive the customer's records (for legal and business purposes, for example) so that you can retrieve the records, if necessary.

Note You don't often have to archive *documents* because documents are usually saved somewhere else as a file. Be sure, however, that you know where you saved the file.

To archive records kept in messages and postings in a public folder, take these steps:

1. Click on the public folder with the customer records you want to archive.
2. Right-click on the message or posting you want to archive, and then select Save As from the shortcut menu.

If right-clicking is unavailable, select the message or posting you want to archive, and then choose the File Save As command.

TIP If you want to archive only the records of a specific customer, set up a filter to display only those records. (For help with filtering customer records, see "Filtering Customer Information," on page 352.)

3. Select the disk and folder in which you want to store the archive file.
4. Type a name for the archive file.
5. Select Message Format in the Save As Type box, and then click on the Save button.

Note If you select more than one item in a folder, you can save the items only in Text Only format. If you want to import the records into a public folder again, you should save each message and posting separately in Message Format.

6. Repeat step 2 through step 5 for each message or posting you want to archive.

Retrieving Archived Records

For many reasons, you might want to retrieve customer information that you've put in an archive. When you're ready to retrieve archived records, take these steps:

1. Open Windows Explorer (or Windows File Manager) and locate the disk and folder on which the messages and postings are archived.
2. Arrange the Explorer or File Manager window and the Exchange window so that you can see both at the same time.
3. Open the public folder in which you want to put the archived records.

4. In the Explorer or File Manager window, select all the message and posting files that you want to retrieve and drag them into the public folder in the message list pane. This action puts a copy of each message and posting in the public folder.

Deleting Records from a Public Folder

After you archive customer records, you might as well delete that information in order to keep the contents of the customer information folder current and to save space on your Exchange server.

To delete records from a public folder, take these steps:

1. Select the items that you want to delete.
2. Click on the Delete button on the Exchange toolbar.

CHAPTER
14

Information for Customers

You know the old saying, "The customer is always right." In any business, it's not only the information that you share with colleagues that makes you successful, but also the information that you share with and provide to your customers and clients. However, keeping track of that information and having easy access to it is another story. By using public folders in Microsoft Exchange, you can store the information that you regularly send to customers, sort through and find the information you need quickly, and, if your customers are up to date, send them the information through electronic mail. In this chapter, you'll learn how.

Scenes from This Chapter

You can easily set up a public folder that contains a mass of materials your organization has prepared for customers. This public folder could contain items such as the following:

- Product information—catalogs and background information
- Marketing materials—brochures, press releases, and advertisements
- Financial information—financial projections, sales performance, and inventory records

From time to time, you need to cull some of this material to satisfy a request from a customer for information about a product or service your organization offers. Finding exactly the materials you need can be time-consuming and even difficult if you have to browse through the list of documents in the folder. Exchange gives you an easy way to find the materials you need. That's the first thing you'll learn in this chapter.

Once you have the materials, you need to send them to the customer. If your customer is electronically enhanced—that is, if your customer can receive documents through e-mail—you can send the materials through Exchange. If your customer is not electronically enhanced, you'll have to do something more old fashioned—print the materials and send them via the postal service or by some other delivery service.

Scenario

Let's suppose that your organization has set up a public folder named Products & Services. In this folder, your organization stores all kinds of information that helps you inform and work with your customers. As the Bozo Bit project has moved along, you've been posting documents about the game in the folder.

You learn from your public relations department that a journalist has called and asked for background materials about the new Bozo Bit game. You need to go through the information in the Products & Services folder so that you can send the appropriate information to the friendly journalist.

Finding Information for Customers

The ways in which you find information in a public folder that's set up to store customer information are more or less the same as those you use in any public folder. One important difference, however, is that the items in a customer information folder will most likely be documents of various kinds (brochures, press releases, sales forecasts, and so on) rather than mail messages or postings. To sort through the variety of documents in a public folder to find the ones you need, follow these steps:

1. Open the public folder that stores the customer information.
2. Choose the Tools Find command.

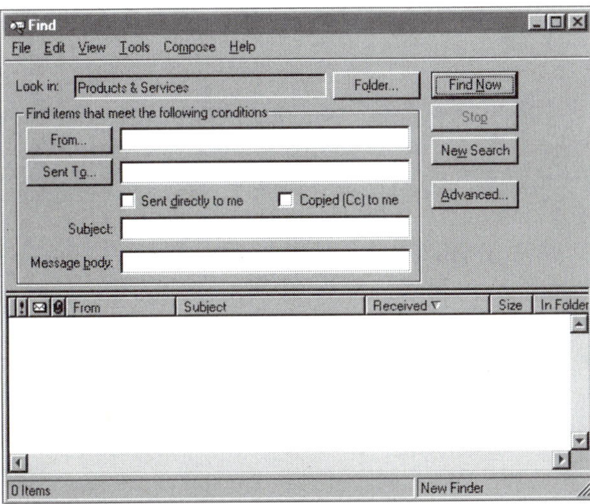

3. In the Find dialog box, click on the Advanced button. In the Show Properties Of area, select the Document option.

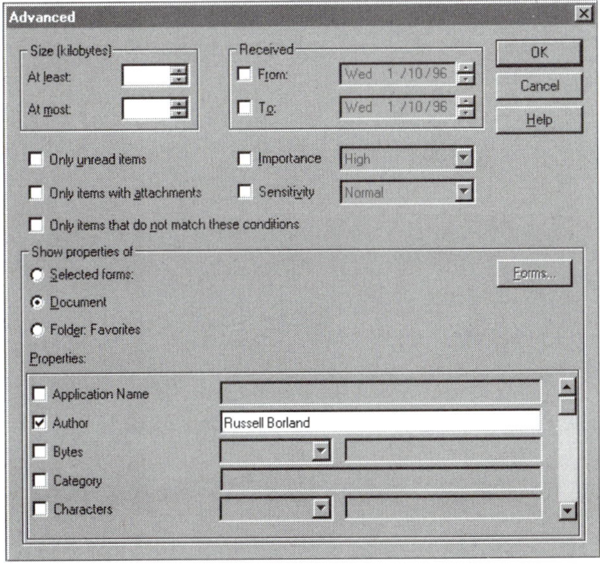

4. Using the check boxes in the Properties area, select the document properties that Exchange should use to find the documents you want.

   For example, you can use the Application Name property to find all the documents of a certain type, such as all the documents created in Microsoft Word. You can also use the Author property to find those documents created by a specific team member.

   To see the entire list of document properties you can use to find documents, scroll the list of properties in the Advanced dialog box. For information about setting document properties, see the sidebar "Setting Document Properties," on page 369.

5. Click on OK in the Advanced dialog box.
6. Click on the Find Now button in the Find dialog box. Exchange searches the folder for documents that match the properties you selected in the Advanced dialog box.

   Exchange then displays the names of the matching documents, as shown here:

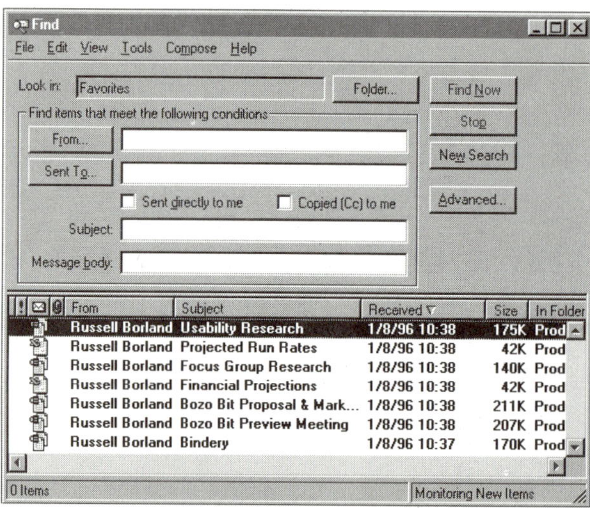

You can now read, print, or send any or all of these documents.

Setting Document Properties

You can use any of the properties of the documents (files) in a folder to select the documents you want to see, work on, or send. However, to have Exchange find a document on the basis of the properties you select, you must have previously set the document's properties. The Find command omits documents that don't have the matching information, such as documents for which the requested information in the Properties dialog box is blank. When you are creating or editing a document in a Microsoft Office application, you can set document properties by choosing the File Properties command and then entering document property information on the Summary tab of the Properties dialog box, as shown here:

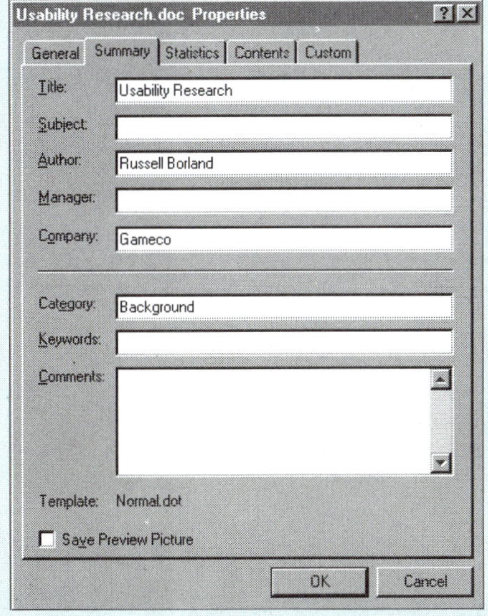

For example, you could type *Background* in the Category box for all the documents that describe the background of a product. Then, when you need to find all the background documents for a particular product, you could use Exchange to search for all documents with the Category property set to *Background.*

For another perspective on document properties, see "Preparing the Contract Documents," on page 336.

Sending Information to Customers

After you have selected the documents you want to send to your customer, you have several choices for how to get the information to them. The conventional way is to print the documents and then send them to your customer via some delivery service. If your customer is up with the times, however, you can send the documents through Exchange.

To send the documents through Exchange, do this:

1. In the Find dialog box, select the documents that you want to send. To select more than one document, hold down the Ctrl key as you click on each document you want to send.
2. Choose the View Toolbar command to display the toolbar, and then click on the Forward button. (If you prefer, you can choose the Compose Forward command instead of turning on and using the toolbar.)

3. Fill in the customer's e-mail address in the To box.

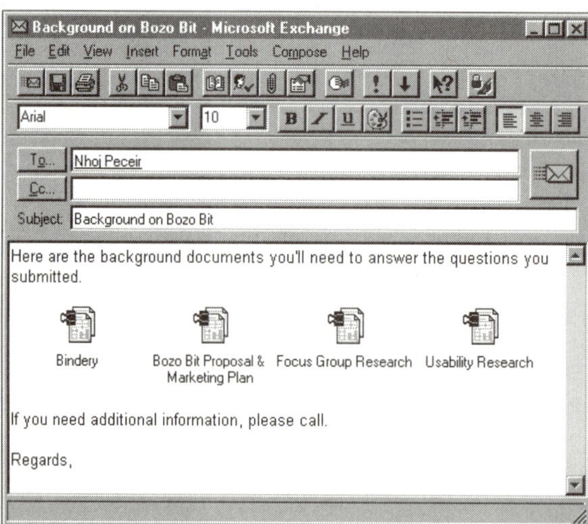

4. Type an appropriate title in the Subject box. For this example, you could type something like *Background on Bozo Bit.*
5. In the message area, type any message you want to send along with the documents.
6. Click on the Send button.

You've done it! You've answered a customer's request for information as easily as that.

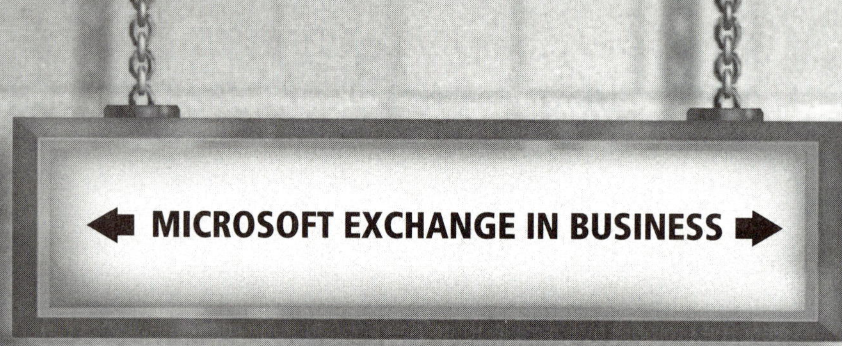

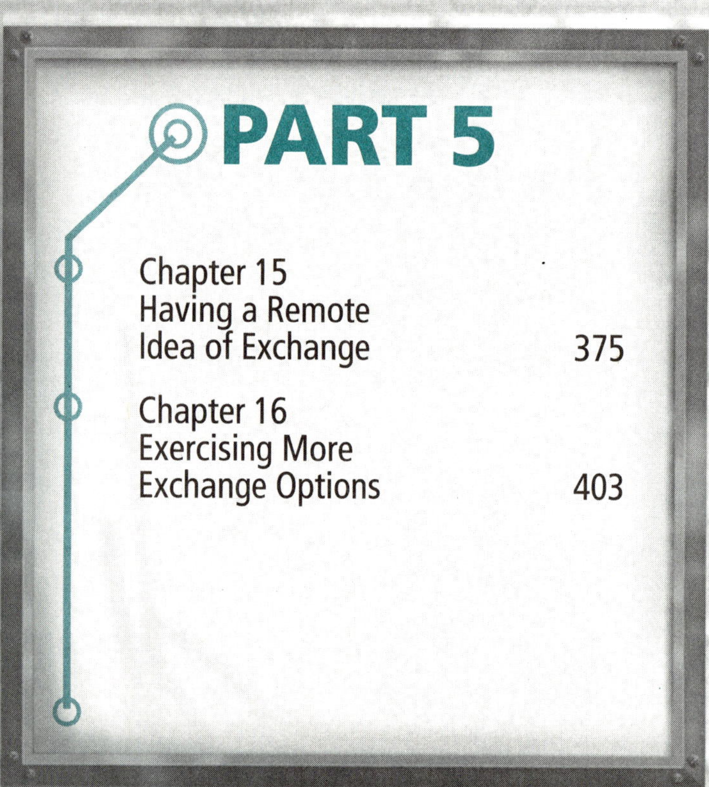

PART 5

You can be quite content using Microsoft Exchange without making a single adjustment or without pushing Exchange beyond its standard setup. But for adventurous souls and for those who like to control their destinies a little more exactly, there are many ways to extend Exchange beyond its basic operating processes.

You can extend Exchange with Remote Mail, which gives you the ability to dial in to and connect to your Exchange server and work with your e-mail and electronic schedule. And whether you're working remotely or at your office, you can set a great many options in Exchange to extend, enhance, control, and alter the way Exchange works for you. We'll cover these topics in this part.

Extending Exchange

CHAPTER
15

Having a Remote Idea of Exchange

When you're lodged in a hotel, you still might want to see the messages, postings, and meetings that are going on at headquarters. For times such as these, you can use Microsoft Remote Mail to work with Exchange. With a Remote Mail connection, you can send and delete messages, set up appointments and tasks, request meetings, and respond to meeting requests. And, with some preliminary setup, you can also see the contents of public folders as well as your server folders. In this chapter, you'll read about setting up and using Remote Mail for these tasks.

Scenes from This Chapter

By using Remote Mail in Exchange, you can connect to your Exchange server and get a list of message headers. Exchange then disconnects from the server to save you from expensive phone charges. You mark the most important messages and tell Exchange to download only those messages. Exchange reconnects to your server, downloads the messages, and disconnects again. You can now read your messages and perform all the actions—reply, delete, forward, move, and save—that you perform with messages when you're connected to your Exchange server through a network at work.

Before you can use Remote Mail, however, you need to take a few preliminary steps while you're connected to your Exchange server, namely:

- Set up folders for offline use
- Download the Offline Address Book
- Set up Remote Mail

Getting into Synchrony

Exchange is set up more or less ready to work with offline. Part of the standard setup of Exchange is that your main server folders—Inbox, Outbox, Sent Items, and Deleted Items—are always set up for online or offline use.

For offline work, however, you might want to see the contents of other folders. If you have set up other server folders or public folder favorites, you can select options to work with any and all of these other folders offline. (Personal Folders are always available offline because they are stored on the hard disk in your computer.) After you set up folders for offline use, you need to periodically synchronize the offline folders with their related folders on the Exchange server. Exchange synchronizes your four main server folders automatically whenever you connect to the network.

In the following section, you'll learn how to make a server folder or a public folder favorite available offline. Then you'll learn about downloading the Offline Address Book. After we cover those topics, you'll learn something about synchronizing folders.

Offline Folders

As mentioned previously, the Inbox, Outbox, Sent Items, and Deleted Items folders on your Exchange server are always available offline as well as online. When you work offline, these folders contain all the items

that were in the folders when you last exited Exchange. You can open and view these folders as you would while working online. You can send messages, move messages, delete messages, and empty your Deleted Items folder—all while you're working offline.

In addition to these folders, you can set up for offline use any other server folders on your Exchange system as well as any public folder Favorites you have established.

To set up a server folder or a favorite public folder for offline use, take these steps:

1. Right-click on the folder you want to set up for offline use, and then choose Properties from the shortcut menu.
2. Select the Synchronization tab.
3. In the This Folder Is Available area, select the When Offline Or Online option, and then click on OK.

If right-clicking is unavailable, click on the folder you want to set up for offline use, and then choose the File Properties command.

Select this option to make a folder available for offline work.

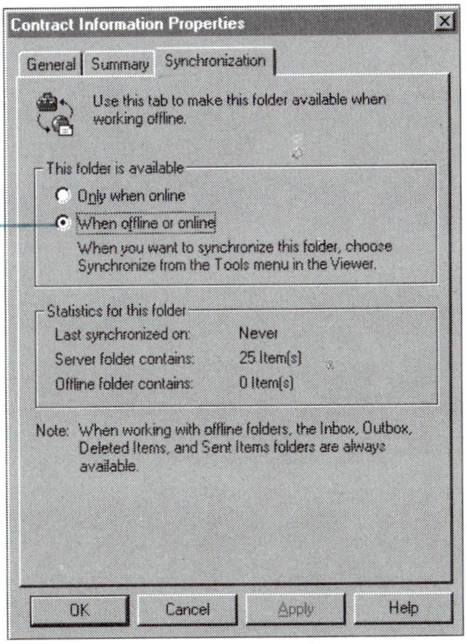

This folder is now available to work with offline as well as online, and Exchange displays a suitcase icon for this folder.

If you no longer want a folder to be available for offline work, select the Only When Online option on the Synchronization tab.

Note You cannot set up your four main server folders—Inbox, Outbox, Sent Items, and Deleted Items—for only online work.

What About My Connections to Other Online Services?

If you have accounts on other online services, such as MSN, the Microsoft online network; CompuServe; America Online; or AT&T, you can set up these services in a profile. If you set up a dial-in information service in a profile, Exchange starts that service when you start Exchange. If you want to connect to the service, follow your usual logon procedure. If you don't want to connect to the service, cancel the logon procedure.

To set up an information service in a profile, follow these steps:

1. Start the Control Panel, and then double-click on the Mail And Fax icon.
2. Click on the Show Profiles button.
3. Select the Profile to which you want to add an information service, and then click on the Properties button.
4. Click on the Add button.

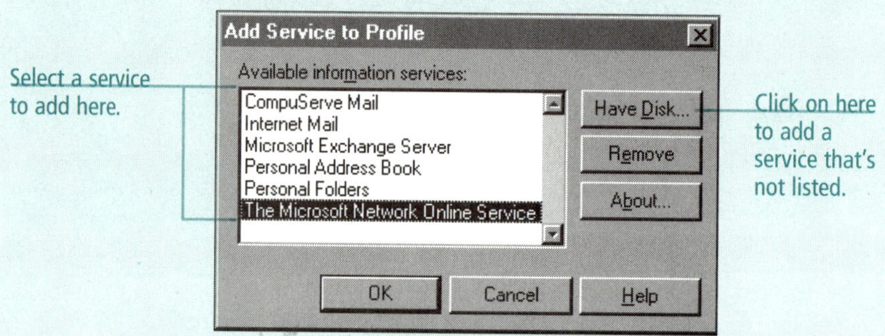

5. Select the information service you want to add to this profile, and then click on OK.

Note You can add only one dial-in information service to a profile, except under unusual circumstances. Why? Each dial-in information service requires a modem and a telephone line. When one service is using the modem and telephone line, a second service won't have access to the line. If, however, you have multiple modems connected to your computer and a telephone line for each modem, you can then set up one dial-in information service for each modem and telephone line.

(continued)

What About My Connections to Other Online Services? *(cont'd.)*

If the service you want to add is not listed, you need a disk that contains the files for the service. To add a service that's not listed, insert the disk in your computer, and then click on the Have Disk button. In the Install Other Information Service dialog box, type the drive letter for the disk that contains the files for the information service, or click on the Browse button to select the disk and folder that contains the files. Click on OK.

6. Click on OK in the Add Service To Profile dialog box, click on OK in the Properties dialog box, and then click on the Close button in the Mail And Fax dialog box.

Although using another information service is similar to using Remote Mail, Exchange works directly with the information service rather than connecting to it by using Remote Mail. Remote Mail is for connecting to your Exchange server.

The Offline Address Book

When you're working offline, you'll probably want to compose new messages to send to others, reply to messages, and forward messages. Before you can specify the recipients of your message or place the message in your Outbox to be sent later, you need to have the Offline Address Book available. If you don't download the Offline Address Book, Exchange tells you you can't compose or otherwise work with a message until you do.

To download the Offline Address Book, do the following:

1. Connect to your network and start Exchange.
2. Choose the Tools Synchronize command.
3. Choose Download Address Book from the submenu.
4. In the Download Offline Address Book dialog box, click on OK.

   You'll see a message that shows you how downloading is progressing. When downloading is complete, you're ready to work with messages.

Synchronizing Folders

Before exiting Exchange, and while you're still connected to your Exchange server, you can synchronize any folders that you have set up to

Using Remote Mail with Public Folder Favorites

While you're working offline, you can't open public folders, at least not directly. Exchange helps you to get around this restriction through public folder favorites. If you've already set up public folder favorites, you're in a good position to take advantage of them during offline work. If you haven't yet set up any public folder favorites, you must do that before you can work with the contents of a public folder offline.

Setting up public folder favorites is quite easy; simply follow these steps:

1. Find and open the public folder you want to add to your Favorites folder.
2. Click on the Add To Favorites button on the Exchange toolbar.

You'll see a message that the folder was added successfully to your Favorites folder. At this point, the folder in the Favorites folder displays the contents of its related public folder, and you can set the folder in the Favorites folder to be available offline.

After you set the folder to be available offline, the favorite folder displays a suitcase icon. When you're working offline, the favorite folder contains the contents of the related public folder as they were the last time you synchronized the folder. You can read items in the folder, post new notes, and reply to postings and messages. You can also delete items and add forms if you have permission to do so. Exchange copies the changes you make in the favorite folder to its related public folder the next time you connect to your Exchange server.

be available offline. To synchronize a single folder, do the following:

1. Select the folder you want to synchronize.

> **Note** You cannot synchronize a public folder directly. If you want to synchronize a public folder, you must select the copy of the folder in your Favorites folder. Public folder favorites that are set up to be available offline will display a suitcase icon.

2. Choose the Tools Synchronize command.
3. Choose This Folder from the submenu.

To synchronize all folders, do the following:

1. Choose the Tools Synchronize command.
2. Choose All Folders from the submenu.

In either case, Exchange will display a window indicating its progress as it synchronizes the folder or folders.

Setting Up Remote Mail

Before you can use Remote Mail, you need to provide Exchange with information about your remote connection. To provide Exchange with this information, you need to start Exchange, start Remote Mail, and then set some options. Follow these steps:

1. Start Exchange.

For directions for starting Exchange, follow the steps listed in "Guided Tour of Exchange," on page 2.

What you see when you start Exchange depends on whether you have created one profile for working both online and offline or you have set up two or more profiles.

- If you have only one profile, skip to step 3.
- If you have two or more profiles, you'll see the Choose Profile dialog box, as shown in step 2 on the next page.

Note If you have multiple profiles set up, but Exchange does not prompt you to choose a profile when you start Exchange, do the following:

1. Choose the Tools Options command, and then select the General tab if necessary.
2. Select the Prompt For A Profile To Be Used option and click on OK.
3. Exit and restart Exchange. This time you will be prompted to choose a profile.

2. Select the profile you want to use, and then click on OK.

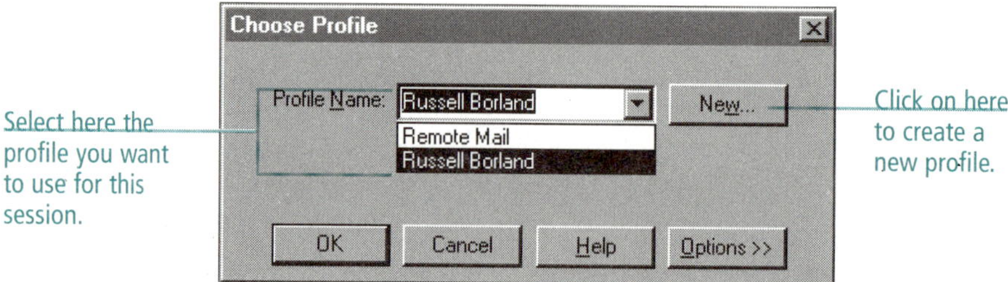

3. In the dialog box that appears, click on the Work Offline button.

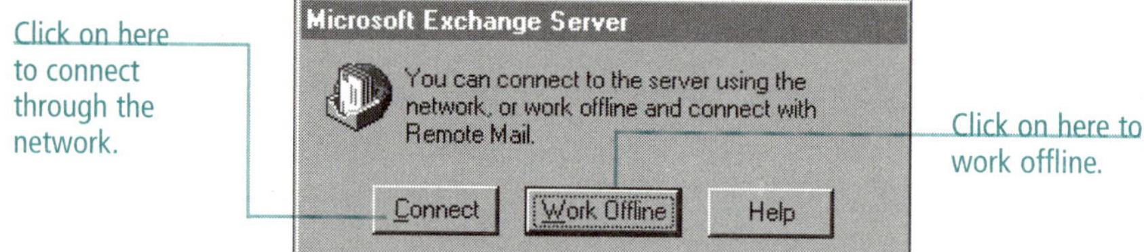

Exchange starts and you see the usual Exchange window. Now you have to start Remote Mail to connect to your Exchange server.

To start Remote Mail, take these steps:

1. Choose the Tools Remote Mail command. You see the Remote Mail window shown here:

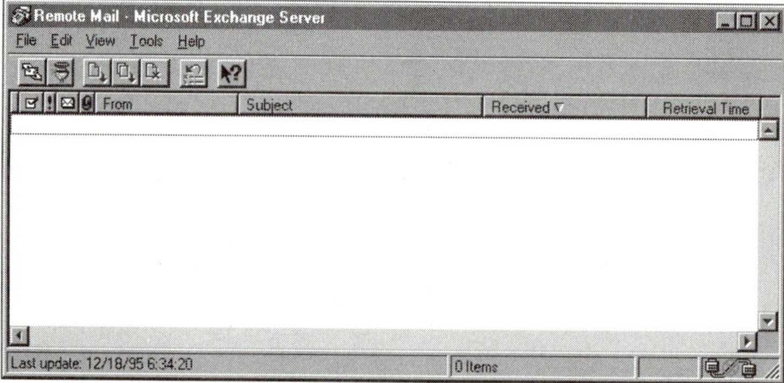

At this point, you need to set Remote Mail options so that Exchange can dial up and connect to your Exchange server.

2. In Remote Mail, choose the Tools Options command.
3. In the Properties dialog box, click on the New button.

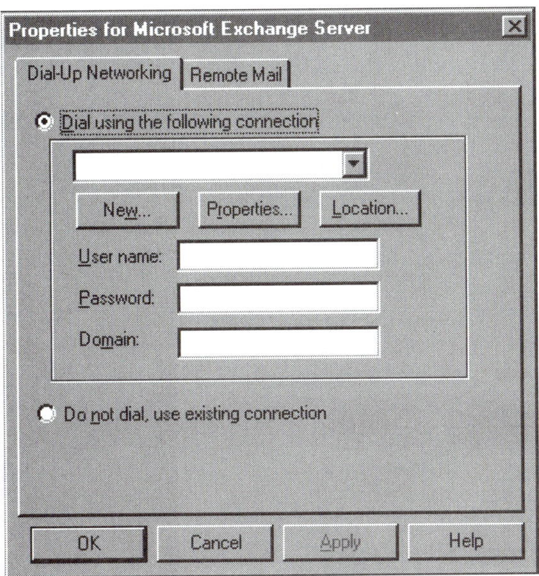

If you do not have a modem installed, Exchange will start a wizard to help you install one at this point. Follow the on-screen directions to install a new modem.

4. In the Make New Connection dialog box, shown at the top of the next page, accept the name *My Connection* or type a new name for your remote connection. If your computer has more than one modem, select the modem you want to use for this remote connection, and then click on the Next button.

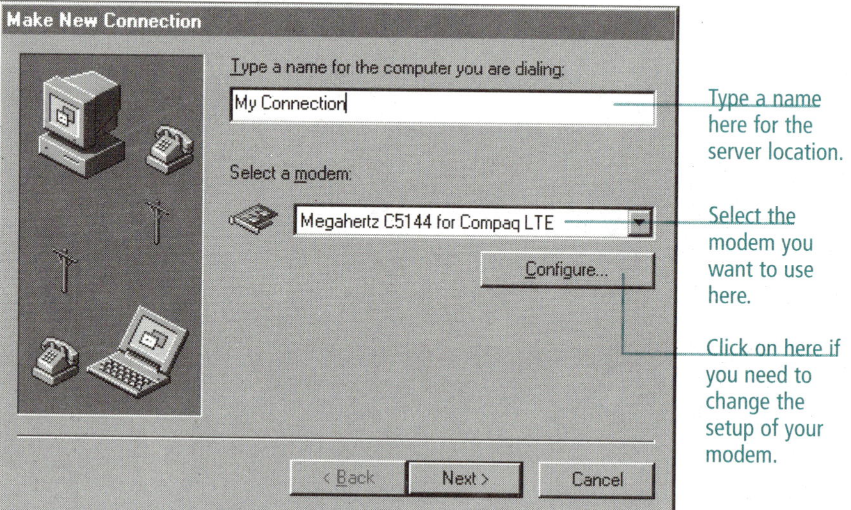

5. Type the area code and telephone number you need to dial to connect to your Exchange server in the next Make New Connection dialog box, shown next. Select the country code for your Exchange server, and then click on the Next button.

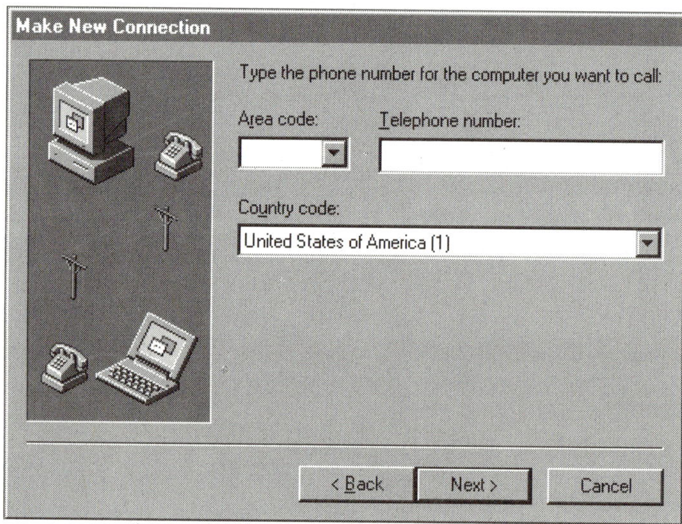

6. Click on the Finish button. The Properties For Microsoft Exchange Server dialog box, shown on page 383, reappears.

7. Click on the Location button. The Dialing Properties dialog box appears, next. You see the location name Default Location. If you'll always dial up and connect from one type of location, you can use this name. If you'll dial up and connect from more than one type of location, you'll need to set up a name for each type of remote location from which you dial. (Different types of locations require different prefixes in order to dial your server location. An office location, for example, might require dialing 9 before the rest of the number.)

   To set up a new location name, click on the New button.

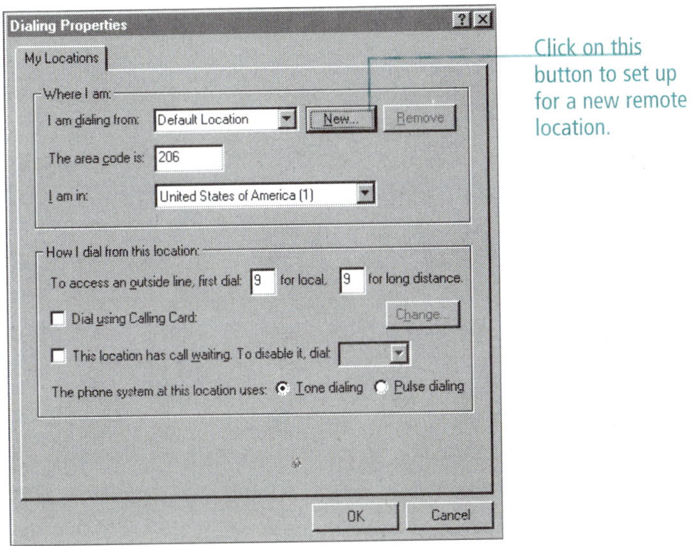

Click on this button to set up for a new remote location.

8. In the Create New Location dialog box, type a name for the location, and then click on OK.

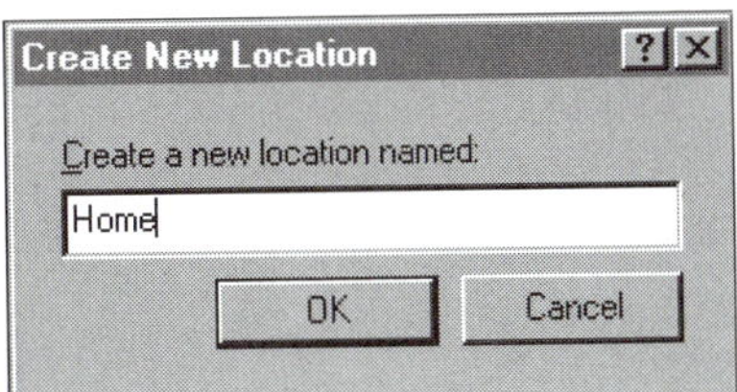

9. Type the telephone area code for your remote location, and then select the country from which you will dial up.

10. In the Dialing Properties dialog box, make other appropriate changes for the telephone system you're dialing from, and then click on OK.
11. In the Properties For Microsoft Exchange Server dialog box, type your network user name, your network password, and then your network domain name, and select the appropriate connection from the dropdown list, if necessary.
12. Click on OK.

You're now ready to connect to your Exchange server through Remote Mail. Jump to step 4 in "Starting Remote Mail," next.

Starting Remote Mail

There are two parts to starting remote mail. The first part is to start Exchange. The second part is to start Remote Mail. Take these steps:

1. Start Exchange.
2. In the dialog box that appears, click on the Work Offline button.
3. Choose the Tools Remote Mail command. You see the Remote Mail window.
4. If you have set up more than one remote location, choose the Tools Options command, select the remote location name, enter your user name, password, and the domain name, and then click on OK.
5. Click on the Connect button.

You'll see a message box telling you that your computer is dialing. When the connection is made, you'll see a message box, like the next one, telling you that you're connected and also a clock that displays your connect time.

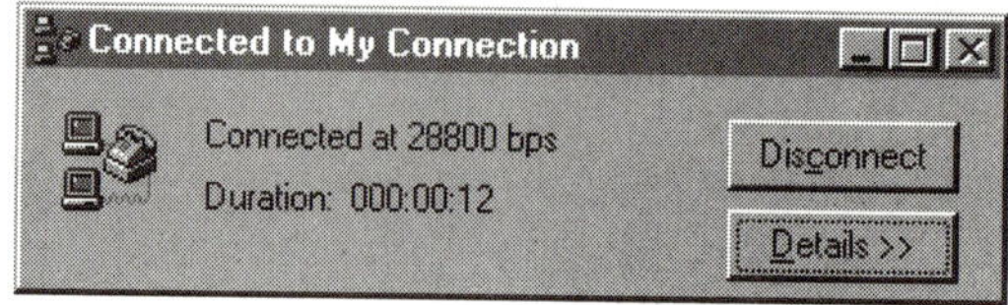

Drag the Connection dialog box away from the Making Connection dialog box if you want to see both dialog boxes.

When the connection is made, you're ready to work with your messages. See "Working with Your Messages," on page 388.

Breaking the Connection and Stopping Remote Mail

Exchange doesn't keep a persistent Remote Mail connection. Remote Mail does its work and then disconnects to save you phone charges.

If you want to break the connection yourself, click on the Disconnect button.

When you're ready to quit Remote Mail, close the Remote Mail window in one of the usual ways.

If you don't want Remote Mail to disconnect automatically, choose the Tools Options command in Remote Mail, click on the Remote Mail tab, turn off the Disconnect After Connection Is Finished box, and then click on OK.

What Happens When You Connect

When you connect to your Exchange server through Remote Mail, four things happen. (These same actions take place when you connect to your Exchange server through the network.)

- Remote Mail downloads the message headers of new messages that have arrived in your server Inbox.
- Remote Mail sends the messages that you have set up to send—new messages, replies, and forwards.
- Exchange deletes messages that you no longer want to keep on the Exchange server.
- Exchange moves messages to the folders to which you have moved them while working offline.

The next sections describe how to set up for these actions to take place when you connect to your Exchange server.

Note Remote Mail can also synchronize other server folders and public folder favorites you have set up for offline work. For more information about this, see "Synchronizing Folders," on page 379.

Big Problem: Can't Download Messages

If your Inbox folder hasn't been synchronized with your server Inbox, you'll see a message telling you that Exchange can't download your messages because there's no delivery point. In this case, you need to assign delivery to your Personal Folders Inbox, at least until you can synchronize your server Inbox. Of course, you have to set up Personal Folders first. To do so, take the steps described in "What About My Connections to Other Online Services?" on page 378, and add the Personal Folders service.

Working with Your Messages

One of the beauties of working with Exchange offline is that you can perform a lot of your work without being connected. You can read new (and old) messages, create new messages, compose replies, and forward messages. You can also delete messages you no longer need or want. Then, when you connect to your Exchange server through Remote Mail, the messages you want to read are downloaded, the messages you want to send are sent to the server for routing, and the messages you want to delete disappear into the Deleted Items folder on your Exchange server.

The following sections treat each of these topics.

Reading Messages

When you want to read the contents of messages in your Inbox, you first mark them for retrieval, and then you connect and download the marked messages.

Marking Messages for Download

Marking a message for retrieval tells Remote Mail that you want to download that message so that you can read and respond to it. To mark a message for retrieval, take the steps on the next page.

1. In the message list pane of the Inbox, select the messages you want to download. To select more than one message, hold down the Ctrl key as you click on each message you want to download.
2. Click on the Mark To Retrieve button on the Remote Mail toolbar.

Use Mark To Retrieve when you want Remote Mail to deliver your messages to your server Inbox. Use Mark To Retrieve Copy when you want Remote Mail to deliver your messages to your Personal Folders Inbox.

The messages are ready to download the next time you connect to your Exchange server.

If you accidentally mark a message that you don't want to download, select it and click on the Mark To Retrieve button again to unmark it.

Downloading Messages

When you are ready to download the messages you have marked, click on the Connect button on the Remote Mail toolbar and make your connection to your Exchange server.

Your Exchange server sends the items you have marked to your offline Inbox. You can now read the messages just as you would read them if you were connected to your Exchange server.

While you're connected, Remote Mail also sends new messages and replies and forwards messages from your offline Outbox to your Exchange server. The Exchange server then sends the messages to their destinations (see "Sending Messages," next). Also, any messages you have marked for deletion are deleted from folders on your Exchange server. (See "Deleting Messages," on page 390.)

Sending Messages

When you're working offline and want to send a message, you simply compose a message as you would when you're connected to your Exchange server. You can also write replies and set up messages for forwarding. These processes aren't mysterious at all. You use the same commands and steps you use when you're connected. The only true difference is that the messages you set up to send don't go anywhere until you connect to your Exchange server. This connection can either be through the network at your office or through Remote Mail.

Note As mentioned several times in this chapter, you need to have a copy of the Offline Address Book in order to set up a message for sending. For more information, see "The Offline Address Book," on page 379.

After you create a new message, fashion your reply to a message, or set up a message for forwarding, the message lives in your Outbox until the next time you connect. Messages that you set up to send are displayed in your Outbox in italics, like this:

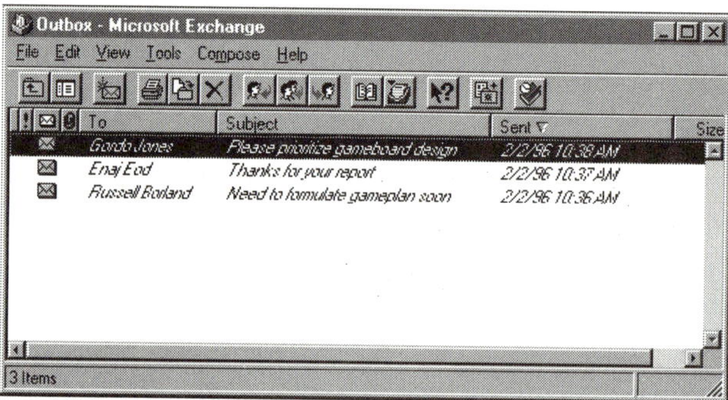

To send messages with Remote Mail, click on the Connect button on the Remote Mail toolbar and connect to your Exchange server.

Deleting Messages

Messages that you no longer want to keep you'll want to delete. You can mark messages for deletion, and the next time you connect to your Exchange server, the messages move to your Deleted Items folder.

There are two types of deletion:

- Deletions from one of the folders in Exchange
- Deletions in the Remote Mail window

Both types of deletions perform the same task—getting rid of the unwanted message.

To delete an item from a folder in Exchange, select the item, and then click on the Delete button on the Exchange toolbar. To delete items from the Remote Mail window, select the items, and then click on the Mark To Delete button on the Remote Mail toolbar.

To complete the deletion, connect to your Exchange server, either through your network connection at work or by clicking on the Connect button on the Remote Mail toolbar.

Moving Items to Different Folders

While you're working offline, you might want to move an item to a different folder. This is a simple process. You simply move the item as you would when you're connected to your Exchange server. The next time you connect to your server, either through Remote Mail or through a network connection, the Exchange server moves the items in the server folders to match the moves you made while you were working offline.

Setting More Remote Mail Options

Now wouldn't it be a shame if you had to give up the fancy tools you use with Exchange simply because you are connected from afar? When you use Remote Mail to work with your messages and folders, you can still use most of the tools—plus some new ones—for working smartly with your messages.

In this section, you'll learn about three types of options that you can set up to make Remote Mail work better for you:

- Filtering Remote Mail so that you don't have to see messages you don't care about when you're away from your office
- Scheduling automatic dial-in times so that you can keep your folders at home as current as you want
- Setting up Remote Mail to dial in using your telephone calling card

Filtering Remote Mail

If you're familiar with the filters you can set up for folders and with the Inbox Assistant, you'll have no trouble setting up filters for Remote Mail. The main difference is that with Remote Mail you have fewer choices about the options you can use to filter incoming messages.

To review, a filter sets up conditions that tell Exchange (in this case, the Remote Mail part of Exchange) which messages to pass through to your Inbox while you're working. For remote work, a filter can be especially helpful because it can screen out messages you don't want to deal with and can pass through only those messages that you do want to see. Filtering provides a means for shorter connection times while Remote Mail downloads the message list. A filter also provides shorter work sessions for you because you aren't wading through extraneous messages.

To set up a Remote Mail filter, take these steps:

1. In the Remote Mail window, choose the Tools Options command.
2. In the Properties For Microsoft Exchange Server dialog box, select the Remote Mail tab.
3. Select the Retrieve Items That Meet The Following Conditions option, and then click on the Filter button.

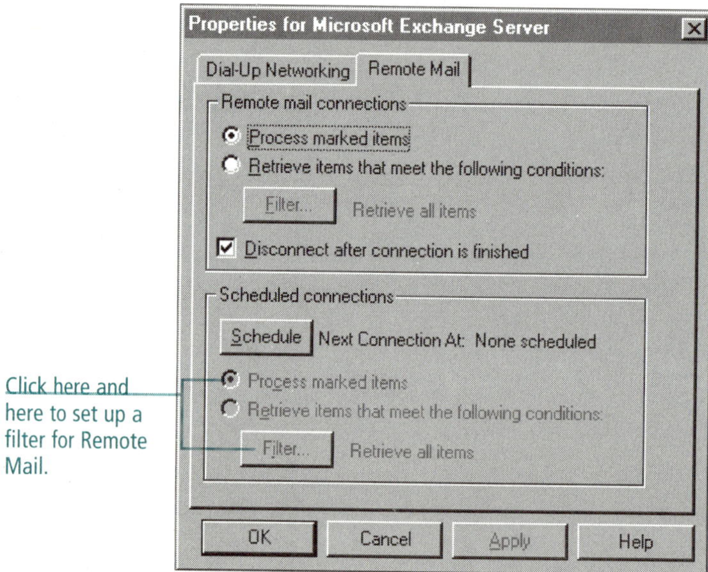

Click here and here to set up a filter for Remote Mail.

4. In the Filter dialog box, set up the criteria for the filter you want to use. Table 15-1, opposite, describes the fields in the Filter dialog box.

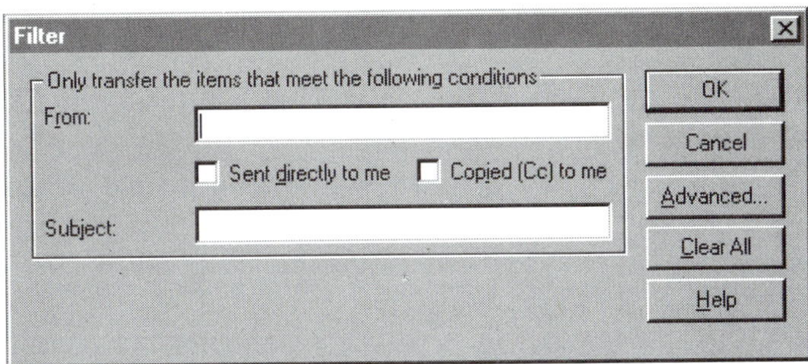

You don't have to fill out the Filter dialog box at all. You can set conditions in the Advanced dialog box either in addition to conditions you set in the Filter dialog box or instead of setting conditions there.

Setting	What Stays
From	Shows only items from a particular sender
Sent Directly To Me	Shows only items with your name in the To box
Copied (Cc) To Me	Shows only items with your name in the Cc box
Subject	Shows only items with subjects that match the exact text you type in the Subject box

Table 15-1

Descriptions of the settings in the Filter dialog box

5. If you want to set up advanced filtering criteria, click on the Advanced button.

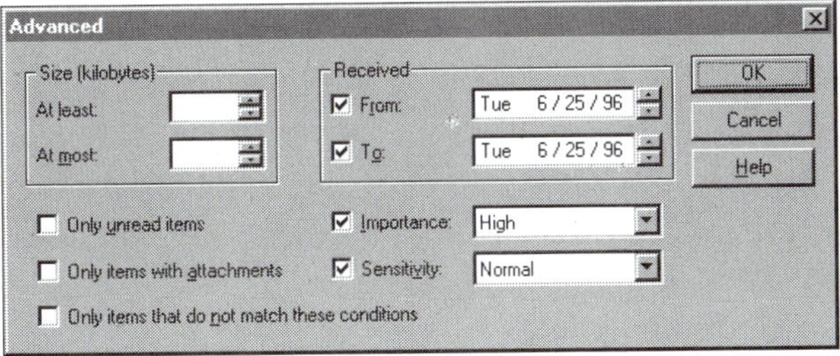

6. Fill in the fields in the Advanced dialog box to suit the types of messages you want to block. Notice the option labeled Only Items That Do Not Match These Conditions. Selecting this option reverses all the other conditions you set up in the Filter and Advanced dialog boxes. Table 15-2 describes the fields in the Advanced dialog box.

Setting	What Stays
Size At Least	Shows only items that are larger than the size you set
Size At Most	Shows only items that are smaller than the size you set
Received From	Shows only items received after the date you set; to see items between two dates, also set a Received To date
Received To	Shows only items received before the date you set; to see items between two dates, also set a Received From date
Only Unread Items	Shows only items you haven't yet read
Only Items With Attachments	Shows only items that contain attachments (files or messages)
Importance	Shows only items set to the specified level of importance—High, Normal, or Low
Sensitivity	Shows only items with the specified level of sensitivity—Normal, Personal, Private, or Confidential
Only Items That Do Not Match These Conditions	Uses the reverse of all the settings in both the Filter and the Advanced dialog boxes; for example, if you turn on the Only Unread Items box and this box, the folder shows only items that you have already read

Table 15-2

Descriptions of the settings in the Advanced dialog box

7. Click on OK in the Advanced dialog box, and then click on OK in the Filter dialog box. In the Properties For Microsoft Exchange Server dialog box, the label beside the Filter button changes from Retrieve All Items to Retrieve Items That Match The Filter.

8. Click on OK in the Properties For Microsoft Exchange Server dialog box.

Turning Off the Remote Mail Filter

There are two steps to turning off a Remote Mail filter.

1. Click on the Filter button, click on the Clear All button, and then click on OK in the Filter dialog box.

   The label beside the Filter button changes to Retrieve All Items. The Clear All button clears both the Filter and the Advanced dialog box settings.

2. Select the Process Marked Items option on the Remote Mail tab.

Scheduling Remote Mail Connections

When you're away from your network connection, you might want to connect with Remote Mail at a specific time or at specific intervals. With Remote Mail scheduling, you can set the time or interval you want Exchange to use to dial in and connect.

To set up a dial-in schedule for Remote Mail, follow these steps:

1. In the Remote Mail window, choose the Tools Options command.
2. In the Properties For Microsoft Exchange Server dialog box, select the Remote Mail tab.
3. Click on the Schedule button.
4. Decide whether you want Remote Mail to connect at a specific time each day or at regular intervals.

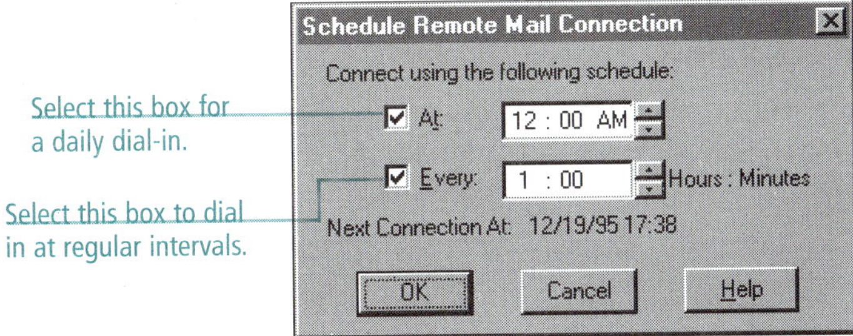

Take one of the following actions:

- To set up a connection for a specific time each day, click on the At box, and then set the time for when you want Remote Mail to dial in. To set the hour, click on the hour number, and then type or scroll to the hour. To set the minutes, click on the minute number, and then type or scroll to the minute. Remember that—depending on your long-distance provider—dialing in between 5:00 P.M. and 10:00 P.M. is cheaper than during the day, and dialing in after 10:00 P.M. is even less expensive.

- To set a dial-in interval, click on the Every box, and then set the interval.

Note You can set both a specific time and an interval for scheduled connections.

5. Click on OK. In the Properties For Microsoft Exchange Server dialog box, you'll see beside the Schedule button an indication of when the next scheduled dial-in will take place. If you have no scheduled dial-in set up, you see None Scheduled beside the Schedule button.

Note Scheduled connections have their own filtering system, which you set up under the Scheduled Connections area of the Properties For Microsoft Exchange Server dialog box. The conditions you can set are the same as for Remote Mail Connections. For help with setting a filter for Scheduled Connections, follow the directions in "Filtering Remote Mail," on page 391.

6. Click on OK in the Properties For Microsoft Exchange Server dialog box.

Calling Card Dialing

For various reasons, you might wish to charge your Remote Mail calls to a telephone calling card. That's easy to set up in Remote Mail. Here's what you do:

1. In the Remote Mail window, choose the Tools Options command.
2. Click on the Location button.
3. In the I Am Dialing From box, select the location from which you want to call using a credit card.
4. Select the Dial Using Calling Card check box. Remote Mail immediately displays the Change Calling Card dialog box, shown on the next page.

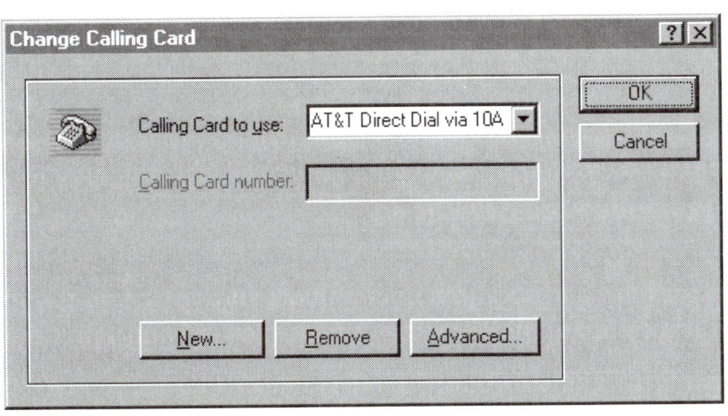

5. In the Calling Card To Use box, select the type of calling card you want to use.
6. In the Calling Card Number box, type the calling card number, and then click on OK. If you need to change the calling card or the number, click on the Change button in the Dialing Properties dialog box, and then repeat step 5 and step 6.
7. In the Dialog Properties dialog box, click on OK, and then click on OK in the Properties For Microsoft Exchange Server dialog box.

Working with Your Appointment Book

For the most part, working with your appointment book is about the same whether you are working offline, connected to the Exchange server at the office, or working with a remote connection. When you work remotely, you might need to set up the time zone so that you schedule meetings at the proper time. You'll also need to have downloaded a copy of the Offline Address Book. (For information, see "The Offline Address Book," on page 379.)

What's My Time Zone?

Schedule+ takes the date and time it uses from your operating system. Because you need to know what time it is where you usually work, your computer is set to use the time zone where you usually work. This time zone is your primary time zone. Many people travel to other time zones, however, or work in a branch office that's in a time zone different from their organization headquarters. These people probably can find a very good reason to set up a secondary time zone. With a secondary time zone set up, you can schedule appointments for either time zone and know that you won't inadvertently misread the time.

Note You don't have to be connected to the network to set up a secondary time zone.

To set up a secondary time zone for your travels and other times away from your primary time zone, take these steps:

1. Start Schedule+.

For directions for starting Schedule+, follow the steps listed in "Guided Tour of Exchange," on page 15.

2. Choose the Tools Options command, and then select the Time Zone tab.
3. In the small box above your primary time zone selection, type an abbreviation for your primary time zone. (You can use as many as three characters—such as PST.)

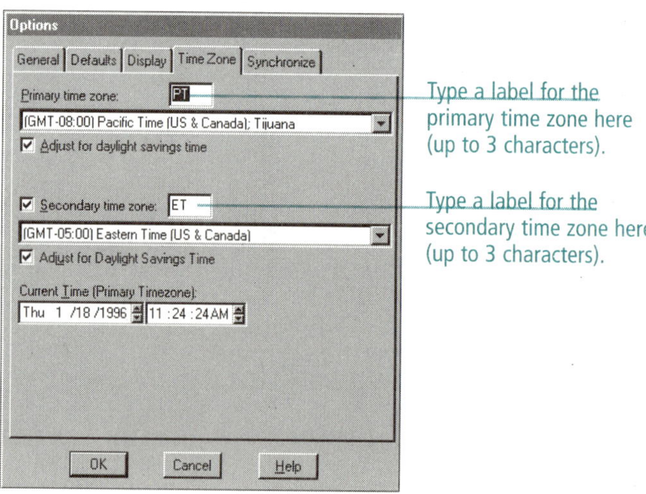

TIP If you have the Adjust For Daylight Savings Time box turned on in Windows 95, your abbreviations don't have to include "S" for "standard" or "D" for "daylight." Instead, you can simply type "PT" for "Pacific Time" and "ET" for extraterrestrial—er—I mean, "Eastern Time."

4. Select the Secondary Time Zone check box, and then type an abbreviation for your secondary time zone. (Again, you can use as many as three characters.)
5. Click on OK.

You'll now see two vertical bands of time in your appointment book, as shown here:

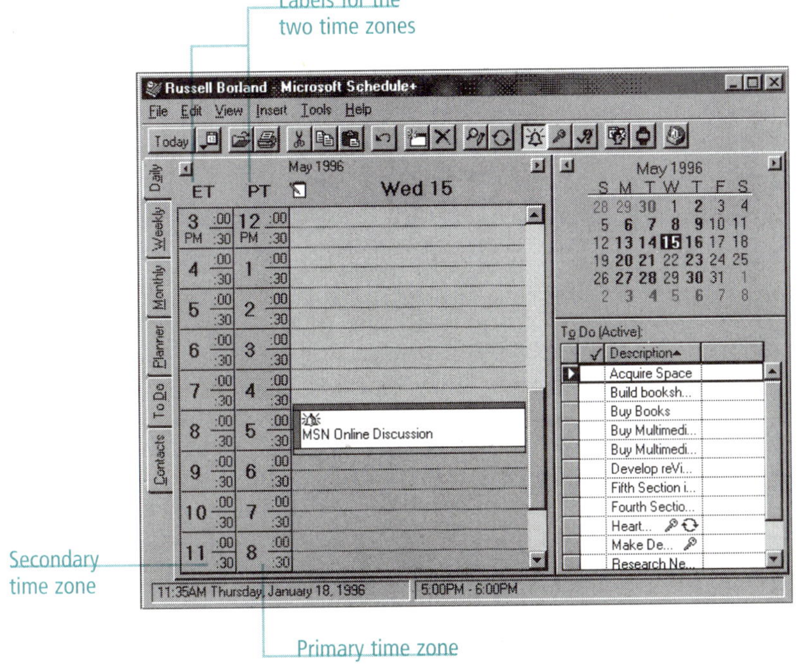

Notice that the abbreviations you typed for each time zone appear at the top of the time bands.

Setting Up Meetings

When you're working remotely, setting up meetings is basically the same as when you're connected to the network. The one requirement Schedule+ needs from you before you can set up a meeting with other people is the Offline Address Book. You must download the offline address book before you can select attendees and resources, unless you have them all listed in your Personal Address Book. Meeting requests are held in your Outbox until you next connect to your Exchange server, either through a network connection or through Remote Mail.

For details about downloading the Offline Address Book, see "The Offline Address Book," on page 379.

Note Be sure to select the times for the meeting in the correct time zone.

Synchronizing Remotely

If you install Exchange on your home computer to make connections to your organization, you won't ever have a direct network connection for synchronizing your offline folders. You'll have to do this remotely. To synchronize offline folders remotely, take these steps:

1. Connect to your organization's network through Dial-Up Networking or RAS.
2. Start Exchange and click on the Connect button.

When Exchange connects to your Exchange server, Exchange automatically synchronizes your main server folders. You can then download the offline address book and set up other folders for offline use and synchronize them. The next time you start Exchange, you can use Remote Mail instead of a Dial-Up Networking or RAS connection.

CHAPTER
16

Exercising More Exchange Options

For many people, the standard Microsoft Exchange setup works fine most of the time, especially when they're first starting out. After a while, however, you might find it beneficial to change some of the options for how Exchange operates so that your work goes more smoothly and using Exchange is more enjoyable. In this chapter, you'll learn about how to set and change options in Exchange.

Scenes from This Chapter

You can make changes to Exchange in a number of ways, which are scattered all over the menus. The Tools Options command controls only the most obvious of the adjustments you can make to Exchange. In this chapter, you'll find reference information about many of the options you can set up in Exchange. For information on changing options for Microsoft Schedule+, see Chapter 2, "Personal Scheduling," and for information on changing Microsoft Remote Mail options, see Chapter 15, "Having a Remote Idea of Exchange."

Favorite Folders

Public folders can provide extensive amounts of information. To help make some sense of it all, Exchange administrators will invariably set up many public folders. And, because a single public folder can contain a wide variety of information about topics that fit within a general category, your Exchange administrator is likely to also set up several levels of subfolders.

For example, if the public folders on your Exchange system include a folder for Internet newsgroups, the newsgroup folder will likely contain a subfolder for each newsgroup area. Many newsgroups will have a large number of subareas, and these subareas can have specialty forums. For example, I'm interested in the Harley forum in the Motorcycles subarea of the Rec (recreation) newsgroup. In Exchange, I need to open six levels of folders to reach the Harley folder—Public Folders, All Public Folders, Internet, Rec, Motorcycles, Harley. When I want to check the latest postings to the Harley folder, I'm loathe to click (and scroll) six times to get there. Instead, I've set up the Harley folder as one of my Public Folder favorites.

The Favorites folder under Public Folders is a place for you to set up shortcuts to public folders that are buried deep within the Public Folders tree. Also, by setting up favorites, you can have access to these public folders for work offline. Of course, the information in a favorite will be only as current as your last synchronization with the public folder it's linked to. For details about setting up a favorite folder for offline work, see "Offline Folders," on page 376.

You have two ways to set up a favorite folder: a command and a toolbar button.

Favorites on command. To set up a favorite folder by command, follow these steps:

1. Open the public folder for which you want to set up a favorite.
2. Choose the File Add To Favorites command.

After Exchange sets up the favorite, you'll see a message telling you that Exchange was successful, as shown here:

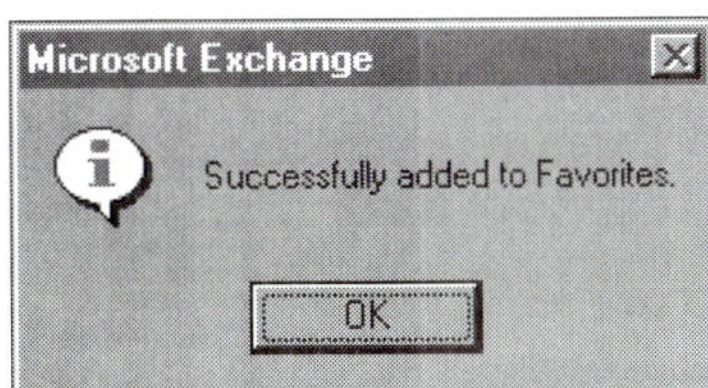

Here is an illustration of several favorite folders I have set up.

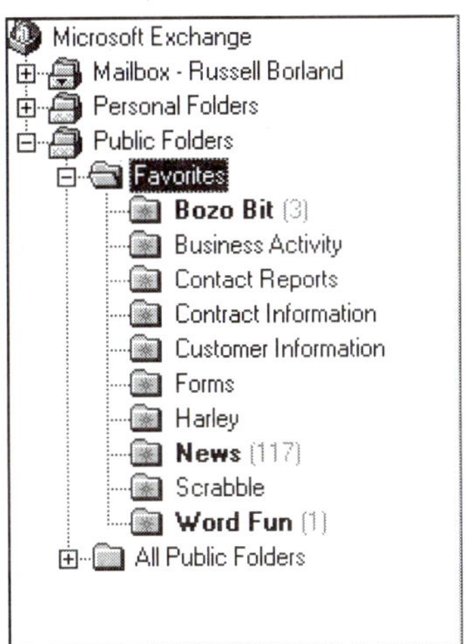

Favorites at the click of a button. Exchange also provides a toolbar button for creating shortcuts to your favorite public folders, shown here:

If the button isn't on your Exchange toolbar, see "Toolbars," on page 417, for instructions for adding this button to your toolbar.

To add a favorite with the click of a button, do the following:

1. Open the public folder for which you want to set up a favorite.
2. Click on the Add To Favorites button on the Exchange toolbar.

Getting rid of favorites. If you no longer have an interest in a public folder and don't need a shortcut to the folder in your Favorites folder any longer, you can remove the shortcut. To do so, follow these steps:

1. In your Favorites folder, click on the folder shortcut that you want to remove.
2. Choose the File Remove From Favorites command.

Folder Shortcuts

Are there folders that you use often? Is there a folder (besides your Inbox) that you like to look at when you start Exchange? You can set up a folder shortcut to any folder in Exchange, not only to public folders.

If you are running Windows 95, you can set up the shortcut on your desktop. When you do, you can double-click on the shortcut to start Exchange and open the folder represented by the shortcut. (In a sense, the Inbox icon on your Windows 95 desktop is just such a shortcut.)

In all versions of Exchange (for all operating systems, including Windows 95), you can set up a folder shortcut in any folder or directory on any disk.

To set up a folder shortcut, take these steps:

1. Open the folder for which you want to set up a shortcut.
2. Choose the File Create Shortcut command. The Create Shortcut dialog box appears, as shown at the top of the next page.
3. In the Create Shortcut dialog box, select the disk and folder (or in the case of Windows 95, the desktop) in which you want to put the shortcut.
4. If you want the name of the shortcut to be different from the folder's name, change it in the File Name box.
5. Click on the Save button.

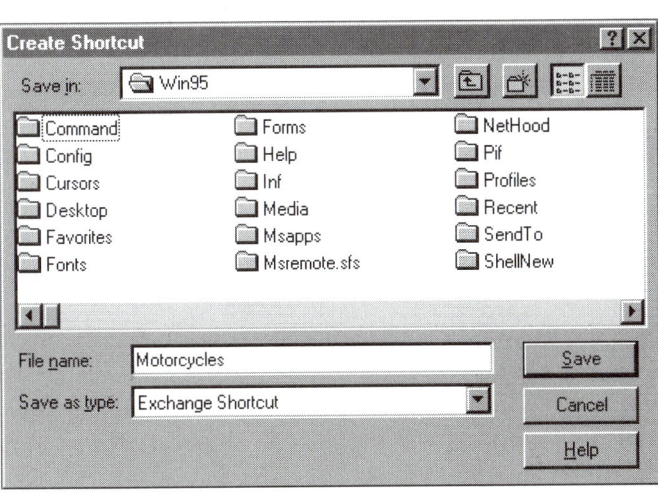

A shortcut icon appears on the desktop or in the folder you selected in the Create Shortcut dialog box. Here's a typical shortcut icon:

CAUTION When you double-click on a folder shortcut icon, you start Exchange and open the folder represented by the shortcut. Each time you double-click on a folder shortcut icon, you start another instance of Exchange. So, if you double-click on the Inbox icon, you start Exchange and open your Inbox folder. If you then double-click on a shortcut for a folder named Customer Information, you start another instance of Exchange and open the Customer Information folder. The same thing happens if you double-click on the same folder shortcut a second time—another instance of Exchange opens to the folder represented by the shortcut. You can end up with several instances of Exchange running at the same time. This might cause your computer to run slowly or might cause more serious problems.

Note, however, that double-clicking on the Inbox icon a second time merely activates and displays the previously opened Exchange window.

Window Options

If you're one of those people who believes that the Exchange window is cluttered, you have three options for straightening it up. Or if you're one of those people who want all the graphical help you can get in order to work your way around in Exchange, you can select options for adding to the "clutter." You have options for hiding or showing folders, for changing the sizes of the folder pane and the message list pane, and for turning on or off the Exchange toolbar and the status bar.

Folders. It could be that the first time you start Exchange you see only a list of messages in your Inbox. If all you ever do with Exchange is read and send messages, this might suit you. But at some time or other, you'll more than likely want to open other folders and then work with the items they contain. The easiest way to do this is to click on the folder you want to open. To do so, you must show the folder pane.

Even if your work takes you frequently from folder to folder, there might be times that you want to see more of the columns in the message list pane without having to scroll horizontally. In this case, you can either hide the folder pane or change the width of the message list pane. (For information about this latter choice, see the next section, "Changing the width of your panes.")

To show or hide the folder pane, click on the Show/Hide Folder List button on the Exchange toolbar, shown here:

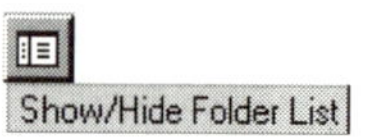

Changing the width of your panes. When you have the Exchange window set up to show both the folder pane and the message list pane, you might want to change their widths, either to see all the folders you've expanded in the folder pane—particularly when the subfolders run several levels deep—or to see more columns in the message list pane.

To change the widths of the panes, do this:

1. Position the mouse pointer on the dividing line between the folder pane and the message list pane. The mouse pointer changes to a vertical line with two arrowheads pointing horizontally, as shown on the next page.

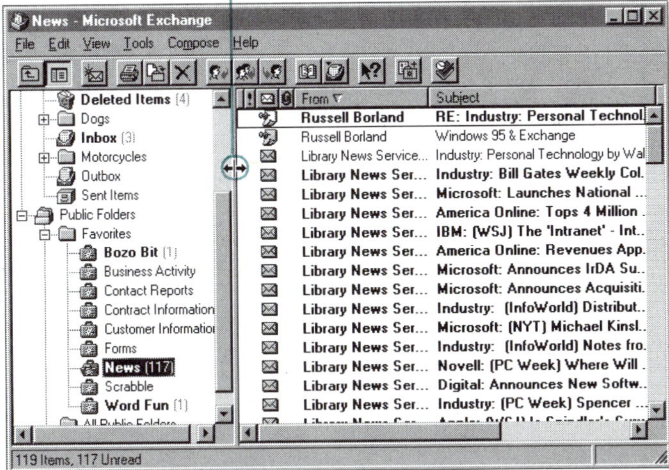

2. Drag the dividing line to the left or to the right to adjust the widths of the panes as you want them.

Toolbar. The Exchange toolbar contains buttons that make working with messages easy. Most of the buttons correspond to menu commands, but the Exchange toolbar can also have buttons that have no equivalent menu command—the Up One Level and Show Schedule buttons are two examples. Also, message windows, form windows, and posting windows can have formatting toolbars. A formatting toolbar contains buttons for applying font and paragraph formatting to message text.

If you prefer to use the window space that the toolbars take up to see more folders or messages, you can do the following:

- Choose the View Toolbar command to display or hide the Exchange toolbar. A check mark beside the command's name indicates the toolbar is visible.
- Choose the View Formatting Toolbar command to display or hide the Formatting toolbar in a message window, form window, or posting window. This command is not available in windows in which you can't use the Formatting toolbar.

Status Bar. The status bar at the bottom of the Exchange window shows helpful information. In many windows, the status bar displays the number of items in the open folder and how many of the items are unread. In message windows and form windows, the status bar shows a message that tells you what commands a menu contains or what a particular command does. In some form windows (if the form's designer set up the form this way), the status bar also shows you messages that indicate what to type or what to choose in a form field.

If none of this information is important to you—if you never or only rarely look at the status bar—you might want to hide the status bar to gain some extra space in the window. To display or hide the status bar, choose the View Status Bar command.

Assistants

Exchange provides three assistants to help you work with items in folders. The Inbox Assistant can be set up to automatically sort messages or to forward messages that you always treat the same way. For folders for which you have an administrative role, you can set up a Folder Assistant, which is a generalized version of the Inbox Assistant. And for those times when you're out of the office, you can set up the Out of Office Assistant to tell people who send you messages that you are away, when you'll be back, and whom to contact or what to do during your absence.

The following two sections describe the Inbox Assistant and the Out of Office Assistant. In the Inbox Assistant section, you'll find a sidebar that discusses the similarities and differences between the Inbox Assistant and the Folder Assistant.

The Inbox Assistant

For a variety of reasons over which you might have little control, your Inbox can become flooded with messages and items that you want to act on in very specific ways. You can, of course, take these actions yourself, attending to each message manually. If you find, however, that there is a category of message that you act on in a specific way every time, you can set up your Inbox Assistant to take care of these actions for you. Inbox Assistant can automatically delete, forward, reply, move, and perform several other actions on items delivered to your Inbox.

Note The Inbox Assistant works and is available for changes only while you are connected to your Exchange server.

To set up your Inbox Assistant, follow these steps:

1. Choose the Tools Inbox Assistant command.

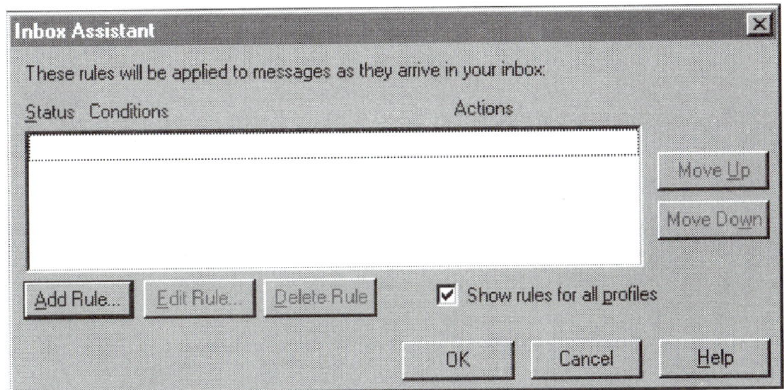

2. Click on the Add Rule button to open the Edit Rule dialog box, shown in Figure 16-1.

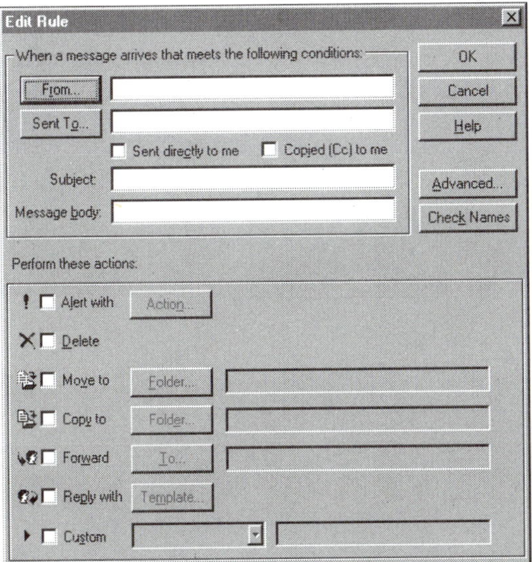

Figure 16-1
The Edit Rule dialog box

3. Set up the Edit Rule dialog box to identify the kinds of items you want the Inbox Assistant to act on. The fewer settings you make in the When A Message Arrives... area, the fewer items the Inbox Assistant acts on. The more settings you make in the

When A Message Arrives... area, the more items the Inbox Assistant acts on. The following table lists which kinds of items the Inbox Assistant can act on.

Setting	What the Inbox Assistant Acts On
From	Items from a particular sender
Sent To	Items sent to a particular recipient
Sent Directly To Me	Items with your name in the To box
Copied (Cc) To Me	Items with your name in the Cc box
Subject	Items with the exact text you type in the Subject box
Message Body	Items that contain the specified text somewhere in the message body

Table 16-1
Edit Rule dialog box options for identifying items

4. Click on the Advanced button to display a dialog box that contains additional settings, as shown in Figure 16-2.

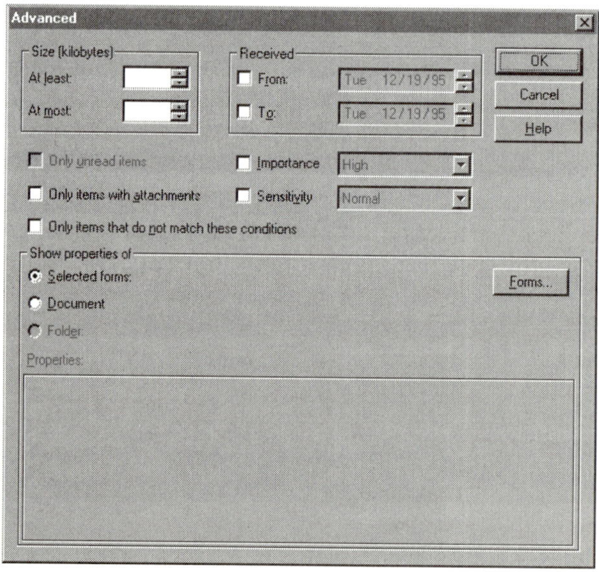

Figure 16-2
The Advanced dialog box

Consult Table 16-2 to determine which advanced settings you might want Inbox Assistant to act on.

Note You can choose settings in the Advanced dialog box without making any settings in the Edit Rule dialog box.

Setting	What Inbox Assistant Acts On
Size At Least	Items that are larger than the size you set
Size At Most	Items that are smaller than the size you set
Received From	Items received after the date you set; for items between two dates, also set a Received To date
Received To	Items received before the date you set; for items between two dates, also set a Received From date
Only Unread Items	Items you haven't yet read
Only Items with Attachments	Items that contain attachments (files or messages)
Importance	Items set to the specified level of importance—High, Normal, or Low
Sensitivity	Items with the specified level of sensitivity—Normal, Personal, Private, or Confidential
Only Items That Do Not Match These Conditions	Uses the reverse of all the settings in both the Edit Rule and the Advanced dialog boxes
Show Properties Of	
Selected Forms	Displays fields in the forms you select with the Forms button
Document	Displays document properties
Folder	Displays fields in the custom forms associated with the folder whose name appears after the Folder label

Table 16-2
Advanced dialog box options for identifying items

5. Click on OK in the Advanced dialog box.
6. After you select the kinds of items you want the Inbox Assistant to act on, you need to select the actions you want the Inbox

Assistant to take. In the Edit Rule dialog box, select the actions you want Inbox Assistant to take on the items you have selected. See Table 16-3 for more information.

7. Click on OK in the Edit Rule dialog box.
8. If you want to add different rules and actions for other types of items, repeat step 2 through step 6.
9. Click on OK in the Inbox Assistant dialog box.

Action Option	How to Set It Up
Alert With	Select the Alert With check box, and then click on the Action button. The Alert Actions dialog box is displayed. To notify you with text, select the Notify With Text box, and type the text for the notification in the box. To notify with sound, select the Play box, and then type the name of the sound file in the Sound box or click on the Sound button, select the sound file, and then click on the Open button. Select the Test button to test the sound notification. When you have made your selections, click on OK in the Alert Actions dialog box.
Delete	Select the Delete check box.
Move To	Select the Move To check box, click on the Folder button, select the folder to which you want to move the items, and then click on OK.
Copy To	Select the Copy To check box, click on the Folder button, select the folder to which you want to copy the items, and then click on OK.
Forward	Select the Forward check box, and then either type the name or names in the To box or click on the To button to select names for the To box.
Reply With	Select the Reply With check box, and then click on the Template button. Follow the directions given in "Automatic Replies," next.
Custom	Select the Custom check box, and then select the action you want from the drop down list. (You will probably find the list empty.)

Table 16-3
Edit Rule dialog box options for actions to take

Folder Assistant versus Inbox Assistant

On the Administration tab of a folder's Properties dialog box, you'll see a button labeled Folder Assistant. When you click on this button, you see a dialog box similar to the Inbox Assistant dialog box. The Inbox Assistant applies only to your Exchange server Inbox. The Folder Assistant applies to those public folders for which you have a role that permits you to set up rules for managing new items in that folder. Otherwise, using these two assistants is the same.

Automatic Replies

To send an automatic reply using the Inbox Assistant, follow these steps:

1. In the Edit Rule dialog box, click on the Reply With box, and then click on the Template button.

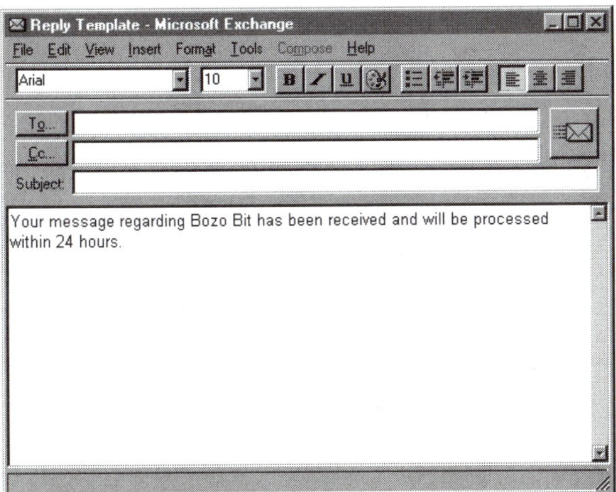

2. In the To box, type the names of any people to whom you want the reply sent in addition to the sender of the item. (You can also click on the To button to select the names.) If it's appropriate, you can also add names to the Cc box.
3. Leave the Subject box blank. Exchange inserts the standard "RE:" as well as the original Subject when it sends the automatic message.
4. In the message area, type a standard message for replies to the kinds of items you have set up.

5. Close the Reply Template window, and click on the Yes button to keep your changes.

Out of Office Assistant

When you're away from your office, on vacation for example, and you want to notify people that you're not available for a while, you can set up the Out of Office Assistant to automatically send a reply when you receive a message. Also, the Out of Office Assistant can act on incoming items to automatically perform specific actions.

To set up the Out of Office Assistant, take these steps:

1. Choose the Tools Out Of Office Assistant command.

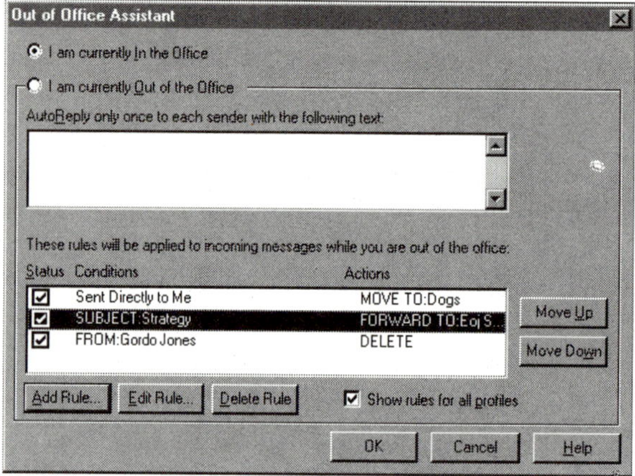

2. In the box labeled AutoReply Only Once To Each Sender With The Following Text, type the message you want the Out of Office Assistant to send to each person who sends you an item. For example, you could type something like the following:

   I'm on vacation until Wednesday, July 10, 1996.

   For emergencies, contact Eoj Eod, who will know how to reach me.

   For Bozo Bit project questions and decisions, contact Enaj Eod.

3. If you want the Out of Office Assistant to also act on incoming items in your absence, click on the Add Rule button.

4. Set up the rules for the types of items you want Out of Office Assistant to act on and set up the actions for those items. You can create as many rules as you need. Consult step 3 through step 6 and Table 16-1, Table 16-2, and Table 16-3 in the section "Inbox Assistant," on page 410, for details about these options.
5. When you're ready to turn on the Out of Office Assistant, select the I Am Currently Out Of The Office option, and then click on OK.

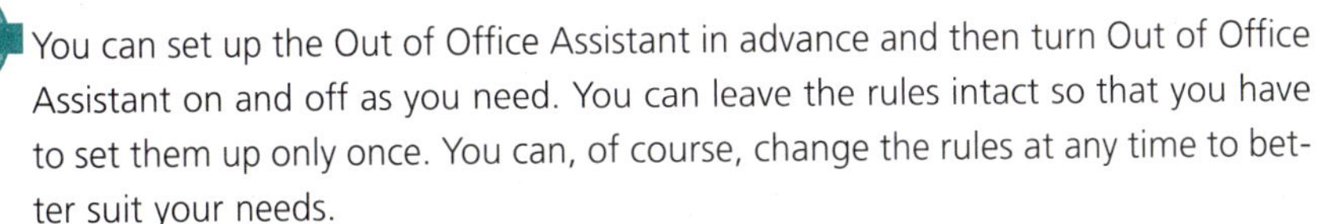

TIP You can set up the Out of Office Assistant in advance and then turn Out of Office Assistant on and off as you need. You can leave the rules intact so that you have to set them up only once. You can, of course, change the rules at any time to better suit your needs.

The next time you start Exchange (if you connect to your Exchange server), you'll see a message that tells you that you are currently registered as being out of the office and asks if you want to turn it off. Click on Yes to turn off the Out of Office Assistant. Click on No to leave the Out of Office Assistant turned on.

The rules stay intact so that you can use them the next time you're out of the office without having to set them up again. The Out of Office Assistant rules are inactive as long as your status is in the office.

Toolbars

Even though the default Exchange toolbar provides buttons for the most commonly used commands for working with folder contents, you might want to put other buttons on the toolbar in addition to the standard ones. After using the Exchange toolbar for a while, you might also find that you'd like to rearrange the order of the buttons or that there are one or two buttons that you never use and can remove.

Adding and Removing Toolbar Buttons

You can customize the Exchange toolbar by adding buttons that you want to have on it or by removing buttons that you don't use.

To add toolbar buttons, take these steps:

1. Choose the Tools Customize Toolbar command. You see the Customize Toolbar dialog box, shown in Figure 16-3.

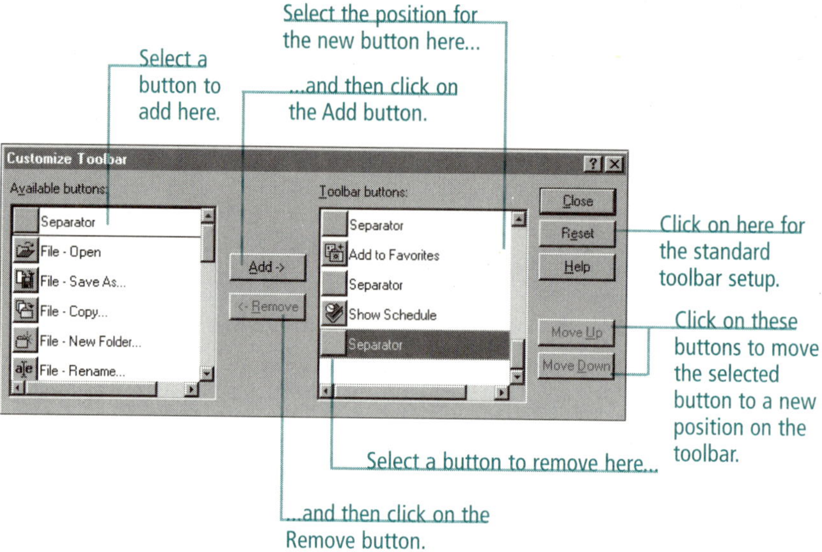

Figure 16-3
The Customize Toolbar dialog box

2. From the Available Buttons list, select the toolbar button that you want to add.
3. In the Toolbar Buttons list, select the button below which you want to add the new button. Exchange will add the new button above the button that you select in the Toolbar Buttons list.
4. Click on the Add button.
5. If you want to add another toolbar button, repeat step 2 through step 4.
6. When you're finished adding toolbar buttons, click on the Close button.

To remove toolbar buttons, follow these steps:

1. Choose the Tools Customize Toolbar command.
2. In the Toolbar Buttons list, select the button that you want to remove, and then click on the Remove button.
3. When you're finished removing toolbar buttons, click on the Close button.

TIP You can remove a toolbar button with the mouse. To do so, hold down the Shift key as you drag the button off the toolbar.

Moving Toolbar Buttons

You have two ways to move toolbar buttons. When you want to move several buttons at once, use the Tools Customize Toolbar command. To move one toolbar button at a time, use the mouse.

To move toolbar buttons on command, take these steps:

1. Choose the Tools Customize Toolbar command.
2. In the Toolbar Buttons list in the Customize Toolbar dialog box (shown in Figure 16-3), select the toolbar button that you want to move.
3. Click on the Move Up or Move Down button to move the toolbar where you want it.
4. If you want to move another button, repeat step 2 and step 3.
5. When you're finished moving toolbar buttons, click on the Close button.

To move a single toolbar button to a new position on the toolbar, do the following:

1. Place the mouse pointer on the button that you want to move.
2. Hold down the Shift key and drag the button to its new position on the toolbar.
3. Release the Shift key and the mouse button.

Other Options

The Tools Options command gives you a number of ways to customize Exchange to suit you and the way you work. The Options dialog box contains ten tabs. This indicates just how much you can muck around with Exchange—the way it works and the way it looks.

To adjust options, choose the Tools Options command, click the appropriate tab, set the options you want to adjust, and then click on OK. The following sections describe the options on each tab.

General Tab

On the General tab of the Options dialog box, you'll find options for what Exchange should do when new mail messages arrive and for when Exchange should permanently delete messages. You'll also find options for what happens when you start Exchange and for ways that Exchange works while running.

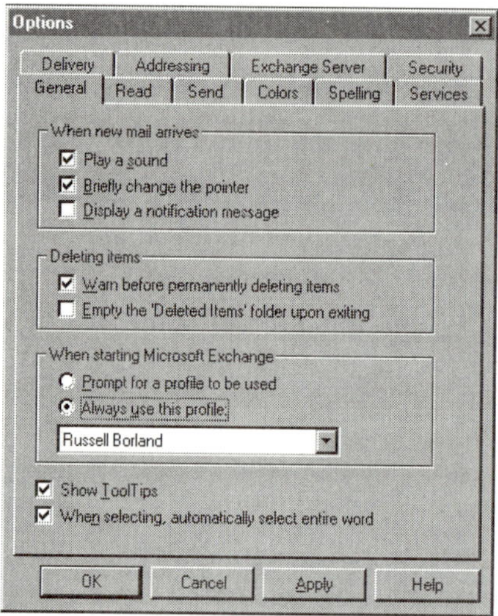

When New Mail Arrives. You have three choices for what Exchange should do when new mail messages arrive. You can set up any combination of the three options.

- Play A Sound—Select this option to hear a beep when new messages arrive. (This option is selected by default.) If you have a sound card installed in your computer, you can set the new message sound to any .WAV file. (You set the sound using the Sounds icon in the Control Panel.)
- Briefly Change The Pointer—Select this option to see the mouse pointer change briefly to an envelope when new messages arrive. (This option is selected by default.)
- Display A Notification Message—Select this option to have the dialog box at the top of the next page appear when new messages arrive.

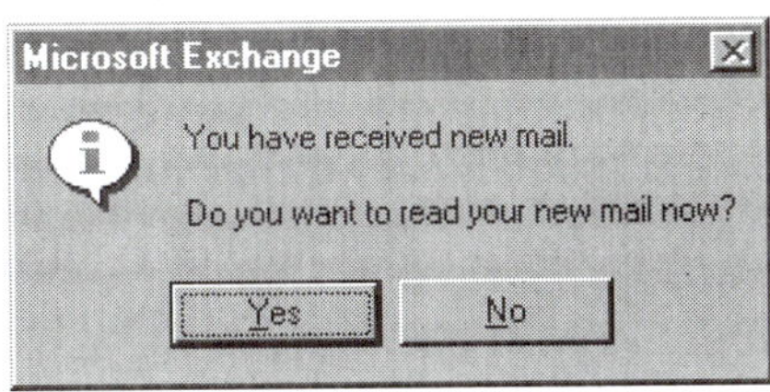

To read the new messages right away, when you see this dialog box, click on the Yes button. When you do, Exchange opens the first new message for you to read, without activating the Exchange window. To read the new messages later, click on the No button.

Deleting Items. When you delete a message from one of your server folders, Exchange moves it to the Deleted Items folder (unless the message was already in the Deleted Items folder). To permanently delete messages, you must clear out your Deleted Items folder. When you decide to clear out your Deleted Items folder, do one of the following:

- Right-click on the Deleted Items folder, and then choose Empty Folder from the shortcut menu.
- Open the Deleted Items folder, select the messages you want to permanently delete, and then click on the Delete button on the Exchange toolbar.

When you use one of these methods to clear out your Deleted Items folder, Exchange prompts you to confirm that you want to permanently delete the messages. (The option labeled Warn Before Permanently Deleting Items is selected by default.) Click on Yes to delete the messages.

The second option on the General tab that's related to deleting items is Empty The 'Deleted Items' Folder Upon Exiting. With this option selected (its standard setting), Exchange empties your Deleted Items folder each time you quit Exchange. If you prefer to clear out your Deleted Items folders more selectively, turn off this option.

When Starting Microsoft Exchange. If you have set up more than one Exchange profile, the options in this area of the General tab are for you. If you switch between two or more profiles because you connect to several online services, or if you travel with your computer and you sometimes connect to your Exchange network, you might want to select the

Prompt For A Profile To Be Used option. If you do, Exchange displays a dialog box when it starts that lists your profiles. Here's an illustration of the Choose Profile dialog box:

When you see this dialog box, select the profile you want to use, and then click on OK.

If you use only one profile, select the Always Use This Profile option, and then select the profile name from the list below the label. This option is most useful when your computer is always in one place and you use the same profile all the time.

Show ToolTips. When you rest the mouse pointer over a toolbar button, Exchange displays a label with the name of the button. These ToolTips help you recall what the button does. (The Show ToolTips option is selected by default.) If you don't want to see ToolTips, turn off this option.

When Selecting, Automatically Select Entire Word. When you're editing a message and start to select text that includes a space, as soon as you select a single character beyond the space, Exchange selects the entire word. This standard setting can be handy if you usually select entire words. But if you need to select parts of two neighboring words, you will find this option frustrating and disruptive. If necessary, you can turn off this option.

Read Tab

On the Read tab of the Options dialog box, you'll find options for what Exchange should do after you move or delete a message you're reading and options for replying to and forwarding a message.

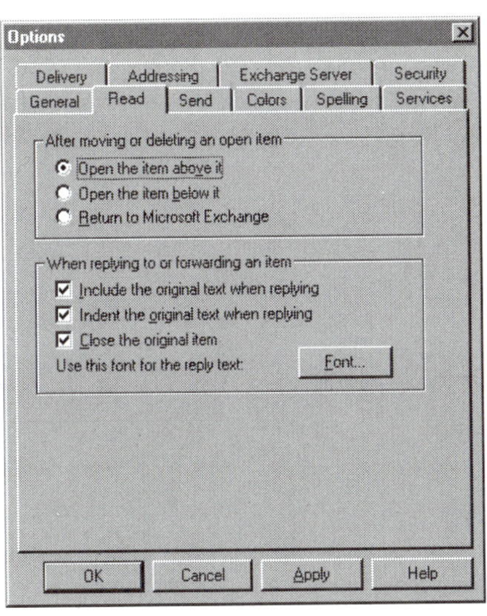

After Moving Or Deleting An Open Item. As part of the process of deleting or moving a message that you've just read, Exchange must close the message window. So, what should Exchange do after closing the window? You can choose one of the following three options:

- Open The Item Above It—This is the standard setting for this option. It relates to the usual sorting order in the message list pane—descending—which places the newest message at the top of the list, and the oldest message at the bottom. With this option turned on and your message list sorted in descending order, you can start reading the oldest message and move up the list to read the newer arrivals.
- Open The Item Below It—Select this option if you sort your message list panes in ascending order (oldest message at the top; newest message at the bottom). With this option turned on and your message list sorted in ascending order, you can start reading the oldest message and move down the list to read the newer arrivals.

- Return To Microsoft Exchange—Turn on this option if you don't want to jump to the next message in the list. This option is especially handy when you have little time to read all your messages and want to select only a message here or there to read.

When Replying To Or Forwarding An Item. Because replies to messages have a conversational context (the reply takes place as part of a conversation among Exchange correspondents), the standard Exchange setup is to include a copy of the message to which someone is replying. Also, to distinguish the original message from a reply, Exchange indents the original message.

If you prefer to reply to messages without including the original message, turn off the Include The Original Text When Replying option. If you don't want the original text indented in your reply, turn off the Indent The Original Text When Replying option.

Exchange is also set up by default to close the original item's window after you send a reply or forward a message. This setting is handy if you're working on a single message here and there. However, if you like to read through all your messages and dispose of them as you go ("disposing" includes replying to and forwarding messages), you might want to turn off the Close The Original Item option so that you can continue to move up or down the message list after you send a reply or forward a message.

For replies, you can also choose the font style you want Exchange to use for the message text in all your replies. You can of course, change the font style for a specific reply by using the Formatting toolbar or the Format Font command. But if you don't like Arial 10-point font in AutoColor as your standard reply font, click on the Font button. Then, in the Font dialog box, select the font, font style, size, color, and effects (strikeout or underline) that you want for your standard reply text, and then click on OK. Exchange will use your settings in the Font dialog box for all your subsequent replies.

Send Tab

On the Send tab of the Options dialog box, you'll find options for the standard font you want Exchange to use for new messages, options for receipts for the messages you send, options for standard sensitivity and importance settings, and options for saving copies of messages you send.

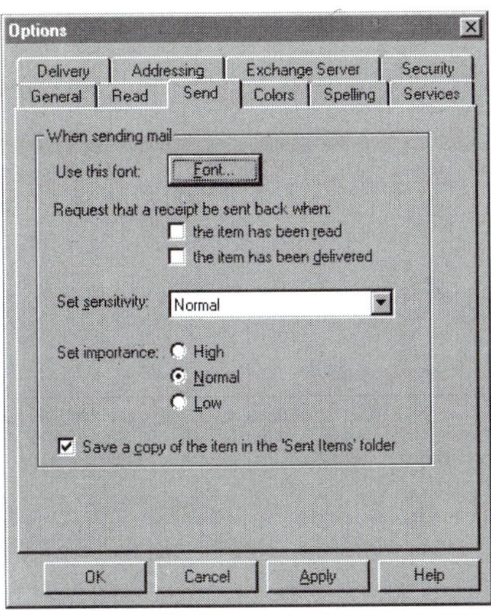

TIP You can format message text for individual messages with the Formatting toolbar or the Format Font command. You can set the sensitivity and importance levels of individual messages in the Properties dialog box for the message by choosing the File Properties command in the new message window. You can ask for delivery and read receipts for individual messages by selecting options in the message's Properties dialog box. If you use these options only rarely, it's better to leave these options turned off on the Send tab in the Options dialog box and set them when you need them in the message's Properties dialog box.

Use This Font. The standard font for new messages is Arial 10-point in AutoColor. If you prefer to use different font options as the standard settings for your new messages, click on the Font button beside the Use This Font label. Then, in the Font dialog box, select the font, font style, size, color, and effects (strikeout or underline) that you want to use, and then click on OK.

Request That A Receipt Be Sent Back When. If you like to know when a message has been delivered to your recipients, select the check box labeled The Item Has Been Delivered. When your message arrives in the recipient's mailbox, Exchange delivers a message to your Inbox that indicates when the message was received.

If you want to know when your recipients have opened your messages, select the check box labeled The Item Has Been Read. When your recipient opens your message to read it, Exchange delivers a message to your Inbox that indicates when the recipient opened your message.

Set Sensitivity. Most messages you send are not particularly sensitive. That's why Normal is the standard sensitivity setting in Exchange. If a message requires a different level of sensitivity, you have three other choices—Private, Personal, or Confidential. The following table lists these sensitivity options and their effect on the messages you send.

Sensitivity	Effect on Messages
Personal	Displays Personal in the Sensitivity column of the message list pane.
Private	Displays Private in the Sensitivity column of the message list pane. This option prohibits recipients from changing your original message when they reply to it or forward it.
Confidential	Displays Confidential in the Sensitivity column of the message list pane. Confidential sensitivity notifies the recipient that he or she should treat the message according to the policies about confidentiality that your organization has set up.

Set Importance. Most messages that you send are of normal importance. That's why Exchange uses Normal as the standard importance setting. If all or most of your messages require top priority, select the High importance option. On the other hand, if all or most of your messages can be read at any time without compromising your work or your recipients' work, select the Low importance option.

A message you send with High importance displays a red exclamation point to the left of its envelope in the message list pane. A message with Low importance displays a blue, downward-pointing arrow to the left of its envelope in the Message List pane. Your Exchange administrator might have set up your Exchange server to deliver messages sent with High importance faster than those sent with Normal or Low importance.

Save A Copy Of The Item In The 'Sent Items' Folder. For your own record keeping, you might want to have copies of the messages you send. Well, maybe you don't want a copy of every message, but it's safer to keep a copy of all the messages you send and then later cull out the ones you don't need to save.

In Exchange, the option for saving copies of the messages you send is selected by default. That means that Exchange puts a copy of every message you send in your Sent Items folder. If you prefer to be more selective about which messages you keep, turn off this option. If you do, however, remember to add yourself to the Cc box for any messages you want to keep for your records.

Colors Tab

The Colors tab of the Options dialog box provides options for setting the color for the number that displays how many messages you've not read, the color for group labels, the color for the line of a message that contains the name of the sender, and the color for the text on that line. For each of these options you have 16 colors to choose from. (The Auto color for these four settings results in whichever color you set as the window text color using the Display icon in the Control Panel.)

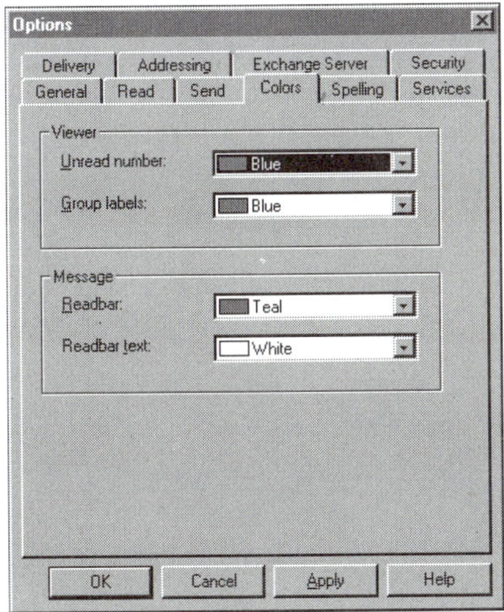

Viewer. The names of the options in the Viewer area of the Colors tab aren't very descriptive. (In fact, the label "Viewer" isn't much of a help either.)

The option labeled Unread Number refers to the number that appears in parentheses at the end of a folder's name. The number tells you how many messages the folder contains that you haven't yet read. The standard color for the number and its parentheses is blue. If you prefer the Unread Number to appear in a different color, select the color from the list box beside the option's label.

Group labels are the titles Exchange gives to the groups you set in a folder. For example, if you arrange folder contents by choosing Group By From (one of the built-in personal views), the names of the senders appear in the standard group label color. The standard color for these labels is blue. If you prefer to use a different color for group labels, select a different color from the list box beside the Group Labels option.

Messages. The From line of every message appears in a color different from the rest of the message heading (To, Cc, and Subject). The standard colors for the From line are teal with white lettering. If you prefer a different background color for the From line, select it from the list for Readbar. If you prefer a different color for the name on the To line, select the color from the list for Readbar Text.

Be sure you don't set Readbar and Readbar Text to the same color—unless you don't want to see who sent the message.

If you want the From line and its text to have the same colors as the rest of the message heading (I don't, but you might), set the Readbar color to Silver and the Readbar Text color to Black.

Spelling Tab

When you check the spelling of messages, Exchange compares the words in your message text with a dictionary file. If the spelling checker can't find the word in its dictionary, the spelling checker shows you the word in a dialog box and gives you a chance to correct the spelling, ignore the word (because it's a special word or a word you made up for the nonce), or add the word to the dictionary.

On the Spelling tab of the Options dialog box shown on the next page, you'll find options for checking the spelling of messages and how (and when) spelling-checking should be conducted.

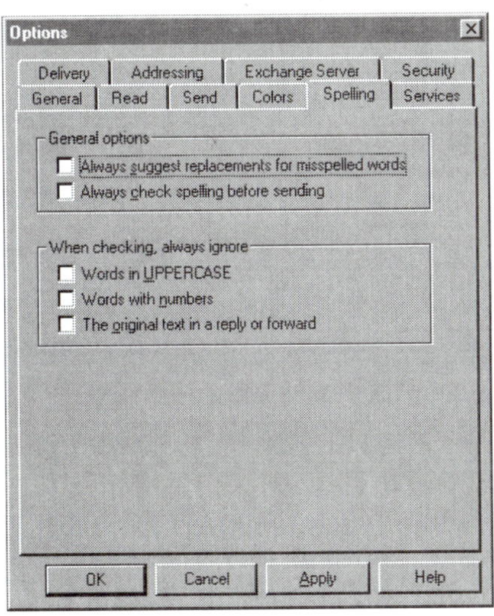

General Options. When you check the spelling of message text, Exchange doesn't automatically suggest correct spellings for words not included in the dictionary file it uses. In cases such as these, you must click on the Suggest button in the Spelling dialog box to get a suggestion out of the spelling checker. If you prefer to always have a suggestion to work from, turn on the Always Suggest Replacements For Misspelled Words check box.

If you're someone who always likes to check spelling before sending a message, the Always Check Spelling Before Sending option is for you. If you turn on this check box, Exchange checks the spelling in your message text after you click on the Send button. This option is a handy way to enforce your wish to always check the spelling in your message text.

When Checking Always Ignore. The spelling checker checks everything in the text of a message, including numbers, words in all capital letters, and any original text in replies and forwarded messages. You can ask the spelling checker to ignore any or all three of these types of information in message text.

To tell the spelling checker to ignore words in all capital letters, turn on the Words In UPPERCASE check box. The spelling checker then ignores words such as FILENAME.

To tell the spelling checker to ignore numbers, turn on the Words With Numbers check box. The spelling checker will then ignore a word that contains a mix of numbers and letters (such as WSJ010846). It will also ignore words that consist entirely of numbers (such as 123456789).

To tell the spelling checker to ignore the original text included in replies and forwarded messages, turn on the The Original Text In A Reply Or Forward check box. The spelling checker then ignores misspellings made by the sender of the original message.

Services Tab

When Exchange is originally set up, you have at least one "service" as part of your profile—Exchange Server. As time goes by (or maybe even right away), you might have access to other services—Remote Mail or an online service such as CompuServe, America Online, AT&T, or MSN, the Microsoft online network.

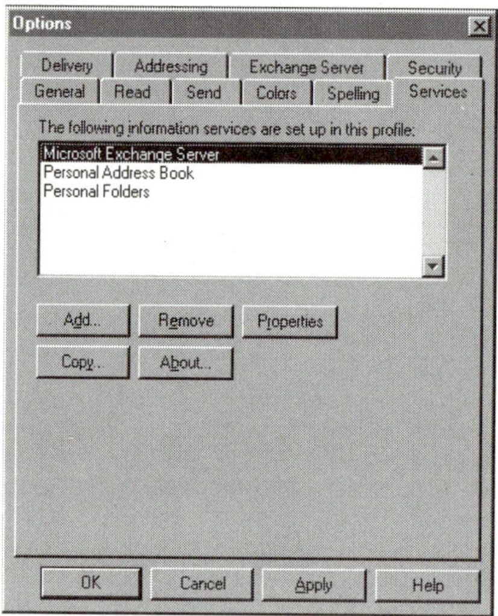

To use these other services to send messages, you need to add them to your profile. And, of course, if you find that one of the services you connect to is too expensive, you will also want to remove that service from your profile.

The Tools Services command displays the Services dialog box, which contains the same options as the Services tab in the Options dialog box. The Tools Services command is simply a more direct way to get to the Services options.

To add services to the current profile, here's what you do:

1. Click on the Add button on the Services tab.

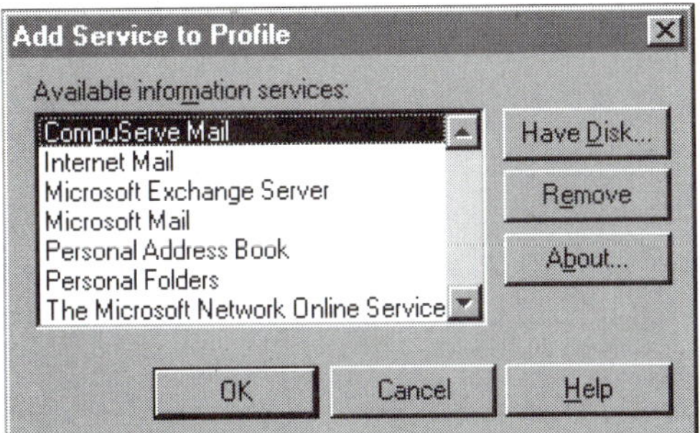

2. Select the service you want to add, and then click on OK.

   If you want to add another service, repeat step 1 and step 2.

To remove a service from the current profile, select the service from the list on the Services tab, and then click on the Remove button.

Copy Button. If you have more than one profile, the Copy button gives you a way to add services to your other profiles from within Exchange. To add services to your other profiles, take these steps:

1. Add the services to your current profile following the steps in the previous procedure.
2. Select a service you want to add to another profile, and then click on the Copy button.

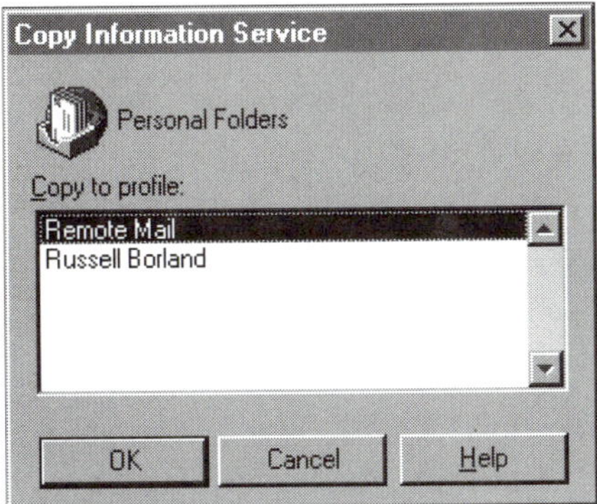

3. Select the profile to which you want to add the service, and then click on OK.

4. To add another service to another profile, repeat step 2 and step 3.

Note To remove services from another profile, you must either start Exchange with that profile and then remove the service or use the Mail And Fax icon in Control Panel, which lets you work on all your profiles at the same time.

Properties Button. Each service that you have set up has its own properties. You can adjust the properties when something about the service changes—for example, if your Exchange administrator moves your mailbox to a different server.

To adjust the properties of a service in your profile, take these steps:

1. On the Services tab, select the service that you want to adjust, and then click on the Properties button. (The following steps show the properties for Microsoft Exchange Server.)

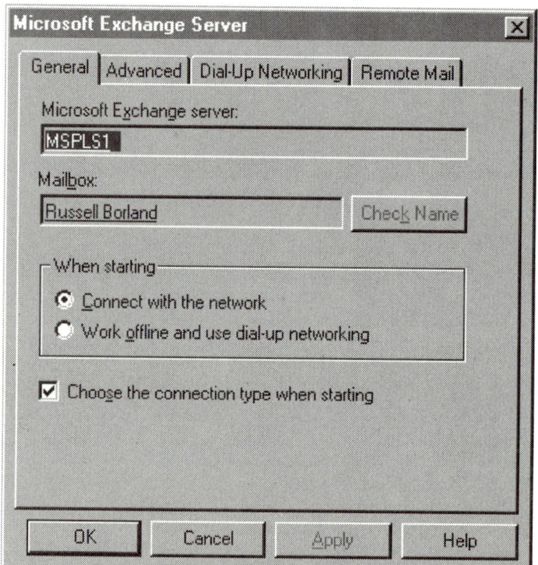

2. On the General tab, you can type the name of your Exchange server. You'll need to do this only if your mailbox has been moved or if you have another mailbox on another server.
3. If your mailbox name needs to be changed, you can type the name of your mailbox. You'll probably change the mailbox

name only if you have a second mailbox or if your name changes on the Exchange server. (This happens most frequently when your legal name changes or when you're given a special name as an ancillary employee and then become a full-time employee, or vice versa.)

4. If you often use Exchange away from the network, you might prefer to set up Exchange to start offline. If so, select the Work Offline And Use Dial-Up Networking option.
5. If you use Exchange about equally for online and offline work, you might prefer to have Exchange prompt you to connect or work offline at startup. If so, turn on the Choose The Connection Type When Starting check box. (This option is on by default.)
6. Click on the Advanced tab.

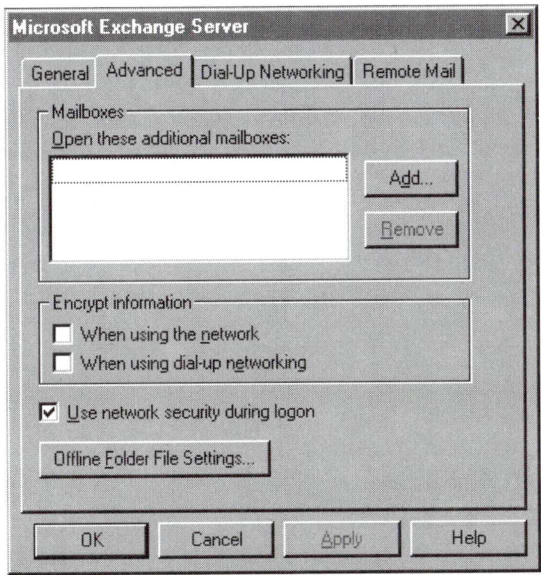

7. If you have access to other mailboxes (for example, if you are an assistant who reads your supervisor's mail or you have responsibility for another mailbox that serves an organizational function such as customer inquiries), you can set up the Exchange server properties to open other mailboxes at startup. To do so, click on the Add button.

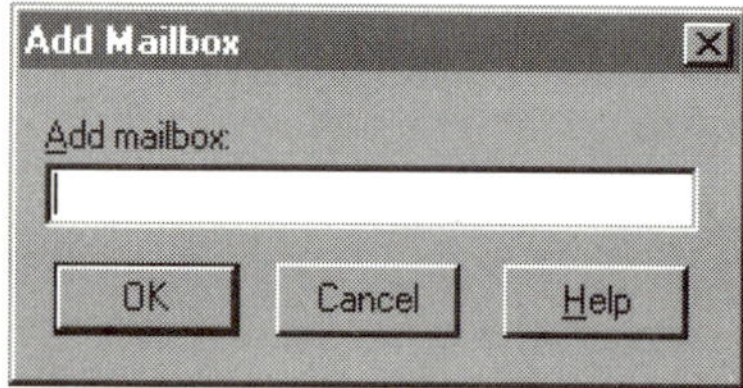

8. In the Add Mailbox dialog box, type the name of the mailbox you want to add to the list on the Advanced tab, and then click on OK.

   If you want to remove a mailbox from the list, select it, and then click on the Remove button. When Exchange asks if you're sure, click on the Yes button.

9. If your Exchange administrator set up your account for encryption, you can choose when to use encryption. If you're working through dial-up networking, encryption might not be available. To encrypt messages you send over your Exchange network, turn on the When Using The Network check box. To encrypt messages you send through dial-up networking, turn on the When Using Dial-Up Networking check box.

10. In most cases, Exchange uses your network logon name to verify you to the Exchange server. If you want to log on to your Exchange server separately from your network logon, turn off the Use Network Security During Logon check box.

11. For your offline folders, you can make some adjustments by clicking on the Offline Folder File Settings button.

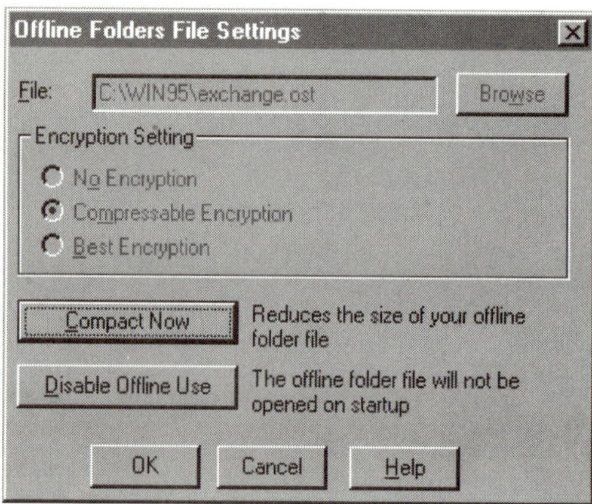

12. If you don't need to use offline folders (because you only use Exchange online), click on the Disable Offline Use button. When Exchange asks if you're sure, click on the Yes button. If you want to enable offline folders, click on the Offline Folder File Settings button again, check that your offline folder filename is correct, and then click on OK.

    If you need to change your offline folders filename, first disable offline use, then click on the Offline Folder File Settings button again, type the name of the new offline folder file (or click on the Browse button and locate the file), and then click on OK.

    If you want to change the encryption level of your offline folders file, first disable offline use, then click on the Offline Folder File Settings button, select the level of encryption you want, and then click on OK.

13. If you want to compact your offline folders file so that it takes up the minimum space on your computer's hard disk, click on the Offline Folder File Settings button, click on the Compact Now button, and then click on OK.

Personal Address Book Properties

The properties for your Personal Address Book provide one option you might find very interesting. To see this property, choose the Tools Services command, select Personal Address Book, and click on the Properties button. In the middle of the Personal Address Book tab you'll see two buttons. Exchange is set up to list names in your Personal Address Book by first name and then last name. Your Personal Address Book is then organized alphabetically by the first names of entries. You might find it more natural, as I do, to have the names listed last name first and then first name—like a telephone book. To list last names before first names, click on the Last Name (Smith, John) button. Before you decide to do this, there's one thing you should know. When you select the Last Name option, the names appear in message headers as last name, first name. For example, if you're sending a message to Enaj Eod, you'll see *Eod, Enaj* in the To box. If you can live with this bit of strangeness, you'll benefit (most likely) from having the names in your Personal Address Book listed by last names.

Note For information about the Dial-Up Networking tab and the Remote Mail tab, see "Setting More Remote Mail Options," on page 391.

Delivery Tab

The Delivery tab of the Options dialog box provides options for where to deliver messages sent to you and how to process messages you send.

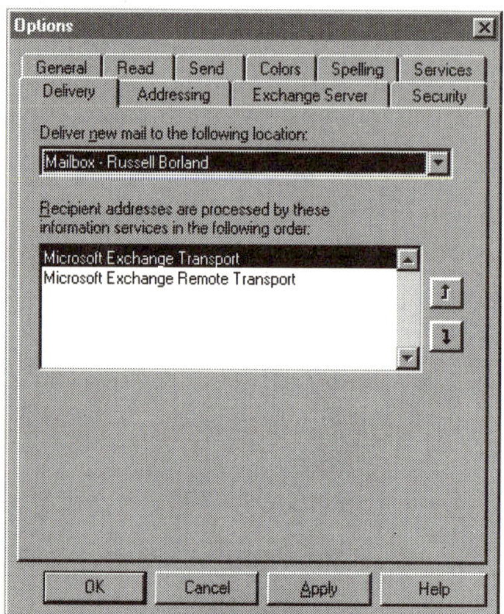

Deliver New Mail To The Following Location. Usually, Exchange delivers messages sent to you to your Exchange server mailbox (your Inbox). If you prefer to have messages delivered to another location, select that location from the Deliver New Mail To The Following Location list. For example, if you have personal folders set up, you could have new messages sent to your Personal Folders Inbox. Or, if you use more than one mailbox (see "Exchange Server Tab," on page 439), you can select from among the mailboxes that Exchange opens for you, such as a mailbox at an online service.

Recipient Addresses Are Processed By These Information Services In The Following Order. In the list under the label Recipient Addresses Are Processed By These Information Services In The Following Order, you'll see all the services set up for the profile you're currently using to run Exchange. When you send a message, Exchange tries to send the message by way of the service listed first. If that fails, Exchange works its way

down the list of services until it finds one that can take the message from your Outbox. For example, if you're working through Remote Mail, your Exchange server isn't available. In this case, Exchange can't send the message through the Exchange Transport, so it tries the Exchange Remote Transport.

If you send messages through a service that uses the same addressing scheme as Exchange, you might want to change the order of the services that Exchange tries for sending your messages. For example, if you have Internet Mail Service set up and you want your Internet addresses processed by your Internet server rather than by your Exchange server (which can also process Internet addresses), you'll want to move the Internet Mail Transport service to the top of the list.

Addressing Tab

On the Addressing tab of the Options dialog box, you'll find options for which address list to show when you first open the Address Book. You'll also find options for where you keep your personal addresses and the order in which Exchange should look through your various address books to verify an address. You can also add address lists, remove them, and check and adjust the properties of your various address lists.

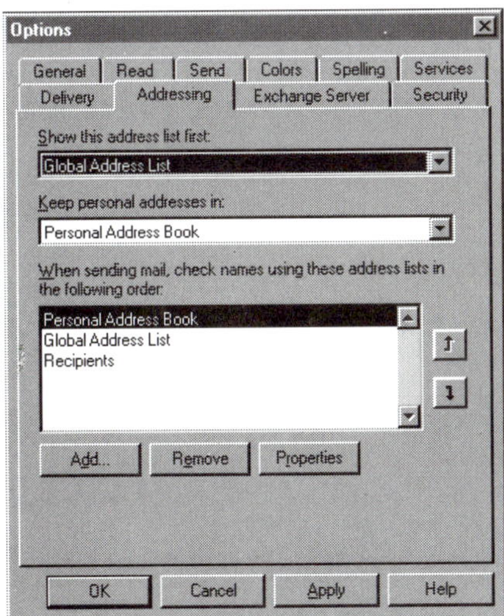

Show This Address List First. From the Show This Address List First list, select the address list you want Exchange to display when you first open your Address Book. If most of the addresses you use are listed in your

Personal Address Book, you might want to select that address list rather than the Global Address List. If you're working offline, Exchange automatically uses the Offline Address Book as the primary address list.

Keep Personal Addresses In. In almost all cases, you'll keep your personal addresses in your Personal Address Book. If the profile you're using gives you access to another address list that you can modify, you might want to select that address list from the Keep Personal Addresses In list. The address list you select is the one Exchange proposes to use when you create a new personal address. (You can still change the destination of a new personal address when you're creating it.)

When Sending Mail, Check Names Using These Address Lists In The Following Order. When you send a message or ask Exchange to check the names of recipients, Exchange looks in the address lists shown under When Sending Mail, Check Names Using These Address Lists In The Following Order. If most of your recipients' addresses are stored in a particular address list, you'll probably want to move that address list to the top. This makes name checking faster.

Add Button. You can add address lists to the current profile by following these steps:

1. Click on the Add button.

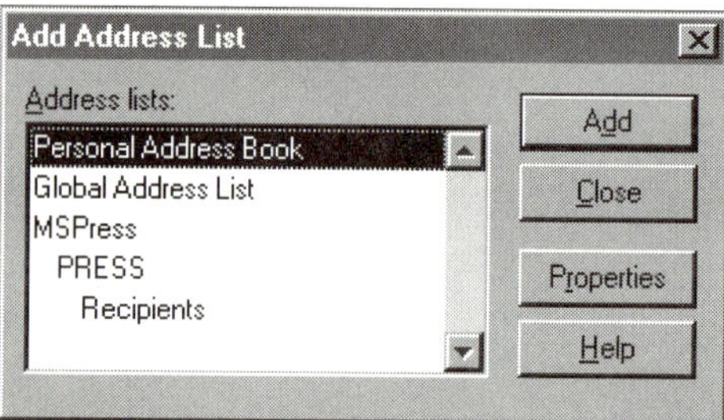

2. In the Add Address List dialog box, select the address list you want to add.
3. If you want to check or adjust the properties of the address list before you add it, click on the Properties button. For more information about the Properties button, see the sidebar called "Personal Address Book Properties," on page 435.
4. Click on the Add button.

5. To add another address list, repeat step 2 through step 4.
6. When you've added all the address lists you want to add, click on the Close button.

Remove Button. If you no longer need to use one of the address lists, you can remove it from your current profile. To do so, follow these steps:

1. Select the address list you want to remove.
2. Click on the Remove button.

Properties Button. When you click on the Properties button, Exchange displays a dialog box, that contains the settings for the selected address list. The properties you see depend on the properties of the selected address list. For more information, see the sidebar called "Personal Address Book Properties," on page 435.

Exchange Server Tab

The Exchange Server tab of the Options dialog box includes options for giving others permission to send messages on your behalf and for setting the amount of disk space you want to set aside for temporarily storing forms for messages and postings that you read. This tab also includes options for managing forms and for changing your Windows NT password.

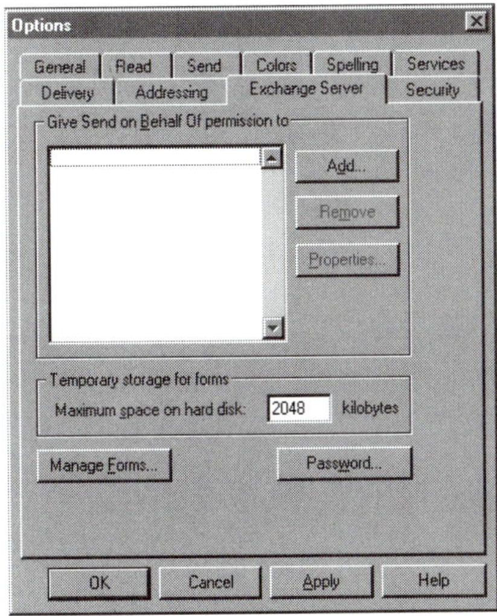

Give Send On Behalf Of Permission To. You're a very busy person, and you have to be away from your office often and for long periods of time. Sometimes you need to have messages sent for you, but the messages still need to carry the weight of your authority. You can grant others permission to send messages on your behalf. For example, you can let your assistant send messages for you when you're not in touch with Exchange.

To give someone permission to send messages on your behalf, take these steps:

1. Click on the Add button.

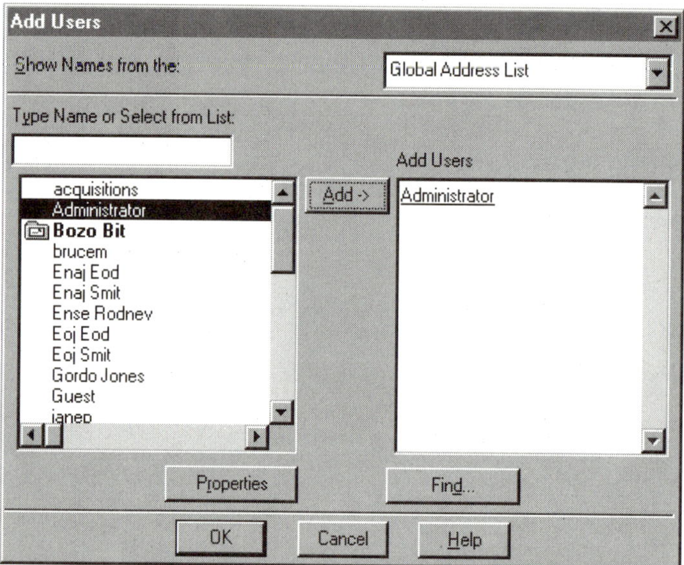

2. From the Show Names From The list, select the address list that contains the names you want to add.
3. From the list at the left of the dialog box, select the name or names you want to add, and then click on the Add button.
4. Click on OK.

To revoke permission to send messages on your behalf, take these steps:

1. In the Give Send On Behalf Of Permission To list, select the name of the person you want to remove from the list.
2. Click on the Remove button.

Temporary Storage For Forms. When you read a message or a posting or create a message or posting with a form that you don't have stored on

your hard disk, Exchange downloads the form and stores it temporarily. This way, if you read or create an item that uses this form again in the next few days, it's ready at hand, and the process goes more quickly.

To prevent forms from taking up hard disk space that you need for other work, you can limit the amount of space Exchange can use for temporarily storing forms. In the Maximum Space On Hard Disk box, type a number (in bytes) for the amount of space you want to set aside for temporary form storage. If you use many different forms frequently, and you have plenty of free space on your hard disk, you might change this value to 2048 or even 5120. Otherwise, the default setting of 1024 is probably appropriate.

When Exchange has filled the space you've set aside, it discards the oldest form stored in temporary storage to make room for the newest form you're using.

Password Button. Changing your passwords regularly (say about every two months) is an important security measure to protect your privacy and confidentiality. You can change your Windows NT password, which also serves as your Exchange password, by clicking on the Password button.

To change your Windows NT password, take these steps:

1. Click on the Password button.

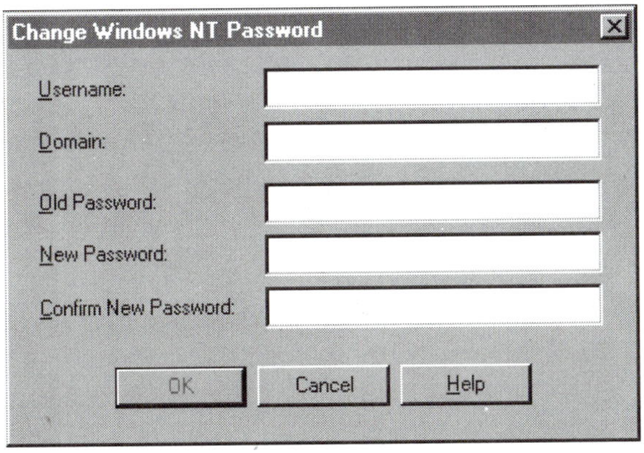

Change Windows NT Password

Username:

Domain:

Old Password:

New Password:

Confirm New Password:

OK Cancel Help

2. In the Change Windows NT Password dialog box, type your network username in the Username box.
3. In the Domain box, type the name of your Windows NT domain.
4. In the Old Password box, type your current Windows NT password.
5. In the New Password box, type the password you now want to use.

6. In the Confirm New Password box, type *exactly* the same password that you typed in the New Password box.
7. Click on OK. You'll see a message that tells you whether the password was changed successfully. If not, click on OK in the message box, and then repeat step 2 through step 7.

Security Tab

On the Security tab of the Options dialog box, you'll find options for encrypting your messages, adding your digital signature to messages, setting your security file, changing your security password, setting up advanced security, and logging off of advanced security.

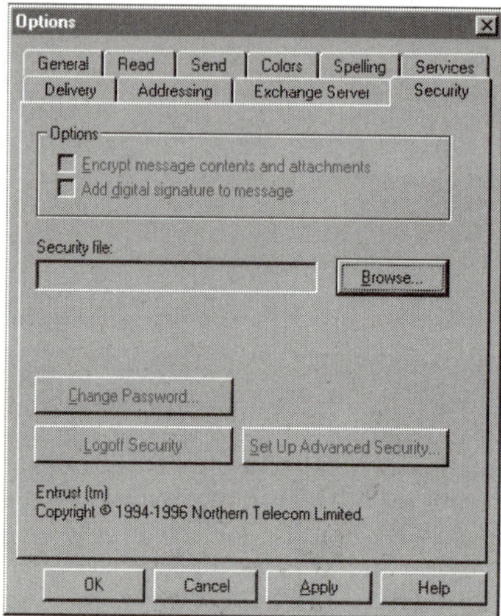

Advanced security provides a layer of protection for your messages. Encryption assures that only someone who logs on to the Exchange server as a valid recipient can read your message. A digital signature assures the recipient that you are really the person who sent the message—in other words, that the message is not some bogus transmission sent by a pernicious computer hacker.

Set Up Advanced Security Button. Before you can use advanced security, you must set it up. To set up advanced security, take these steps:

1. Send a request for advanced security for your Exchange account to the Exchange administrator.

2. Your Exchange administrator must set up and turn on advanced security for your Exchange account.
3. The Exchange administrator sends you a token.
4. You choose the Tools Options command, select the Security tab, and then click on the Set Up Advanced Security button.

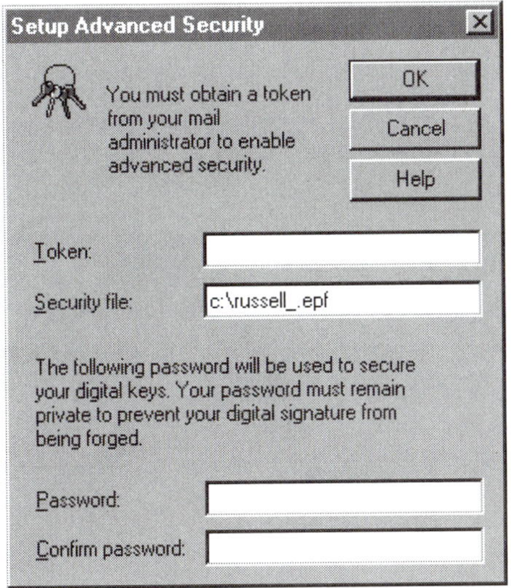

5. In the Set Up Advanced Security dialog box, type your unique token in the Token box. Choose a password to use for Advanced Security, enter it in the Password box and in the Confirm Password box, and then click on OK.
6. Click on OK in the dialog box telling you that a message has been sent to your Exchange server. Click on OK in the Option dialog box.
7. Your Exchange server verifies your token and returns a message to you that your account is now set up for advanced security. You must open the message from the Exchange server and enter your password in it before you can use advanced security.
8. At this point, you should check the Security tab of the Options dialog box to be sure that the Encryption and Digital Signature boxes are turned on.
9. From now on, when you send a message, Exchange requires access to your security file, which has its own password (the one you chose in step 5, above). Type the password, and then click on OK to open your security file and send the message.

10. If a recipient doesn't have Exchange advanced security, you'll see a message that tells you this. You have two choices for delivering the message:
    - Click on the Don't Encrypt button to send the message anyway. When encryption is turned on, this is the only way to send a message to a recipient who doesn't have advanced security.
    - Click on the Cancel Send button if you decide not to send the message to those who don't have advanced security.

You can, of course, turn off encryption and your digital signature on the Security tab of the Options dialog box. For details, see "Options," on page 419. If you do so, you can encrypt a single message or add your digital signature to a single message by clicking on the Seal Message With Encryption or the Digitally Sign Message button on the new message window toolbar. You can use these buttons to turn off security for an individual message.

When you receive a message with a digital signature, click on the Read Digital Signature button on the message window toolbar to verify that the message is authentic.

Exchange requires access to your security file before reading a digital signature.

Options. When you have advanced security available to you, you'll probably want to use it most of the time. If, however, some of your recipients don't have advanced security, you have to send the message without encryption or a digital signature. To save yourself from having to answer the message that appears each time you send a message to a recipient without advanced security, you might want to turn off options for using encryption and a digital signature. Without encryption, your messages are sent as readable text. Without a digital signature, your recipients must trust that the messages they receive from you are really from you and not from someone else.

Security File. This box lists the name of your security file. If the filename isn't listed (but you have advanced security set up) or you have another security file you want to use, type the filename or click on the Browse button to locate the advanced security file.

Change Password Button. You can change your advanced security password by clicking on the Change Password button. To change your advanced security password, do this:

1. Click on the Change Password button.

2. In the Change Security Password dialog box, type your current advanced security password in the Old Password box.
3. In the New Password box, type the new advanced security password.
4. In the Confirm Password box, type *exactly* the same password that you typed in the New Password box.
5. Click on OK.

Logoff Security Button. When you're using advanced security, Exchange requires access to your security file. When Exchange needs this access, you see a dialog box in which you type your advanced security password. This dialog box also contains the Don't Prompt For Password Again Until Next Exchange Logon check box. If you turn on this check box you don't have to type your advanced security password every time you send a message or read a secured message. However, selecting this option means that your Exchange account is open to anyone who sits down at your computer and sends a message. To prevent unauthorized use of your account while you're away from your computer, you can log off of advanced security.

To log off of advanced security after you have turned on the Don't Prompt For Password Again Until Next Exchange Logon option, choose the Tools Options command, click on the Security tab, and then click on the Logoff Security button.

This button is active only after you have turned on the Don't Prompt For Password Again Until Next Exchange Logon option. When you return to your computer and send a message or read a secure message, you'll once again see the dialog box that asks for your security password.

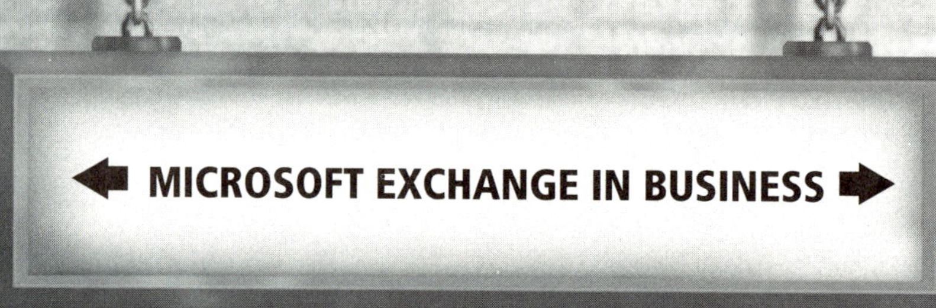
MICROSOFT EXCHANGE IN BUSINESS

PART 6

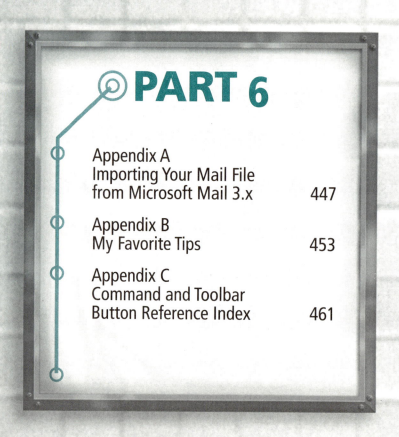

Appendix A

Importing Your Mail File from Microsoft Mail 3.x

Moving up to Microsoft Exchange doesn't mean that you lose your messages and personal address book from Microsoft Mail 3.x (3.0, 3.1, and 3.2). In fact, it's a relatively simple matter to move your messages and personal address book to Exchange.

Before you bring your messages and personal address book from Microsoft Mail to Exchange, you must make a backup copy of your MAIL.MMF file, which is where your messages and personal address book are stored.

To make a backup copy of your MAIL.MMF file, take these steps:

1. Log on to Microsoft Mail.
2. Choose the Mail Backup command.

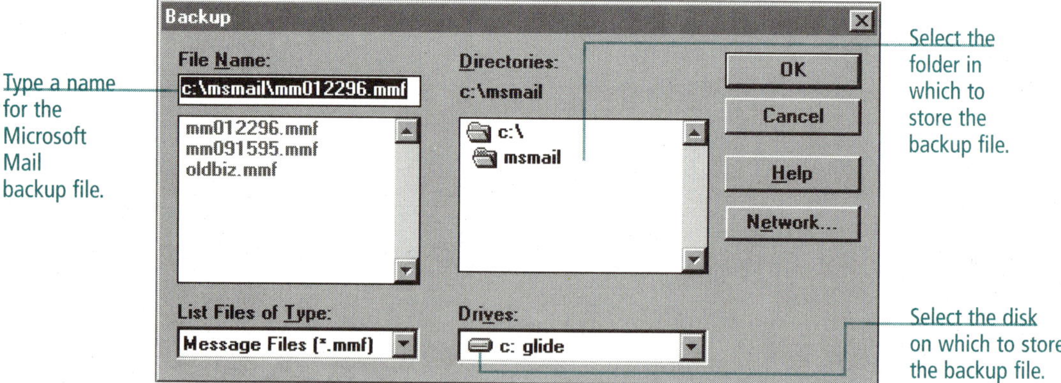

3. Select a disk and folder in which you want to store your backup file. This folder can be the same folder in which your mail file is normally stored, for example, C:\Msmail.
4. Type a name for the backup file, and then click on OK.
5. Choose the File Exit And Sign Out command if you want to quit Microsoft Mail.

To bring your messages and personal address book from Microsoft Mail to Exchange, take these steps:

1. Start Exchange.
2. Choose the File Import command.

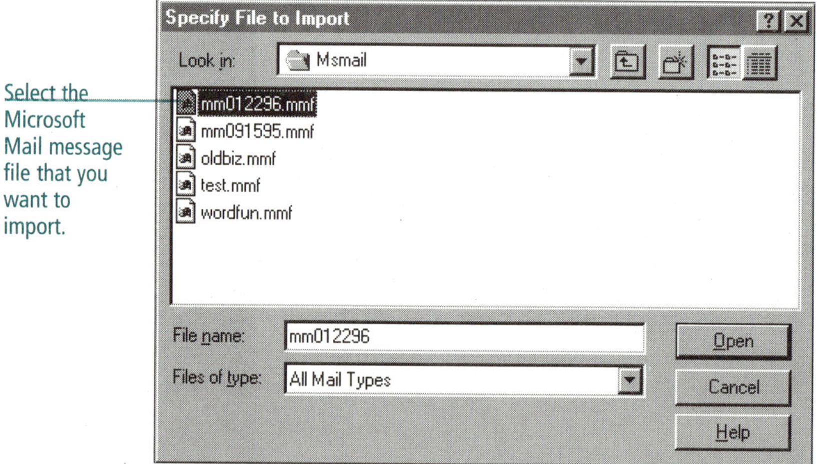

3. In the Specify File To Import dialog box, switch to the disk and folder in which you stored the backup copy of your MAIL.MMF file.
4. Select the backup copy of your MAIL.MMF file, and then click on the Open button.

TIP I recommend against importing your regular MAIL.MMF file. If something goes wrong when you import the file, you'll want to be able to try again. For that, you'll need your .MMF file in its original condition.

5. In the Import Mail Data dialog box, type your Microsoft Mail password.

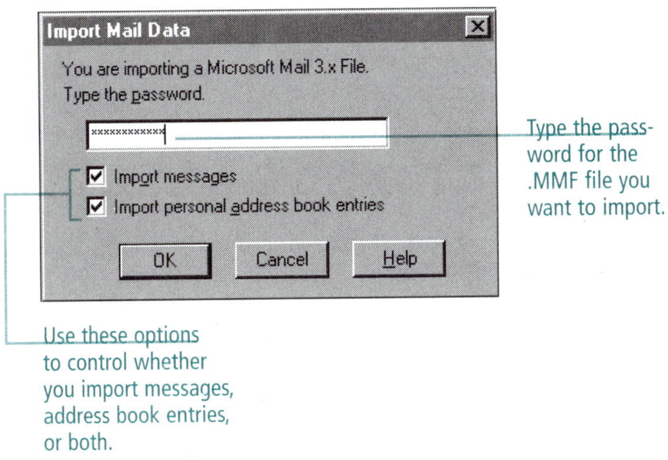

Type the password for the .MMF file you want to import.

Use these options to control whether you import messages, address book entries, or both.

6. If you want to import both messages and personal address book entries from Microsoft Mail, leave both check boxes in the Import Mail Data dialog box turned on. If you want only one of these two items, turn off the check box for the item you don't want to import. (If you want neither of these items, why are you putting yourself through all this?)
7. Click on OK.

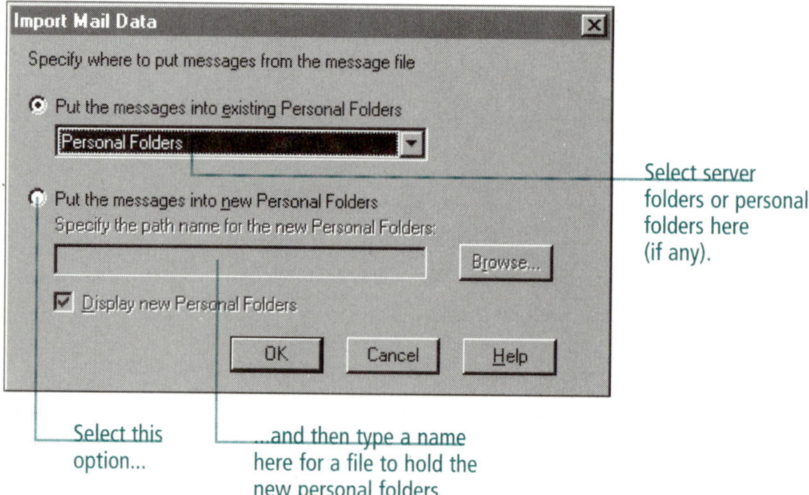

8. In the second Import Mail Data dialog box, select the personal folders into which you want to import your Microsoft Mail folders. If you want to use existing personal folders, select the Put The Messages Into Existing Personal Folders option, and then click on OK. You can use the drop down list box to choose between putting the messages from your .MMF file in your mailbox (stored on the Exchange server) or in your Personal Folders (stored on your hard disk).

   If you don't want to modify your current personal folders (or you don't have any), select the Put The Messages Into New Personal Folders option, and then type or select (by using the Browse button) the name of the file in which you want to store the imported folders. Click on OK. If you typed the name of a file that doesn't already exist, you must also type a password for the file. After you type the password and click on OK, Exchange creates the new personal folders.

Exchange imports your folders and their messages and then imports your personal address book. You'll see a dialog box that displays the progress of the importation.

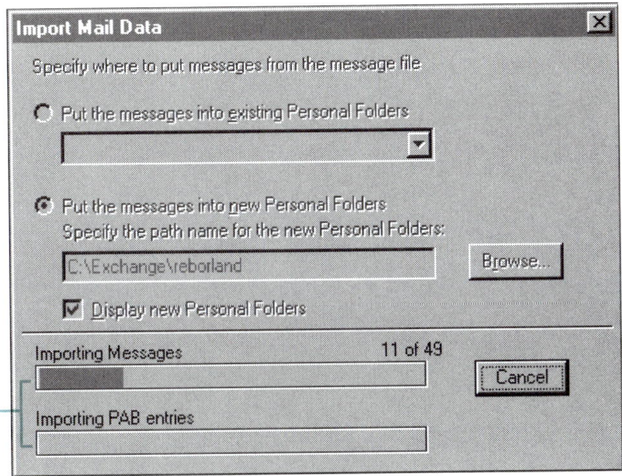

Exchange shows its progress on these two lines.

TIP Exchange doesn't check whether your personal address book from Microsoft Mail contains entries that also appear in your Exchange Personal Address Book. You have to open your Exchange Personal Address Book and delete duplicate entries.

Appendix B

My Favorite Tips

This appendix describes some of my favorite tips for using Microsoft Exchange. Not all of these tips are profound or even difficult to pick up; it's just that sometimes we (for "we" read "I") forget them, and it's nice to have a short list to refresh one's memory.

Keep clicking on the Next or the Previous button.
When you're reading a list of new messages (or reviewing messages that you've already read), keep clicking on the Next or the Previous button. It doesn't matter in which direction you're moving through the list of messages—when you get to the last message in the list Exchange closes the message window. This is handy because you don't have to worry whether you're at the end of the list and should close the window instead of clicking on the Next or the Previous button.

Press Alt+K to check names.
When you're addressing a message, type the first part of the name in the To (or the Cc or Bcc) box, and then press Alt+K, which chooses the Tools Check Names command. Exchange will then try to match what you typed with a valid entry in the address book. If Exchange finds several entries that could match, it presents the list of possibilities in a dialog box.

Insert smiley face characters.
If you choose the Compose WordMail Options command, then turn on the Enable Word As E-mail Editor option, and then click on OK, you can use the Word Insert Symbol command to insert "smiley face" characters—☺, 😐, ☹—in your messages. These characters are in the Wingdings character set.

Note Your recipients must be able to receive your messages in Exchange Rich Text Format in order to see these characters.

Set up your Inbox to show the newest messages at the *bottom* of the message list pane.
To do this, click on the Received column heading twice. You'll see a downward pointing arrow to the right of the Received label. Now choose the Tools Options command, and then click on the Read tab. Select the Open Item Below It option, turn off the Close The Original Item option, and then click on OK.

With this setup, you read down the list of messages, which seems natural to me. And by reading from older messages to newer messages, you read the messages in the order they were sent. This way, you see an original message before you start reading the replies to it.

Also, by using this setup, when you click on the Next button, Exchange opens the next newest message. When you read a message and then click on the Delete button on the Exchange toolbar, Exchange opens the next newest message. And when you move an open message, Exchange opens the next newest message.

When you reply to a message or forward it, Exchange returns to the message you just worked on. You can then click on the Next button to see the next newest message.

Save yourself some spelling aggravation.

Choose the Tools Options command, click on the Spelling tab, turn on the check box labeled The Original Text In A Reply Or Forward, and then click on OK. Now when you check your spelling in a reply or in a forwarded message, Exchange won't check the spelling in the original message. This setup saves you the trouble of dealing with the spelling "errors" that get checked in the header lines of the original message as well as the spelling errors of others. This tip can be especially rewarding when you reply to or forward a message that contains multiple replies or a long original message.

Rename the Deleted Items folder "Trash."

To do this, right-click on the Deleted Items folder and choose Rename from the shortcut menu. (If right-clicking is unavailable, select the Deleted Items folder, and then choose the File Rename command.) In the Rename dialog box, type *Trash*, and then click on OK. Renaming the Deleted Items folder "Trash" (or any other name you prefer) doesn't affect how Exchange uses the folder.

Set up AutoSignatures.

AutoSignature puts any closing you want at the end of your messages. You can set up several AutoSignatures and then insert the one that fits the message you're sending and its recipients.

To set up an AutoSignature, follow these steps:

1. Choose the Tools AutoSignature command.
2. In the AutoSignature dialog box, click on the New button.
3. Type a name for the AutoSignature in the Name box, and then type the text in the Contents box.
4. Format the text for the AutoSignature any way you want. Click on the Font button to format the font. Click on the Paragraph button to align the text or to add bullets. You can format each character and each paragraph of an AutoSignature differently.
5. Click on OK.
6. To add another AutoSignature, repeat step 2 through step 5.
7. Click on the Close button.

To insert an AutoSignature in all messages you send, do this:

1. Choose the Tools AutoSignature command.
2. Select the AutoSignature you want Exchange to insert automatically.
3. Click on the Set As Default button.
4. Turn on the Add The Default Selection To The End Of Outgoing Messages check box.
5. If you also want Exchange to add your AutoSignature to replies and forwards, leave the Don't Add Selection To Replies Or Forwards option turned off.
6. Click on the Close button.

To select and insert an AutoSignature for a particular message, do this:

1. Compose the message.
2. After you finish the message but before you send it, choose the Tools AutoSignature command from the message window menu bar.
3. Turn off the Add The Default Selection To The End Of Outgoing Messages option.
4. Select the name of the AutoSignature you want to use for this message.
5. Click on the Insert button.

Note If you want Exchange to insert the AutoSignature you selected in future messages, choose the Tools AutoSignature command from the Exchange menu bar, and turn on the Add The Default Selection To The End of Outgoing Messages check box again.

Check mark completed tasks.

When you finish a task, the easiest way to mark it completed is to click in the blank box for the task in the ✔ column. When you do this, Schedule+ marks the task as 100% complete.

You can mark the task complete in the Daily Reminder window that appears each day, on the To Do tab, and in the task list on the Daily tab. (You can also use the Weekly Schedule and Monthly Schedule tabs if you have added these to your appointment book.)

Avoid security messages, if possible.

If you have Exchange advanced security set up (and you have encryption and digital signatures turned on for all messages) and you know that the recipient of your message doesn't have advanced security set up, you can select options to avoid seeing message boxes that Exchange displays when you send a message. To avoid these message boxes, click on the Seal Message With Encryption and the Digitally Sign Message buttons on the message window toolbar to turn off these security features. You must turn off both buttons. When you do, you forgo encryption and your digital signature for a single message.

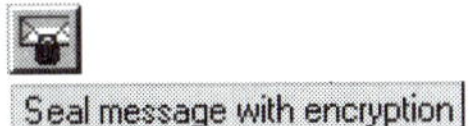

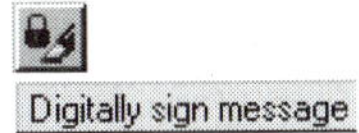

Create personal folders for private items.

Personal folders reside on your computer's hard disk, not on the Exchange server. This means that items in personal folders are as private as you can make them on your computer.

To set up personal folders, take these steps:

1. Choose the Tools Services command.
2. Click on the Add button.

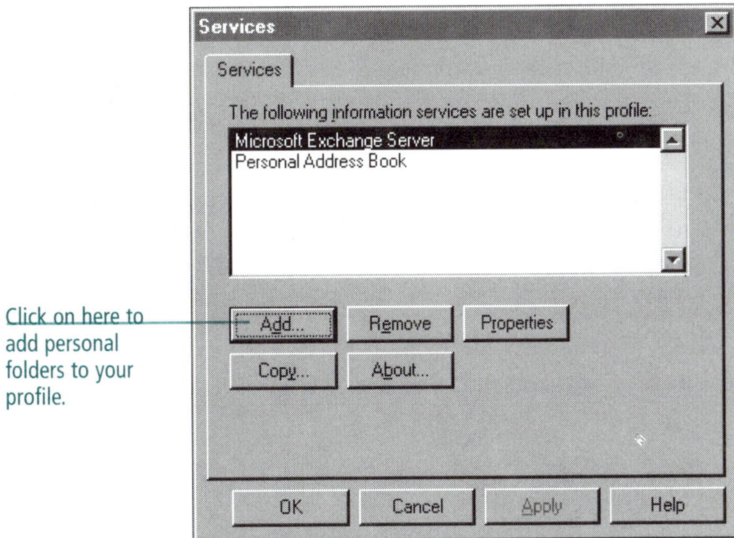

Click on here to add personal folders to your profile.

3. Select Personal Folders, and then click on OK.

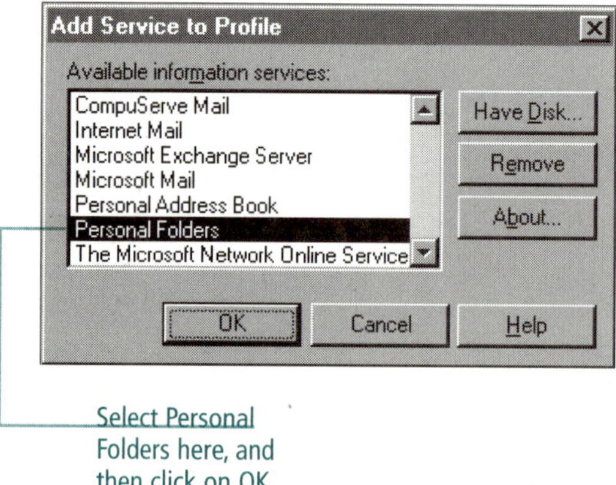

Select Personal Folders here, and then click on OK.

4. Select the disk and folder in which you want to store your personal folders. In the File Name box, type a name for the file that will store your personal folders, and then click on the Open button.

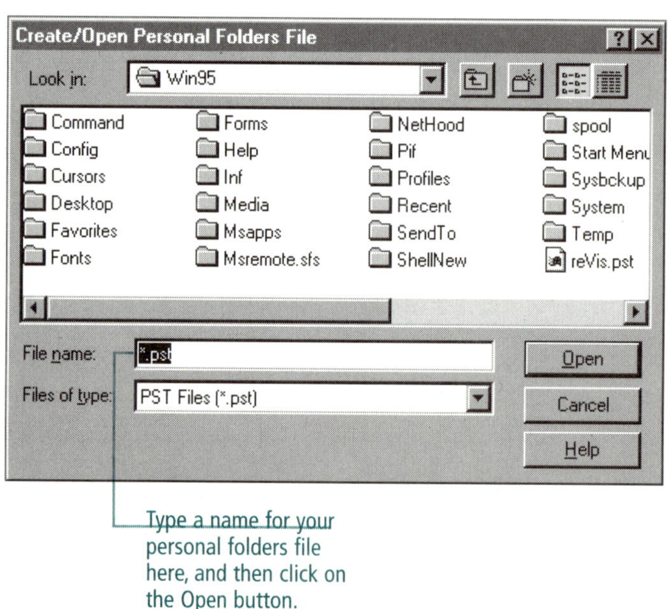

Type a name for your personal folders file here, and then click on the Open button.

5. Make any changes you want in the Create Microsoft Personal Folders dialog box, and then click on OK.

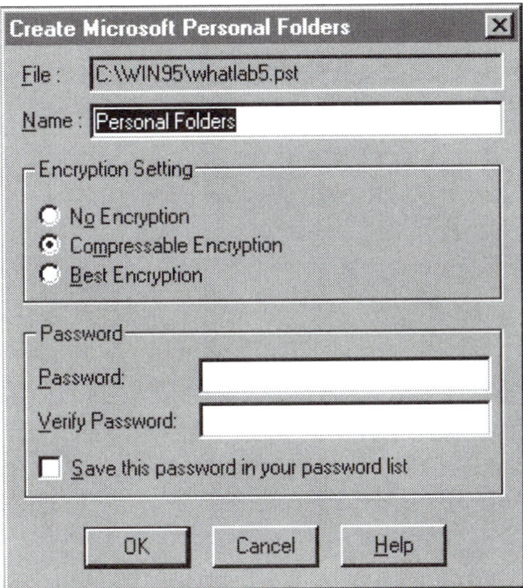

6. Click on OK in the Services dialog box.

Personal Folders contains folders for Inbox, Outbox, Deleted Items, and Sent Items, just as your Exchange server folder does. You can add any number of folders to Personal Folders, and, of course, you can add as many subfolders and layers of subfolders as you want.

In the folders inside Personal Folders, store your private messages, postings, documents, and other files that you want to view and work with in Exchange. You can add any kind of item to your personal folders that you can add to any other Exchange folder.

Add new Address Book entries from messages.
Most people receive at least a few messages from someone outside their organization (or at least from someone who isn't listed in any of your available address books). For the nonce, you can reply to the message and not worry about the address. At another time, however, you'll want to have the address handy to send a new message to that person. It's easy to add a new address to your address book from a message you have received. To do so, follow the steps on the next page.

1. Open the message.
2. Double-click on the sender's name. You'll see a Properties dialog box for the sender, as shown here:

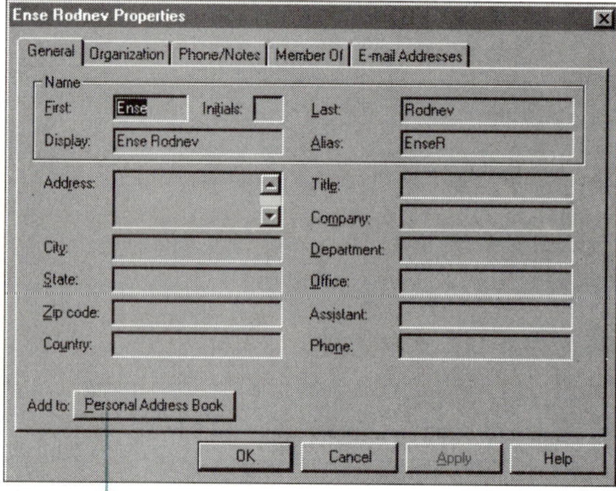

Click on here to add the sender's name and e-mail address to your Personal Address Book.

Note This dialog box is the same one you see if you open your address book, select a name, and then click on the Properties button on the Address Book toolbar.

3. Click on the Add To Personal Address Book button, and then click on OK.

Appendix C

Command and Toolbar Button Reference Index

This appendix lists many of the menu commands and toolbar buttons in Microsoft Exchange that are used to perform the tasks and procedures described in this book. In the tables in this appendix, you'll find:

- The command or toolbar button name.
- A brief description of the task or tasks for which you use the command or button.
- Page references for the sections in the book in which the tasks are discussed.

Electronic Mail

This table lists selected commands and toolbar buttons you use to create and manage e-mail messages in Exchange.

Command or Toolbar Button	Task	Page Reference
Address Book button	Manage your address books	"Opening an Address Book," 56; "Switching Address Books," 56; "The Gang's All Here: Personal Distribution Lists," 61
Compose WordMail Options	Activate WordMail tools	"Creating a Project Message Template," 256
Delete button	Delete a message or a folder	"Keeping Things Tidy: Dealing with Messages," 45; "Deleting Unwanted Folders," 49
File Import	Import message (.MMF) files into Exchange	"Importing Your Mail File from Microsoft Mail 3.x," 447
File New Folder	Create a new folder in Exchange	"Moving Messages," 46
File Save As	Save a message as a text, .RTF, or message (.MSG) file; save a message attachment	"Saving Messages in Files," 51; "Saving Message Attachments," 52
Find button (Address Book toolbar)	Locate an entry in an address book	"Finding Someone by Other Means," 58
Format Font	Format the font, font size, and other font effects in a message	"Getting the Word Out: Sending a Message," 27
Format Paragraph	Format paragraphs, idention, and alignment in message text	"Getting the Word Out: Sending a Message," 27

(continued)

continued

Command or Toolbar Button	Task	Page Reference
Forward button	Forward a message to another recipient	"Passing the Buck: Forwarding a Message," 44; "Sending Information to Customers," 370
Insert File button	Attach a file to a message; attach an existing message to a new message	"Getting the Word Out: Sending a Message," 27; "Attaching Messages," 35
Insert Object	Attach an object created in another application to a message	"Getting the Word Out: Sending a Message," 27
Mark To Retrieve button	Mark a message for retrieval with Remote Mail	"Marking Messages for Download," 388
Move Item button	Move a message or other item to a different folder	"Moving Messages," 46
New Entry button (Address Book toolbar)	Add an entry to your address book	"Adding Someone," 59 "Contact Information," 310
New Message button	Open a new message window	"Getting the Word Out: Sending a Message," 27
Reply To All button	Reply to the sender and all recipients of a message	"Take That! Replying to a Message," 42
Reply To Sender button	Reply to the sender of a message	"Take That! Replying to a Message," 42
Show/Hide Folder List button	Show or hide the folder list in the Exchange window	"Window Options," 408
Tools AutoSignature	Set up an autosignature to use when sending messages	"Stamping Your Signature," 37; "Set up AutoSignatures," 455

(continued)

continued

Command or Toolbar Button	Task	Page Reference
Tools Customize Toolbar	Customize the Exchange toolbar	"Toolbars," 417
Tools Deliver Now Using	Retrieve and send messages from online services	"Gathering Messages from the Beyond," 41
Tools Inbox Assistant	Set up the Inbox Assistant	"The Inbox Assistant," 410
Tools Options	Set options in Exchange for working with e-mail messages, starting Exchange, checking the spelling of messages, and for display colors, security, and passwords	"Take That! Replying to a Message," 42; "Other Options," 419; "Setting More Remote Mail Options," 391
Tools Out Of Office Assistant	Set up the Out of Office Assistant	"Out of Office Assistant," 416
Tools Remote Mail	Start remote mail	"Setting Up Remote Mail," 381
Tools Synchronize	Download the Offline Address Book for remote mail	"The Offline Address Book," 379
View Formatting Toolbar	Show or hide the formatting toolbar	"Window Options," 408
View Toolbar	Show or hide the Exchange toolbar	"Getting the Word Out: Sending a Message," 27; "Window Options," 408

Personal and Project Schedules

This table lists selected commands and toolbar buttons you use to set up and manage tasks and appointments in Schedule+.

Command or Toolbar Button	Task	Page Reference
Delete button	Cancel a meeting	"Canceling a Meeting," 277
Edit button	Edit the properties of an appointment, task, or other item; assign, reassign, and track tasks	"Remind Me Again What I'm *Supposed* to Be Doing: Setting Reminders," 78; "Scheduling a Special Meeting," 270; "Assigning Tasks to Team Members," 289; "Tracking Task Progress," 292
Edit Edit Item	Edit the properties of an appointment, task, or other item	"Changing a Task," 87
Edit Edit List Of	Edit the list of events and annual events	"Massaging the Entire List of Events or Annual Events," 94
Edit Edit Recurring	Change the properties of a recurring appointment or task	"Changing a Recurring Task," 89; "Changing Further Occasions of a Regular Meeting," 276; "Canceling All Further Occasions of a Regular Meeting," 277
Edit Find	Locate the date for a particular appointment, task or event, or find a contact	"Finding a Date," 73

(continued)

continued

Command or Toolbar Button	Task	Page Reference
Edit Go To	Jump to a particular date	"Finding a Date," 73
Edit Move Appt	Change the time of an appointment	"Moving an Appointment," 80; "Moving a Special Meeting or One in a Series of Meetings," 274
File Archive	Archive schedule information	"Archiving Project Scheduling," 279
File New	Create a new appointment book	"Giving a Project Its Own Appointment Book," 284
File Open	Open an appointment book	"Archiving Project Scheduling," 279
Insert Annual Event	Add an annual event to an appointment book	"Anniversaries and Other Annual Events," 92
Insert Event	Add an event to an appointment book	"Special Events," 91
Insert New Appointment button	Create a new appointment	"Scheduling an Appointment," 75
Insert New Contact button	Add contact information to an appointment book	"Keeping Your Little Black Book," 96; "Schedule+ Contacts Tab," 313
Insert New Task button	Add a task to an appointment book	"Just the One-Time Task," 84
Insert Project	Set up a project name in the To Do List of an appointment book	"Setting Up a Project Name," 285
Insert Recurring Task	Set up a recurring task in an appointment book	"You're Going to Do It Over and Over Until You Get It Right: Recurring Tasks," 88

(continued)

continued

Command or Toolbar Button	Task	Page Reference
Insert Related Item	Set up a task from an appointment or an appointment from a task	"Task Appointments, Appointed Tasks," 287
Insert Task	Set up a project task	"Scheduling a Task," 286
Private button	Mark an appointment private	"Public and Private Appointments," 78
Recurring button	Create a recurring appointment or make a one-time appointment recurring	"Let's Set Aside Every Tuesday at 2 O'Clock: Recurring Appointments," 81; "Scheduling a Regular Meeting," 264
Reminder button	Set a reminder for an appointment	"Remind Me Again What I'm *Supposed* to Be Doing: Setting Reminders," 78
Tools Options	Set up options for Schedule+	"Making Schedule+ Your Own: Adjusting Options," 104
View AutoSort	Automatically sort items in a folder	"Sort Now and AutoSort," 304
View Number Of Days	Set the number of days displayed in Daily or Weekly view	"What's Going on Today? Daily View," 70
View Sort Now	Perform a one-time sort of items in a folder	"Sort Now and AutoSort," 304
View Tab Gallery	Change the tab setup in Schedule+	"Adding Tabs," 116

Project and Public Folders

This table lists selected commands and toolbar buttons you use to manage items and information in both project folders and public folders.

Command or Toolbar Button	Task	Page Reference
Compose New Post In This Folder	Post a new notice in a public folder	"Adding Information to a Public Folder," 125
Compose Post Reply In This Folder	Respond to a posting in a public folder	"Adding Information to a Public Folder," 125
Delete button	Remove items from a public folder	"Removing Inappropriate Exchanges," 197 "Deleting Records from a Public Folder," 362
File Add To Favorites	Add a public folder to your Favorites folder	"Public Folder Favoritism," 126 "Favorite Folders," 404
File New Folder	Create a new folder	"Setting Up the Discussion Forum Folder," 177; "Creating the Project Folder," 202
File Properties	Set the properties of a public folder; add and remove participants in a project folder or public folder	"Following a Thread" 161; "Adding Your Voice to a Discussion," 163; "Setting Properties for Your Discussion Forum," 177; "Adding and Removing Participants," 183; "Setting Up a Roster of Team Members," 203
File Remove From Favorites	Remove a public folder from your Favorites folder	"Cutting Off Your Favorites," 127; "Favorite Folders," 404

(continued)

continued

Command or Toolbar Button	Task	Page Reference
File Save As	Save the selected item or items in an archive file	"Archiving and Deleting Customer Information," 360
Tools Application Design	Start the Exchange Forms Designer	"Creating a Project Report Form," 228; "Designing Customer Information Forms," 319
Tools Find	Find information in a project or public folder	"Finding Materials in the Project Folder," 211; "Finding Customer Information," 349; "Finding Information for Customers," 366
Tools Services	Set up personal folders for private items	"Create personal folders for private items," 457
View Columns	Change the columns displayed in the message list pane	"Columns Right, March: Changing Column Number and Order," 159; "Worlds of Views: Columnbining, Grouping, Sorting, and Filtering Tasks," 295; "Sorting Customer Information," 359
View Define Views	Create a new personal view or folder view for a folder	"Taking It Personal: Setting Up Personal Views," 155; "Doing It All at Once: Folder Views," 169; "Grouping Customer Information," 354
View Filter	Set up a filter for a folder	"Filtering Discussions," 166; "Filtering Tasks," 304; "Filtering Customer Information," 352

(continued)

continued

Command or Toolbar Button	Task	Page Reference
View Group By	Set up groupings for a folder	"Grouping Tasks," 300
View Personal Views	Change to a different view of a folder	"Teasing Out a Thread: Organizing a Discussion," 152
View Sort	Sort items in folder	"Sorting Tasks," 302

Index

Special Characters

A

B

C

D

E

F

G

H

I

K

L

M

N

O

P

Q

R

S

T

U

V

W

Russell Borland started as a technical writer for Microsoft Corporation in 1980 and rose to Manager of Technical Publications. In 1984, Bill Gates asked him to join a team to design and develop a new product, code-named Cashmere. This project evolved into Opus, the code name for Word for Windows version 1. Borland helped develop the product specification, the interface design, and the messages in version 1 and wrote the printed documentation. He has been an intimate of Word for Windows since its inception.

Borland transferred to Microsoft Press in 1988 to write a book about Word for Windows version 1, titled *Working with Word for Windows.* He has since revised this book several times under the title *Running Microsoft Word for Windows.* Borland, now a Master Writer, is also the author of *Microsoft WordBasic Primer, Microsoft Word for Windows 2.0 Macros, Getting Started with Microsoft Windows 3.1,* and *Running Microsoft Mail for Windows 3.* He is also coauthor of *Windows 3.1 Companion* and *Windows for Workgroups Companion.* All these books are published by Microsoft Press.

Borland earned a bachelor of arts degree from Whitworth College, a master of arts degree from Portland State University, and a Ph.D. from the University of Washington. His graduate studies focus was nineteenth-century (Victorian) British fiction, with special emphasis on the novels and short stories of Thomas Hardy.

Borland recently retired after a six-year stint as editor-in-chief of *The Journal of Computer Documentation,* the official quarterly publication of SIGDOC, the ACM special interest group on documentation. Borland is currently a member of SIGMM, ACM's special interest group for multimedia, and the IEEE Computer Society. He is past president of the Whid Isle Brittany Club and has acted as field trial chairman for the club on five occasions during his six years of club membership.

Borland lives on a five-acre farm near Sauk, Washington, at the base of Sauk Mountain, with his Brittany "Rusty" (Lazaruss Acre Racer), Loretta Lazar and her Belgian Tervuren "k.d." (Arrivées Chloë), their shared dog "Society Zoë," and their shared cat "Suddenly Seymour." Zoë and Seymour were both adopted from the Humane Society.

In 1992, at the age of 46, Borland took up motorcycle riding. His first bike was a 1992 Harley-Davidson FXRS-Con Low-Rider Convertible. He named this bike "Gloria." In 1993, Borland traded Gloria for a 1993 Harley-Davidson FLHS Electra Glide Sport, which he named "Blake." Whenever possible, Borland rides Blake back and forth the 90 miles to the Microsoft corporate campus.

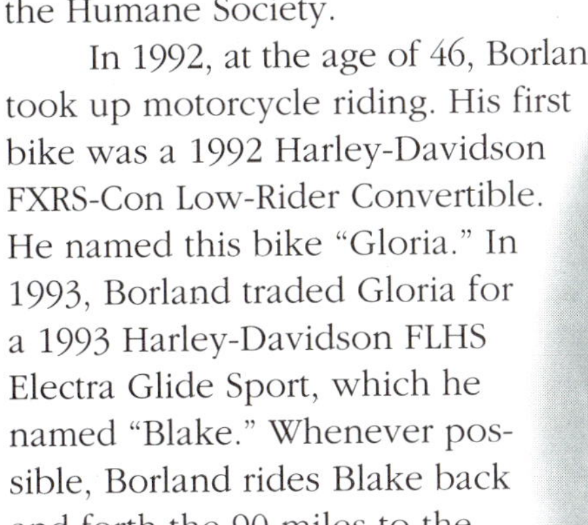

The manuscript for this book was prepared and submitted to Microsoft Press in electronic form. Text files were prepared using Microsoft Word for Windows 95. Pages were composed by Editorial Services of New England using Quark XPress for Windows 3.31. The text is set in ITC Garamond with display type in Adobe Frutiger. Composed pages were delivered to the printer as color-separated electronic prepress files.

Cover Designer
Greg Erickson, Team Design

Cover Color Separator
Color Service, Inc.

Cover Photographer
Tom Collicot

Interior Graphic Designer
Kim Eggleston

Principal Typographers
Peter Whitmer, Mark Heffernan, Sean Donahue

Principal Word Processors
Laura Meister, Patricia Porter

Principal Proofreaders
Bridget Leahy, Bernadette Murphy, Heather Kelly

Indexer
Matthew Spence

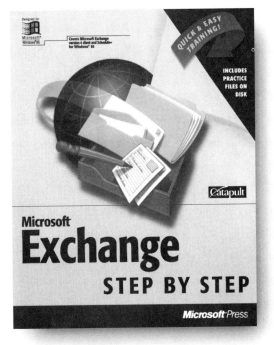

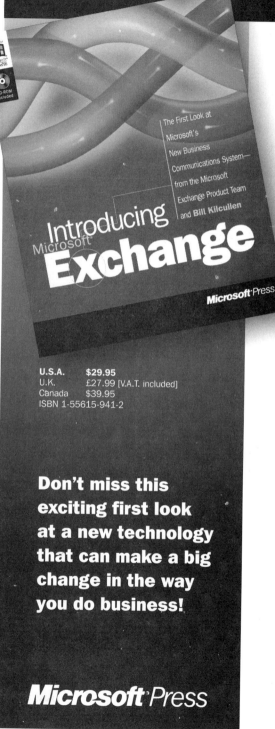

Register Today!

Return this

Microsoft® Exchange in Business

registration card for a Microsoft Press® catalog

U.S. and Canada addresses only. Fill in information below and mail postage-free. Please mail only the bottom half of this page.

1-57231-218-1A ***MICROSOFT® EXCHANGE IN BUSINESS*** ***Owner Registration Card***

NAME

INSTITUTION OR COMPANY NAME

ADDRESS

CITY STATE ZIP

NO POSTAGE
NECESSARY
IF MAILED
IN THE
UNITED STATES

BUSINESS REPLY MAIL
FIRST-CLASS MAIL PERMIT NO. 108 REDMOND, WA

POSTAGE WILL BE PAID BY ADDRESSEE

MICROSOFT PRESS REGISTRATION
MICROSOFT® EXCHANGE IN BUSINESS
PO BOX 3019
BOTHELL WA 98041-9946